PELICAN BOOKS

A533

CHORAL MUSIC

EDITED BY ARTHUR JACOBS

Choral Music

A SYMPOSIUM

EDITED BY

ARTHUR JACOBS

PENGUIN BOOKS

BALTIMORE · MARYLAND

Penguin Books Ltd, Harmondsworth, Middlesex
U.S.A.: Penguin Books Inc., 3300 Clipper Mill Road, Baltimore 11, Md
AUSTRALIA: Penguin Books Pty Ltd, 762 Whitehorse Road,
Mitcham, Victoria

—

First published 1963

—

Copyright © Arthur Jacobs, 1963

—

Made and printed in Great Britain
by Hazell Watson & Viney Ltd
Aylesbury and Slough
Set in Monotype Baskerville

CONTENTS

ACKNOWLEDGEMENTS

Permission has been gratefully received from the following publishers to reproduce copyright material: Associated Music Publishers: Ives, *67th Psalm*. C. C. Birchard & Co.: Bloch, *Sacred Service*; Hanson, *Lament for Beowolf*. Boosey & Hawkes: Britten, *Hymn to St Cecilia*; Copland, *In the Beginning*; Delius, *A Mass of Life*; Kodály, *Psalmus Hungaricus*; Prokofiev, *Alexander Nevsky*; Stravinsky, *Canticum Sacrum*. Cranz & Co.: Bryan, *Gothic Symphony*. J. Curwen & Sons: Holst, *The Planets*. Durand: Debussy, *Le Martyre de St Sébastien*. Foetisch Frères: Honegger, *Le Roi David*. Novello & Co.: Elgar, *The Dream of Gerontius*. Oxford University Press: Dyson, *In honour of the City*; Walton, *In honour of the City of London*. Éditions Salabert: Poulenc, *La Figure humaine*. Stainer & Bell: Stanford, *The Blue Bird*. Hinrichsen Edition Ltd for Suvini Zerboni: Dallapiccola, *Canti di liberazione*. Universal Edition: Bartók, *Cantata Profana*; Janáček, *Glagolitic Mass*; Mahler, Symphony No. 9; Schoenberg, *Three Satires*; Webern, Cantata No. 2.

NOTES ON CONTRIBUTORS

F. Ll. Harrison is senior lecturer in music, University of Oxford; Caldwell Titcomb is associate professor of music, Brandeis University (Waltham, Mass.); Elizabeth Cole was formerly assistant librarian of the Royal College of Music; J. Merrill Knapp is professor of music, Princeton University; Denis Arnold is reader in music, Extra-Mural Department, the Queen's University of Belfast; Sir Jack Westrup is professor of music, University of Oxford; Walter Emery, musicologist, works for a London music publisher; Roger Fiske, musicologist, is a former member of the BBC's Music Division; Richard Franko Goldman has taught at Princeton University, Columbia University (New York) and the Juilliard School of Music (New York); J. H. Elliot is Manchester music critic of the *Guardian*, Manchester; Theodore M. Finney is professor of music, University of Pittsburgh; Mosco Carner is a music critic for *The Times*, London; Deryck Cooke, author and musicologist, was formerly a member of the BBC's Music Division; Charles Reid is a writer on music for the *Daily Mail*, *Punch*, and *High Fidelity* (U.S.A.); Dika Newlin is professor of music and head of the Department of Music, Drew University (Madison, N. J.); Gerald Seaman has carried out post-graduate musical study at the Leningrad Conservatory of Music; Ernest Bradbury is music critic of the *Yorkshire Post*, Leeds; Rollo H. Myers, sometime music editor of the *Listener*, London, was formerly the British Council's music officer in France; Peter J. Pirie, musicologist, has contributed to many British and American journals; Robert Sabin was formerly editor of *Musical America* magazine.

INTRODUCTION

THIS book is designed as a companion for all interested in choral music – listener, performers, conductors, and even (who knows?) composers. Choral music occupies, in current musical life, a place neither as dominating nor as well-defined as it did fifty or a hundred years ago. It is the editor's hope that this book, by putting the heritage of choral music in historical and aesthetic perspective, may make some contribution towards its re-establishment.

The range between a motet by Lassus and Stravinsky's *Symphony of Psalms*, between Bach's *St Matthew Passion* and Carl Orff's *Carmina Burana*, is more extensive than the range covered in the previous books of the present series.* The contributors to the present volume were therefore not asked all to adopt identical methods of treatment. But all were asked not only to give a general outline of the music falling within their chapters, but also to treat a few selected major works in some detail. Moreover, they were asked to indicate the relationship of the music to the general social life of its time. If such an indication is necessary for truly historical treatment of any musical phenomenon, it is particularly necessary in treating choral music – bound up, as it has been, with the ritual of the Churches and with the developing relationship between professional and amateur musicians.

The term 'choral music' has been interpreted to include madrigals, part-songs, and the like (that is, works which may have been primarily designed as 'vocal chamber music' to be performed with only one or two voices to each part) where such music has entered the repertory of choral groups today. But, especially in the later periods, emphasis has naturally been placed on the music for larger choral forces. All works referred to are for mixed voices (women's,

* *The Symphony*, edited by Ralph Hill (1947); *The Concerto*, edited by Ralph Hill (1952); *Chamber Music*, edited by Alec Robertson (1957) – all published by Penguin Books.

or boys', and men's voices), unless a contrary indication is given. The letters SATB indicate soprano (or treble), contralto (or male alto), tenor, and bass.

An effort to avoid the parochial outlook so often associated with choral music has been made in the allotment of space to composers. No apology is offered for the fact that Stainer's *Crucifixion* is dealt with in one sentence, Stravinsky's *Canticum Sacrum* in three pages. British readers will, it is hoped, be refreshed by the contribution of American scholars (Messrs Titcomb, Knapp, Goldman), Finney, and Sabin, and Miss Newlin) to the book. Deliberately, the editor has adopted throughout the book a 'mid-Atlantic' vocabulary – choosing, for example, the logical American *quarter-notes* and *eighth-notes* rather than the British *crotchets* and *quavers*, but on equally logical grounds preferring such British usages as twelve-*note* (not twelve-*tone*) and leading-*note* (not leading-*tone*). On this point see the Introduction to the editor's *A New Dictionary of Music* (Penguin Books).

The editor is also responsible for the decision to use English rather than foreign-language titles of works whenever possible (an exception being made for ecclesiastical Latin); and the cross-references between chapters are the editor's own.

At the end of the main text are lists (by Joan Pemberton) of recommended books and musical editions, incorporating suggestions from the authors of the individual chapters, and a list (by Stanley Sadie) of recommended gramophone records. Nicholas Maw also prepared the index; Dr Sadie also prepared the music examples for the press and read the book in proof, to its great profit. To them I am indebted for their specialized and meticulous collaboration.

Two appendices follow. Appendix 1 gives the Latin text and English translation of the Ordinary of the Mass, and of the Requiem Mass (in part). These texts have been so often set by composers (such settings, indeed, being mentioned in almost every chapter of this book) that an understanding at any rate of their literal meaning is vital to the understanding of choral music. It is perhaps remarkable that, apparently, none of the better-known general musical reference books in English print these texts and translations. The translations given here are those of a Latin-English Roman Missal (Burns, Oates), except that the 'Dies irae' (rendered in the Missal into English verse) is here given in the literal prose translation of William Mann, by his kind permission.

Appendix 2 deals with the *continuo* – a term still widely misunderstood, though of increasing importance now that historically correct interpretation of choral (and other) music is more strongly felt desirable.

General histories and dictionaries of music are not included in the list of recommended books. But one particularly useful reference book (not, unfortunately, available in English), listing thousands of choral works by category and publisher, may be mentioned here: the *Handbuch der Chormusik* by Erich Valentin, published by G. Bosse, Regensburg (Germany). The English agents are Hinrichsen Edition, Ltd.

ARTHUR JACOBS

London 1962

I

Choir and People in the Later Middle Ages

c.1000–c.1470

F. LL. HARRISON

IF we define polyphonic music as music in which two or more independent vocal or instrumental lines are heard simultaneously, then it may be said that, by the end of the twelfth century, composers had been writing polyphonic music for some two and a half centuries. Although at least two composers, Léonin and Pérotin of Notre-Dame in Paris, had achieved individual fame during the twelfth century, almost all music composed earlier than the fourteenth century was written anonymously. A few famous names are known from the fourteenth century, but it was not until after 1400 that a composer's name was commonly attached to his music.

The century after 1400 also saw the rise of choral music in our sense of part-music sung with two or more singers to each part. Earlier polyphony was vocal or vocal-instrumental chamber music, normally performed with one singer or player to each part. Group singing was confined to the unison singing of plainsong, often called Gregorian chant because of the role which Pope Gregory I (590–604) is said to have played in its organization. In the early Church the congregation had taken part by singing such chants as hymns and simple responses, but by the time of Gregory I plainsong had become a highly developed art, taught to singers in the song-school (*schola cantorum*) attached to every large church. The singers were taught from boyhood the musical idioms of the chant, and memorized the greater part of the music they sang in the services.

With the development of an established cycle of daily

services, ordered and varied according to the seasons and
festivals of the Church year, it was essential that the work of
the choir should be correspondingly organized. This was
done by means of a recognized hierarchy of duties and
functions, assigned according to the rank of the individual.
In descending order of importance, the members of the
choir responsible for the music were the Precentor, who was
nominally in charge; the Succentor, his active deputy; the
Rulers (one to four according to the importance of the day
in the Church calendar) who were stationed at floor-level
and directed the chants; the more accomplished musicians
who sang at a lectern, in groups of two to four, the elaborate
passages of the plainsong; and the choir (*chorus*) of men and
boys who formed the general body. Within this systematized
framework of ritual and musical functions, the art of polyphony as we understand it in western Europe was born and
developed.

The members of a medieval choir were in the first place
members of a church community, whether they were monks
observing the rule and fulfilling the duties of their order, or
lesser ministers in a cathedral or large church run by secular
(non-monastic) priests. The choir of a large medieval church
was separated from the rest of the building by a series of
solid screens, and the services were carried out by and for the
church community, with no participation by those outside
the choir. In a parish church there was some degree of
participation by the congregation, since there the screen
was of open-work and the altar could be seen from the nave.
However, it was not until the end of the Middle Ages and
the early Renaissance (about 1450, as far as England is concerned) that parish churches began to have polyphonic
music in their services.

The function of early polyphony was essentially festive
and ornamental. On the great feasts of the Church the
soloists were permitted to add an air of jubilation to their
parts of the chant by singing a second part (descant) above
the plainsong. This festive elaboration of plainsong was one
of the many manifestations of the Romanesque period
(ninth to twelfth centuries) in the arts. The impulse which

created Romanesque architecture by elaborating the basic plan of the early Christian basilica also created new liturgical and musical forms by elaborating the basic framework of the services. Among these forms were the 'tropes', interpolations of prose and poetry into the standard liturgical texts; the 'Sequence', a sung poem to follow the Alleluia of the Mass; and the liturgical plays, stories with action inserted into the ritual. Polyphony was a purely musical method of festive decoration, though it was often associated with the verbal method of the insertion of tropes. This insertion is called 'troping', and such a phrase as a 'troped Alleluia' means 'an Alleluia with a trope inserted'. Some of the earliest polyphonic music known is contained in a manuscript of tropes and other festival music from Winchester Cathedral written about the year 1000. The two-part music in the *Winchester Troper*, or *Cantatorium* as it is more properly called, was written in 'neumes', a form of musical notation which did not indicate exact pitch. While it cannot be transcribed with certainty, its general characteristics can be discerned.

By the eleventh century, a form of staff notation was in general use, and the next two notable collections of polyphonic music, both from the first half of the twelfth century, can today be accurately transcribed as to pitch, though the rhythm is still free and unmeasured, as in plainsong. One of these collections, which is contained in four manuscripts, comes from the Abbey of St Martial in Limoges (France)[1]* and is chiefly music for the Christmas season, while the other is from Compostela in Spain[2] and is entirely concerned with the feasts of St James, the patron saint of that famous centre of pilgrimage.

The St Martial piece is a troped Gradual, the Gradual being part of the Proper of the Mass† (Introit, Gradual, Alleluia or Tract, Offertory, and Communion); the setting from Compostela is a troped Kyrie (from the Ordinary of the Mass, consisting of Kyrie, Gloria, Credo, Sanctus, and

---

* In this and the following chapter, small figures indicate reference to the list of recommended editions at the end of the book.

† For the Mass, see Appendix 1, p. 397.

Agnus Dei). It may be assumed that these pieces were performed by voices alone.

In the twelfth century, composers' settings of the soloists'
parts of the chant – such as the Responds (responsorial
chants) of the Office of Matins and Vespers, the Gradual
and Alleluia which are the responsorial chants of the Mass,
and the troped Kyries – were based on the plainsong as the
lower part; while free composition without a plainsong basis
was used in settings of non-ritual words, such as the tropes
inserted into the 'Benedicamus Domino' ('Let us bless the
Lord') at the end of the Office, and in the Conductus which
accompanied the reader of a lesson to the lectern. 'Conductus'
(see also p. 21) here indicates a processional piece. As such,
conductus also had a place in the liturgical drama found in
England, France, and Spain during the twelfth and thirteenth centuries. *The Play of Daniel* (known today in a
thirteenth-century copy of a twelfth-century French original)
shows how effective in this context a unison choral chant
can be.

In the time of Léonin of Notre-Dame (active *c.*1160–80)
a notation for measured (i.e. exactly rhythmical) music
was devised. Léonin himself achieved the unprecedented
feat of composing two-part music for all the important feasts
of the year in his *Great Book of Polyphonic Music of the Mass and
Office for the Enrichment of the Divine Service* (*Magnus liber
organi de gradali et antiphonario pro servitio divino multiplicando*),
which was written when the new Gothic cathedral of Paris
was being built. His work marks the end of Romanesque
polyphony and the birth of Gothic. Clothed in an animated
triple rhythm, his melodies embodied the same aesthetic
aims as the new architecture, in their spirited lines and
enlivened detail.

Léonin's successor, Pérotin (active from *c.*1183), supple-
mented the existing two-part polyphony with works in three
and four parts, including magnificent four-part settings of
the Graduals for Christmas Day (*Viderunt*,[3] 'All the ends of
the earth have seen the salvation of our God'), and for the
following day, St Stephen's Day (*Sederunt*,[3] 'Princes sat and
spoke against me'). The plainsong given to the soloists, com-

Ex.1. (a) [♩.= c. 90] Léonin (probably)
Voice
(Upper part vocalized)
Organ
[Vi-
de - (runt)]

(b) [♩.= c. 90] Pérotin
T1 T2
(Upper parts vocalized)
T.3
Organ
[Vi-
de - (runt)]

prising the opening words and the verse – in *Viderunt*, the words *Viderunt omnes* and the verse beginning *Notum fecit Dominus* – is freely extended, so that each note becomes a time-unit of some length, while the upper parts disport themselves around it in a musical representation of a celestial dance. These upper parts were probably not sung to words but merely 'vocalized' (sung to a vowel). The lower parts were probably given to instruments, but in musical quotations it is conventional to put under the notes the words of the original plainsong – given above in square brackets. Pérotin's development of the style of Léonin may be illustrated by comparing their settings of the opening of *Viderunt* (Example 1). In a complete performance plainsong and polyphonic sections (in which the tenor, as the lowest

part was called, was probably played or doubled by organ)
should alternate thus:

> Polyphony: *Viderunt omnes*
> Plainsong: *fines terrae salutare Dei nostri:*
> *jubilate Deo omnis terra.*
> Polyphony: *Notum fecit Dominus salutare suum:*
> *ante conspectum gentium revelavit*
> Plainsong: *justitiam suam*

All the ends of the earth have seen/the salvation of our God. Sing
joyfully to God, all the earth./ The Lord hath made known his
salvation: he hath revealed his justice in the sight of the Gentiles.

It was probably Pérotin who composed the third surviving
four-part work of this period, the text of which is the single
word *Mors* ('Death').[4] We are told by a monk of Bury St
Edmunds who studied in Paris about the middle of the
thirteenth century that Pérotin wrote many compositions
belonging to this type, which was called the *clausula*. It
was based on a short phrase of plainsong usually repeated
once or more to make a *clausula* or set of *clausulae*. The
clausula was not, strictly speaking, a part of the liturgy,
but a piece which the solo singers were allowed to perform
after the Sanctus at Mass on festivals. The word *Mors*,
together with the music used for the tenor (the lowest part)
in Pérotin's setting, occurs in the Eastertide Alleluia with
the verse *Christus resurgens ex mortuis*.

The importance of the *clausula*, a short-lived form in
musical history, lies in the fact that it gave birth to the
motet. In its medieval sense – that is, a polyphonic composition based on a phrase of plainsong – the motet lasted
until the middle of the fifteenth century. Initially a *clausula*
was made into a motet by adding words (*motet* is the dimi-
nutive of the French *mot*) to the upper parts, a different
poem being set in each part. For this reason, the titles of
motets are given by citing the different opening words of
each voice. Thus the *clausula Mors* became, with the same
music, but with words added, the motet which we refer
to as *Mors a primi patris/Mors quae stimulo/Mors morsu/*
(Tenor) *Mors*.[4] The *clausula* soon went out of existence, and

motets were now composed as original works, not by adding words to an existing *clausula*. In France, where the form of the motet was chiefly cultivated, there were relatively few motets entirely using religious texts, though a tenor taken from a liturgical chant was almost always used as the basis.

In France the thirteenth-century motet seems to have become the recreative music of clerics and aristocrats; in England it was turned solely to religious purposes, and there are extremely few English secular polyphonic pieces from the Middle Ages. It is all the more surprising that one of the most famous pieces of medieval music, *Sumer is icumen in* (*c.*1240), should be English and should have secular words. Though the English words fit it like a glove, it is by no means certain that it was first composed for them, rather than for the religious text beginning *Perspice christi-cola* ('Look, O worshipper of Christ') which are also written under the music in the manuscript.[5] In this music the technique of *rondellus* (repetition with exchange of parts between voices) is combined ingeniously and uniquely with that of *rota* (canon at the unison). *Rondellus* was a special feature of English church music for a century after *Sumer is icumen in*. In secular music, on the other hand, there is nothing else remotely like this *rota-rondellus* to be found in medieval England. Moreover, the five notes F – G – F – G – A, which are sung alternately by the two lowest parts in their *rondellus*, are the first five notes of the well-known antiphon for the Easter season, *Regina caeli* ('Queen of Heaven'). If the composer was conscious of this, and it is difficult to believe he was not, the piece was written with religious use in mind, and thus partakes of the nature not only of *rota* and *rondellus*, but of motet as well. It is, further, the only known six-part work earlier than the fifteenth century.

Whether this little masterpiece was created in a religious or a secular context, or in some way in a combination of both, it shares its lively melodic and rhythmic style and its *rondellus* technique with many English conductus (the Latin word is both singular and plural) of the second half of the thirteenth century. The term conductus, which we earlier encountered as used of a piece to accompany movement in Church ritual or in a liturgical play, was soon transferred to the troped form of the *Benedicamus Domino* sung at the end of the Office; and thence also to pieces which were sung in place of this *Benedicamus*. Like their prototypes, these conductus were settings of religious but non-liturgical poems; and, unlike motets, they were musically free compositions, not based on plainsong. English composers used the method of *rondellus* (exchange of parts between voices) not only in the conductus – an example is *Rosa fragrans* ('Fragrant rose') which has been recorded – but also in preludes and interludes (freely composed vocal additions) to the Alleluia of the Mass, and in the motet too. Examples are the delightful *Alleluia psallat*[6] from Worcester; the motet for Epiphany, *Balaam inquit*/(Tenor) *Balaam*[7] of *c.*1300; and the motet from Bury St Edmunds *Ave miles*/(Tenor) *Ave rex* (a motet in honour of St Edmund)[8] of *c.*1340. Another characteristic style of English polyphony during this period was a simple manner of writing in three parts, often moving in parallel fifths or sixths with thirds, which has become known as 'English descant'. This style, the successor of the earlier descant writing in two parts, is exemplified in a *Gloria in excelsis* from Worcester.[9]

While English composers were pursuing such varied methods of composition, their French contemporaries, led by Philippe de Vitry (composer, theorist, poet, and Bishop of Meaux, 1291–1361) and Guillaume de Machaut (composer, poet, and Canon of Reims, *c.*1300–77), enlarged the design of the motet and introduced new methods of notation which embraced duple as well as triple subdivisions of rhythm. Numerical order and proportion, expressed in melody, rhythm, and form, became the basis of their musical thought. In place of the frank release of festive joy which was the dominant note of thirteenth-century music, church music in France was now distinguished by solemnity and cool restraint. It preserved inviolate its own order of beauty, almost untouched by what we call 'expression'. Through the medium of its architectonic framework the words were displayed in an aura of ceremonial depth and dignity.

Here, too, the tenor part was probably performed on, or doubled by, the organ; as to the use of other instruments, we have no convincing evidence until the fifteenth century.

In technical terms the governing formula in the design of a fourteenth-century motet was the principle which modern scholars call isorhythm ('the same rhythm'). The tenor of the thirteenth-century motet had foreshadowed this method, since (as we have seen) it was invariably laid out in a short rhythmic pattern continuously repeated. The isorhythmic motet of the fourteenth century went further. Here, the tenor, still a phrase of plainsong, was laid out in rhythmically identical sentences (each sentence called a *talea*, 'cutting'), and repeated once or more in the same or in exactly proportionate *taleae*. Isorhythm was also applied to the upper parts, though less often and more freely. One of the characteristic devices used in the upper parts was 'hocket', the fragmentation of a melodic line by rests. Hocket was usually combined with the proportionate quickening of the *talea* in the tenor to produce a rhythmically cumulative effect in the final section of a motet. In the following example from de Vitry's *Rex quem metrorum*[10] the tenor and countertenor at the end (2b) go twice as fast as at the beginning (2a) and the upper parts (called *duplum* and *triplum*) reinforce this (in 2b) with hocket.

It will be noted that in this motet the two lower parts (the lowest being the tune of the plainsong *Rex regum*) were probably given to instruments; the highest part was sung to a text meaning 'It must be proclaimed openly at the meeting-places, the abominable madness of these ages, the demented frenzy of dogs, launched on the world by the eternal Satan . . .'; and the next highest part (*Rex quem metrorum*) meant 'O King whom I represent in the first letter of these lines. . . .' Thus the text yields the acrostic 'Robertus'. The work is thus a political motet concerned with the struggle for possession of Sicily between the Angevins, led by Robert d'Anjou (1278–1343) and the Aragonese. Curiously enough this motet was copied into an English manuscript, as was also, more understandably, the equally fine *Vos qui admira-*

mini/Gratissima virginis species/(Countertenor)/(Tenor) *Gaude gloriosa* in honour of the Virgin Mary.[11] This was not only copied in England but was cited by an English theorist writing about 1350, from whom we know it to be by de Vitry.

The twenty-three motets of Machaut pursued and developed the methods of de Vitry, though in subject-matter they are closer to the thirteenth century, most being secular pieces with French texts. Three of his five religious motets are in four parts,[12] and, like the two of de Vitry just mentioned, could effectively be performed by giving the upper parts to two groups of voices and the two lower parts to instruments. Though his motets are relatively little known, Machaut's *Notre-Dame Mass* has been several times printed[13] and recorded, and much discussed. Other Masses from the fourteenth century have been discovered,[14] but Machaut's remains the first important example of a form which has been cultivated in every subsequent period of musical history, as well as one of the great works of its own time.

For the shorter movements he followed the procedure of the motet in the isorhythmic design and in the disposition of his four-part texture, though here the lower parts (tenor and countertenor) need not be given to instruments and are quite suitable for vocal performance. The longer movements (Gloria and Credo) are essentially vocal in style, and the words are treated in largely syllabic fashion, apart from the long section sung at the end of each movement to the single word 'Amen' (isorhythmic in the Credo). Machaut rounded off his Mass with an isorhythmic setting of *Deo gratias*, the choir's response to the celebrant's *Ite missa est*, from which the service of the Mass (Latin *Missa*) took its name.

Machaut's secular polyphonic part-songs or *chansons*, like his secular motets, hardly come within the sphere of choral music because they are more appropriately performed by single voices and instruments. This is true also of most music of the time in Italy, where polyphonic church music is relatively rare throughout the Middle Ages. But attention must certainly be drawn to the Italian genre of part-song called the *caccia*. This is a vigorous type of piece, usually depicting a hunt with its attendant sounds (though a market scene and a fishing expedition are found as subjects), composed in the form of two-part vocal canon over one or two supporting instrumental lines. They are eminently suitable for group performance.[15]

While northern France provides much of the music we have discussed, the papal court at Avignon and its neighbouring kingdoms had a flourishing musical culture in the second half of the fourteenth century. There is also a sizeable amount of English church polyphony in the fourteenth century, most of it still unpublished. The strength of this indigenous tradition and the marked influence of music from the north and south of France are equally apparent in the first 'school' of named English composers, whose work was written into a large choirbook for the Household Chapel of Henry IV (1399–1413) and Henry V (1413–22). This choirbook is the Old Hall Manuscript, so called from St Edmund's College, Old Hall, near Ware, Hertfordshire, which has been its home since 1893. The Old Hall Manuscript (now available in modern printed form) marks the first great period in the musical history of the Royal Household Chapel. Among the composers included in it is Roy Henry, whom John Harvey (see his *Gothic England*, 1947, pp. 86–7) from his work on the archives, and Manfred Bukofzer* from his analysis of the musical style, considered to be Henry V. In my *Music in Medieval Britain** I have detailed my reasons for believing him to have been Henry IV, who reigned from 1399 to 1413, and who is said by a contemporary chronicler to have been 'brilliant in music'. The royal composer's *Gloria In Excelsis*[11] is in the sophisticated style which English composers derived from the French *chanson*, while his *Sanctus*[17] is in the simpler flowing manner of 'English descant' which, as we have seen, had long been a feature of English polyphony. A wide range of style and technique characterizes the Old Hall collection, which contains movements from the Mass (excluding the Kyrie) in styles from descant to isorhythm and canon (Pycard's canons are especially clever and complex), antiphons (see below) in descant and *chanson* styles, and isorhythmic motets (one, or perhaps two, by a French composer, Mayhuet). There is a haunting beauty in the descant pieces, no less in the simpler style of Leonel Power's antiphon *Beata progenies* ('Blessed progeny')[18] than in Byttering's slightly frenchified

* See Bibliography.

Ex. 3.   [♩ = c. 72]   Byttering

Ne- sci-ens ma- ter vir-go vi- rum

setting of *Nesciens mater virgo* ('Knowing no man, the Virgin Mother brought forth the Saviour'; see Example 3).[19]

Leonel Power (*d.*1444) lived in Canterbury Cathedral as a lay member of the community for the last few years of his life. He was the most famous English composer before Dunstable (*d.*1453), his later music appearing in Continental manuscripts from *c.*1430 alongside that of Dunstable himself and others of their countrymen. The interchange of styles between France and England was the most important single factor in the evolution of choral music in the first half of the fifteenth century. The graceful idioms of the French *chanson*, which the Old Hall composers had allied to the smooth sonority of English descant, was developed along the same lines by Dunstable, chiefly in the same categories of Mass, isorhythmic motet, and antiphon. It was during Dunstable's lifetime that the musically unified ('cyclic') Mass originated, which has ever since been a potent form in the hands of the great composers. (In its plainsong form the Mass had been a set of separate pieces without interconnexions.) English musicians almost certainly took the lead in this conception, and Power's Mass *Alma redemptoris*[20] is one of the earliest examples. The usual method of integration, as in this instance, was the use of a plainsong in the tenor, repeated for each movement. The plainsong was thus the underlying basis (or *cantus firmus*, literally 'fixed song') of all four movements (five movements, the Kyrie being included, in

Continental Masses). This form, which came to be called the
'*cantus firmus* Mass', was an extension of the idea of the isorhythmic motet, and the tenor of a Mass was in fact sometimes laid out isorhythmically. Masses built in this way on a
plainsong are identified by the name of that plainsong, as
the *Alma redemptoris* Mass mentioned above.

As to Dunstable himself, it is not entirely certain that he
composed a complete *cantus firmus* Mass, for the Mass *Rex
saeculorum* in honour of St Benedict[21] is attributed to him in
a contemporary manuscript and to Power in a later one.
But we do have from Dunstable's pen two individual movements for each of two isorhythmic *cantus firmus* Masses: a
Gloria and Credo on the plainsong of *Jesu Christi Fili Dei*[22]
and a Credo and Sanctus on the plainsong *Da gaudiorum
praemia*.[23] His most famous works, and the most frequently
copied in his own century, are the isorhythmic motet to a
text invoking the Holy Spirit, *Veni Sancte Spiritus et emitte/
Veni Sancte Spiritus et infunde/Veni Creator Spiritus/*(Tenor)
Mentes tuorum,[24] and the secular song *O rosa bella*[25] to an
Italian text. This motet, like the Credo and Sanctus on the
plainsong *Da gaudiorum praemia*, already mentioned, may
have been composed for the coronation of Henry VI as
King of France in Notre-Dame in 1431. It is a fine example
of Dunstable's art in its clarity of design and plasticity of
melody.

The effect of Dunstable's style on the Franco-Flemish
composers Gilles Binchois (*c.*1400–60) and Guillaume Dufay
(*d.*1474; his name is pronounced Du-fa-ee) was commented
on by Martin le Franc, court poet of Philip the Good of
Burgundy, who remarked that both composers had adopted
la contenance Angloise ('the English manner') and followed
Dunstable. Binchois had been with William de la Pole,
Earl of Suffolk, in Paris about 1425 before he joined the
Burgundian court in 1430. Some of his church works have
clear similarities to English style, while those of Dufay show
a gradual change to the new English-inspired style during
the 1430s, the decade of most of his large isorhythmic
motets. This development was consummated in the three-
part Latin hymns and Magnificats, in the five later Masses

(all in four vocal parts) written at Cambrai, and in the
beautiful antiphons *Ave regina caelorum* ('Hail, queen of
heaven') and *Alma redemptoris mater* ('Gracious mother of the
Redeemer').[26] The former was written ten years before his
death for performance at his death-bed, and into its text he
inserted prayers for his salvation, mentioning his own
name – *Miserere tui labentis Dufay* ('Have mercy on thy failing Dufay'). In his Mass on the same plainsong, also a late
work, Dufay quoted music from the antiphon. In such works
as these, and in the earlier Mass *Caput* (a plainsong also used
by Ockeghem, Obrecht, and Richard Hygons of Wells)
and Mass *Se la face ay pale* (named after his own secular
chanson, 'If my face is pale', used as the tenor of the Mass),
the fully choral style was achieved on which succeeding
composers were to build:

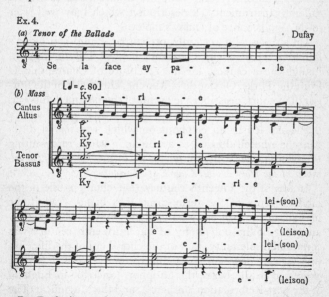

In Dufay's work we may observe not only profound
changes in the function and style of music, but also the connexions of his art with some of the historical events of his
time. In 1417 the so-called Great Schism, with rival Popes

at Rome and at Avignon, came to an end and the Papacy was firmly re-established in Rome under Martin V. He brought to Rome craftsmen and painters of the early Renaissance from northern Italy, and also singers and composers from France and the Low Countries for his chapel. Dufay, who had joined the papal singers in 1428, composed a motet in 1431 to mark the election of Eugenius IV as Pope, and two years later a motet to celebrate the Treaty of Viterbo between Eugenius and the Emperor Sigismund. In 1436, while with the papal chapel in Florence, he wrote a motet for the dedication of Brunelleschi's dome for the cathedral of Santa Maria del Fiore there. We are told by one who was present that at the Elevation during the dedicatory Mass 'every part of the cathedral resounded with the symphonious harmony and with the simultaneous sounds of different instruments', a description which may well refer to the performance of Dufay's motet.

Dufay was also certainly present at Philip the Good's fabulous 'Feast of the Pheasant', held at Lille in 1454 to inaugurate a crusade for the recapture of Constantinople from the Turks. Olivier de la Marche, chronicler of the Burgundian court, describes the events of the banquet, and tells us that in the final representation a Saracen armed with a battle-axe led in an elephant on which was seated de la Marche himself dressed as a woman in white, representing the Church, while the musicians performed Dufay's *Lamentation of the Holy Mother Church of Constantinople*.

It was in the fifteenth century that choral music in the modern sense of the term came into being. And if the prevailing spirit of early polyphonic music was festive joy and that of the polyphony of the fourteenth century was ceremonial solemnity, that of the choral era of the fifteenth was fervent devotion, particularly to the Blessed Virgin, expressed in the Mass, the antiphon (ancestor in England of the post-Reformation 'anthem'), and the Magnificat. The inception and growth of these forms coincided with a decline in the musical culture of the monasteries and a rise in that of cathedrals and churches of secular (i.e. non-monastic) priests, of colleges, and of private chapels. In France the

King and the Dukes of Burgundy, Berry, Orleans, and Savoy (where Dufay spent seven years in a chapel which was called 'the best in the world') vied with each other in the perfection of their chapel music. In England the chief centres included Edward III's foundations of St George's at Windsor and St Stephen's at Westminster, the Royal Household Chapel, and a succession of colleges, among them Queen's College, Oxford, Eton College, and King's College, Cambridge. In the royal chapels and the colleges the services were attended only by the members of the institution. From the early fifteenth century a parallel development to this rise of new choral foundations took place both in the secular (non-monastic) cathedrals and in the larger monasteries. There, however, the new devotional choral music was definitely aimed at a lay congregation. In secular cathedrals the choir of vicars-choral and boys sang votive Masses and antiphons in the Lady Chapel or nave; in monasteries a choir of laymen (not monks) and boys was maintained for similar functions, which also took place outside the choir, independently of the regular monastic services there.

In France and the Netherlands, after Dufay, the creative impulse of choral music passed to Ockeghem, Obrecht, and their contemporaries, in England after Dunstable to the composers whose choral works (for four to nine voices, mostly for five) were copied about 1500 into a splendidly executed choirbook for Eton College. The outstanding figure in this group of writers of brilliantly elaborate choral music is John Browne whose *Stabat Mater* (a setting of the devotional Latin poem about the vigil of Mary by the Cross)[27] ranks among the greatest works of his time. Not far behind him come Walter Lambe of Windsor, Richard Davy of Magdalen (Oxford) and Exeter, and Robert Wylkynson of Eton, while Robert Fayrfax and William Cornysh the younger are represented by early works. (See also p. 54.) The Eton choirbook (now available in a modern printed edition) was almost exclusively devoted to antiphons and Magnificats, but also contains Davy's *St Matthew Passion*,[28] in Latin, for four voices, the first Passion by a known composer. Its

combination of restraint and vigour make it a notable land-
mark in the history of the form. It is a setting of the words of
the crowd and of all personages in the Passion except Christ
himself. The antiphons and Magnificats, large in scope and
exacting in technical requirements, are more representative
of the florid style which these composers cultivated. In
splendour of conception and wealth of detail they rank
worthily with such contemporary accomplishments in architecture as the chapels of Eton and King's. The music of these
founders of the English choral tradition is a challenge to the
choirs of today to match in technical prowess and expressive
resource those of one of the richest periods in the history of
choral music.

2

From Ockeghem to Palestrina

c.1470–c.1590

CALDWELL TITCOMB

By the last decades of the fifteenth century, we find polyphonic choral composition in full swing; and it enjoyed a
peak period throughout the sixteenth century.

The story of Franco-Flemish and Italian choral polyphony in the High and Late Renaissance is essentially the
story of the music of the Roman Catholic Church, which
was at this time the chief patron of music as well as of the
other arts. Choral polyphony quite naturally appeared first
in liturgical music, since for centuries choirs had been on hand
to perform the extensive corpus of monophonic plainsong.

Composers of the period devoted themselves largely to
two types of choral music: the High Mass (*missa solemnis*)
and the motet. A polyphonic Mass would be a cycle of five
(or six) movements set to the invariable texts of the Ordinary
of the Mass: Kyrie, Gloria, Credo, Sanctus (with or without
a separate Benedictus), and Agnus Dei. Being wholly functional music, the movements were performed at the appropriate points during the service, so that only the first two
movements came without a considerable lapse of time
between.*

The motet was a single piece, set to words taken from the
Scriptures (often the Psalms) or the liturgy. Although motets
were often sung during the Mass, they were intended
primarily for use during the Divine Offices. These Offices
– also known as the Canonical Hours and the Office
Hours – theoretically took place every three hours round the
clock; the eight daily services were, starting about midnight:

* See Appendix 1, p. 397.

Matins, Lauds, Prime, Terce, Sext, None, Vespers, and
Compline. Vespers were musically the most noteworthy,
and frequently featured a polyphonic setting of the Magnificat. The other important offices, from a musical point of
view, were Matins (with its Te Deum) and Compline (with
its four antiphons of the Blessed Virgin Mary); and Easter
week elicited a number of special choral settings. One other
occasion inspired a fine body of choral music: the Requiem
Mass (*Missa pro defunctis* or Mass for the Dead). Save for
the vestigial Greek of the Kyrie in the Mass, the texts for all
this music were in Latin, the official tongue of the Catholic
Church.

Franco-Flemish composers enjoyed a clear musical hege-
mony in the High Renaissance. Often referred to as 'the
Netherlanders', they worked in what is now northern France,
Belgium, and Holland. The late fifteenth century had two
chief practitioners: Johannes Ockeghem (1430–95) and
Jacob Obrecht (*c.*1451–1505). With the advent of Ockeghem
one can really speak of a 'school of composers'; he trained
almost all of the important composers of the time, while
spending his last four decades in the service of three successive French kings. Nevertheless, his own choral output
was surprisingly small (though some works have been lost):
we have today only eleven complete Masses, a few other
movements from Masses, the earliest extant polyphonic
Requiem, and no more than ten motets.

Ockeghem's music marks a considerable departure from
the typical three-voice, short-phrased, treble-dominated
style of his teacher, Dufay (see Chapter 1). He increased the
normal texture from three parts to four. Although there are
a few isolated instances earlier, Ockeghem is thus the first
to employ consistently a real bass part in the modern sense,
with lines that go down as low as cello C (below the bass
stave). His interest in extending the vocal ranges downwards is contemporary with a similar extension in the ranges
of instruments and with eager exploitations of depth in
painting through the use of perspective.

Adopting the sonority of full triads (although it would be
several decades before the *final* chord of a piece was regu-

larly allowed the luxury of containing a third), Ockeghem aims at achieving a true contrapuntal style with embroidered tracery in all the voice-lines equally. Reflecting a distaste for unfilled or unintegrated space – an oft-observed feature in the Renaissance arts – he avoids internal stops as much as possible; and his lines float on and on without much aim or contour. He shows little concern for harmony as such, and the progression from chord to chord tends to be arbitrarily erratic. Contrary to general belief, his church polyphony does not on the whole make much use of thematic imitation among the voice-lines (his secular works do, however). Even the canons in the Masses, of which writers have made such a fuss, usually show such a time-lag that the canonic basis is all but imperceptible to the listener. A characteristic feature in Ockeghem is a build-up of tension and complex activity in the approach to the final cadence, as may be seen in several works available in modern editions.[1]*

Obrecht's choral legacy consists of two dozen Masses and a similar number of motets (including one Magnificat). Although he shares with Ockeghem a prevailing four-voice texture and a fondness for a climactic drive to the final cadence, Obrecht is a more progressive and more masterful figure. His lines, though less fussy than Ockeghem's, are more vigorous and kinetic; and they indulge in a good deal of easily audible imitation. The pulse is strong, with a pregnant use of short, recognizable motives. The texture is richly varied – both in the number of vocal strands and in the mixture of contrapuntal and chordal writing. The phrases are beautifully shaped arches, supported on the clearly defined pillars of dominant-to-tonic internal cadences. And, in fact, Obrecht is the first real master of consciously expressive harmony in the history of music. He moved rather often from job to job – both in northern Europe and in Italy – and his Church music[2] betrays the influence of Italian secular music (the *frottola*) and Netherlandish folk-music.

* In this and the previous chapter, small figures indicate reference to the list of recommended editions at the end of the book.

The High Renaissance comes to a climax in the early sixteenth century with an extraordinary fraternity of creative artists in all fields. In particular, these years witness the culminating maturity of a supreme quadrumvirate within our purview: Donato Bramante (1444–1514) in architecture, Raphael (1483–1520) in painting, Josquin des Prez (c.1445–1521) in music, and Leonardo da Vinci (1452–1519) in practically everything (the paragon of the versatile 'Renaissance man').

Though a northerner, Josquin des Prez (also spelt as Després and in other ways) spent the middle of his life working in Italy, including an eight-year stint as a singer in the papal choir. He was universally idolized as the greatest composer and teacher of his time; and his works gained unusually wide circulation through being printed and reprinted by Ottaviano dei Petrucci in book form from 1502 on – a rare privilege for any composer before the second half of the century. We have from Josquin's pen a choral repertory of about two dozen Masses and a hundred motets. Preferring a four-voice medium, he wrote music of admirable clarity, balance, and restrained expressiveness. He was not afraid to present sections more than once, either through straight repetition or variation; and he took great care in mixing contrapuntal and chordal writing. His music betrays a special fondness for contrasting high and low duet passages; and in general it reflects an innate concern for the importance of choral colour. The greatest composer who had yet lived, Josquin synthesized and intensified the musical techniques of his predecessors, and added a few new features of his own. He fused the Franco-Flemish-Gothic tradition and the Italian tradition into an exemplary universal style. And he bequeathed a rich arsenal of procedures, which almost all the rest of sixteenth-century choral music was content to adopt or adapt.

Consequently, this would seem an appropriate point to specify the chief techniques in composition at the time of the High and Late Renaissance. In the Mass, with its several movements, a special need was felt for some solid, unifying structural device. A favourite method was (as was shown in the preceding chapter) the employment of a pre-existing melody as a *cantus firmus*, which constituted the basis of the successive movements. The *cantus firmus* usually appeared in the tenor voice, written in either normal or relatively long note-values; and it might also permeate other voices as well. Composers drew their *cantus firmi* from several sources. One source was plainsong. Another was the secular song – the best-known example being the popular fifteenth-century French tune *The Armed Man* (*L'Homme armé*), which provided the material for Masses by Josquin and at least thirty other Renaissance composers. A third type of *cantus firmus* came from the use of an abstract fragment of an ascending or descending scale; and another resulted from linking up the vowels of a series of words with the corresponding solmization syllables – that is, the names of notes, *ut* (modern *do*), *re, mi, fa, sol, la*. This is a procedure analogous to the practice of some modern composers in fashioning thematic material from the letters of someone's name or from the numbers in a telephone directory. The names given to Masses (for instance Palestrina's Mass *Veni sponsa Christi*, below) generally refer to their source-material as an identification.

A second method of construction yielded the so-called 'parody' Mass. (The word 'parody' here carries none of the customary derogatory connotations.) Here a composer took over as a basis not just a single melodic line, but rather the entire polyphonic fabric of an existing piece – either by himself or by another, and either to a religious text (motet) or a secular one (*chanson* or madrigal). In some instances, the composer just substituted the text of the Mass for that of the original (a procedure known as *contrafactum*); but in most cases he interlarded sections of the original with new ones of his own, or reworked his model drastically and elaborated it into a fresh edifice that often all but obscured its source entirely. A significant point to realize is that very few Renaissance settings of the Mass were completely original products cut out of whole cloth. This by no means betokens a lack of creative power. The composers felt that, in their borrowing, they were paying homage to their mater-

ial, or were elevating its stature by incorporating it into the
Mass. Anyhow, the quality of works of art depends little on
the provenance of their material and largely on the way
the material is treated (the plays of Shakespeare providing
the classic instance).

Now these structural techniques were also used for motets.
But another procedure, present in many of Josquin's motets,
became by far the most universally characteristic, as the
motet itself increasingly throughout the sixteenth century
attracted composers more strongly than did the Mass.
(In fact, other kinds of composition written in this way –
both in the Renaissance and since – are said to be 'in motet
style'.) The composer broke his motet text up into its
constituent phrases. For each phrase, he fashioned a separate melodic idea, which was then presented imitatively by
successive voices – the whole presentation of one phrase
being known as a 'point of imitation'. A motet would then
consist of as many 'points' as there were phrases of text. At
first, imitations occurred mostly at the unison or octave, but
the interval of the fifth and fourth soon became increasingly
common. Occasionally, a 'point' might, for variety, be
homophonic rather than contrapuntal. In general, voices
were rhythmically independent and of equal importance.
The texture of a typical motet was continuous, since a new
point began in one voice before the previous point was
finished – except when a composer might choose to clarify
a major textual division by interrupting the flow of the
music.

A fine example of this technique, and of Josquin's style, is
the Annunciation motet *Ave Maria*,[3] which freely derives
some of its thematic material from a plainsong setting of this
much-used text. In Josquin's version, there are nine successive points of imitation. The excerpt in Example 5 shows
the portion from the end of point *a* to the beginning of point
d, point *c* ('Benedicta tu') illustrating the composer's
favourite device of contrasting duets. All the illustrated
points overlap; but later in the work, to emphasize the
only big break in the text, Josquin clearly separates points
e and *f*, and he underlines the articulation here, as in

Ex. 5.   Josquin, *Ave Maria*

numerous other works, by changing temporarily from his customary duple metre to triple metre.

The entire sixteenth century is often termed 'the golden age of polyphonic choral music'; and it is perfectly true that this period enjoyed the creativity of an astoundingly large number of highly gifted composers. Among Josquin's contemporaries the most notable figures are Isaac, de la Rue, and Mouton. Heinrich Isaac (*c*.1450–1517) not only

composed two dozen Masses[4] – that is, settings of the invariable Ordinary of the Mass; he also composed the first
polyphonic setting of all the texts for the Proper of the Mass,
that is, the part that varies with the day of the liturgical
year – a voluminous collection called the *Choralis Constan-
tinus*. The forty or more Masses[5] of Pierre de la Rue
(*c.*1460–1518) include the oldest known six-voice setting of
the Ordinary. Jean Mouton (*c.*1470–1522) was almost
exclusively a church composer, and second only to Josquin
in his easy mastery of counterpoint.[6]

I have already mentioned the increasing tendency of
Late Renaissance composers to favour the motet rather than
the Mass. This trend is partially explained by the fact that
the motet offered musicians a temptingly freer rein in the
personal choice of text and the methods of expressive musical
treatment. The preference is reflected in the work of the
two chief Franco-Flemish masters of the post-Josquin
generation. Nicolas Gombert (*c.*1490–1556) left us 10 Masses
and 169 motets, and Jacobus Clemens (*c.*1510–*c.*56) 15
Masses and 231 motets. Both composers, as was typical of
their generation, employed a five-voice texture about as
often as a four-voice one; and both favoured the 'point'
technique of Josquin. Gombert's motet *Super flumina* ('By
the rivers of Babylon'),[7] although it has thirteen points,
observes the same general textural and metrical organization as Josquin's *Ave Maria*; and about half his motets,
taking a clue from the text, are clearly divided into two
large sections, called the *prima pars* and *secunda pars*. Clemens's motet *Vox in Rama* ('In Rama was there a voice
heard')[8] has only four points, but each is considerably
developed.

In the middle of the century, the Catholic Church, as
part of its Counter-Reformation activities, held in Rome
the historic Council of Trent (1545–63). Meeting sporadi-
cally, this body, together with a special commission of
cardinals (1564–5), deliberated over the proper style for
church music. Its somewhat vague pronouncements advo-
cated the avoidance of anything 'lascivious or impure'
(such as the basing of liturgical music on material of

secular origin), and urged the employment of a lucid and dignified choral style in which the music should serve the text by setting the words in an easily intelligible and un-ostentatious manner.

During the second half of the century, musical leadership passed from the Franco-Flemish northern part of Europe to Italy. Many northern musicians continued to emigrate and work in Italy, but a host of native Italian composers also attained prominence. The most important nucleus, as one might expect, was the Roman school of composers, of whom by far the foremost was Giovanni Pierluigi da Palestrina (c.1525–94), who took the name 'Palestrina' from the town of his birth. From his own time right down to the present day, Palestrina's works have been held up by the Church as the supreme models of ideal liturgical style. No innovator, he was a conservative summarizer. Using all the Josquin techniques, he produced restrained, euphonious, unemotional, and balanced music through a masterful mixing of beautiful melody, harmony, and rhythm; and his treatment of melodic contour and of dissonance was even stricter than that of his predecessors. In the Palestrina style, the chief dissonance was the suspension, which was always prepared as a consonance of the same or longer time-value, and subsequently resolved downward by step to another consonance. Thus, in the following example from Palestrina's *Pope Marcellus* Mass, the alto part contains two suspensions – the first slightly embellished by a rhythmic anticipation of the resolution, and the second unadorned.

Incidentally, this passage (and what precedes it) demonstrates one aspect of the remarkable rhythmical flexibility characteristic of the composer. The combined effect of the participating voices can be interpreted metrically in many different ways. I am probably the first to choose to transcribe the passage in triple ($\frac{3}{2}$) metre. One can, however, hear the music as starting on the first beat in duple ($\frac{2}{2}$) time; or, again, as starting on the last beat in quadruple ($\frac{4}{2}$) time (see the accompanying diagrams). And there are still other possibilities.

Ex. 6. Palestrina, *Pope Marcellus Mass*

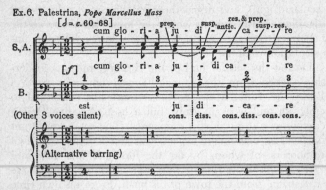

Palestrina's *Pope Marcellus* Mass, for six voices, is his most famous work and one of the rare specimens (in that period) of a Mass not based on prior material, so far as we yet know.

Palestrina left us 105 masses, of which 41 are for four voices, 38 for five, 22 for six, and 4 for eight. A good example of the style of his Masses is the first 'Agnus Dei' from the four-voice 'parody' mass *Veni sponsa Christi*[9] (about four-fifths of his Masses use 'parody' or a similar technique), which consists of three points of imitation. He also wrote about 500 motets and other sacred works. His four-voice motet *Sicut cervus* ('As the hart panteth'),[10] following the Gombert two-section scheme, has a *prima pars* of three points and a *secunda pars* of five; while the motet *Adjuro vos* ('I charge you, O daughters of Jerusalem')[11] displays a thicker, six-voice texture. Palestrina did not reach the heights of two other sixteenth-century composers, Byrd and Lassus, and owes the pre-eminence of his reputation largely to an unflaggingly elevated level of craftmanship. Musically, he was always on his best behaviour – even though, on the side, he gave up the priesthood to marry a rich widow and to engage in the worldly pursuit of managing a fur-trading business.

Among Palestrina's pupil-successors, two – sometimes called 'the Little Romans' – stand out. One is Giovanni Maria Nanino (*c.*1545–1607), whose six-voice motet *Hodie* *nobis coelorum rex* ('Unto us this day is born the King of Heaven') is still sung in the Sistine Chapel every Christmas morning. The other is Felice Anerio (*c.*1560–1614), Palestrina's immediate successor as composer to the Papal Chapel, several of whose works were for a long time assigned to his master. A similar misattribution characterized more than two dozen pieces by the talented chapel-master of Cremona Cathedral, Marc'Antonio Ingegneri (1545–92). All three men used the Palestrina style, but with a little less severity and a little more personal feeling.

A colony of Roman-trained composers was also active in Spain, of whom the two most eminent were Cristóbal de Morales (*c.*1500–53) and Tomás Luís de Victoria (1549–1611). Both devoted themselves exclusively to church music with an intensity that well mirrored the fanatical zeal with which Spain espoused the Counter-Reformation. Morales, the first great Spanish composer, brought a stark, mystical power to his works, such as his masterpiece, the penitential motet *Emendemus in melius* ('Let us make amends')[12] (one of several examples of his simultaneous use of two different religious texts in the same work) and the last of his sixteen settings of the Magnificat, in the eighth mode.[13] Victoria, perhaps the greatest composer that Spain has ever produced, has deservedly been called 'the Spanish Palestrina'. Utilizing the Roman techniques, he added his own emotional fervour (at times approaching fever), together with a freer treatment of dissonance, more chromatic harmony, and melodic intervals forbidden in the Palestrina style. His music is often dramatic, with repeated notes, and does not flow evenly. Victoria had a preference for the minor mode, and for texts dealing with personal ideas or events rather than with abstract Church dogma – as in the highly expressive motets *O magnum mysterium* ('All wondrous mystery')[14] and *O vos omnes* ('All ye that pass by').[15] Some of his works were strongly influenced by the progressive style of the Venetian school of composers.

In fact Venice was, next to Rome itself, the most important musical centre in Italy during the late Renaissance. The city's musical uniqueness stemmed largely from the special character of Venice itself – a region rather aloof from the life of the four other major states; a luxurious, semi-oriental capital carrying on continued intercourse with the East. Its environment was one of visual splendour – above all, in the dazzling polychrome exteriors of its architecture – which was increased by the glittering reflections in the water. The byword of Venetian life was 'colour'. Just as a magnificent treatment of colour characterizes the work of the great Venetian painters of the time like Titian, Tintoretto, and Veronese, so Venetian music could not help being similarly influenced.

St Mark's Cathedral was the nucleus of Venetian life – political, religious, and musical. The grand emergence of Venetian music dates from the appointment in 1527 of an imported Fleming, Adrian Willaert (c.1490–1562), to the much-coveted post of music director at St Mark's. During his tenure of thirty-five years, he wrote church music (mostly motets), ran a singing school, and trained a flock of native Italian composers and theorists. He modified his inherited Franco-Flemish techniques in favour of a richer, thicker, more harmonically oriented style, in which the individual voice lines are less interesting melodically – though they are impeccably adjusted to the text-syllables, as in the *prima pars* of his Easter motet *Victimae paschali laudes* ('Praises to the paschal victim').[16] And on occasion he wrote separate parts for accompanying instruments.[17]

But Willaert's best-known contribution was the stimulus to polychoral composition he provided by writing and performing, some time before 1550, eight Psalm-settings that required two separate four-voice choirs to sing alternately and together. Now Willaert did not, as often stated, 'invent' this polychoral technique – there are a number of considerably earlier examples; but he did prove to be the necessary catalyst in the right place at the right time. Three contributing agents were: the age-old antiphony characteristic of the orient, kept alive through constant contact with Byzantine culture; the contrasting-duet technique of Josquin; and the architectural design of St Mark's – the only great church in western Christendom built on the plan of a Greek cross – with its two organs in opposing apses. Polychoral writing became a Venetian speciality, whose influence would extend far and wide; it was developed further in Venice, especially by Willaert's pupil Andrea Gabrieli (c.1520–86), and reached a peak of opulence, with brilliant, idiomatic parts for brass and other instruments, at the hands of the latter's nephew, Giovanni Gabrieli (see p. 95).

It need hardly be added that Italy and Spain produced no non-Catholic church music; although Protestantism did have some success in Switzerland, France and the Low Countries, its churches did not have trained choirs, and played little if any role in the story of Renaissance polyphonic choral music. Choral groups today might, however, look into the French ensemble settings of the Psalms, written for home use, by the Protestant convert Claude Goudimel (c.1505–72) and other composers.[18]

The corpus of secular Renaissance polyphonic compositions is, properly speaking, not choral music at all. It was written for informal and usually intimate performance, with one singer on each part (or, sometimes, one singer on the top part and instruments on the rest). But, just as we have evidence that once in a while choral works for the Church were performed with only one (strong-voiced) singer on a part, records exist of occasional performances of secular pieces with two singers on a part. At any rate, modern choruses have eagerly embraced the secular Renaissance repertory along with the religious; and it would be uncharitable, to say the least, to take it away from them. Consequently, our present purposes demand some mention of the two secular genres that have enjoyed widespread choral appeal: the sixteenth-century French *chanson* and the Italian madrigal. Of course, most of the composers already mentioned wrote both church and secular music; but it is nevertheless a valid generalization that Renaissance composers tended to excel in one or the other.

The rage for the writing and performing of *chansons* began in 1528, when Pierre Attaignant, the first French printer to use movable type, issued two *chanson* collections –

the earliest publications of polyphonic music in the country. At his death in 1552 he had issued some 1,500 *chansons*. So popular was this genre that there arose a particularly entertaining sort – the well-named *fricassée* – in which composers would incorporate dozens of phrases from other *chansons*; one of these [19] contains some fifty quotations from familiar *chansons*. Of the earlier practitioners of the *chanson*, the most significant are Claudin de Sermisy (*c*.1490–1562) and Clément Janequin (*c*.1485–*c*.1560), a pupil of Josquin; and the foremost later master is Claude Le Jeune (*c*.1530–1600).

Some *chansons* are close to the contrapuntal style of the motet, while some are entirely chordal; but most represent some sort of compromise, like Crécquillon's *Pour ung plaisir* ('For a delight') [20] and Costeley's *Allon, gay, gay* ('Come now, gay, gay shepherds'). [21] A characteristic *chanson* would have: a vernacular French text (often of high quality); four or five voices; a strong, lively rhythmic pulse in duple metre; an opening motive containing repeated notes, or the rhythm of a half-note and two quarter-notes (or both); internal breaks at cadences; and recurring sections with the same or different text. So the musical scheme of *Pour ung plaisir* is *a a b c c*, and that of *Allon, gay, gay* is a rondo – *a b a c a d a e a'*.

Janequin (also spelt Jannequin), of whose *chansons* nearly 300 survive, is especially famous for his body of descriptive or programmatic *chansons*. The call of the lark is imitated in *L'alouette*; [22] other *chansons* depict the Battle of Marignan, the hunt, the songs of an entire aviary, the capture of Bologna, the cries of Paris, the cackling of women. These pieces had many imitators. Another significant type was the *chanson mesurée*, practised by Le Jeune and others. The texts were poems, mostly by Baïf, that revived the ancient Latin quantitative prosody; in setting them, the composers allotted exactly twice the time-value to a long syllable as to a short. The result was music with irregular accents or constantly shifting metres, like Le Jeune's *O rôze reyne des fleurs* ('O rose, queen of flowers') [23] or *D'une coline* ('As I walk upon a hill'). [24] But the most frequently performed specimen, which also gives an idea of the general *chanson* flavour, is Le Jeune's attractively jaunty *Revecy venir du printans* ('Here comes springtime once again'),[25] the first portion of which is shown in Example 7. Its over-all scheme, typical of the *chanson mesurée*, is the same as that of *Allon, gay, gay* mentioned above. Specifically, there are five statements of a two-line refrain for a full, five-voice texture; alternating with these are four long strophes, which successively increase the texture from two voices to five. The metrical pattern yields, in effect, an oscillation between $\frac{6}{4}$ and $\frac{3}{2}$ time (known as *hemiola*), which incidentally continued to be a favourite rhythm right through to the end of the Baroque period in the eighteenth century.

The Italian madrigal, which dealt mostly with aspects of love, grew out of the *frottola* (a simple, sectional, dance-like vocal-poetic genre popular in northern and central Italian aristocratic circles)[26] with considerable assistance from the *chanson* and the motet. The first madrigals so termed appeared in 1530. For three or four voices, the early madrigals were written by such Franco-Flemings as Philippe Verdelot[27] and Jacob Arcadelt,[28] and by the first important native madrigalist, Costanzo Festa.[29] But the great period of the madrigal begins with the works of the immigrant northerner Cipriano de Rore (1516–65), who chose fine texts (often by Petrarch), preferred a five-voice texture in which all lines were equal, and adopted a rather continuous non-strophic style in which he carefully expressed the emotion of the poem phrase by phrase – sometimes through dramatic use of chromaticism.[30] A superb, serious exponent was the Belgian-born Philippe de Monte (1521–1603), who also wins the prize for quantity by having composed some 1,200 madrigals.

But the finest madrigalist of all was a native Italian, Luca Marenzio (1553–99), whom his contemporaries called 'the divine composer' and 'the sweetest swan in Italy'. His seventeen books of madrigals (the majority for five voices) show him as a superlative master of imitative counterpoint and homophony, though he leaned to a vertical harmonic emphasis.[31] The perfect bond between notes and text makes each madrigal unique. A frequent user of chromaticism, he moulded an expressive, dramatic, pliant, and polished style in which he raised the techniques of word-painting to a sophisticated art.

Consider, for instance, Marenzio's *S'io parto i' moro* ('If I leave, I die'),[32] whose opening phrase is shown in Example 8.

The sadness of parting calls for slow motion. And the idea, as often with Marenzio, is underlined by juxtaposing notes in both their unaltered and altered forms (the B natural and B flat in the first and second tenor, the F natural and F sharp in the bass and soprano). The word 'die' is emphasized by the jump downwards of the two upper voices,

Ex. 8. Marenzio, *S'io parto*
[*Andante*]

and by the alto's affecting *appoggiatura* on E flat and following suspension of the note D – while the soprano is so choked with emotion that she has to take a momentary rest, and the first tenor is unable even to utter the word. Later in the madrigal, after a quickening of pace, the music again slows down at 'the dolorous parting slays me', the second statement of 'slay' containing rising, dissonant tension in the tenor. 'Those whom Love has joined, how divide them?' has, in its first phrase, a closely wedded duet in the upper parts; while the second is conveyed by dividing the flow of one voice into small note-values and by setting off the phrase in another part by rests.

The extremes in radical harmony and chromaticism came in the 'manneristic' madrigals by the daring, murdering Carlo Gesualdo (*c.*1560–1613) and in some by Claudio Monteverdi (see Chapter 5). The influence of Marenzio on the flowering of the madrigal in England is noted in Chapter 3.

I have saved till last the mention of the greatest of all Renaissance composers – Roland de Lassus (1532–94) – who represents a grand culminating synthesis of the Renaissance musical mind. Thrice kidnapped as a boy because of his beautiful voice, he became known as 'the Belgian Orpheus', proceeded to hold successive jobs all over Europe, and was knighted by both Emperor Maximilian II and the Pope. ('Orlando di Lasso' is an Italian version of his name.) Lassus, Josquin, and William Byrd (see Chapter 3) make up the reigning triumvirate of all Renaissance vocal composition.

A composer of incredible versatility and inexhaustible creative power, Lassus left more than 2,000 works, including more than 1,000 motets and at least 53 Masses (mostly of the 'parody' type). Furthermore, he was a master of the Italian madrigal, the French *chanson,* [33] and even the German *lied* ;[34] and he would doubtless have written to English words too had the need arisen. His work betrays a cosmopolitan fusion of northern and southern national elements, as well as an interpenetration of religious and secular influences. He used everything from a two-part to a twelve-part texture, with a predominance of five-voice writing. Some of his church works are Franco-Flemish, some are severely Roman, some are brilliantly polychoral in the Venetian manner. His writing of Masses[35] is no greater than Palestrina's; but he is incomparable in the motet field – examples being the celebrated *Penitential Psalms,*[36] the five-voice *Adoramus te, Christe* ('We adore thee, O Christ')[37], and *Tristis est anima mea* ('My soul is exceeding sorrowful'),[38] and the six-voice *In hora ultima* ('At the last hour shall die all things').[39] Compared with Palestrina, Lassus employs a richer palette, is more human and deeply expressive, as well as more harmonically oriented. In general, his style falls between that of Palestrina and de Monte on the one hand and that of Victoria and Marenzio on the other. He wonderfully summarizes the entire Renaissance while at the same time looking forward to the Baroque.

There remain to be mentioned a number of general points about Renaissance vocal music that are not widely enough recognized. Most of these concern the large disparity between what a composer wrote and what the listener heard, particularly in church music. It may seem to us that there was an appalling imprecision and indifference on the part of composers, but we must realize that these men were not writing for distant posterity but primarily for specific occasions at hand, often ones that they personally would be charged with supervising.

Frequently, then, composers did not put the words underneath the proper notes, but wrote them all together in one place. In the case of well-known texts, such as the Mass, they would indicate just the first word, and leave the detailed fitting of the words to the performers (who were used to this, as we are not). Although the music was ostensibly written in the old modes, the modal harmony was somewhat undermined in performance by the customary practice of automatically applying unwritten accidentals (*musica ficta*), notably the sharpened leading-note at cadences (e.g. C sharp, not C natural, when rising to a final D). Not only this, but the music as written was likely to be modified by all sorts of improvised embellishments, especially in the top voice and at cadences. (For a good summary, see Imogene Horsley's article in the *Journal of the American Musicological Society*, Spring 1951.)

During the period, vocal music was not available in full score, nor was it provided with bar lines. No attempt was made to align the notes in one part with the corresponding notes in another. Thus a singer was forced to concentrate on conveying the flexible rhythms of his own part without being unduly influenced by those of his colleagues. For secular music, in fact, singers generally had a part-book – whether hand-written or printed – containing nothing but, say, tenor parts. Part-books were sometimes used for church music; but most frequently a huge folio choirbook (usually hand-copied) was employed, and all the singers read from the same copy. In this connexion, I should make clear that a normal sixteenth-century church choir had only twelve to sixteen singers, while the papal choir hovered consistently around twenty-four members. Even for a festive Venetian work for two choirs, St Mark's could not count on rounding-up more than sixteen singers for each choir. (Lassus, when at Munich, had available for a time a body of sixty-odd singers and thirty instrumentalists, but this was virtually unique.) Furthermore, no women were allowed to sing in church; the upper parts were sung by boy sopranos or adult falsettists, or – increasingly as the sixteenth century progressed – *castrati*.

Now the impression persists that the Renaissance ideal

was the *a cappella* (unaccompanied) choir. The *a cappella* ideal was actually an invention of the Baroque. Polyphonic Renaissance church music was almost always accompanied on the organ, and often by other instruments too (doubling the voice parts) – except in the Sistine Chapel, where the choir gallery was too small to accommodate anything but the body of choristers. Moreover, composers did not provide directions for dynamics or expression. Many recent editions of Renaissance music preserve the original note-values (which were much faster then), so that a piece may contain only breves, semibreves, and minims. This is largely responsible for the dreadful funereal tempo so often adopted in present-day performances (conductors please note). Finally, there was in that era no accepted standard of pitch; hence no violence is done to this music today by transposing it up or down, within reasonable limits, to suit the convenience of the performers.

The execution of this repertory is indeed fraught with dangers, yet it has proved tempting and worthwhile to countless twentieth-century choral groups throughout the world. Still, much of this music remains untapped; performers today, amateur and professional alike, would benefit by increasing their acquaintance with the rich legacy of vocal music bequeathed by the bright galaxy of Renaissance masters.

3

Tudor England and After

c.1470–c.1625

ELIZABETH COLE

STRICTLY speaking, choral music is that which is sung by a choir. But in England from 1470 to around 1625 large choirs were to be found only within the church; secular vocal music was normally sung with one voice to each part. Today, however, it does not matter if one sings a motet or a madrigal in a group of four to six soloists or in a larger choir; the effect of working in a group – and there is nothing quite like it – is a most stimulating experience which gains in proportion to the increase in numbers. We cannot in our musical organization today reproduce the conditions found in Tudor England, so we must sing, to borrow a phrase from the old country-dance books, 'longways as many as will'.

Even church music, at this time, was not as church music is today. The closed communities of the Church – the friaries the monasteries, and the great schools – were the seats of learning, with an international language of Latin. There is no choral music of this period designed for men and women to sing together, not because the composers were misogynists, but because the Church was exclusively male. Choristers were organized in chapels, and the word 'chapel' meant the whole of the choral establishment – 'children' and 'gentlemen' (i.e. boy singers and men singers), choirmasters, organist, schoolmaster, vestments, plate, service-books, and all. Apart from the cathedrals, the King maintained his own Chapel Royal, and sometimes took the members of it with him when he went on a journey; royal patronage in fact tended to reflect the personal interest of the reigning monarch. Richard III, who reigned from 1483–5, instituted the practice of taking choristers from provincial choirs (by press-gang methods if necessary) to serve in his own Chapel Royal.

Once inside a choral establishment, strict rules governed every moment of a boy's life, as can be seen from this extract from the early sixteenth-century regulations of Wells Cathedral:

When the boys are seated [at table] they should behave like gentlemen . . . eat their food slowly and not ravenously . . . they should not clean their teeth with their knives. . . . Let them jump into bed so that in each bed there be boys lying in the manner following, viz: two small boys with their heads at the head of the bed, and one elder with his head at the foot of the bed.

The composer John Redford (c.1485–1543) bears this out, for he writes of his early days as a chorister in a set of semi-humorous verses which include the lines:

We have so many lashes to learn this peelde* song
That I will not lie to you, now and then among,
Out of our buttocks we may pluck the stumps thus long.

A decline in English music had followed Dunstable's death in 1453. But about 1500 there again arose a notable school of English composers, which includes Robert Fayrfax (1464–1521), William Cornysh (c.1465–1524), John Taverner (c.1470–1545), Hugh Aston (?1480–1522), Christopher Tye (c.1498–1572), and John Redford. Great numbers of Masses and motets testify to the quality of their art. The contribution of Fayrfax and Cornysh to the Eton Choirbook (c.100) was mentioned in Chapter 1.

Christopher Tye began as a chorister at King's College, Cambridge, and came to the Chapel Royal by way of the organ-loft of Ely Cathedral. His best-known work is the Mass for four voices written round an old folksong *Westron Wynde*. This practice of taking a well-known popular tune (purged of its sinful rhythms) is an interesting phenomenon of the early Tudor period. The idea, originally from the

---

* 'Peelde': wretched, miserable.

Netherlands (see the previous chapters), did not bring such a fresh look to church music as might be imagined, since the popular tunes were all but unrecognizably buried among the other independent parts. But at least it showed a slight weakening of the domination of the traditional plainsong as a source-material for polyphonic composition.

John Taverner began his working life as Master of the Children (that is, the choirboys) at Wolsey's College (now Christ Church) at Oxford. In 1528 he was imprisoned for heresy in 'a deep cave under the ground of the College, where salt fish was laid, so that through the filthy stink thereof they were all infected'. However, he seems to have survived this ordeal and was pardoned – 'being but a musician'. In 1538 he gave up his musical appointment to become a political agent for Thomas Cromwell in the suppression of the monasteries. Taverner's music is typical of the whole period. A single word is often squeezed out over interminably long musical phrases, stretched through the beautiful but tortuous alleyways of polyphony, until it vanishes. And when the word has disappeared, the effect is almost of instrumental music, not choral. Taverner was perhaps the greatest master of music of his time, but he shows no feeling for words.

More attractive as a personality was Henry VIII's personal friend William Cornysh (c. 1465–1524), under whom the choir of the Chapel Royal must have enjoyed itself immensely. He first appears in the records as Master of the Singing Boys in 1479/80, and served three successive kings at a salary of 13s. 4d. a quarter. In his time he played many parts – as composer, playwright, and provider of pageants, paving-stones, lavatories, and guttering. In 1513 he took the choir to France and gave a series of one-night performances in several towns. In June 1530 he was there again for the ceremonies of the Field of the Cloth of Gold, and received 103s. 4d. for the keep of ten children at the rate of 2d. per head per day. In the British Museum is a manuscript of songs, most of them in three parts, in which many of Cornysh's works appear together with thirty-eight compositions of Henry VIII himself. One of Cornysh's most attractive songs is *Blow thy horn, hunter*, a refreshingly simple piece which has a sense of harmonic progression which was modern at the time (Example 9).

Ex.9. Cornysh, *Blow thy horn*

[*Fast*]

A.,T.

[*mf*] Blow thy horn, hun - ter, and blow thy horn on high. There

B.

is a doe in yon-der wood, in faith she will not die   Now

Now blow

blow thy horn, hun-ter, now blow thy horn, jol-ly hun - ter.

thy—

Cornysh was a rare spirit; his contemporaries were far more academic and conservative. If the choral music of this period, now available in the fine *Tudor Church Music* series, seems somewhat monotonous to us, we must remember that it was more or less old-fashioned even when it was written. English composers were apparently little affected by the sudden quickening of pace observable on the Continent in the work of Josquin des Prez and his successors.

A few of the massive manuscript choirbooks of this time can still be seen today. These were stood on lecterns, and the choir gathered round them to see the huge notes in the dim light of the church. Copying had to be done laboriously by hand, and it was customary for individual members of the choir to write out all the treble parts of several works, all the tenor parts, and so on, and stitch them together. To make a modern edition of a work of this period depends on our being able to obtain a copy of *each* voice-part; and when (as often happens) one or more parts are lost, then we can only conjecture what the whole work would once have sounded like. It is true that the printing of music in England is reckoned as having begun with the arrival in London in 1477 of Wynkyn de Worde as assistant to the famous William Caxton; but not until the middle of the sixteenth century did printing come to be widespread enough to rank as an active force in the spreading of choral (or instrumental) music.

The most important single event in the first half of the sixteenth century, as regards music, politics, and social life in England, was the dissolution of the monasteries by Henry VIII in 1539-40. Thousands of choristers were turned out of the friaries and monasteries, and obliged to look for other work in what must have seemed to them an alien world. 'The loss to music', so the textbooks tell us, 'was incalculable.' Nothing could be further from the truth. Forcibly scattered throughout the country, the church musicians with their knowledge and discipline were directly responsible for the flowering of secular music in the succeeding Elizabethan age.

In any case, Henry VIII was by no means as ruthless towards his musicians as the Dissolution might suggest. He arranged for the establishment of a 'New Foundation', to include paid choristers (boys and men) as well as clergy. And under his son, Edward VI, the Reformation proceeded in a careful and orderly fashion, with some curious omissions. When the chantries (endowments for the chanting of Masses) was dissolved in 1547, for instance, an exemption was made for the Royal Chapel of St George's, Windsor; and Latin Mass continued to be celebrated there right up to the reign of Elizabeth.

The most distinguished member of the Chapel Royal at this time was Thomas Tallis (*c*.1505-85), who had what Taverner and his contemporaries had generally lacked – a feeling for the beauty of words. Tallis's output was enormous, and some of his works (the Morning and Evening

Service in the Dorian mode, and several hymns) are still in frequent use today. As a visual illustration of the revolution brought about by the Reformation, compare the two short extracts of Example 10 – the first from Taverner's Mass *O Michael* (the name is that of a plainsong used in the composition of this Mass) and the second from a 'Benedictus' by Tallis.

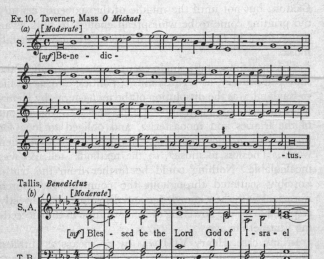

With the passing of the Act of Uniformity in February 1549, Protestantism became the official religion of the country and English replaced Latin as the language of the liturgy. The first English Prayer Book appeared in the same year, and it was ordained that no language except that 'understanded of the people' was to be heard in the churches.

Tallis, who composed equally happily to Latin and English texts, was one of a group of otherwise little-known composers who actually anticipated the demand for a new and simpler music for worship. In the Bodleian Library at Oxford are three of a set of four part-books (the tenor part is unhappily lost) which show how the break-away from elaborate polyphony took place. These part-books form part of what is known as the Wanley manuscript, after the man who gave them to the library in the eighteenth century, and contain more than eighty works set to English words – canticles (settings of obligatory texts) for morning and evening service, harmonized settings of plainsong, a great many anthems, and no less than ten English settings of Holy Communion. In these settings, simplicity is prized, and the principle of one-note-to-one-syllable is very carefully observed.

In 1550 John Merbecke (*c.*1510–85) published his *Book of Common Prayer Noted*, which is still in use today. In parts of it he adapted old plainsong melodies to the new English liturgy, so that they could be learned by heart by the congregation. It is believed that he did this under the supervision of Archbishop Cranmer, who drew up the words. Later, Merbecke dropped out of musical life, and became a writer of tracts of theological invective.

The reign of Elizabeth, from 1558 to 1603, is often said to be the 'golden age 'of English music. The position of the composer in society, however, was that of a superior kind of servant. He was obliged by law to wear the livery or badge of the nobleman in whose service he was employed, or run the risk of being locked up as a rogue or vagabond. Unattached musicians often turned out to be spies, for there was much subversive activity in Elizabeth's reign. Yet the status of music was higher than it had ever been, and the salaried composer might become the friend of the family he served. There was music for every occasion – birth, marriage, entertaining guests, in the theatres, indoors and out of doors, Sundays and weekdays, for hunting, at meal-times, and at death. And anybody who laid claim to an education, however rudimentary, could, and did, sing. Vocal music set the pattern for instrumental music. The works for small or large combinations of strings or wind which poured out of the presses in the last twenty years of Elizabeth's reign and throughout that of James I (1603–25) were built on solid principles of vocal writing. The feeling for our modern harmonic sense, based on major and minor keys, grew, and the use of the medieval modal scale declined.

The motet (previously a composition to a Latin text not an obligatory part of the service) now took on, in post-Reformation England, a divided form. Some works were still written in Latin, though they could no longer be used in the Established Church. These were known as *cantiones sacrae* ('sacred songs'). But for the liturgy, the motet was replaced by the anthem with English words. The term *anthem* itself is distinctively English, and is usually derived from 'antiphon'. But the old spelling 'antempne' – as in a thirteenth-century reference, 'after the Hympne come the Antempnes and Psalms' – suggests a derivation from 'hymn', as though the 'antempne' is to the 'hympne' what the anti-masque is to the masque – that is, that an anthem comes *after* the hymn. Queen Elizabeth's injunctions in 1559 gave official sanction to the use of anthems, and an enormous number of them were written during her long reign.

Thomas Morley (1557–*c*.1605), a great innovator, is best known for his secular vocal music (see p. 62) and for his activities as a music publisher. But the anthem *Out of the Deep* for tenor solo and five-voiced choir was one of his most successful experiments, anticipating the 'verse anthem' of the Restoration period. (See Chapter 6.) Morley evidently had in his choir one singer with a strong tenor voice (most choirs have) and gave him lines to sing alternately with the choir. The balance and contrast of the one with the many, in always ascending passages, is intensely personal and moving. Another supreme example in this style is *Behold thou hast made my days*, by Orlando Gibbons (1583–1615), whose madrigals we shall consider later. Gibbons's best-known anthem is *Hosanna to the Son of David*, a massive full-choir setting. The text was similarly set as an anthem by Thomas Weelkes (?–1623).

John Dowland (1563–1626) became a Roman Catholic (later returning to Protestantism), and, failing to obtain a place at Elizabeth's court, worked variously in Germany, Italy, Denmark, and England. His distinctive contribution to vocal music is the ayre (this old spelling of 'air' is commonly kept for this special use), a type of solo song to be sung to the lute or to viols and other combinations of instruments. These are not quite outside the choralist's repertory for many of the ayres have alto, tenor, and bass voice-parts as an alternative to the lute accompaniment below the soprano melody.

Dowland's preface to an ancient musical treatise which he translated contains some cutting remarks of an internationally travelled musician:

The English do carol, the French sing, the Spaniards weep, the Italians ... caper with their voices, the others bark, but the Germans (which I am ashamed to utter) do howl like wolves.

The ayre, with its concentration of melodic interest in the uppermost voice, is distinguished from the madrigal, which in principle was a contrapuntal composition in which all voice-parts made equally important contributions to the web of sound. On many of the original printed part-books of English madrigals are to be found the words 'apt for voices or viols'. It was indeed a common practice for a viol either to act as a replacement when one of the voices was missing, or to back up a weaker voice. Since viols correspond closely in pitch to our modern family of strings, it is entirely permissible today to play a soprano part on a violin, an alto part on a viola, and tenor or bass parts on a cello, in substitution or accompaniment.

The 'English' madrigal is a myth. Its origins were purely Italian. The madrigal form came to England in the travelling-bags of noblemen and musicians, and the 'Italianate Englishmen' of the last half of the sixteenth century, heartily despised and secretly envied by their more insular countrymen, are of the utmost importance to the development of English secular music. They went abroad for many reasons – on errands of politics or business, or to improve their education, or for reasons of religion. The Roman Catholic composer Peter Philips (?–1634) won fame abroad as Pietro Filippi, and John Cooper (c.1575–1626) became known as Giovanni Coperario. Traffic of this type brought back to England hundreds of printed part-books of Italian madrigals, and many new ideas. In 1588, the year of the Armada, Nicholas Yonge as publisher and Thomas Este as printer brought out the first book of *Musica transalpina* – 'madrigals translated, of 4, 5, and 6 parts, chosen out of divers excellent authors, with the first and second part of *La Verginella* made by Master Byrd upon two stanzas of Ariosto, and brought to speak English with the rest'. Yonge writes in his Introduction that he had found

Italian madrigals to be singularly well liked, not only of those for whose cause I gathered them, but of many skilful gentlemen, and other great musicians, who affirmed the accent of the words to be well maintained, the descant not hindered, and in every place due decorum kept.

The composers represented included Marenzio (Dowland's personal friend), Palestrina, and Lassus. The second volume of *Musica transalpina* was published in 1597, the year when music-printing in England reached a new peak. Among the records of the Stationers' Company for this year are books of madrigals by Kirbye and Weelkes, Dowland's *First Book of Ayres*, Morley's five- and six-part canzonets (similar to madrigals), and Morley's *Plain and Easy Introduction to Practical Music*, the most famous textbook on music of the whole period. With the madrigal went the subsidiary form known as the ballett – dance-like (as its name implies), strongly rhythmical, and with a fa-la refrain. Morley, as in *My bonny lass she smileth*, was a master of this type of composition.

The greatest composer of the Elizabethan age was William Byrd (1543–1623), who wrote music that was (in his own phrase) 'framed to the life of the words'. Like Gibbons, he was discriminating in his choice of texts. His music, properly performed, has a swinging stride that later editors have too often shackled with bar-lines that the composer neither wrote nor intended. Everything Byrd wrote is important, from the *Psalms, Sonnets, and Songs of Sadness and Piety* of 1588 (which contains some of his most gay and airy madrigals, as well as magnificent settings of metrical versions of the Psalms) to the Latin motets in his *Gradualia* of 1605. Of this work the entire first edition vanished, since it was held to have subversive political implications. We may well wonder how, in those stormy times, Byrd managed to live to be eighty years of age. He was a Roman Catholic, and whenever a major plot was afoot, his house was searched. Yet his person remained untouched. The problem of divided loyalty did not bother him, for he remained faithful to Rome, and at the same time was the most respected member of Elizabeth's Chapel Royal. His three Latin Masses (for three, four, and five voices), all conjecturally dated about 1605, are among the great classics of the age.

In the considerable output of Orlando Gibbons there is only one slim volume of madrigals, printed in 1612 as *The First Set of Madrigals and Motets of Five Parts: Apt for Viols and Voices*. The printer evidently believed he would soon have the pleasure of producing a second set, but this was not to be. The lyric of the second madrigal in this book gives us the key to Gibbons's character –

> O that the learnéd poets of this time
> That in a love-sick line so well can speak,
> Would not consume good wit in hateful rhyme,
> But with deep care some better subject seek.

Gibbons himself was fastidious, and always sought the subject of his settings 'with deep care'.

Since madrigals were written primarily for the pleasure not of an audience but of those who sang them, we need not consider it a criticism that the complexity of texture often makes it difficult for a listener to distinguish the words. But the madrigals of Thomas Weelkes (*c.*1575–1623) and John Wilbye (1574–1638) are deliberately written so that the significant words should 'come through'. These two men are among the twenty-six different composers who contributed to the *Triumphs of Oriana*, a collection which Thomas Morley edited in 1601. Each of these madrigals ends with a refrain it is impossible to miss, whatever the ramifications that have gone before:

> Then sang the shepherds and nymphs of Diana:
> Long live fair Oriana.

After nearly 350 years, the identity of 'Oriana', previously assumed to be Queen Elizabeth, has lately been questioned.

'Diana' was one of Elizabeth's nicknames, and nobody seems to have thought it odd that 'Diana' and 'Oriana' (which should rhyme, by the way), were made out to be one and the same person. Recently, however, the present writer has pointed out a stronger claim to the title of 'Oriana'. The name seems properly to belong to Anne of Denmark, the young wife of James I, who came to the throne in 1603. On her journey south from Scotland, after her husband's accession, 'Anna' (as she liked to be called) was greeted by Ben Jonson and others in a masque in the following style:

> Long live Oriana
> To exceed, as she succeeds, our late Diana.

It seems probable that the 'shepherds and nymphs' of Queen Elizabeth would want to welcome the new queen consort with a collection of madrigals, especially since she was known to love music and dancing. Moreover, the composer Thomas Greaves published, well over a year after the death of Queen Elizabeth, a collection of music which includes a madrigal with these lines:

> Sweet nymphs that trip along the English lands
> Go meet fair Oriana, beauty's queen.

There is no question that the 'Oriana' of this madrigal is Anne of Denmark. Moreover, James I was hailed as 'Orian, Master of the Ocean', and Jonson speaks of Oriana as 'Oriens Anna' – Anne of the rising sun.

One of the longest and most satisfying madrigals in the *Triumphs of Oriana* is Weelkes's six-part *As Vesta Was from Latmos Hill Descending*, which has ten principal subjects or ideas, exactly corresponding with the verse. Thus in the first four bars, at the word 'descending', the alto starts running down the scale, to be followed by the soprano with the drop of a sixth, and so on. The same thing happens in reverse at the words 'she spied a maiden queen the same ascending', which the tenor leads upwards. The whole of the first forty-six bars is a continuous movement up and down. At bar forty-seven there begins a remarkably effective passage, with a literal illustration in turn of 'two', 'three', 'together', and 'all alone':

Ex. 11. Weelkes, *As Vesta was from Latmos hill descending*

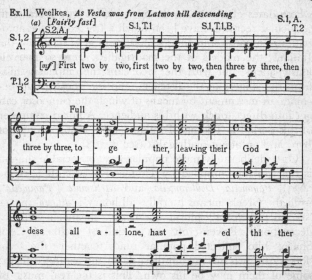

The madrigal becomes purely harmonic at bar seventy-two, with the words of the refrain 'then sang the shepherds and nymphs of Diana':

Though the rest of the work, from bar 79 to 114, is concerned with this refrain only, and very thickly scored, the word 'Oriana' is continually placed on very high notes, tossed from part to part like a single ball among six players – a ball which must never fall to the ground.

Weelkes and Wilbye were the first of the great Jacobean madrigal school, which includes Francis Pilkington (*c*. 1562–1638), Michael Este (?–1648), son of the printer Thomas Este, Thomas Bateson (*c*. 1570–1630), and John Ward, whose dates of birth and death are unknown. Weelkes in particular seems to have been much attracted by the acrobatics of anguish and the gymnastics of grief in which the Italians, the models of the madrigalists, were so marvellously adept. But with the Jacobeans the emphasis shifts from the singers to the listeners, and the vocal group becomes an instrument by means of which the composer can get into direct touch with his audience. A noted composer of this period is Thomas Tomkins (1572–1656), a pupil of Byrd and an adept madrigalist (see p. 108).

On a deliberately more popular level of sociable singing is the triptych compiled by Thomas Ravenscroft (*c.*1590–1633), *Pammelia*, *Deuteromelia*, and *Melismata* ('*Pammelia*', from the Greek, means literally 'all honey'; '*deutero*' means 'second'; '*melisma*', plural '*melismata*', means 'a musical decoration'). Ravenscroft was a kind of Jacobean Cecil Sharp, who collected popular tunes together (the term 'folk music' was not used in those days) and arranged them; some of them may be his own. This is the real music of the common people – rounds, catches, canons – singing in which anybody could join after a good dinner and drinks in the local tavern. It is indeed music for fun, and any choral group would find much value in it. All the numbers are unaccompanied, and can be sung at any pitch. In modern editions most of them are printed, as they should be, without bar-lines, and provide excellent practice on the eternal triangle of melody, rhythm, and harmony. Ravenscroft himself writes:

Music . . . may seem somewhat niggardly and unkind in never, as yet, publicly communicating but always privately retaining . . . this familiar mirth and jocund melody. But it may be Music hath hitherto been defective in this vein, because this vein indeed hath hitherto been defective in music.

Another 'popular' touch is evident in settings of *The Cries of London* by Dering, Weelkes, and Orlando Gibbons, for five and six voices with accompaniments for consort of viols. In these are preserved over 150 sets of words and tunes originating in the cries of street-traders as they hawked their wares through Queen Elizabeth's London, woven into highly organized musical fantasias.

James I reaped where Henry VIII and Elizabeth had sown; during his reign the madrigal school, the stage, poetry, and architecture all came to full flower. And new impetus was given to the choral music of the future by the publication in 1611 of the Authorized Version of the Bible, which regenerated church music and was directly responsible for the development of oratorio a century later.

4

Germany and Northern Europe, before Bach

c.1470–c.1705

J. MERRILL KNAPP

By modern standards, medieval and Renaissance choirs were never very large. Figures are generally lacking until the sixteenth century, but an illustration of the famous Netherlands composer, Jean Ockeghem (see Chapter 2), and his chapel choir at the court of France shows only eight singers beside himself. They are singing from a large choir-book, the notes of which are large enough to be read at a distance by the whole group. Before the invention and spread of music-printing (c.1500) and, even afterwards in the church, choral music was performed in this manner.

Around 1500, the average choir probably numbered no more than fifteen at the most. Even sixty or seventy years later, the papal choir in Rome had about twenty-five singers (in 1586 it was twenty-one), and this was considered large. Of these the majority were probably boys (women were not allowed to sing in church: *mulier taceat in ecclesia*) because the light voices of boys had to be doubled or tripled to balance the men. That the number increased over the years is seen in the picture of Heinrich Schütz (1585–1672), surrounded by his choristers in the chapel of the Elector of Saxony in Dresden. Presumably it shows a complement of singers about the middle of the seventeenth century, yet even here they number only about thirty. The figures are significant because they probably indicate that, with the exception of festive occasions and special churches like St Mark's in Venice, the choral sound desired was not massive. Rather it emphasized clarity, balance, and clean performance.

Outside the Church, the concept of a chorus hardly existed. Secular music such as madrigals, *chansons*, *lieder*, and canzonets were performed by groups rarely having more than one voice to a part. Here, obviously, the ecclesiastical prohibition of women did not apply: contemporary pictures often show a group of two or three women and the same number of men, clustered around a series of part-books at a table, happily singing madrigals. However, this vocal chamber music can be profitably sung by a small chorus today as long as the proper dimensions of the music are kept in mind. Instrumental accompaniment is not necessarily to be ruled out. Although the unaccompanied (*a cappella*) performance was, as an ideal, a strong feature of Renaissance style, not only in Italy and the Netherlands but probably also in northern Europe, it was only one of several possibilities in performance. Instrumental doubling of the voices or the replacement of voices by instruments was if anything more common – for the simple reason that few choirs outside royal chapels and large cathedral centres were capable of good performance without instrumental support.

The ecclesiastical style established by Josquin and his followers about 1500 swept Europe, and at first there was little difference between Masses and motets heard in Italy, France, and Germany. But the Protestant Reformation in the first quarter of the sixteenth century eventually wrought as far-reaching a musical revolution in Germany as it did a political one. The new transforming element was the German chorale or hymn which Luther and his musical helpers placed at the heart of their service. (The proper German noun is *Choral*, but in English usage the mock-foreign word *chorale* has become accepted.) To trace its influence from about 1550 to Bach's time is to be granted an insight into the whole course of German church music.

The stylistic changes which characterize the end of the Renaissance in Italy about 1600 and the beginnings of the so-called Baroque music – the rise of pure instrumental music, of opera, of the continuo* principle, and of Venetian

* See Appendix II, p. 403.

polychoral and instrumental effects – were slow to take
root in conservative Germany. But composers like Schütz
and his contemporaries who brought these innovations to
the North were able to produce a fine amalgam of German
solidity and Italian grace unique unto itself. They were the
real creators of a national style, and consequently our attention will be largely directed to them and their successors.

There was no sudden break with the past or even with
the Mother Church when Martin Luther (1483–1546)
posted his theses on the church door at Wittenberg in 1517,
signifying the beginning of the Reformation. As an Augustinian monk well versed in the liturgy and music of Catholicism, Luther recognized the value of preserving tradition
as well as of introducing new elements into it. Long after his
death, for instance, the Lutheran service remained partly in
Latin and partly in German, and only gradually in the
musical portion did German chorales take the place of
Latin sequences, proses, and hymns.

But Luther knew the power music could have in the life
of the Church. He himself was a devoted amateur of the art,
playing the flute and the lute and singing regularly. His
knowledge was, therefore, more than a superficial one. He
wrote: 'Next to the word of God, only music deserves to be
extolled as the mistress and governess of human feelings.' He
also made the study of music a mandatory part of the curri-
culum for the schools under his auspices. His ministers had
to understand music as a prerequisite to ordination. His
insistence on the use, though partial, of the native language
so the congregation could understand the text of the liturgy
(the Word), and his desire to see the congregation participate individually in the musical service started a movement
in the Lutheran Church that helped to shape its whole
character. The priesthood of all believers demanded a
music of all believers, and it was found in the Protestant
chorale.

The tunes were printed in song-books, sometimes by
themselves, sometimes in polyphonic arrangement with the
melody in the tenor part. The first collection of the second
type was the 1524 *Wittenberg Sacred Song-book* (*Wittembergisch*

Geistlich Gesangbuch) of Johann Walther (1496–1570), Luther's musical adviser, containing thirty-five melodies in five parts. Another publisher and composer, Georg Rhau (*c.*1488–1548), put out a well-known collection in 1544 of *New German Sacred Songs* (*Newe Deudsche Geistliche Gesenge*) which was particularly arranged for school use.

The sources of these tunes were fourfold:

(1) official Latin hymnody translated into German – thus the hymn to the Holy Spirit, *Veni, sancte spiritus* became *Komm, heiliger Geist*;

(2) pre-Reformation popular hymns rewritten or expanded – e.g. the hymn on the birth of Christ, *In dulce jubilo*;

(3) secular songs with new words – thus *Mein g'mut ist mir verwirret, das macht ein Jungkfrau zart* ('My peace of mind is shattered by a tender maiden's charms') became at first *Herzlich thut mich verlangen* ('My heart is filled with longing') and later *O Haupt voll Blut und Wunden* ('O sacred head, now wounded');

(4) original hymns – e.g. *Christ lag in Todesbanden* and *Ein' feste Burg*, the words of which were written by Luther himself and are known in English as 'Christ lay in death's dark prison' and 'A stronghold sure'.

Ein' feste Burg, familiar today to all the Protestant world, became the battle-cry of the Reformation. The words to this stirring tune are a paraphrase of Psalm 46 ('God is our refuge'), and the music may also have been written by Luther. The original version was written in free rhythm without bar-lines or any regular stress: Example 12a reproduces the opening. Below it (Example 12b) is the version Bach knew some 150 years later: the so-called free rhythm has become metrical, with four beats to the bar and a march-like tread emphasizing the outline of the melody.

At first these tunes were probably sung unaccompanied in unison, like plainsong. If treated polyphonically, they became spiritual motets of the sort described above in Walther's song-book. When the melody shifted to the top voice towards the end of the sixteenth century, the lower voices

Ex. 12. *Ein' Feste Burg*

fell into chords rather than imitation, and the familiar hymn-pattern emerged. Wherever they appeared, the tunes were easily learned and recognized by ordinary people who could lift up their voices in praise of God in the language they knew.

Meanwhile this new surge in church music meant no cessation of interest in lighter music, particularly if it emanated from Italy. The great Roland de Lassus (see p. 49), international in training and taste, wrote some charming German songs during his residence in Munich as composer to the Duke of Bavaria, but they are primarily a mixture of the madrigal, *chanson*, and *villanella* he learned in Italy and France. There are others who managed the same fusion with perhaps more emphasis on their native tradition. The best of these is a native German who belongs to the generation after Lassus and produced some superlative results: Hans Leo Hassler (1564–1612).

Born in Nuremberg, Hassler was one of three musical brothers, and spent most of his life in Augsburg, Nuremberg, Ulm, and Dresden either in the service of the Fugger family of bankers or of German royalty. (His connexion with the Fuggers enabled him to carry on some profitable commercial enterprises.) But his musical training had been Italian, and this formed the definitive element in his style.

In his youth he studied at Venice with Andrea and Giovanni Gabrieli. From Andrea probably came Hassler's affinity for the madrigal and its lighter relation, the *canzonetta*, the forms of his first published works. Giovanni Gabrieli, who pioneered the Venetian polychoral style, must have inspired Hassler's church works in this genre. But some of his lighter secular pieces (vocal chamber music) show more clearly the blend of solid, contrapuntal texture with Italian rhythmic clarity and tonal definition which characterize his best work.

Example 13 is a jolly little German part-song resembling the Italian *canzonetta*. There are three fairly well-defined sections. The first, corresponding to the first two lines of text, is repeated; the next section sets the next two lines of verse; the final section sets the final three lines and is repeated. The piece begins imitatively, and the first phrase almost mirrors the words by going up the scale after a decisive '*nun*' (now) at the start of each voice. The second phrase ('Last Instrument', etc.), homophonic in contrast, suggests instruments themselves by its rhythmic animation. There is contrast again between the second and third parts of the song. '*Lieblich zu musicieren*', etc., is given in longer note-values, creating the effect of slower tempo; there is also a temporary change of tonality, though the chordal structure continues. The last line returns to imitation, suggested by the words '*schlagt und singt*' ('play and sing'). It is as if everybody liked the idea and said so separately. The gaiety of this unpretentious but effective little piece is fetching, and it breathes more of the spirit of the times than many a more imposing work.

One of the great musical figures in northern Europe at the end of the sixteenth century and the beginning of the seventeenth was the Dutch organist and composer, Jan Pieterszoon Sweelinck (1562–1621), all of whose career was spent in Amsterdam. His pupils, mostly German (Samuel Scheidt was the most famous), became musical leaders in the next generation and made his influence felt far and wide.

Sweelinck is primarily known for his organ music, but his works (published in ten volumes) also include Psalms, sacred

Ex. 13. Hassler, *Nun fanget an*

songs (*cantiones sacrae*), *chansons*, and some delightful *French and Italian Rhymes*, published at Leyden in 1612 (*Rimes francoises et italiennes à deux et à trois parties*) which the composer in his preface says were written 'at the request of several amateurs'. Most of this music is in the traditional sixteenth-century style – contrapuntal parts around a fixed melody for many of the Psalms; freer contrapuntal techniques for the sacred songs, *chansons*, and *rimes*. Sweelinck, although he travelled little and is commonly thought of as a solemn church organist, must have possessed that open spirit and breadth of interest which makes the Renaissance age such a fascinating one.

We may now turn our attention again to Germany, where, in the closing years of the sixteenth century, the innovations of the new style coming from Italy were beginning to penetrate the conservative stronghold of German Protestant music. These innovations – such as solo song, double choirs, and the regular combination of voices with instruments – were associated with secular forms like opera and madrigal comedies, and the Church was reluctant to adopt them. Yet progressive musicians were inevitably affected, and their work often betrays a pull between the old and the new.

One of these German musicians was Michael Praetorius (1571–1621), an extraordinarily fertile composer, equally important as a theorist and musical historian. His book *Musical Treatise* (*Syntagma musicum*, 1615–20, in three parts) is one of the most important sources for seventeenth-century music. Part I is an historical treatise in Latin treating the English, Italian, German, and French music of the time; Part II deals with instruments; Part III with musical composition. Praetorius was chamber-secretary to the Duke of Brunswick and also served as Kapellmeister (literally chapelmaster, i.e. musical director) in Dresden and Magdeburg. He was well acquainted with Venetian practice, and his own works include German and Latin motets for double and triple choirs with all kinds of instrumental combinations. His chief collection of music, in nine parts, was called *The Muses of Zion* (*Musae Sionae*, 1605–10). It contains German psalms and religious songs for the whole Church year in every conceivable vocal arrangement, from quadruple and triple choirs down to *bicinia* (works for two voices). The voluminous prefaces in Latin and German give directions for performance as well as incidental information about general musical practice. Most of these pieces are based on German chorales. In general, the style is conservative. The continuo is hardly used, and the music belongs more to the sixteenth than to the seventeenth century. Publications of 1619 and 1620, however, begin to show the influence of Italians like Caccini. They are more progressive, with continuo, solo voices, ornamented melodic lines, and all the paraphernalia of the Italian style of the time.

Although the new styles of composition were artistically freer than those based on the chorale, the chorale text and tune were still the backbone of the Lutheran service. The texts of the chorales now had the weight of tradition and were the equal of the Bible in authority. Thus Praetorius's preoccupation with the chorale in *Muses of Zion* was understandable. Since the square-cut stanzas of the text and the tune did not allow much musical licence, the problem for the composer in constructing a composition around a chorale was to give the appearance of freedom even though the structure was largely determined in advance. We may indeed derive an interesting picture of musical development by considering the different types of arrangement a chorale tune received from the late sixteenth century up to the time of Bach. The melody is the same for all of them, but the style and treatment differ in each case.

Praetorius can serve as a good starting point, and we may choose a melody going back to the early days of the Christian Church, although taken over by the Lutherans in adapted form in the first half of the sixteenth century. It is *Nun komm der Heiden Heiland* ('O come, thou Saviour of the Gentiles'), a chorale for the Advent season, modelled on the old Latin hymn, *Veni Redemptor gentium*, which is given in modern notation as Example 14a. The text of the original is by St Ambrose, the fourth-century Bishop of Milan. By the sixteenth century, the melody had changed somewhat (see Example 14b for first phrase), but the original contours are still visible even though the second phrase goes up instead of down. When translated into German, further re-arrangement was necessary. The chorale as it finally appeared is seen in the soprano line of a setting by Praetorius for four parts, published in his *Muses of Zion* (Example 14c). At first glance the simple note-against-note treatment looks like a modern hymn. But the tonality is too ambiguous. There is a

mixture of medieval mode and G minor in the first phrase
(F sharp in the bass of 'Heiden'; but no F sharp in the alto
of the cadence on 'Heiland') as well as in the rest of the
setting.

Ex. 14. *Veni Redemptor gentium*

(d) Praetorius, *Nun komm der Heiden Heiland*

Praetorius treated this melody in a number of different ways. Another setting shows a three-part piece for discantus (soprano), mezzo-soprano (alto), and tenor, with the melody in the soprano (Example 14d). The tune is straightforward except for a few minor rhythmic changes. The two lower voices act as accompaniment in duet fashion. They are independent, somewhat contrapuntal, and in a few places imitative (the tenor voice, bars four and five, anticipates the melody of the second phrase, bars six to eight).

The chief problem for the composer is the treatment of his subordinate voices. In some cases they may have no melodic or rhythmic relation to the melody; but for most of the time they anticipate the melody by developing fragments of musical phrases based on it. And the voices must also bring out the meaning of the text, either by word-painting or in general mood. If there were a number of verses with the same music, Praetorius provided variety by indicating different vocal and instrumental combinations for each verse. In the *Musical Treatise* he gives seven possible arrangements for a ten-part motet by Lassus, *Quo properas* ('Wither hastenest thou?') probably written for some festive occasion in honour of the Duke of Bavaria.

In *Muses of Zion*, from which this example is taken, Praetorius speaks of three methods of chorale arrangement. He calls them 'motet fashion', 'madrigal fashion', and '*cantus firmus* fashion'. In the first method the chorale is not presented intact but penetrates the contrapuntal texture of all the voices like a sixteenth-century Mass based on an already established tune. In the second method, the chorale is also broken up, but is formed into little motives tossed back and forth between pairs of voices and supported by continuo accompaniment. In the third, the chorale remains intact, and the other voices provide direct imitation or counterpoint.

Johann Hermann Schein (1586–1630) was cantor at St Thomas's Church in Leipzig (a post later held by Bach) from 1615 until his death. He left an arrangement of *Nun komm, der Heiden Heiland* which is an interesting mixture of Praetorius's second and third methods. Schein, one of the German pioneers of the new movement in music proceeding from Italy, called the collection from which it is taken, *The New Work* (*Opella Nova*) or *Sacred Concertos* (*Geistliche Concerten*); Part I, 1618; Part II, 1626. The term 'sacred concerto' is one found consistently in the seventeenth century. 'Concerto' today normally means a work for solo instrument and orchestra, but the word was originally used by the Gabrielis and their pupils to distinguish vocal compositions with instrumental accompaniment from unaccompanied music. It implied contrasting bodies of sound – instruments and voices separately, or solo voice and chorus separately. This stylistic use of the term persisted up through Bach's lifetime (several cantatas by him were called 'concerti'), and to make matters more confusing existed alongside the more characteristic, purely instrumental use of the word.

Schein's arrangement of *Nun komm der Heiden Heiland* is scored for two sopranos, tenor, and instrumental bass, in addition to a continuo part. Other strings may have doubled the vocal parts.

(e) Schein, *Nun komm der Heiden Heiland*

The chorale melody is in the tenor, and, except for the last few bars appears as an unchanged *cantus firmus* whose four phrases are separated by interludes. The interludes (bars three and four begin the first one) show the two upper voices imitating each other in dialogue fashion with motives based on the first few notes of the chorale phrases. The instrumental bass acts as harmonic support along with the continuo bass, which it mostly doubles. The last interlude, a coda, temporarily forgets the idea of developing motives and abandons itself to a series of tumbling, descending scales. The final measures bring back echoes of the chorale. Schein is striving for a more subjective interpretation of the melody than Praetorius, and his nervous rhythms in the outer voices make more vivid the jubilation which should accompany the music of the text. For the chorale is a song of rejoicing which anticipates the coming of Christ's birth.

The greatest composer of German Protestant church music in the seventeenth century is a man whose music has only recently been heard extensively outside his own country. Heinrich Schütz (1585–1672) may well have a renaissance in the twentieth century that will parallel the one Bach had in the nineteenth. He links the worlds of High Renaissance and Baroque, and his creative fusion of Italian and German styles results in music of exceptional interest.

Schütz lived to a ripe old age in spite of wars and turmoil in his lifetime. In his youth (1619) he studied in Italy with Giovanni Gabrieli; at his death, Buxtehude, whom Bach as a young man walked miles to hear play in Lübeck, was already thirty-five years old. During this long and fruitful career Schütz was almost totally absorbed in vocal music to religious texts. Only his first published work, a book of eighteen madrigals (Venice, 1611) dedicated to his teacher, and the lost music to a German opera, *Daphne* (performed in Torgau, 1627), were of a secular nature. The loss of his wife after a few years of marriage and the havoc of the Thirty Years' War (1618–48), which thoroughly disrupted his career, may account for this stern adherence to one branch of the art.

That during a highly disturbed, hazardous life Schütz was able to write as much music as he did and also get it published seems remarkable. His chief works are: *Psalms of David* (1619), compositions in German for two, three, and four choruses with instruments, after the polychoral style of Gabrieli; *Sacred Songs* (*Cantiones sacrae*, 1625), motets on Latin texts in the old contrapuntal style with continuo added only at the insistence of the publisher; *Sacred Symphonies* (*Symphoniae sacrae*; Part I, 1629; Part II, 1647; Part III, 1650), Latin and German religious songs in the new style with specified instrumental ensembles – really vocal chamber music; *Little Sacred Concertos* (*Kleine geistliche Konzerte*; Part I, 1636; Part II, 1639), solo pieces for one voice or several voices and continuo on German texts; and lastly, several oratorios and passions. The word '*symphonia*', by the way, was used by both Giovanni Gabrieli and Schütz to signify a work for voices *and* instruments.

Very little of this music utilizes the chorale. A variety of factors may have been the cause: Schütz's Italian training; his service in the Saxon court chapel where the tastes of the Elector were probably for a service in the nature of a 'church concert'; or his own preference for the Gospels and Psalms – sources not limited as the chorale texts were. Dramatic and subjective elements are present in all his works – a heritage from his Italian masters and a result of his own independent thinking.

Schütz did not wholly neglect the chorale, however. There are four arrangements among the twenty-four pieces in the first part of the *Little Sacred Concertos*. One of these is *Nun komm der Heiden Heiland*, the developments of which we have been considering. In his preface, Schütz speaks of the devastation his country had suffered and of how these modest compositions, written for a few voices, might serve chapels or churches bereft of singers and instrumentalists. Example 15 (a and b) is scored for four voices and continuo.

The four lines of the verse are clearly divided in the music

Ex. 15 Schütz, *Nun komm der Heiden Heiland*

to make four sections. Schütz has gone over to the second
manner indicated by Praetorius, in which the chorale is
broken up into little motives and treated in turn by different
voices. Yet the rhythm of each section invariably holds one's
interest. To be noted are certain Italian mannerisms – scale
passages, a string of thirds between two parts, the alternation of high and low voices, the quasi-imitation. The absorption of those mannerisms within the framework of Protestant austerity gives the piece its charm. (For a treatment
by Bach of the same chorale, see p. 140.)

To represent Schütz, the honoured Dresden Kapellmeister, only by this music would be unjust. For his forte lay
in dramatic realism, in making a perfect union of words and
music, in using the resources of the new style to make vivid
the words of the Scriptures, particularly the Psalms. Most
of his works of this kind are for solo voice, and thus fall outside our discussion, but towards the close of his career, when
he had all but retired from active musical life, Schütz wrote
(1666) three Passions, according to St Luke, St Matthew,
and St John. These works were written in an archaic style –
solo recitative and choruses, without any instrumental
accompaniment. Schütz foreshadowed this conservatism in
1648 when he expressed his alarm at the decline in technical
prowess among the younger generation and proposed a
return to the study of strict counterpoint with less reliance
on the mainly harmonic outlook as represented in the use of
the continuo. Yet the Passions were not so much a study in
counterpoint as an expression of what the ageing composer
felt to be the true style of such composition.

The story of the Passion – the events of Holy Week leading up to Christ's crucifixion and resurrection as told by the

four Evangelists in the New Testament – is an integral part of both Roman Catholic and Protestant faiths. The custom of having it sung goes back in time to the earliest days of the Church. The first settings were in plainsong with a deacon varying the pitch and expression of his voice to indicate the Evangelist, Jesus, Pilate, Peter, and the crowd (soldiers, Jews, onlookers, each group called a *turba*, Latin for 'crowd'). Gradually, different voices came to be assigned to each role – Evangelist, a tenor; Jesus, a bass; the other parts, sometimes several voices in harmony; and the crowd, a chorus. During the sixteenth century, there were 'motet Passions', set chorally all the way through; but later, with opera in the background, the natural tendency was for the ancient story to be dramatized by using recitative, arioso, and aria as well as chorus.

Schütz's solution, then, was doubly conservative, for it went back to the Middle Ages. It was, none the less, highly intensive and highly effective. The recitative frankly imitated the old Gregorian reciting tone with a purposefully narrow range and all the attributes of chant. Schütz even set each Passion in one of the old modes, not in one of the major or minor keys. Each Passion began, as was customary, with an Exordium, a choral setting of the introductory words: 'The passion of our Lord Jesus Christ as it is described by the holy Evangelist (Matthew, John, etc.)'; and concluded with a chorus of thanks. These and the *turbae* choruses are the only choral sections. There are no interpolated arias or reflective chorales, such as are found later in Bach's Passions.

But Schütz's four-part choruses are vivid and dramatic. In the St Matthew version, where Jesus at the Last Supper predicts that one of his disciples will betray him, the chorus representing the disciples comes in one by one with 'Lord, is it I?' ('*Herr, bin ich's?*'), each part speaking in turn. Another vivid episode occurs when Pilate questions Jesus and then turns to the crowd saying, 'I find no fault in him.' He speaks of the custom of freeing one prisoner at Passover, and asks if it should be 'the King of the Jews'. The crowd cries: 'Not this one, but Barabbas.' Now in Bach's *St Matthew Passion*

Ex. 16　Schütz, *St. John Passion*

the cry 'Barabbas' is as of one person – a great choral shout. Schütz, however, in Example 16d, portrays the group in scattered cries by rising, delayed entries in a quasi-imitative structure. It still generates tremendous force. Note how carefully the composer declaims each set of words – three quarter-notes for '*Nicht diesen*' ('Not this one'); two eighth-notes, a dotted quarter-note, and an eighth-note for '*sondern Barabbam*' ('but Barabbas'). This is the art that conceals art.

It may be difficult for English-speaking people to appreciate this great German master because of the barrier of language. The union of text and music Schütz achieved was similar to the one Purcell achieved in English, and for this reason he is particularly difficult to translate. But his works deserve a high place in the history of music.

During the seventeenth century some centres in Germany were spared war's destruction, and music retained its function as the handmaid of worship. One such city was Lübeck in the north, which, though threatened for a time, managed to maintain its cultural life. The great church of the town was St Mary's (Marienkirche), where for decades several of the best-known composers in Germany were organists and choirmasters. To this church, in 1703 and 1705 respectively, young Handel and young Bach came separately to hear the famous *Abendmusik* (Evening music in Advent) of Buxtehude (1637–1707), one of the finest organists of his time and an influential composer.

Buxtehude married the daughter of his predecessor at St Mary's, Franz Tunder (1614–67), a younger contemporary of Schütz and organist at Lübeck from 1641 until his death. Tunder's church compositions were not published during his lifetime, but were found subsequently at the Royal Library in Uppsala, Sweden. They show the kind of music cultivated in northern Germany during the middle and later seventeenth century, and throw light on the conservative Lutheran practice which Buxtehude and then Bach knew. Most of Tunder's music is based on chorales: a varied instrumental or choral treatment of them. He takes each verse separately in an attempt to vary the musical texture according to shades of meaning. He particularly draws on instruments and solo voices to create his effects. There is a certain stiffness in the music, but one can see the model which others were to use with such richness of imagination.

Tunder's son-in-law, Diderik (Germanized as Dietrich) Buxtehude, was by birth a Dane who spent most of his life in Germany. We know very little about his early years, and unfortunately a great deal of his music has been lost. Fifty to seventy-five years ago he was primarily esteemed for his organ music, which strongly influenced Bach. More recently, attention has centred on his cantatas, some 124 of which survive from the period 1678–87. (If he maintained the same rate of production for the rest of his career, he must have written over 400.) Those that survive are extra-ordinarily varied. Most of them are for solo voices, but a number can be performed by a small chorus. They show vividly Buxtehude's mastery of both operatic and church idiom. Many of his arias and ariosos are warmly lyrical – a quality not generally associated with north-German music of this period. The texts to these cantatas are either in Latin or German and are taken at will from the Bible (mostly Psalm verses), the chorales, or free poetry. Orchestral accompaniment is an important feature. Most of the can-tatas begin with an introductory overture or *sinfonia*, the motives of which are often worked into the voices at the end of the work in an Alleluia or Amen coda.

Some of Buxtehude's cantatas, however, are chorale can-tatas on the model of Tunder. A splendid example of this type is *Jesu meine Freude* ('Jesus, my joy') based on Johann Franck's chorale (1653) of six stanzas. Scored for two sopranos, bass, two violins, bassoon, and continuo, the can-tata opens with an instrumental piece (here called a *sonata*) of three sections (fast, slow, fast), the first and last of which start fugally but end in the style of the contemporary trio sonata (that is, with two upper melodic lines and a continuo bass). Verse 1 is a straightforward harmonic setting of the tune, with the melody in the soprano and with instrumental interludes between the phrases. Verse 2, which speaks of the protection Jesus affords against all enemies, is a soprano aria dominated by a lively eighth-note figure. Verse 3 for bass emphasizes '*trotz*' ('*In spite of* the serpent, death's tor-ment, and fear, I stand calm, in peace, at rest'). Similarly with Verse 1, the strong word is '*Weg*' ('*Away* with all treasure, Thou art my delight'). Verse 5 reverts to the solo voice and breathes the spirit of resignation ('Fare thee well that's mortal'); the cantata ends by returning to the straight harmonic pattern of Verse 1.

From here the step to Bach (who himself set *Jesu, meine*

Freude, known in English as *Jesus, priceless treasure*) is but a short one. Yet Schütz and Buxtehude are not predecessors; they are great artists in their own right, and their language is a powerful reincarnation of that militant spirit engendered by Luther and his followers many years before. With them we come to the close of a rich period in German music – a period marked by many revolutionary changes. Yet these changes, successfully incorporated into an older tradition, emerged in new, resplendent colours.

5

At the Courts of Italy and France

*c.*1590–*c.*1730

DENIS ARNOLD

THE ideas which were to kill the madrigal were well established by 1594, the year of Palestrina's death. In Florence, the intellectuals who were interested in music were saying that, if music was to have a future, it must abandon its present frivolity and return to the high seriousness described by Plato and other ancient philosophers. To this end, counterpoint must go. It must go because it made it impossible to hear the words, impossible to savour the poem which must feed the intellect as the musical sounds feed the senses. But paradoxically, the same Greek philosophers who gave these ideas to the theorists were indirectly responsible for a final, late flowering of the madrigal itself; for their ideas were sufficiently vague to give rise to another interpretation. According to this, it could be held that the audibility of the words was less important than that music should match and emotionally enrich the verse.

The two great composers of this ultimate stage in the madrigal both make this idea the basis of their style. The first of these, Prince Carlo Gesualdo da Venosa (*c.*1560–1613), is one of the most remarkable composers in all musical history. The monarch of a minor principality in southern Italy, he gained notoriety in his time for the murder of his first wife and her lover, caught in the act of infidelity. But musically more significant was his second marriage to Leonora d'Este of Ferrara, for he spent some years in his wife's home and learned a great deal from her court musicians. It was there that he rediscovered a curious chromatic harpsichord built over forty years earlier in an attempt to solve the mysteries of ancient Greek intonation. Gesualdo had composed conventional and slight madrigals in his early life. Now his music took on a completely new style as he experimented with strange chromatic harmonies and sudden modulations. He chose verse full of paradox and erotic imagery (something rather like that of the metaphysical poets in England), and set it in a kind of inspired improvisation. The phrases are short, the texture usually homophonic. There is no attempt at contrapuntal flow. Each line, sometimes each word of the poem suggests a new musical motive. Violent changes of tempo and even more violent changes of key (for any semblance of adherence to the old modal system has gone) give a nervous discontinuity. There is little sheer ease of enjoyment for the singer, for this is virtuoso music, nor is there time for musical word-painting of the conventional kind. But it is undeniably effective in its neurotic stimulation, the era's final word in passion and continuous excitement.

Gesualdo's music could only have been written by an amateur, that of Monteverdi only by a professional. Claudio Monteverdi (1567–1643) studied with a master of the old contrapuntal style, and his first book of madrigals (1587), written while he was still living in his provincial home town of Cremona, is conventional both in technique and sentiment. In his second book (1590) he shows his complete mastery of this style and his liking for painting the concrete images of the verse, much as the English madrigalists do. One madrigal portrays the excitement of the hunt, in a series of close canons; the opening words of another, '*Non si levava ancor*' ('The dawn is not yet risen'), suggest a rising figure in one part negatived by a descending scale in another; and the little masterpiece *Ecco mormorar l'onde* finds a series of appropriate motives to convey the murmuring waves, the rustling leaves, and the mountains catching the glow of morning – motives which are then worked out contrapuntally in a most magical way.

His third book (1592) was written after his move to the elegant court of Mantua, and is inspired by the technique of some virtuoso singers and by the discovery of the Greek ideals of combining verse and music. Monteverdi now chooses more passionate poetry and interprets it more vividly. Sometimes he writes deliberately angular melodic lines, using awkward intervals to create tension. Dissonance becomes a primary means of expression, and the agony of love seems to require one discord to resolve into yet another. The climax of this style comes in the fourth and fifth books (1603 and 1605), where Monteverdi combines the realism of his second volume with the emotional power of the third. Monteverdi again chooses the lamenting erotic verse in which the lover's anguish is expressed by pointing out the difference between his hopes and fears. The musician makes this contrast even plainer. *A un giro sol* is a fine example. 'When you turn your eyes, the air itself smiles,' says the poet: and Monteverdi provides first a 'turn' (musical ornament) for the word *giro*, then a *melisma* (long chain of notes to one syllable) for the Italian word *ride* ('smiles'). This literally makes the singer seem to smile. The approval of sea and winds is given in a gentle, consonant motion, as near to realism as music can be. Suddenly the concrete images disappear; the lover laments, 'Only I am sad, being killed by your cruelty'; and the music immediately becomes agonized with a chromatic change (sudden, but not wilful, as Gesualdo's so often seem). Dissonance and awkward intervals rend the heart.

Ex. 17. Monteverdi, *A un giro sol*

It is interesting to see how Monteverdi, for all the difficulties in performing his music, is nevertheless a joy to the
performer, for his sections are always sufficiently developed
contrapuntally to provide a strong feeling of continuity.
Although often gloomy, his music is never neurotic, and is
tense without being overwrought.

These madrigals were probably sung with one voice to a
part. (Mantua was famous for its virtuoso singers, especially
women – helped by recruitment abroad, in which Mantuan
ambassadors participated.) In his fifth book, Monteverdi
introduces a number of works in which a keyboard instrument is necessary to accompany solo voices which are given
passages on their own. Now, for these soloists, Monteverdi
provides voluptuous, decorative lines and accompanies
them with harmonies which are themselves rich. In between
these solo sections, *tutti* passages in simple chordal harmony
act as refrains. In his later books, even where the music is
not avowedly accompanied, there is a feeling that it is
designed for the display of virtuosity rather than domestic
delight. The arrangement of a scene from the opera
Ariadne (1608) which appears in his sixth book (1614) shows
in its declamatory lines how the older idea of the madrigal
had disappeared. Gloriously dissonant and beautifully
linked together in form, it is a most moving piece – for the
listener.

The rest of Monteverdi's madrigals are duets and trios
which scarcely belong to a history of choral music – the rest
of them, that is, with the exception of certain numbers
published in the last volume of all (1638). In this book he
returns to his former love of pictorial 'realism' in music
which he justifies in a preface in which he explains how
Plato has affected his thinking. Plato demands that music
should express three kinds of emotion – the calm, the amor-
ous, and the warlike. Having found no example of this last,
Monteverdi tries by various devices to provide it. *Hor che'l
ciel e la terra* ('Now that heaven and earth') shows his attempt to express all three of Plato's categories. A calm section expressing the peace of the night, the cries of the lover
as he lies awake lamenting, the fanfares of his 'war' against the

cruel beloved are all woven into a fine emotional web which is the logical culmination of Monteverdi's earlier style.

By 1638 Monteverdi was a survivor from a distant age. Secular vocal music now meant songs and duets, which could be printed in their hundreds and which required less musical skill on the part of the amateur performer than had the ensemble madrigal. Church music also turned to the soloist; but here, links with the past were stronger. The style of Palestrina's church music had been musically canonized by this time, and, with a conservatism typical of church musicians, Palestrina's pupils and followers in Rome ignored almost completely the new ideas. They continued to write smooth polyphony, with perfectly vocal melody and a consonant harmony which deliberately avoided the expressiveness of the late madrigal. Even Monteverdi, whose main interests were certainly in 'advanced' music, learned to write in the '*stile antico*' ('antique style'), as it was called; 'learned' is to be taken literally, for, as he admitted, in writing his first unaccompanied Mass he had deliberately to study the style afresh. This was a 'parody' Mass (in the sense explained on p. 37), using ten themes taken from a motet of the Netherlander Gombert, written decades before. These themes are worked out with all possible artifice in a texture thick with imitations. The harmony rarely contains a dissonance, and the whole setting seems impersonal in a way certainly not known to Palestrina himself. Monteverdi's later Masses are less academic, and, one feels, more fresh. The melody is still smooth and the harmony consciously purged of any harshness, but there is a more regular accentuation and a diatonic melody which clearly came to the composer more naturally. For these reasons the Mass in G minor (1651) is splendid to sing, more especially since it leaves its customary impersonality at the end of the Crucifixus, where there is some effective dissonance, and in the iterations of 'Hosanna', which have some virile rhythm.

Most of the succeeding composers, such as Antonio Lotti (c.1667–1740) in Venice and Francesco Durante (1684–1755) and Alessandro Scarlatti (1660–1725) in Naples, adopt such a compromise solution. They use a vocal style in general modelled on that of Palestrina, but convey a new expressiveness by adding chromatic harmonies, sequential phrases, and a respect for the regular accentuation of the bar-line which all give a much more modern flavour. Lotti's eight-part *Crucifixus*, for example, is written in a style nearer to the expressive madrigal than to the purity of Roman church music; and, although it preserves a classical manner, it can scarcely be called unemotional.

The real future of church music stemmed not from conservative Rome but from the independent states of northern Italy and in particular from the Venetian Republic. The musical individuality of Venice has already been commented on in a previous chapter (see p. 43). In many ways Venetians considered themselves superior to Romans. Theirs was a richer community, for it was still a great centre of international trade; it had a unique and much-studied constitution, with an elected head of state, and had avoided the squabbling which had disfigured the papal succession; and in St Mark's it possessed a unique church, with a liturgy which had an antiquity of its own and an architecture which, with its raised choir galleries and ornate decoration, again stood apart from Roman traditions. This separateness affects Venetian music in every way. Magnificence rather than devotion is its theme, and by dividing the approximately sixty singers and players into groups which were hidden in the several choir galleries (each having its own organ) it adds an air of mystery to mingle with its grandeur.

The greatest Venetian composer, Giovanni Gabrieli (1557–1612), was to lay the foundations of a style which lasted until the nineteenth century. In his earliest work he followed the idioms of his masters, Lassus and his own uncle Andrea Gabrieli (see p. 45). He wrote counterpoint which involves much more rhythmic virility than Palestrina had used, in motets both for single choir and for multiple choirs. By his middle years, counterpoint as such interested him less, vocal and instrumental colour far more. When writing for a single group, he clearly exploited total tone-quality at the expense of his individual vocal lines, some of which are frankly dull. The resulting richness of tone-colour is indescribable, as can be heard in such a motet as *Exaudi Deus* ('Hear, O God') of 1597 in which the seven lines are all written for baritones and basses, no doubt accompanied by trombones.

The motets which Giovanni Gabrieli wrote in this period for choirs placed apart from each other show even more interest in colour. It is rare for the groups to be evenly matched. The boys may be contrasted with the men – the motet, *Beata es Virgo* ('Blessed art thou, O Virgin') of 1597 is an especially beautiful example – or a group including instruments may be set against an unaccompanied choir. Three or four choirs may be placed in different parts of the church, and solo voices may be given the accompaniment of strings or trombones to heighten the contrasts. Every device for making the music more splendid and sonorous is used, and the rapidity of the dialogue between the various groups keeps the listener constantly amazed, as the sound comes from each different direction. There is a tremendous *joie de vivre* in these motets, which often break into a dancing triple time wherever the gaiety of the words suggests it. Gabrieli's settings of the words 'Alleluia' and 'Hosanna' are unforgettable.

In the work of his final years, Gabrieli develops in two ways. In his Passiontide motets he uses the jagged intervals and astringent harmonies of the late madrigal. Man's fear and humility are vividly expressed. On the other hand, in his motets for Easter Day and Christmas, he brings the splendour of Venetian music to its climax. With the application of the continuo principle* the use of solo voices became easier, and the new possibilities of the thirty-strong orchestra of St Mark's attracted him immensely. The motet *In Ecclesiis* ('Praise God in the churches') shows this final splendour. Soprano and tenor soloists sing their praise of the Lord against only an organ accompaniment. The choir responds with an 'Alleluia' refrain which intoxicatingly leads into an orchestral interlude, full of the dotted rhythms and lively ornaments of instrumental music. A series of duets ensues,

* See Appendix II, p. 403.

again interrupted by the choral cries of 'Alleluia'; and then comes the final glory. To the words 'In eternity', the soloists sing out their florid ornaments over a stern and solid choral tone and massive orchestral writing. The tension is maintained by a dominant pedal which seems almost to belong to the nineteenth century.

Ex. 18. G. Gabrieli, *In ecclesiis*

(The orchestra holds the same chords.)

The revolutionary nature of this style lies in its complete reversal of the traditional contrapuntal techniques. Whereas Palestrina's interlocking jigsaw of phrases and sections imposed on the composer a natural unity of mood throughout a work, it is contrast which is the basis of the new music. And since contrast and sudden change are the requirements of any passionate human music, Gabrieli's motets and all the other church music in the Venetian tradition bring a secular air into church. This can be seen at its most obvious in the Vesper Psalms and motets (commonly known as the *Vespers*) published by Monteverdi in 1610. It is customary nowadays to perform these as a unity, but they were probably not designed as one. Instead, the book was really conceived to show any prospective employer how Monteverdi (at the time looking for a new job) had mastered all the styles of church music available at the time. Here is the erudite unaccompanied Mass to please the Romans; the Vesper Psalms to please the Venetians; and the skilful solo motets to please any prince who was more interested in his virtuoso singers than in the dullness of papal choir music. The *Vespers* also include the *Sonata sopra Sancta Maria* (which bears no resemblance in form to the later sonata), a set of free variations on a plainsong theme which is sung by a soprano. It uses an orchestra of wooden cornetts (old wind-instruments, unrelated to the modern cornet), trombones, and strings. It is to be noted that instrumental pieces were often played during Mass at this time, much as organ interludes are today. As the north Italian courts had large instrumental ensembles available, these interludes were sometimes extended orchestral works.

The Vesper Psalms, with the introductory piece *Domine ad adiuvandum* ('O Lord, make haste to help me') and the instrumental *Sonata sopra Sancta Maria* are less remarkable for their secular technique than for Monteverdi's attempt to combine the new humanism with older tradition. He uses plainsong themes, as had been the common practice of all church musicians for centuries; but he always finds a new use for them. In the opening piece, for example, he gives a chant on a single chord to the choir – something known in all church music – but insists that his Venetian-style orchestra simultaneously plays a secular piece, and that no less than the fanfare overture to his opera *Orpheus* (1607).

Then the first Psalm-setting, *Dixit Dominus* ('The Lord hath said', Psalm 110) mixes passages in chant with duets and trios which are reminiscent of the accompanied passages in the fifth book of madrigals, while the organ accompaniment provides the plainsong themes. Even *Nisi Dominus* ('Except the Lord build the house'), which appears to be a double-choir piece in the manner of Gabrieli, is less secular than Venetian music, in the way that the plainsong is worked into the tenor part of each choir. In the hymn *Ave maris stella* ('Hail, star of the sea'), after a rather conventional-looking first verse for double choir, Monteverdi turns the plainsong into a bewitchingly beautiful triple-time song to which we might have expected secular words, and provides a dance-like interlude between each verse. This strange mixture of techniques is seen at its finest in the great Magnificat which, like *In Ecclesiis*, is frankly divided into a series of short sections, bound together with a repeated plainsong melody. But the music set around the plainsong is as emotionally rich as anything in the history of church music. A dialogue between upper and lower choirs, an echo scene borrowed from Act IV of *Orpheus*, duet sections where tenors or sopranos weave dotted rhythms and roulades around the slow-moving plainsong, and others where instruments paint the words (trombones for 'the lowliness of his handmaiden', angelic flutes for 'shall call me blessed') – these dazzle the listener. Yet the intensity of harmony and virtuoso melody is more truly passionate and less purely splendid than in some of the grandiose music of the Venetians.

The solo music of the *Vespers* is less unexpected, in that it borrows unhesitatingly from secular music without any restraint. *Nigra sum* ('I am black but comely') is a setting of voluptuous verses from the *Song of Songs*, and here Monteverdi writes a passionate operatic love song, with its climax at the King's bidding: 'Arise, my beloved, and come.' *Duo Seraphim* ('Two seraphim') is a typical chamber-duet, and its sobbing ornaments (*trilli*), dotted notes, and scales remind us that the Duke of Mantua's virtuoso singers were among the finest of their day. The inevitable echo piece *Audi coelum* ('Hear, O heaven') is a direct descendant of the echo scenes so fashionable in pastoral plays and early operas.

With the aid of the *Vespers*, Monteverdi was appointed to be director of music at St Mark's in Venice (the Psalm-settings were probably used as his test-piece); but although his interest in church music might have expected to have increased in his later years, in fact his Venetian liturgical music is less interesting. This is not, as has sometimes been suggested, for spiritual reasons – his religious songs and solo motets are very fine – so much as for technical ones. The psalms and other liturgical texts which were required to be set, often contained too little emotional variety to inspire him, and since there was no question of altering them (as there was with an opera libretto), there are long neutral passages in his music. His writing usually takes the form of a loose series of duets and trios, punctuated with occasional *tutti* passages. The solo sections are rarely complete in themselves, and for this reason the long Psalm-settings seem to be rather formless and lacking in climax. He is at his best when a definite shape is suggested by the words, as in his Gloria for seven voices, which becomes a rondo; or where he can impose a shape on them, as in his delightful setting of the psalm *Beatus vir* (Psalm 112), in which he uses a fragment from his chamber duet *Chiome d'oro* ('Tresses of gold') as a refrain.

Monteverdi was the last great Italian composer to write a considerable amount of church music. His successors in Venice were mainly opera composers to whom their ecclesiastical duties were secondary, and who wrote scholastically in the old style, or efficiently but rarely enthusiastically for soloists and string orchestra. In Rome, the best of the church musicians was Orazio Benevoli (1605–72) who took the polychoral technique of Gabrieli and froze into it the contrapuntal style of Palestrina, but did not develop the Venetian novelties of form. Elsewhere it was minor composers – the ill-paid choirmasters and organists – who made progress. In the works of the north Italians we find the basic idea of Monteverdi's great Magnificat developed. They split up the psalms and movements of the Mass into short sections, each of which is set to music in such a way that it is reasonably complete in itself. There are arias and duets, choruses and orchestral interludes. The duality of style is now very obvious: the arias and ensembles are usually written in an up-to-date manner which reminds us of opera, while the choruses are often contrapuntal and rather old-fashioned.

This duality of style dominates the eighteenth century, as we can see in Vivaldi's famous Gloria for two soprano solos, chorus, and orchestra. The composer divides the text into twelve sections. Eight of them are given to the chorus, which either sings in a grand solidly chordal style while the orchestra develops its own concerto-like material, or joins in a fugue, complete with scholarly subjects and counter-subjects. The other four movements are for soloists, and comprise a duet, a pastoral aria very reminiscent of Handel, an aria with choral interpolations (rather like the penultimate number of Bach's *St Matthew Passion*), and a cheerfully operatic aria in triple time. Exceptionally in Roman Catholic church music, female voices for solo and choral parts were envisaged here, since Vivaldi's Gloria is among the music he wrote for the girls' orphanage in Venice where he was music-master and where the high standard of performance was famous. He himself was a Venetian (1685–1741).

Although the setting of the liturgy declined after about 1650, religious music was not dead, for a new form began to flourish: the oratorio. This was the direct result of the needs of the Roman Catholic Church after the secession of Luther. Protestants had succeeded in bringing a new understanding of religion to the common man, and Filippo Neri (St Philip Neri, 1515–95) deliberately set out to do something parallel for Roman Catholics. To supplement the sacraments and priestly office, he and his followers met together with a greater informality, to hear a sermon and to sing hymns (called in Italian *laudi*) in the vernacular tongue, not in Latin. The music of these hymns was deliberately simple and their poems were usually lyrical, although one or two turned to Bible stories for their subject. These meetings took place in the 'oratories' (a kind of chapel) in the Roman churches, and it is from this that the term 'oratorio' in its musical sense originated. Although the music of these *laudi* did not in the first place take a dramatic form, the temptation to dramatize in music was there, and it only required a small incentive for a true dialogue to suggest itself to the composer.

This came when Emilio de' Cavalieri (*c.*1550–1602) wrote a kind of religious opera which was performed in costume, complete with action and dances, in the Oratory of Vallicella, Rome, in 1600. *The Representation of Soul and Body* (*La rappresentazione di anima e di corpo*) is, to all intents and purposes, a mystery play set to music in the manner of a Florentine opera. The characters are allegorical figures – the Spirit, the Body, Time, and so on; the action is a simple story in which the World and the Body are shown to be shoddy compared with the splendours of eternity. The mainspring of the music is the newly invented operatic recitative style. With the aid of the spectacle, there can be little doubt that the play was most effective; and even without the spectacle, some of the *arioso* pieces are extremely beautiful. The monologue of Time is quite lovely, and anticipates Monteverdi's use of significant motives which are repeated to give shape to the recitative. There are also a number of simple choruses.

After this, there were several possibilities open to composers. Some, such as Michelangelo Rossi (*c.*1600–?), followed de' Cavalieri in writing religious operas, which gained emotional power as much from the scenic grand manner as from the musical recitative. Others developed the quasi-dramatic dialogue. Using the story-telling hymn texts of the Oratorians, the works of these composers divide the words between the various characters, with, if necessary, a narrator to hold the story together. These soloists sing not the recitative of opera, but an *arioso* developed from the motet lines of the Venetians. The chorus usually acts as an observer, and sings madrigals of the sort used in the old pastoral plays of the sixteenth century, full of great sonority (especially when instruments double the voices, as they usually do). In all, the dialogue can hardly be said to be really dramatic. Its main aim seems to be to give a new understanding of the text to a congregation which otherwise would take the story for granted. The style is less that of a religious drama than of a dramatized motet. It is this non-stage musical form which we now call oratorio.

It is no coincidence that the first master of the oratorio in this sense, Giacomo Carissimi (1605–74), flourished at a time when the operatic idiom was itself softening the drama into a lyrical form, where aria and *arioso* is more important than dynamic action. Unlike the earlier Oratorians with their Italian texts, he preferred to set the Old Testament stories in the Latin version of the Bible; but his choice of subjects was much the same. In musical style, his work is a curious mixture of secular and religious. His forms are often very near those of Monteverdi's late motets, and his recitative derives from church music rather than opera. Yet he is capable of a big *scena* of tremendous dramatic power. His *Story of Hezekiah* (*Historia di Ezechia*) is virtually an extended motet, similar to the psalm-settings of Monteverdi in its use of short duets and solos, held together by a short *ritornello* for violins. The two sopranos represent the angels, the bass speaks God's words, Isaiah is a male alto and Hezekiah is a tenor. As in the earlier dialogues, there is comparatively little drama in the piece until we come to Hezekiah's great prayer to be spared for yet a few more years. This is constructed over a chromatic bass which is kept the same for three verses, while the melody is changed to express the detail of the words. No power of dissonance and expressive declamation is spared. This is Monteverdi's *Lament of Ariadne* in terms of religious music, and the joyful aria and chorus which conclude the work contrast with the prayer most effectively.

The same mixture can be seen on a more extended scale in Carissimi's masterpiece, *Jephtha*. In this, the least dramatic element is the recitative, which tells the story in the biblical words. Much of this is given to a narrator, who sings in an unemotional, neutral style. But everything else is full of dramatic life. The opening scene in which Jephtha defeats the Ammonites has a tremendous warlike chorus, reminiscent of Monteverdi's 'realism', and a superb bass solo based on strong, virile rhythms. The daughter's aria and the choral cries of thanksgiving are equally powerful. Then suddenly – as suddenly as the arrival of the messenger bearing the news of Eurydice's death in Monteverdi's *Orpheus* – comes Jephtha's realization that he must sacrifice his daughter. His lament and his daughter's cry of agony to the mountains which echo her plaintive cadences are as moving and as real as anything in opera; and the final chorus ('Lament, lament!') is a great dissonant madrigal, which the English singer will find curiously like the great melancholic works of Wilbye.

Ex. 19. Carissimi, *Jephtha*

Most of the later Italian composers wrote oratorios, in Latin or Italian. Some of these are undeniably effective, such as Vivaldi's *Juditha triumphans* (1716, based on the story of Judith, from the Apocrypha). This is another work displaying 'warlike' music. But a more consistent flowering of the manner of Carissimi is to be found in France, where he was honoured as 'the greatest musician that Italy has produced' as the French writer on music, Lecerf de la Viéville (1674–1710), called him. In both church music and in oratorio the French composers follow the Italian style but add their own distinctive flavour. There are two main veins: a grand manner which matches the splendours of Versailles, and a more intimate and delicate atmosphere.

The most influential composer of the French school, Jean-Baptiste Lully (1632–87), gave of his best in the first manner. It is no coincidence that he seems to have strong affinities with the Venetians. Not only was he an Italian by birth; but, just as the music of St Mark's glorified the state and its Doge, so Lully's magnificence reflected the glory of 'le roi soleil', the 'sun-king', Louis XIV. All the stateliness of the court can be found in his celebrated *Miserere* ('Lord, have mercy') which appropriately enough takes up from Gabrieli the Venetian tradition of using a double choir. One of these choirs is a group of soloists, who sometimes sing independently in short arias and ensembles and then come together to contrast with the full choir. But Lully's melody is much more regular in rhythm than Gabrieli's and the harmony leaves a much colder and more formal effect than that we find in the Venetians.

There is more passion in the motets of Michel Richard Delalande (1657–1726),* although he is more conservative than Lully in some ways, since his choral idiom is based on the old contrapuntal techniques. He uses decorative French melody for the soloists and the square rhythms which reflect French courtly pomp so well; but his harmony seems richer and more emotional. There can be no doubt of the true human spirit in his motet *De profundis* ('Out of the deep'), 1689.

For the modern listener, however, the most readily attractive French choral music of the time is to be found in the work of two masters, Marc-Antoine Charpentier (1634–1704) and François Couperin (1668–1733). Charpentier studied in Rome and learned a great deal from Carissimi. He wrote in Carissimi's oratorio forms, as well as liturgical

* The surname is often given as Lalande.

music. He lacks the human warmth of his master, for like other French composers he tended to replace the freedom of the recitative *arioso* by a straightforward melody with clear-cut rhythms and less dissonant harmony. Yet this is the very basis of Charpentier's delightfulness. Much of his power comes in the astonishingly sonorous choruses, and his peculiarly French solo writing gives a great air of charm, especially when organized in symmetrical rondo and *ritornello* patterns. His cantata *In nativitatem Domini Nostri Jesu Christi canticum* ('Song for the Birth of Our Lord Jesus Christ') makes an attractive use of this gift, especially in the aria of the angel who announces the arrival of the infant to the shepherds, and in the final rejoicing of the shepherds themselves.

Couperin wrote less church music than Charpentier, but on the whole he shows a more delicate emotional sense. He has the same lack of passion, but brings to his motets an engaging sweetness. His purity of style is at its finest in the *Four Extracts from a Motet Composed on the Order of the King* (*Quatre Versets d'un motet composé de l'ordre du Roy*) written about 1703 for women's voices. It begins with a lovely and serene unaccompanied duet for sopranos: ornamented and elegant, this has only an occasional dissonance to disturb its purity. The solo with violin *obbligato* which succeeds it seems more ordinarily operatic, although in different company this too would seem pure enough. Then comes a tender movement, with flutes accompanying a solo soprano; and since the bass-line of the harmony is given to the violins, there is scarcely a note below middle C. The angelic quality of the sound as soloists and chorus alternate is difficult to put into words but remains unforgettable.

The same impression of magical innocence is left by Couperin's motet in praise of St Susanna (*c.*1698), even though male voices (a baritone and countertenor) are used with the soprano. The opening aria for countertenor is very like Handel, both in its rhythmic motives and its *roulades*. The duet in which the soprano joins him is so mellifluous, in its thirds and sixths, that the composer's direction '*doux*' ('sweetly') seems to fit much more than the echoing cadential phrases over which it is written. A recurring chorus, strong and in chordal homophonic style, acts as a refrain between other solos, which include a delicate soprano aria, less ornamented than usual and richer emotionally in its gentle dissonances. In a final recitative, the bass calls us to praise Susanna over a bare single bass note on the organ. 'Here', as Wilfred Mellers has written, 'the paradox of a sensuousness of harmony that is united with a virginal spirituality of line finds its loveliest expression'; and this paradox of sensuousness in the service of pure religious feeling is something which is typical of the whole of the seventeenth century. It is a sign of the strength of religious music that a French writer could declare: 'The passions of an opera are cold compared with those which are depicted in our church music.' Only when church music loses this passion does it become unworthy of its subject.

6

Church and State in England

c.1625–c.1715

J. A. WESTRUP

CHURCH and State in seventeenth-century England were rocked to their foundations by the Civil War. The twenty years that elapsed between the end of the Long Parliament and the Restoration were not long enough to make a complete break with tradition. But by the time music at the court and in the Church was resumed in 1660 a good many changes had occurred in the development of music on the Continent, and these were inevitably reflected in the music of the young composers who came to the fore in Charles II's reign. In the meantime the suspension of the monarchy and the ban on church music (other than metrical psalms) caused widespread unemployment among professional musicians. The majority of these had been in the service of Charles I or the cathedrals, and quite a number of them had managed to combine both activities. The Puritan régime compelled them to depend on private patrons, or to make a living by teaching or to find other sources of income. The full tale of hardship has never been told. The encouragement of secular music by the Puritans, however, provided opportunities which many of them were quick to take. It is significant that the Commonwealth saw a notable development in music-publishing, which continued after the Restoration.

The emphasis on secular music had already begun in the reign of Charles I. The death of Orlando Gibbons (see p. 60) in 1625 virtually marked the end of an era in English church music. Thomas Tomkins (1576–1656) survived till the last years of the Commonwealth, but he was a lone

figure among composers of lesser stature. That he was held
in honour after his death is evident from the posthumous
publication of his church music in 1668; and the fact that
so many of his anthems are 'verse anthems' (that is, having
solo passages, sometimes with a considerable degree of
elaboration for the solo voices) shows that he was ready to
follow a tradition already firmly established in the work of
Gibbons. But we have no means of knowing how many of
these works actually belong to the reign of Charles I; and
in any case there was a growing tendency to continue using
the best church music of the past – a tendency which has
lasted to the present day and has left its mark on the work
of composers of widely different periods. This tendency is
strikingly illustrated by the publication in 1641 of the first
part of an anthology of *Selected Church Music*, edited by John
Barnard. (He was a minor canon, i.e. a member of the choir
in holy orders, of St Paul's Cathedral.) All the composers
represented in this collection were deceased, though Barnard intended to include living composers in a second part.
Unfortunately he had chosen a very unsuitable time for his
publication, and the second part was never issued.

The massive part-books which make up the collection
were intended for the use of the Chapel Royal, cathedrals,
and college chapels. Cathedral choirs have never been large,
but in the seventeenth century they had far fewer boys than
we should normally expect at the present day. Apart from
the Chapel Royal the men were part-time singers, often
engaged in trade, frequently uneducated, and in some cases
wholly irresponsible. Complaints of drunkenness and misbe-
haviour in the choir occur over and over again. It is a tribute
to the idealism of composers that they continued to write good
music even though they knew it might be inadequately
performed. We do not know how many copies of Barnard's
collection were printed, but it is a reasonable guess that the
majority of the cathedrals bought sets before it was too late.
Many copies must have perished in the Civil War. The
Puritan zeal for the abolition of church music led in many
cases to the wholesale destruction of choir-books and also to
the wrecking of organs. The destruction was not universal.

Some organs were spared, others were removed, and some were prudently dismantled before the soldiers could get at them. We know that some copies of Barnard's collection survived the Commonwealth, and these must have helped to provide the material for restoring cathedral services in 1660.

The problem at the Restoration was not so much the material one of replacing music and building organs as the difficulty of finding singers. Some of the choirmen of Charles I's reign had died, others were too old to return to service. But since twenty years is not an impossibly large gap in a man's life, there were a sufficient number to revive the traditions of the past and to hand them on to younger men. Boys were quite another matter: until they could be re-cruited and trained the services had to be sung by men only. But this obstacle was overcome surprisingly quickly, parti-cularly in the Chapel Royal, where Henry Cooke (c. 1616–72) vigorously pursued the time-honoured practice of taking boys away from the provincial cathedrals. Where there was delay in rebuilding or replacing organs the old system of supporting the voices with cornetts (see p. 98) and trombones was found to be very useful and died out only gradually.

Inevitably we know most about conditions in the Chapel Royal. Here the existing repertory of church music made a solid foundation on which to build; and we may guess that in the cathedrals it provided the principal material for services for some time to come. But in the Chapel Royal this material was soon augmented by new music. Cooke himself was an indifferent composer, and older men like William Child (1606–97) were not very happy at adapting them-selves to a new age. But the choir included a number of clever boys who soon showed a gift for composition, and as they grew up came to provide most of the new anthems for the Chapel Royal. Pelham Humfrey (1647–74) in particular attracted the attention of Charles II and was given a grant at the age of seventeen to enable him to travel to France and Italy. It is evident from his anthems that he learned a good deal from his visit, though he must also have learned something from Cooke, who was noted as a singer in the Italian style.

The Restoration composers inherited the pre-Commonwealth tradition of verse anthems, with passages for solo voices accompanied by organ or strings, but modified it in several ways. The most important of these changes was the introduction of what is sometimes called, rather ambiguously, a declamatory style – in other words, a form of recitative. Recitative, which had its origin in Italy in the late sixteenth century, was not unknown in England before the Restoration, but it had little chance then of penetrating into church music. After the Commonwealth it was so familiar in secular works and in devotional music for private use that it was quite natural for Humfrey, particularly with his continental training, to use it in anthems. In his hands it became a vehicle for pathetic expression, which often verged on sentimentality; and if the pathos is distributed between three voices, as it often is, the effect is even more fulsome, e.g. in Example 20, from *Hear, O heavens*:

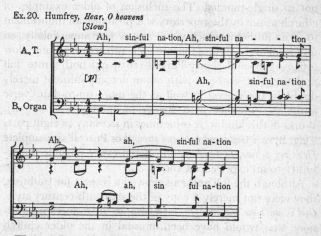

Ex. 20. Humfrey, *Hear, O heavens*

The modern listener may feel that this goes beyond the reasonable limits of devotional expression; but a seventeenth-century congregation would have recognized it as the counterpart of the extravagant religious poetry of the time. The Restoration age was one of violent contrasts – on the one hand a coarseness on the stage and in popular catches which would not be tolerated today, on the other an intense awareness of sin and a passionate desire for God's mercy. The temper of the times was individualist: it was this, rather than any inadequacy in the Chapel Royal choir, that induced Humfrey to give the chorus relatively little to sing. The voices were now accompanied by the organ; the pre-Commonwealth practice of using viols was obsolete, because the viol family itself was thought to be old-fashioned. At the same time Charles II liked to have instruments playing in the Chapel, no doubt because this was the practice at Versailles, and in consequence his string orchestra of twenty-four players (violins, violas, and cellos) was used to play preludes and interludes in the anthems. According to the diarist John Evelyn, this happened for the first time in December 1662.

Nearly all Humfrey's anthems use a string orchestra in this way. His contemporaries and immediate successors were not so single-minded. The inclusion of older examples of church music in the repertory was probably an inducement to write anthems which were, at any rate superficially, an imitation of the style of the late sixteenth century. John Blow (1649–1708) and Henry Purcell (1659–95) both wrote 'full anthems' (i.e. anthems with organ accompaniment merely doubling the voices) as well as the more up-to-date 'verse anthems' (whether with strings or merely with organ). Works of this kind were sometimes in as many as eight parts – e.g. Blow's *God is our hope and strength* or Purcell's incomplete *Hear my prayer, O Lord* – and offered every possible opportunity to an experienced choir.

Although the full anthems showed a respect for tradition, they were not merely a copy of the sixteenth-century style. *God is our hope and strength*, for example, introduces progressions that would have been unusual in the older church music, though they were familiar enough in madrigals, and the harmonic structure is more firmly anchored to a bass. We find the same thing to an even more marked degree in Purcell. One of his earliest anthems, a setting of the funeral

sentence *In the midst of life we are in death,* plunges into extravagantly chromatic harmony at the words 'deliver us not
into the bitter pains of eternal death'. Purcell also had his
own ways of resolving dissonance, and both he and Blow
retained the outmoded habit of using harmonic clashes
resulting from the combination of two different scale systems (e.g. Example 22, bar 3 – B flat and B natural), particularly in cadences: we find examples also in the work of
Blow's fellow-chorister Michael Wise (*c*.1648–87).

To the present-day listener such passages may sound
curiously modern, whereas in fact they are the survival of an
old tradition which Thomas Morley criticized as early as
1597. We may suppose that Blow and Purcell used this convention because they had grown up with it in the Chapel
Royal. Nor was this the only thing they had learned from
singing the music of Byrd and Gibbons. The older composers had taught them better than any master how to combine voices in independent lines: the result is that their full
anthems make them worthy heirs of a great tradition. Purcell never lost his interest in this aspect of his art. His passion
for ingenious contrapuntal combinations is brilliantly illustrated in his chamber music, and it sometimes turns up in
the most unexpected places in his music for the stage.

Anthems with strings were designed for more festal occasions than the full anthems and in consequence are often
brilliantly assertive, particularly if the text is of a jubilant
character. The strings have the function of emphasizing
this brilliance and also conveying an atmosphere of pomp
and ceremony. Their interludes are sometimes directly
related to the vocal sections, sometimes independent. On
occasion they accompany the singers, but for the most part
this task is assigned to the organ: the result is a clear-cut
contrast between singers and orchestra. The coronation of
James II in 1685 offered a particular opportunity for elaboration, since more than one choir was employed. Both
Blow and Purcell excelled themselves here with the composition of large-scale works – Blow with *God spake sometime
in visions* and Purcell with *My heart is inditing*. No quotation
can give an adequate idea of the way in which the large

forces available were used, but a brief extract from Blow's anthem may help to suggest the splendour of the occasion (Example 21).

A short summary of Purcell's *O sing unto the Lord* may also serve to illustrate the relationship between solo voices and chorus in a typical verse anthem of the period. The music is continuous and the sections are numbered here merely for convenience:

1. Prelude for strings (related to No. 2)
2. Bass solo (with organ): 'O sing unto the Lord'
3. Chorus (with strings): 'Allelujah'
4. Bass solo (with organ): 'Sing unto the Lord, all the whole earth'
5. Chorus (with strings): 'Allelujah'
6. Interlude for strings (related to No. 5)
7. Quartet (with organ): 'Sing unto the Lord and praise his name'
8. Bass solo (with strings): 'Declare his honour unto the heathen'
9. Chorus (with strings): 'Glory and worship are before him'
10. Duet (with organ): 'The Lord is great'
11. Interlude for strings (a continuation of No. 10)
12. Quartet and chorus (with organ): 'O worship the Lord'
13. Bass solo and chorus (with strings): 'Tell it out among the heathen'
14. Quartet and chorus (first with organ, later with strings): 'Allelujah, Amen'.

Purcell must have learned a good deal from Humfrey and Blow, as well as from Matthew Locke (1630–77), who was a good deal older than either of the others; but he learned even more from his own experience. He was a boy chorister in the Chapel Royal, and succeeded John Blow as organist at Westminster Abbey in 1679; in 1682 he became one of the organists of the Chapel Royal as well. He also had a curiously original mind which liked to find new ways of doing familiar things. Naturally enough, there is much in

Ex. 21. Blow, *God spake sometime in visions*

his church music that is the common property of the period;
but there are also individual twists which have no exact
parallel in the work of his contemporaries. On the whole he
was at his best in anthems of an intimate and devotional
character. Where pomp and brilliance were required, his
feelings were less actively engaged, unless, as in the coronation anthem, the occasion appealed strongly to his imagination. Even in works which begin triumphantly, such as
Blow up the trumpet in Sion, he would seize the opportunity to
indulge a penitential mood (Example 22). The most

Ex. 22. Purcell, *Blow up the trumpet in Sion*

moving passages of the festal *Te Deum and Jubilate*, written
for St Cecilia's Day in 1694, are those which express a
humble and a contrite heart. The rest of the work is largely
a matter of sonorous trumpeting.

Most of Purcell's anthems date from the reign of Charles
II (1660–85). The reason for this is partly the decline of the
Chapel Royal under James II and William III (in particular, the abandonment of orchestral participation) and partly
the fact that in the latter part of his life Purcell became
more and more engrossed in composition for the theatre.
His interest in the stage is evident to anyone who knows his
dramatic music; but it did not lead him to confuse categories. The most cheerful movements in his anthems are
quite distinct from his theatrical work. Their cheerfulness is

not a sign of secular influence, as has sometimes been supposed, but an acceptance of the current formulas for praising God. Any apparent similarity with triumphant or jolly music in the dramatic works in only superficial. The regular rhythms of Purcell's songs and dances have no exact counterpart in his music for the church.

The Chapel Royal, the cathedrals, and the college chapels were the only places where seventeenth-century listeners could regularly expect to hear a choir. Choruses occur in the dramatic music of the time, but they are generally incidental to the performance. The only other works with chorus are the odes, most of which were written for the Royal family and hence were heard only by those invited to attend at court. No one knows exactly when the first ode was composed, but the practice certainly did not exist before the Restoration. The idea may have come from Continental operas in which tribute was paid to a ruler in the prologue. As England had no operas of this kind the ode was a suitable means of expressing loyalty, often in the most extravagant terms. The principal occasions for works of this kind were New Year's Day, royal birthdays, and weddings, and the return of the monarch from some provincial excursion. Once the custom became established it hardened into a tradition which lasted right into the nineteenth century.

Humfrey, Blow, and Purcell all wrote odes for the court, as did a number of other seventeenth-century composers, including Purcell's younger brother Daniel (c.1663–1717). In form these works are short cantatas for solo voices, chorus, and orchestra, built on a plan rather similar to that of the larger anthems. The style of Purcell's odes frequently recalls that of his dramatic music; and on two occasions he actually introduced popular tunes of the day. But though the music is often tuneful, it can also be serious. The occasions for which these works were composed were not frivolous; and though the words may strike us today as ludicrous, we must suppose that the courtiers took them seriously. Certainly there is never a hint that the composers set them with their tongues in their cheeks.

Some of the finest choral writing of the period is to be found in these court odes, most of which are unknown today because their texts are unsuitable for any other purpose than the one for which they were designed. Purcell's odes cover the whole period of his creative life. The best are those which he wrote for Queen Mary's birthday, culminating in the splendid *Come, ye sons of art, away* (1694), which includes the well-known duet *Sound the trumpet* for two counter-tenors. It is difficult to know what models the English composers had for their choral writing. Some knowledge of contemporary Italian music must be presumed: the style often suggests Carissimi in its insistence or clear-cut rhythms and a brilliant melodic line. A good example is Example 23 (using the Latin equivalent for 'Hurrah!') from Purcell's ode *Now does the glorious day appear*, written for Queen Mary's birthday in 1689 (the year of *Dido and Aeneas*).

As I have suggested, the court odes were heard by only a limited number of people. Occasions for hearing choral music elsewhere were few and far between. The most important was the celebration of the feast of St Cecilia on 22 November. It is not known when these celebrations began. The earliest ode we have was written by Purcell in 1683, a setting of verses beginning:

> Welcome to all the pleasures that delight
> Of every sense the grateful appetite.

Blow followed with the ode *Begin the song* in 1684, performed in Stationers' Hall, which became the normal London meeting-place. A further development was the holding of a special choral service (with sermon) in St Bride's, Fleet Street. The purpose of these meetings was to glorify the art of music, and composers seem to have been very ready to contribute, though in fact the annual celebration lasted only twenty years. Some of the best-known poets of the day provided texts, and in some cases the same text was set more than once. Dryden's *Alexander's Feast* and *Ode on St Cecilia's Day*, set by Handel in 1736 and 1739 respectively, were originally written for the celebrations in 1697 and 1687, the music of the first being by Jeremiah Clarke (*c.*1673–1707),

Ex. 23. Purcell, *Now does the glorious day appear*

of the second by Giovanni Battista Draghi (c.1640–c.1710), an Italian resident in London. The finest of all the seventeenth-century odes is Purcell's *Hail, bright Cecilia* (1692), which uses the chorus with a breadth and freedom unequalled until Handel's oratorios.

Handel (see Chapter 8) arrived in England in 1710, but by that time most of the Restoration composers were dead. Those who survived were not men of great consequence. Thomas Tudway (c.1650–1726) is remembered not as a composer but as the compiler of a remarkable collection of manuscript church music for Edward, Lord Harley, who became the second Earl of Oxford in 1724. John Eccles (c.1663–1735) was known to his contemporaries chiefly by his music for the stage, though in his capacity as Master of the King's Music from 1700 onwards he was assiduous in the composition of court odes, which indeed seems to have been his only activity in the latter part of his life. William Turner (1651–1740) outlived them all and died at a ripe old age, but did little to justify the promise he had shown as a choirboy when he combined with Humfrey and Blow to write the so-called 'Club Anthem'.

Apart from the anthems in the old style, choral music played only a subsidiary part in the music of the time. The emphasis, both in church music and in the odes, was on solo singing, and the chorus, like the orchestra, was used mainly for contrast. It remained for Handel, in his anthems and oratorios, to give choral singing a new dignity and importance; and even in his oratorios the choruses are often relatively few. No such thing as an amateur choral society existed at this time or for many years later. The singers in the cathedrals may have been part-time employees, but they were paid; and the Chapel Royal choir was completely professional. Purcell and his contemporaries in London wrote for trained singers who were competent to undertake solo parts as well as to sing in the chorus. In the theatre, at court and at public manifestations composers could count on musicians who could give a respectable performance with the minimum of rehearsal.

It is a curious reversal of fortune that much of the music

of this period has become the preserve of amateurs. This does not necessarily mean that our performances are inferior to those of the seventeenth century. But there is inevitably a shift of interest; and where a modern conductor uses a large choir he is creating a sound quite foreign to the seventeenth-century convention of a small and expert body. It is also not easy for us to realize that most of the choral music of the time was tied to the liturgy or court ceremonial. But it is one of the virtues of music that it outlives successfully the circumstances for which it was composed. Many of the anthems of this period are still part of the cathedral repertory, and more and more choirmasters are taking what opportunity they can to perform them with orchestra. The odes present a different problem; but a generation that can listen happily to the extravagant texts of many of Bach's cantatas should be able to stomach the language in which the Restoration poets paid homage to their kings and queens.

7

Bach and his Time

c.1705–c.1760

WALTER EMERY

Of the choral music covered by this chapter, comparatively little has found its way into the current repertory. For one thing, all the other composers are overshadowed by J. S. Bach – more so than is altogether fair. For another, most of this music, including Bach's own, suffers from serious practical disadvantages. The texts, whether religious or secular, are sometimes tasteless, if not downright ridiculous. The solos are inconveniently numerous, and are apt to be difficult. Few of the religious works fit naturally into present-day church services, or can be made effective with organ accompaniment; and for concert purposes they, like the secular works, require just those things that are nowadays most difficult to provide, for financial reasons – a small but highly efficient choir and an orchestra that must be about equally numerous, must understand the performing conventions of the period, and must include a skilled continuo player. In recent years the broadcasting and gramophone companies have done a little to rectify this state of affairs; but to most of us, even in the 1960s, the title of this chapter means one or two of Bach's major works, three or four of his church cantatas, and precious little else. Much of it, moreover, we know only from indifferent performances.

Bach's period was one of drastic changes both in musical style and in fundamental thought about musical aesthetics. Some of these technical changes are supposed to be related to the general idea that the arts ought to appeal to the emotions of the layman, rather than to the intellect of the expert; though it seems likely that they represent collateral developments rather than the direct consequences of that one idea. The latter was nothing new; so far as religious art is concerned, it went back to the Council of Trent. It was put forward in more general terms by Roger de Piles in the 1670s, and by Du Bos in 1719 (both in France). The writings of Telemann (see p. 131) and of J. D. Heinichen (1683–1729), director of music to the court at Dresden from 1717, show that in the Leipzig area, during the first few years of the eighteenth century, musicians talked a good deal about a 'new school of melodic composition' (involving tunefulness, with a direct emotional appeal), as against the 'unmelodious artifices' of their predecessors. By the 1750s such authors as J. J. Quantz (1697–1773), Avison (see p. 127), and C.P.E. Bach (see p. 135) make it perfectly clear that music must arouse the passions (emotions), and that the performer must feel the passions he seeks to arouse in his audience.

This change of emphasis is apparent in the librettos of church cantatas, where the decisive step was taken by Erdmann Neumeister (a priest, not a composer) in 1700. Previously librettos had normally been put together from Bible quotations and verses of chorales (traditional hymn-tunes; see p. 69) with little or no original material. (Bach's Cantatas Nos. 4, 106, and 131 are of this type, though written after 1700.) But Neumeister's first librettos were entirely original, and consisted exclusively of recitatives and arias. The arias were the highlights, presenting various states of religious emotion; the recitatives served as links; and the whole scheme was consciously modelled on the contemporary opera, a form brought to Germany from Italy. *Daphne* by Schütz (see p. 81), performed in 1627 at Torgau (Saxony), is historically reckoned the first German opera; but the first substantial growth of the form occurred at Hamburg from 1678, in which year *Adam and Eve* by Johann Theile (1646–1724) became the first *Singspiel* (German opera with spoken dialogue) to be publicly performed.

This borrowing from opera brought a revolutionary change in the church cantata; the impersonal dignity of the old libretto, compiled from the Word of God, and the

hardly less sacred voice of the Protestant Church, was replaced by a description of the religious feelings of an individual, whose value depended entirely on the sincerity and
literary ability of the author. In his later publications Neumeister was less extreme; he admitted choruses in 1708, and
chorales and the Bible crept back in 1711; but his general
scheme remained operatic, and provided the model for
practically all subsequent cantata texts. Similarly, original
Passion poems began to appear (as in Handel's *Brockes
Passion*, *c*.1716, and Graun's *Death of Jesus*); so that here also
the simple dignity of the traditional material was either
rejected altogether, or half submerged by an emotional
commentary, in language that is often exaggerated or dis-
gusting. Strange as it may seem, composers welcomed such
texts; presumably the exaggerations stimulated them.

As is well known, there was at this time a decline of
interest in counterpoint. Bach himself wrote much less
counterpoint than he is commonly given credit for; in his
choral works, as in his suites, there are many movements
that can only be described as accompanied melodies, even
if the accompaniment is rather more elaborate than was
customary. It is easy – probably all *too* easy – either to say
that this was because composers became increasingly anxious
to appeal direct to the emotions by writing expressive tunes,
instead of relying on the intellectual interest of intricate
counterpoint, or to see the change as a reflection of the
gradual transfer of patronage from a supposedly intelligent
aristocracy to a supposedly stupid and sentimental middle
class. One ought also to remember the rise of the solo song
and of music for solo instruments with continuo accompaniment – seventeenth-century developments, whereby the top
part tended to become the only one that mattered. Certainly music became increasingly difficult to execute, so
that the top parts could only be played or sung by star
performers; and instead of taking an intelligent interest in
music that they could have played or sung themselves,
audiences gradually became content to sit back and be
stunned by virtuosity. (A parallel phenomenon in England
is shown in the memoirs of the lawyer and musical dilet-

tante, the Hon. Roger North: see Bibliography.) Anyway, for whatever reason, counterpoint declined; and when, about 1750, there was a revival of interest in this old-fashioned technique of 'unmelodious artifices', the results tended to be stiff and self-conscious. See, for instance, the academic fugue on *Christ unto us hath left an example*, No. 10 of Graun's *Death of Jesus*.

In its crude treatment of chorales, this work (1755) seems to reflect another aspect of this appeal to the emotions of the layman. The chorales are harmonized in the baldest and most perfunctory way; and there is nothing comparable to Bach's allusive use of them, as in the first chorus of the *St Matthew Passion*, or more strikingly in the bass recitative (No. 9) of Bach's Cantata No. 70. In Bach, these allusions are extremely effective, in much the same way that entries of Wagner's leading-motives are effective; and since even a modern listener can get some idea of their meaning and emotional force by learning the chorale melody and glancing at the words, eighteenth-century audiences ought to have had no difficulty in understanding this allusiveness. However, a certain intellectual effort is undoubtedly required; and, slight as it must have been, it appears to have been too much for Graun and his contemporaries.

Here there also arises the question of symbolism, which needs to be discussed in some detail because, in certain otherwise excellent books, it is greatly over-emphasized and presented in such a way that it puzzles the listener and makes the composer look a fool. The devices covered by the term 'symbolism' are of several different kinds, but they all have two things in common: they invite the listener to make an intellectual effort, and to find a meaning in some feature of the music that he does not normally listen for.

For instance, Bach is said to have used a whole system of 'motives', standing for grief, joy, and other abstractions. This notion might have been acceptable if Bach had used his motives fairly consistently, as Wagner used his. In fact, he did not. Chromaticism is not always associated with grief. The so-called 'Joy Motive' is also associated with shouts of 'Crucify Him!' Most of these abstract motives are simply stock rhythms, or stock melodic figures, or stock harmonic progressions. They make their musical effect; beyond that, they have no definite meaning. A list of Wagner's motives is worth learning; a list of Bach's *abstract* motives is not even worth looking at.

Pictorial symbolism is a different matter, since Bach undoubtedly used it. Even so, one has to ask whether he used it as a means of expression – in other words, whether he thought his audiences would take it in.

Morley, in his *Plain and Easy Introduction to Practical Music* (1597), taught pictorialism as a matter of course:

You must have a care that when your matter signifieth ascending, high heaven, and such like, you make your music ascend . . . for as it will be thought a great absurdity to talk of heaven and point downwards to the earth, so will it be counted great incongruity if a musician upon the words 'he ascended into heaven' should cause his music to descend . . .

This was in accordance with the ancient view that the arts make their effect by imitating nature. Once it was realized that no art can be completely explained in that way – and music least of all – the whole idea of pictorialism was bound to be questioned. Kuhnau (1660–1722) used pictorialism in his Bible Sonatas for clavier (1700)* but only with reservations that he took pains to explain in his preface. Heinichen, in 1711, regarded pictorialism less as a means of expression than as an aid to invention. He explains in great detail that if a composer has to set dull words in a hurry, and is stumped for an idea (which must have been a common situation in those days), he can help himself out by trying to find something in the libretto that will suggest pictorial figuration. For instance, a dull poem about love may nevertheless suggest 'the fires of love'; and the composer can picture those fires by a flickering figure (very much like Wagner's 'Fire Music'). By the 1750s, owing to the increasing emphasis on emotional communication between composer and audience, musicians had become positively

---

* A famous early example of illustrative music.

suspicious of pictorialism. The Newcastle composer and organist Charles Avison (1709–90), in his very readable *Essay on Musical Expression* (second edition, 1753) says of Handel:

What shall we say to excuse this same great Composer, who, in his Oratorio of *Joshua*, condescended to amuse the vulgar Part of his Audience, by letting them *hear the Sun stand still*?

J. S. Bach's son, Emanuel (C. P. E.) Bach, writing to Forkel (his father's biographer) in 1774, was careful to point out that his father had always paid due attention to the general drift of his texts, without the undue emphasis on individual words that so often sounded ridiculous.

All these authors were right, up to a point. Avison and Emanuel Bach were right in saying that pictorialism becomes ridiculous when it is overdone. But Morley also was right. Pictorialism is impossible in a hymn or a strophic song, where the same music serves for several verses and totally different words; but whenever the general scheme of a work admits of emphasis on individual words, it is absurd to avoid what is in fact a fundamental musical instinct. Pictorialism occurs in the works of all the most important composers from the madrigalists to the present day. And finally, Heinichen was right: if a composer cannot think what to do next, pictorialism may provide the answer.

In recent years, commentators on Bach's period have written a great deal about number-symbolism. This is a reasonable device, so far as it is pictorial. It is natural that a single voice should sing of someone who is walking all alone, and that when the person walking is joined by others, other voices should join in. It is not unnatural that a fugue concerned with the Ten Commandments should contain ten entries of the subject; though one may doubt whether anyone but a modern commentator would have bothered to count the entries, and suspect the composer of a pious joke. No doubt there are many genuine examples of pictorial number-symbolism; but some of those that appear in books on Bach prove only that twentieth-century numerologists cannot count.

As for the more elaborate forms of number-symbolism that have been imagined by musical Baconians, it is doubtful whether composers of the Bach period ever used them – except perhaps as a joke, in the canons and other musical puzzles that they presented to their friends. It is true that seven is a 'sacred' number (though no one seems to know exactly what that means); true that there were ten Commandments and twelve disciples; and true that these numbers, or their multiples, can be discovered in movements that contain forty-nine fugal entries or eighty-four bars. It is also true that if numbers are assigned to the letters of the alphabet, BACH adds up to fourteen, and J. S. BACH to forty-one (I and J both count as nine): and that these numbers also can be discovered in certain movements. Unfortunately, it is easy to find any number somewhere, if one has time to waste on looking for it. Besides, it is as well to remember that when Printz explained to Telemann how music could be used as a code for sending messages, Telemann was most immoderately amused. As he thought the story worth telling in his autobiography, he probably dined out on it for years; and it was after the Printz episode that he met Bach.

On the whole, it seems likely that the German composers of this period had no serious use for any kind of symbolism but plain pictorialism; that at the beginning of the century they regarded even pictorialism less as a necessary means of expression than as a handy aid to invention; and that they used it less and less, as time went on, because they became more and more afraid of making themselves ridiculous.

It is certain that Bach attached no particular significance to his own pictorialism, for he left it unaltered when he adapted movements to fresh words. The best-known examples occur in the *Christmas Oratorio*, much of which was borrowed from secular cantatas. (Certain English authors have maintained that the secular cantatas were borrowed from the oratorio. It is charitable to suppose that they never saw the original manuscripts.) In one of the secular arias, Hercules refers to the serpents that attacked him in his cradle. The serpentine bass part shows that Bach reacted instinctively to a suggestive word. This aria became the familiar *Prepare thyself, Zion*; the serpents are still there in the music, although no one has ever explained what they have to do with Zion. In other words, once Bach had written his bass part, he forgot its connexion with serpents; it meant nothing more to him than so many notes and chords.

The question of borrowing and adaptation is another that needs a word of explanation, chiefly because there is really so little to be explained. In spite of the increasing emphasis on emotion as the mainspring of artistic expression, in the early eighteenth century it was not felt, as it is today, that a work of art ought to be a unique manifestation of a unique personality, and the artist's own property, in the sense that no one else could have produced it. In a word, the idea of copyright hardly existed, and borrowing was common form. Turning to London architecture, Flitcroft's steeple at St Giles-in-the-Fields, a barefaced imitation of Gibbs's design at St Martin's, aroused no indignation among his contemporaries. When one artist might borrow from another, there was no reason why a composer should not borrow from himself, even if his only motive was to save time and trouble; and that was not always the only motive, at any rate with Bach. Some of his adaptations are admittedly perfunctory; but sometimes the second version is so different from the first that it probably took him longer to adapt than it would have taken him to write fresh music. The original music must have struck him as so very suitable for the fresh words that it was not worth his while to start again.

Conditions of employment do not seem to have changed much during this period. Like Bach himself, a composer might be a church organist, eking out what was sometimes a miserable existence by teaching; or an employee of a town council; or a member of an aristocrat's musical establishment. From this point of view, it is difficult to see that the middle classes had any more influence in 1780 than in 1700. Publication became commoner, and presumably increasingly profitable as a sideline; and composers who wished to sell their music had to cater for the general public. But even so, middle-class taste cannot have had much effect on choral music in this particular way, for comparatively little was published.

As for performing conditions, the standard of singing varied from the star soloist employed by a lucky composer with a wealthy patron, down to the village choirboy. In between, there were local professionals or semi-professionals, such as Anna Magdalena Bach, who, according to her husband, had 'a very clear soprano'. She was employed as a singer both before and after her marriage. The same is true of instrumentalists. Some composers wrote for professional orchestras, with expert continuo-players like Emanuel Bach. Others had to make do with what they could get. J. S. Bach's post as director of music at St Thomas's Church, at Leipzig, was by no means unimportant; but he was largely dependent on choir boys and other musicians who were not full-time professionals. The only generalization that can be made about performers is that their sight-reading and general musicianship must have been extraordinarily good.

Bach's early cantatas were written for small-town resources; but modern performers do not find them particularly easy. At Leipzig he sometimes put on a new church cantata every week. On 8 December 1733 he performed a secular cantata (No. 214), to celebrate a royal birthday. This work contains two big choruses, which afterwards became Nos. 1 and 24 of the *Christmas Oratorio*, and the showy bass solo that is now familiar as *Mighty Lord*. The full score was finished the day before the performance. Anyone who knows how long it takes to make modern performers do justice to Bach will sympathize with the question asked by W. G. Whittaker (see Bibliography): 'What must the performance have been like?' But the answer must be that the performance was at any rate decent, and that Bach knew there was no serious risk of a breakdown. This does not mean that his performers were in every way incomparably better than ours. It must be remembered that they understood the performing conventions of the period. Half the trouble today is that we have to reconstruct those conventions, and that as we cannot reconstruct them completely, they are a perpetual source of worry.

Apart from the works of J. S. Bach, very little of the choral music of this period is available except in expensive and more or less unpractical learned editions. Such composers as J. J. Fux (?1660–1741), J. Ludwig Bach (1677–1731), G. P. Telemann(1681–1767), Gottfried Kirchhoff (?1685–1746), C. H. Graun (?1703–59), W. F. Bach (1710–84), C. P. E. Bach (1714–88), and J. C. F. Bach (1732–95) can hardly be said to have found their way into the regular repertory, or even to have much chance of doing so. It would be unprofitable to do more than indicate the sort of music they wrote, and suggest that some of it may deserve at least an occasional hearing.

Fux stands somewhat apart from the other men mentioned, being an Austrian, a Roman Catholic, and considerably older. Very little is known of his early years; but he was influenced by Corelli, and it is supposed that he somehow contrived to study in Italy. In 1698 he became attached to the Imperial Court at Vienna, and from 1715 onwards he was Kapellmeister (director of music) there. At Vienna he had a considerable musical establishment at his disposal: a five-part choir of some forty or fifty voices, and an equally numerous orchestra of the type usual at the period, including some expert performers. He is now best known as a theorist – his *Gradus ad Parnassum* ('Steps to Parnassus') of 1725, a Latin textbook on counterpoint, had an enormous and lasting influence, and to this day remains both instructive and delightful to read. His music, like Bach's, dropped out of use after his death; and, unlike Bach's, has not been revived. Naturally, it is considerably more old-fashioned. Along with broad melodies of the type that we think of as Handelian (though it was really Italian-international) there are false relations and clashes of major and minor that remind one of the Purcell period. There may perhaps be too many clichés; without actually hearing the music, it is difficult to say. A few performances of his Masses and oratorios would help us to assess the compositions of the last and greatest figure of the native Austrian Baroque.

Ludwig Bach was a good composer, and the family knew

it; during 1726 J. S. Bach copied out and performed eighteen
church cantatas by his remote relative. The only one that
is readily accessible is that which has hitherto been published as J. S. Bach's Cantata 15; Whittaker, who naturally
accepted it as an early work of J. S. Bach's, bears testimony
to its attractions. The other cantatas would be well worth
exploring. They were presumably written for the court of
Meiningen, at some time after 1699; most of them are
lightly scored, although a fair-sized orchestra seems to have
been available.

Like Handel, Gottfried Kirchhoff began as a pupil of
Zachau's; and he succeeded his master at St Mary's, Halle,
in 1713. He must have known Bach, who declined the Halle
appointment in 1713, and examined the organ in 1716.
Only two of his cantatas have been preserved; and only the
second of them (*How short is our time*, for the New Year) can
really be called a choral work. Even that is scored for only
three voices (SAB) and strings. It is tuneful, in that quasi-
Handelian way we have noted, and has a good deal of
simple-minded charm.

Opinions differ about Telemann. In Germany he is considered worthy of a Collected Edition; elsewhere he is apt to
be dismissed as a mere note-spinner. As with Elgar and
Sibelius, national differences of taste may be concerned. In
his lifetime he was enormously successful. While still more or
less a student he became director of the Leipzig Opera, and
from 1704 onwards he held a series of lucrative appointments, sometimes several at once; in 1721 he became Cantor of the Latin School and Director of Music in the five
principal churches of Hamburg. He knew both Bach and
Handel; and it is evident from his autobiography (translated in *The Consort*, London, July 1953) that he was a man
of great personal charm. No doubt that had much to do
with his success; but he was also fortunate in that his own
taste was the fashionable taste. From his Leipzig days
onwards he was all in favour of thin textures and straightforward tunefulness. Although he enjoyed immense technical
skill (Handel said he could write in eight parts as easily
as anyone else could write a letter), his choral writing tends

to be homophonic, and is usually simple. Example 24 is from his setting of Psalm 117:

Ex. 24. Telemann, *Psalm 117*

The most accessible of his vocal works are probably those that have been falsely ascribed to J. S. Bach, and published as the latter's Cantatas 141, 160, 218, and 219; besides these there is the above-quoted setting of Psalm 117, and a semi-secular cantata *Times of the Day* (*Die Tageszeiten*) with sections for Morning, Noon, Evening, and Night. There is no denying that Telemann wrote too much; but neither is there any doubt about the attractions of his music, at its best. *Times of the Day*, a sort of forerunner of Haydn's *Seasons*, comes remarkably close to the early classical (Haydn-esque) style in places, and would be well worth hearing.

Graun also had a successful career, partly as a singer. In 1725 he went to the Brunswick Court Opera as a tenor; about 1727 he was appointed deputy musical director there. In 1733 began a lifelong friendship with the Crown Prince Frederick (the Great), of Prussia, whom he served at Rheins-berg from 1736, and (as court musical director) at Berlin from 1740. He and Hasse were the chief composers of the Italianate opera school that was then fashionable; he was also a member of the Berlin group that included Quantz and C. P. E. Bach, and he earned the respect of J. S. Bach. His operas were soon forgotten, but his *Te Deum*, and the Passion cantata known as *The Death of Jesus*, remained in the repertory for a long time; the latter, to which reference has already been made on p. 124, is said to have been as popular in Germany as *Messiah* is in England, and not until the 1880s was it displaced by Bach. Its libretto resembles that of Stainer's *Crucifixion*, and is so unpleasant that it prevents one from seeing any good in the music; only a drastic change in public taste could justify a revival. The *Te Deum* does not suffer from this disadvantage. It was written in thirteen days to celebrate a victory at Prague (1757), and is by no means profound; but it serves the Lord cheerfully, somewhat in the manner of Haydn, and is tuneful and effective.

W. F. Bach (eldest son of J. S. Bach) was organist at St Sophia's Church, Dresden (1733–46), and succeeded Kirch-hoff at St Mary's, Halle. He resigned this important post in 1764, for reasons that are not clear, and afterwards lived as best he could. His choral works were written at Halle. They do not show him at his best; he imitated his father too closely, whereas in his instrumental works he developed a style of his own. However, some of the single movements (especially the more homophonic ones) deserve attention.

Another of J. S. Bach's sons, Carl Philipp Emanuel, took a leading part in the musical life of Frankfurt-on-Oder while still a law-student. In 1738 he moved to Berlin, and almost immediately entered the service of the Crown Prince Frederick (the Great) as accompanist. In 1768 he succeeded his godfather Telemann as director of music in the chief churches of Hamburg. A vast amount of music had to be provided, and it is not surprising that Emanuel borrowed extensively from his father and Telemann, and that a good deal of his original work was turned out by the yard. His best choral works are said to be a Magnificat (1749; written in Berlin), Passion and Ascension Cantatas, an oratorio called *The Israelites in the Wilderness*, and a German *Sanctus* for double choir (which was published in 1779, and, according to its composer, sold as fast as the hot pastry in front of the Stock Exchange).

One thinks of Emanuel either as the author of that fascinating book, the *Essay on the True Art of playing Keyboard Instruments* (see Bibliography), or as that depressing thing, a Precursor (of Haydn). In fact, he is a grossly neglected composer. His style can be fairly accurately described as a mixture of his father's and Haydn's, but the point is that the mixture was his own. He was no fumbling amateur who made a few lucky shots, but a fine musician and a very considerable personality in his own right.

Another son of J. S. Bach, Johann Christoph Friedrich Bach – often referred to as Friedrich Bach, and not to be confused with his brother Johann Christian Bach – was appointed chamber musician to the Count of Lippe, at Bückeburg, in 1750, and became Konzertmeister in 1759. (A Konzertmeister was usually a harpsichordist or string player, not necessarily a First Violin, who conducted from his place in the orchestra.) He was not very well paid, but made only one attempt to break away – when he applied, unsuccessfully, for Telemann's post at Hamburg. He seems to have been a quiet, unambitious man, content to have employers who were on the whole sympathetic, and an orchestra that became one of the best in Germany. This impression is confirmed by his music. An oratorio, *The Childhood of Jesus*, is available in a modern edition; and Geiringer found the right words when he wrote of its 'gentle charm'.

Johann Sebastian Bach (1685–1750) began his professional career as a chamber musician at Weimar, where he spent a few months in 1703. (He was employed by Duke Johann Ernst, the father of the boy-composer of the same name; it was not until 1708 that he served Duke Wilhelm Ernst.) Thereafter he was organist at Arnstadt (August 1703–September 1707); at Mühlhausen (till June 1708); chamber musician and organist to Duke Wilhelm of Weimar, becoming Konzertmeister in March 1714, with the duty of composing cantatas; director of music to Prince Leopold of Cöthen (December 1717); and from May 1723 onwards, Cantor of St Thomas's School at Leipzig. Here he supplied choirs for four churches, and himself conducted at St Thomas's and St Nicholas's alternately.

In discussing Bach's vocal works it must be emphasized that the 'traditional' chronology (set up in 1880) has been so thoroughly upset, by discoveries published during the last few years, that there is at present no trustworthy discussion of the subject as a whole in print. The biographical and critical works referred to in the Bibliography can still be read with profit; but many of the dates are wrong, and inevitably the generalizations are wrong also. Needless to say, although the new chronology is well established as far as it goes, there still remain some gaps and controversial points.

Many of Bach's vocal works have been lost; but even the remnant is of formidable dimensions. To mention only those works that are most likely to be heard, and are most profitable to study – and allowing also for the possibility that some of them will soon be proved spurious, like Cantatas Nos. 15, 141, 142, 160, 189, 218, and 219 – we have about 16 secular cantatas; 6 motets; about 190 church cantatas; and 6 major works.

Of the secular cantatas, eight are entirely for solo voices

and need not be considered here (though the *Peasant
Cantata*, No. 212, is a masterpiece of humour). The others
are Nos. 201, 205–8, and 213–15. Many of the movements
are already well known in later adaptations to religious
texts; but that does not justify us in neglecting the original
secular versions as we do. Take, for instance, the first
chorus of the *Christmas Oratorio*, with its opening words
'Christians be joyful, and praise your salvation'. It is a good
movement; but it would sound even better with its original
words – the words that inspired the scoring (Cantata 214;
Example 25).

Ex. 25. Bach, *Cantata 214*

Cantata 208 is the earliest of these works, and the only one
written before Bach went to Cöthen. It dates from 1716, and
was performed at Weissenfels to celebrate the Duke's
birthday. The other cantatas of this group were written for
occasions of private or public rejoicing, and some of the
words are so closely connected with these occasions that
they are unsuitable for general use today. Someone ought
to rewrite them.

There is an excellent discussion of the motets in Whittaker's *Fugitive Notes* (see Bibliography), and little need be
said of them here. It seems that they were all written at
Leipzig, for funerals or other special occasions. The best
of them are those known in English as *Jesu, priceless Treasure*

(in five parts); *Come, Jesu, come*; *Be not afraid*; and *Sing ye to the Lord* (all for double choir, i.e. in eight parts). It must be emphasized that the motets are not show-pieces for un-accompanied choir. They ought always to be accompanied, by the organ at least and preferably by other instruments as well; not only because that is how they were originally performed, but also because choirs sing them so much better when there is an accompaniment to give them confidence.

Of the church cantatas, about nine were written before Bach became Konzertmeister at Weimar; about twenty at Weimar, between 1714 and 1716; a few, perhaps, at Cöthen; most of the remainder during Bach's first three or four years at Leipzig. Not more than ten church cantatas are known to have been written after 1735. Setting aside works in which the choir sings only a plain chorale, or not at all, the total number is about 140.

The earliest works are Nos. 131 (1707), 71 and 196 (1708), 106, 4, 150, 18, 21, and 63; the last three may be as late as 1714. Of the others, No. 4 is not the most typical; but in some ways it is the most difficult to understand. At first sight this grim grey work, all in E minor, seems the oddest piece of Easter music ever written. The explanation is that every movement is based on the Easter chorale *Christ lay in death's dark prison* (*Christ lag in Todesbanden*, 1524), with Luther's words (see p. 71). This chorale was one of the finest products of a period when men fought for their religion, and regarded the Resurrection as the greatest fight of all; hence the savagery of the words, the tune, and the cantata as a whole.

The work probably dates from Easter 1708, and certainly is not much later. Bach revived it at Leipzig in 1724, but left it substantially as it was; it still shows several early features. The libretto is Luther's hymn, unaltered. The scoring is old-fashioned, with two violas, making a five-part instead of the usual four-part string ensemble. The intro-ductory Sinfonia (overture), though extremely expressive, is shapeless; it quotes the first line of the chorale melody, but so casually that no one would notice it unless he already knew the melody. The first chorus is of the antique type

in which each line of the chorale is fugued separately; it
is therefore incoherent, if judged by purely musical criteria.
When coherence is aimed at, as in verses 2, 3, and 6, it is
obtained by quasi-*ostinato* methods (compare Purcell's
passion for *ostinato* figures). There is a tendency towards
short phrases, marked off by perfect cadences, most conspicuous in verse 3; and here and there (verse 1, bars 50–57)
the vocal figuration is full of hacking repetitions (Example
26: *Gott loben und ihm dankbar sein*).

Ex. 26. Bach, *Cantata 4*

By March 1714, when it became Bach's duty to compose
cantatas regularly, he had been studying Italian music for
five or six years and his style had undergone a profound
change. In 1714 he wrote Cantatas Nos. 182, 12, 172, 54
(solo), 199 (solo), 61, and 152 (solo); in 1715, Nos. 80, 31,
and six others: in 1716, Nos. 70, 147, and two others. No.
61 (Advent Sunday, 1714) is as typical as any.

The libretto is from Neumeister's collection of 1714, and
is of his latest type, containing chorale and Bible quotations
as well as original recitatives and arias. As in No. 4, there
are two viola parts; but the violins are mostly in unison.
It looks as if Bach was temporarily short of violins, but had
plenty of violas. The first movement is a vocal adaptation of
an instrumental form: it is a French Overture (first and last
sections in a slow dotted rhythm; middle section, a fast
fugue). During the first slow section the choir sings the
first two lines of the Advent chorale, *Now come, thou Saviour
of the Gentiles* (see p. 77); during the last section, the fourth
line; and the subject of the fugue is a decorated version of

the third line. As the fourth line (Example 27b) happens to be the same as the first (Example 27a), there is what amounts to a varied repetition of a recognizable theme; and a strong impression of coherence is produced by this purely musical

Ex. 27. Ouverture

ihm be- -stellt.

method. Both the arias have complete *da capo* repetitions (the repetition includes the *whole* of the first section, not just the instrumental introduction); this is characteristic of the arias of 1714. The *da capo* idea cannot have been new to Bach; but it does look as if this was his first opportunity of spending a year or so on seeing what could be done with it. The most striking features of the work, as compared with No. 4, are the breadth and smoothness of the melodic lines, and the lack of anything that can reasonably be called counterpoint (except in the fugue and the short last chorus). Telemann stood godfather to Emanuel Bach in March 1714, and at this time J. S. Bach, like his more immediately successful friend, was reacting against 'the unmelodious artifices of the ancients' and supporting 'the new school of melodic composition'. Cantata No. 61 has always been popular, and rightly so. It is not profound, but it is extremely attractive; the only thing to be said against it is that the last chorus (based on only half a chorale) is too short to be entirely convincing as a finale.

Bach began his regular duties at Leipzig on the First Sunday after Trinity, 30 May 1723, and for two years he took them seriously. Admittedly he drew upon his early works to some extent; but he also produced a vast number of fresh cantatas, sometimes at the rate of one a week. Most of the 'chorale cantatas' date from this period; not, as was supposed until recently, from 1735 to 1745. During the next year, ending at Trinity 1726, he seems to have composed very little; and as far as church music is concerned, he was never again so continuously prolific as formerly. In 1729 he became conductor of the Collegium Musicum (Musical Society), and thereafter he seems to have been chiefly interested in instrumental music and secular cantatas. Apart from the *Christmas Oratorio* and the Mass in B minor, he is not known to have written much church music – just occasional cantatas, to fill gaps in the annual cycles that he had already written. Cantata No. 140 (1731) appears to be one of these. It is *Wachet auf!*, known in English as *Sleepers, wake!*

In this cantata, the parable of the Ten Virgins provides the underlying idea of the text. The first verse of the chorale *Sleepers, wake!* serves as an introduction. In a *secco* recitative (that is, accompanied only by continuo), the tenor narrator announces the arrival of the Bridegroom. Bride and Bridegroom sing a duet (soprano and bass). There follows the second verse of the chorale (tenors in unison), which has been interpreted as the dance of the bridesmaids. In a recitative, this time with a sustained accompaniment for strings, the Bridegroom calls the Bride to him; the pair then sing a kind of love duet, and the cantata ends with verse 3 of the chorale.

The first and second verses of the chorale are treated as 'concerto chorale preludes', of a type that Bach had developed at Weimar both in cantatas and in organ works (and see Cantata No. 4, verse 3). Such movements begin with a *ritornello*, or orchestral introduction. This, or a portion of it, recurs at intervals in various keys, and also concludes the movement, thus establishing a scheme of repetition and modulation. Between the *ritornello* entries the chorale lines are presented – sometimes singly, sometimes in small groups. They correspond to the solo passages in a concerto movement; and, as in concertos, there is sometimes a relationship between the solo and the *ritornello* passages. Such a relationship can be traced in this first verse, but it is tenuous and may be accidental; in the second verse there is none.

The first duet is another *ritornello* movement, though it has nothing to do with the chorale; the *ritornello* form (that is, one in which a section recurs in the course of a movement) is so elastic that, so long as it is slightly modified, it can be used several times in a single work without inducing monotony. Here the voices use the opening phrase of the introduction, but are otherwise independent. The second duet is a straightforward *da capo* movement; the last verse of the chorale is set as a congregational hymn. As the tune and words are familiar in England it is easy – for once – to see that the highlight of this cantata is neither the elaborate first chorus nor the famous tenor verse nor either of the charming duets, but the plain final hymn-tune; and the same is true of the many other cantatas that are similarly constructed.

Bach's major choral works are the Magnificat (in E flat, 1723; revised version in D, *c*.1730); the *St John Passion* (1724, revised later); the *Easter Oratorio* (1725, with later performances); the *St Matthew Passion* (1729, revised later); the *Christmas Oratorio* (1734–5); and the Mass in B minor. The two oratorios contain a great deal of good music, but do not show Bach at his best. The Magnificat does; it is a first-rate piece of work, all the more attractive because it is hardly longer than the average cantata. Unfortunately it requires a five-part choir, and receives fewer performances than it deserves.

Both the Passions use Bible words for the narration (tenor recitatives). The speeches assigned to single characters are set as recitatives for appropriate voices, and occasionally as *ariosi*; those assigned to the disciples as a group, or to the mob, as choruses. A devotional commentary on the more significant situations is provided by *ariosi* and arias, and by carefully chosen chorale verses; the solo movements tend to speak for the individual Christian, the chorales for the Church at large. The scheme is rounded off by big meditative choruses based both on chorale verses and on original words.

The *St John Passion* is badly planned. Admittedly, this Gospel is less suitable for music than St Matthew's; but there was no need to overload it with arias, or to weaken the dramatic effect of the crowd choruses by making them too long. These defects are not entirely due to haste, for the work was performed more than once, and Bach had plenty of time for revision.

In both respects the *St Matthew Passion* is far superior. It is well planned, and the crowd choruses are shorter; note especially the tremendous effect made by the single shout of 'Barabbas' – which, by the way, comes off only when the German pronunciation is used, and the *first* syllable is stressed. Moreover, the dramatic effect of these outbursts is heightened by the general reticence of the narration. Compare, for instance, the scourging episodes. In the *St John* (No. 30) the narrator forgets his impersonality in a vulgar display of pictorialism. In the *St Matthew* he merely states the facts; emotional expression is confined to the following *arioso* (No. 60), where it is appropriate. See also the treatment of Peter's weeping. Another small refinement is worth noting: the sayings of Jesus are now distinguished from those of the other characters by a *sustained* string accompaniment, except the last two (in Nos. 52 and 71), where, it is supposed, Bach wished to stress the Saviour's humanity.

The *St Matthew Passion* avoids the grosser faults of the *St John*; but, like any other Bach work that lasts more than about twenty minutes, it is not a flawless masterpiece. The chorus of priests (in No. 76) is needlessly elaborate (like the soldiers' chorus, No. 54, of the *St John*). The bass aria, No. 51, 'Give me back my Lord', is wildly inappropriate; and if commentators could only bring themselves to admit that great composers sometimes make mistakes, it would be generally agreed that two or three of the other arias are dull. But in a big work of seventy-eight numbers, occasional failures of imagination are to be expected, and are hardly noticed; the general effect remains extremely impressive.

It happens that we have some idea of Bach's vocal and instrumental resources at the time when the *St Matthew Passion* was first performed. There were about thirty-four singers, divided into two choirs, and thirty instrumentalists; the significant point is the balance, not the actual numbers. For present-day purposes, the continuo ought to be played on the organ throughout. It is true that a harpsichord part has been preserved, but it contains only the movements sung by the second choir, and was probably made only because that choir was smaller and less efficient than the first, and needed extra support. As the Narrator belonged to the first choir, there is no excuse whatever for accompanying him on the harpsichord, thus introducing a contrast of tone-colour in the accompaniment that breaks the conventions of the period.

Whereas the Passions are easy to understand, the Mass in B minor presents a problem that not even the new chronology established by recent scholarship has solved. Why did the Protestant Bach write a Latin Mass?

A few years ago it was fashionable to cut the knot by saying that Bach did no such thing: the various sections of the Mass were written separately, for various more or less hypothetical occasions, and were bound up together by accident. This explanation is outmoded, and the problem remains. The facts seem to be as follows.

The Sanctus was originally written for Christmas 1724, and there were at least two later performances. The Kyrie and Gloria *may* have been performed on 21 April 1733, when the new Elector received the homage of Leipzig. Kyrie and Gloria together constitute a *Missa*, a portion of the liturgy that was common to Protestants and Roman Catholics. As an offering from Bach to his Catholic sovereign, such a performance would have been appropriate; but there is no certainty that it took place. However, the *Missa* was complete by 27 July, when Bach sent a set of parts to the Elector and applied for the post of Court Composer. There is no evidence that the *Missa* was ever performed complete after 1733; but three movements of the Gloria were adapted for use as a Christmas cantata (No. 191) at some time after 1735.

The other sections of the Mass were put together during the last few years of Bach's life; many of the movements are adaptations. At the same time Bach revised the Sanctus, and seems to have tinkered at the *Missa*. There is no evidence that he performed these sections of the Mass, or even single movements from them.

It thus seems clear that Bach did deliberately write a complete Latin Mass, although there was no room for it in the Leipzig liturgy – or anywhere else, for the work is half as long again as Beethoven's Mass in D and lasts about two hours. Until a better explanation is found, it seems reasonable to regard the Mass as 'paper-music', comparable not with the Passions but with such collections as Bach's *Little Organ Book (Orgelbüchlein)* and the first three parts of the *Clavier Exercise (Clavierübung)* – whose schemes were dictated by logic or convenience, not by musical necessities. We do not spend two hours listening to the six Clavier Partitas, played in numerical order, just because Bach published them together. Perhaps it is equally foolish to listen to complete performances of the Mass; and certainly such performances are hardly ever successful.

If a satisfactory gramophone recording ever becomes available, it will be possible to take the Mass in smaller doses, and much easier to enjoy it. Whether or no it is in any sense 'paper-music', it is a very great work. It is true that the arias and duets are not particularly remarkable, and that the choruses can more or less be matched by individual choruses in other works. But the movements, as a group, maintain an exceptionally high standard; and to see how absurd it is to object to eighteenth-century borrowings, one need only refer to the Sanctus. Bach had written several settings of these words, and probably knew he would never write a better one. No one ever has.

8

England in the Age of Handel

c.1715–c.1740

ARTHUR JACOBS

To an English-speaking reader, the words 'choral music' probably suggest Handel rather than any other composer. In particular they may call to mind the customary performance of *Messiah* by a mixed-voice amateur choral society – several hundred voices accompanied by an orchestra of about fifty in a concert-hall, or a few dozen voices accompanied by the organ in church or chapel. It is hard to realize how extensive is the difference between this musical world and the musical world of George Frideric Handel (1685–1759) himself. (That was the form of English name which Georg Friederich Händel adopted on being naturalized in 1726.)

Handel – like Purcell (see p. 112) – knew no amateur choral societies. His choruses were of professionals, and the soprano parts were sung by boys, the altos by men. A performance of *Judith* by Thomas Arne (see p. 185) in 1773 was stated to be the first at which an oratorio was performed in London with a female chorus, and even then the women sang soprano parts only, not alto. Handel's chorus in oratorio, moreover, was habitually smaller than his orchestra. 'It was very magnificent,' commented a contemporary on Handel's *Deborah* (1733): 'near a hundred performers, among whom about twenty-five singers.' The monster chorus is sometimes thought to have been the product of the great Handel Commemoration Festival held in Westminster Abbey in 1784 – but even there, though 275 singers took part, an orchestra of 250 balanced them.

Handel generally gave his oratorios in theatres, never in

churches (except for some late performances of *Messiah* at the Foundling Hospital, London). The London public went to oratorio as an alternative to opera, not as an alternative to a religious service. Moreover, although *Messiah* is now a hundredfold more familiar than all its fellows, it is in some sense not a typical Handel oratorio. It is not merely that *Messiah* (1742) has a Christian subject, and all Handel's other oratorios save *Theodora* (1750) have subjects drawn from the Old Testament or later Jewish history. A more important point is that Handel's general pattern in oratorio was to present a kind of drama, with each soloist impersonating one or more named characters, but *Messiah* has the soloists as commentators on the story, not as participants in it. To know *Messiah* is not to know Handel's oratorios: and even to know Handel's oratorios would not be equivalent to knowing Handel fully as a choral composer. We must also consider his anthems and cast a glance, at least, at his operas.

It was as a composer of Italian opera, the fashionable entertainment of the day, that Handel first came to Britain. *Rinaldo* (1711) was his first work for the London stage. Certain elements of musical style, indeed, which today we think of as 'Handelian' come in fact from the common tongue of the Italian operatic composition of the time. In general Handel's operas have no choral parts, though Handel used the word *coro* (Italian for *chorus*) as a heading for the concerted vocal piece in which the soloists joined together to end an opera or an act. But in *Julius Caesar* (1724) Handel had an off-stage choral effect to represent a group of conspirators; because it was off-stage, this could be sung by soloists. *Alcina* (1735) is the only opera in which the use of a genuine chorus on stage seems to point forward to the splendidly dramatic use made of the chorus in the operas of Gluck, who greatly admired Handel.

In oratorio, however, Handel made a prime element of his chorus. Here he did not use the example of Italian opera. He may have noted the use of the chorus in English operatic and semi-operatic works such as those of Purcell and of John Eccles (*The Judgement of Paris*, staged in 1701), but a more obvious stimulus was given him by two other choral tech-

niques nearer to hand. The first was the tradition of German
'Passion Music' (see p. 85), in which the chorus both represented the voice of the crowd in the Passion story and
moralized from a modern audience's viewpoint. Handel
himself wrote two such German 'Passions', dated 1704 and
approximately 1716. The other technique of choral usage
which must have stimulated Handel was that of the Church
of England anthem (especially the 'verse anthem', in which
choral and solo voices were contrasted, and in which the
organ was sometimes replaced by orchestral accompaniment
in works designed for festal occasions), together with the
anthem's near-relation, the ceremonial secular composition
typified by Purcell's odes for St Cecilia's Day.

Before ever he came to compose English oratorio, Handel
himself wrote a splendid series of festal anthems for solo
voices and chorus with orchestral accompaniment, a series
whose present neglect is almost as unjustified as that of the
oratorios themselves. These are the eleven Chandos Anthems,
written for the chapel of the Duke of Chandos, an English
nobleman whose private musical director Handel became in
1717. (A twelfth anthem sometimes included in the set,
called *O praise the Lord, ye angels of his*, is either spurious or a
later composition: it is not to be confused with the authentic
Chandos anthem, *O praise the Lord with one consent*.) There are
two anthems entitled *Let God Arise*, a shorter one in A and a
longer one in B flat, partly making use of the same material.
The Chandos Anthems are marred by faults of accentuation
which show Handel's unfamiliarity, at this stage, with the
English language. But musically they show rich, sometimes
inspired invention. The choruses alone are worth the attention of performing groups, even if it is not always desired to
sing the anthem as a whole.

Often the anthems give a foretaste of Handel's later
glories. *My song shall be alway* concludes with a 'Hallelujah'
chorus. The final chorus of *Let God arise* (both versions) also
has a chain of triumphant Hallelujahs. The second version
has a choral setting of the words 'Both the horse and the
rider are fall'n' with that musical evocation of physical
movement which Handel also summoned at the setting of

similar words in *Israel in Egypt*. The anthem *Have mercy upon
me, O Lord* has the 'agonized' discords familiar in 'Surely
He hath borne our griefs' from *Messiah*; and the familiar
'Blessing and honour' from the latter is anticipated in the
chorus 'Glory and worship are before him' from the Chandos anthem *O come let us sing unto the Lord*. The whole of this
last-named anthem radiates Handel's mastery, though the
fact that its choral scoring is soprano-tenor-tenor-bass (no
altos) presents a certain difficulty to most choirs today.

The anthem *O praise the Lord with one consent* is striking
from its very first choral line, in which the title-words are
set to the notes known today as those which open the hymn-
tune *St Anne* ('O God our help in ages past'). (Perhaps
Handel himself knew it: see p. 161 for a discussion of its
conjectural composer, William Croft.) It is typical of Handel, who had a feeling for the massive, simple choral effect
as well as the more involved type of choral counterpoint,
that this line is set in a way that absolutely fits the directness
of the words. 'O praise the Lord' sing the sopranos, and *all*
the chorus join at 'with one consent'. What is more, Handel
exceptionally makes thematic use of the opening four notes,
bringing them back twice in later choruses. Example 28
shows one of these recurrences.

Ex. 28. Handel, *O praise the Lord*
(a) Andante e staccato
S., A. [f] O praise the Lord with one con-sent
T., B. (With full orch.)

(b) Allegro ma non presto
S., A. With cheer-ful notes let all the earth
T., B. (With full orch.)

The four Coronation Anthems (1727, for George II) like-wise display Handel's festive eloquence. Of these *Zadok the Priest* has been performed at every coronation since.

We may now turn back to Handel's period of service to the Duke of Chandos. At Cannons, the Duke's estate in Middlesex, Handel composed *Acis and Galatea*, a work of the type which is historically tabulated as a masque but which we shall not be far wrong in thinking of as a short opera with a pastoral plot and a deliberately artificial air. It has a choral part. It was probably produced, in stage form, at Cannons in 1718. Also at Cannons Handel presumably first performed, as a stage work, *Haman and Mordecai* (1720). This work was revived in private performance in London in April 1732, with a new title, *Esther*, but still in stage form; and then, one month later, it was given with a newly lengthened musical score and in concert form (not staged). Thus *Esther* became the first English oratorio.

The reason why Handel presented *Esther* to the London public as a concert work, not a stage work, is uncertain. The usual account is that the Bishop of London, in his capacity as Dean of the Chapel Royal, forbade the participation of his choirboys in such a profane undertaking as the putting of a biblical story on the stage. This account, though accepted by Mr Winton Dean, the leading present-day authority on Handel, is based on no authoritative evidence whatever, but only on hearsay repeated half a century later by two par-ticipants in the concert performance of 1732. It is at least as likely that Handel decided on a concert form for his work on the ground of economy and practicality. In the twenty-seven years after 1732, during which Handel continued to write oratorio, we have no hint that he ever contemplated presenting them except in concert form ('in still life', as his contemporary, Burney, put it), nor that he even so much as regretted this circumstance. Some of the oratorios *can* be staged and have been; but such staging should be regarded as an expedient, not as a fulfilment of Handel's plan.

Handel's oratorios are in general, none the less, dramatic in form. (*Messiah* is, as we have seen, an exception; so is *Israel in Egypt*, 1739, which is like some vastly extended

anthem.) The very word 'oratorio' was described in Gras-
sineau's English musical dictionary (1740) as 'a sort of
spiritual opera', and the terms 'oratorio' and 'sacred drama'
were at that time virtually interchangeable. A Handel
oratorio was divided into 'acts' (where a modern score
probably says 'Part One', Handel wrote 'Act One'); and
librettos with a large or small helping of imaginary stage
directions were sold to audiences. But the stage *was* imaginary, and so Handel could naturally – and quite properly
– employ effects of purely musical construction which
go against the pace and directness that would be desirable
in theatrical presentation. The heavy inflation of *Esther*
which Handel permitted when he turned it from a stage
to a concert work points to this. In general, the use of the
chorus in Handel's oratorios – now supposedly participating in the action, now commenting – would be clumsy in
the theatre.

We must, then, judge most of the oratorios as a kind of
musical drama, but a non-theatrical drama. These oratorios are, today, all but unknown, save for *Messiah*. And,
save for *Messiah* (in the edition by Watkins Shaw), not one
is available in Britain today in vocal score in an edition
prepared in conformity with modern scholarship. Bad old
editorial errors, omissions, and falsifications abound. The
words have suffered equally with the music. 'Blest the
day when I was led To ascend the nuptial bed' is the admirable sentiment of the queen in *Solomon* (1749), altered
in the Victorian (and current) Novello score to 'Blest the
day when I was brought To behold this favour'd spot' –
a bowdlerization astonishingly accepted in Sir Thomas
Beecham's gramophone recording, or not so astonishingly
in view of his lack of fidelity to Handel's musical intentions.

Indeed, as to the actual manner of performing Handel,
most existing traditions are bad traditions. Audiences who
expect to hear Mozart and Tchaikovsky more or less as
their composers intended are regaled with out-of-period,
out-of-style performances of Handel. Stylistically bad performances of Handel are more common than of Purcell,
Bach, and Vivaldi. 'The Lord is a man of war' from *Israel*

in Egypt is still sometimes heard as a ponderous duet for massed choral basses instead of a lively duet for two bass soloists; 'Deeper and deeper still' is still sung by recitalists, quite wrongly, as the recitative before 'Waft her angels' in *Jephtha*; the middle section of 'He was despis'd' is almost always cut from *Messiah*. This is to say nothing of the reluctance of singers and conductors to learn eighteenth-century conventions of ornamentation. We may also classify as deadweight the custom of the audience's standing in the 'Hallelujah Chorus' of *Messiah* – originally the gesture of an audience who could not possibly sit when George II decided to stand at this point, and now a gesture which merely encourages the bad habit of counting a performance of *Messiah* as a quasi-religious rite.

Handel's use of the chorus in oratorio was admirably characterized by the American scholar R. M. Myers:

Generally, Handel's chorus supplies the place of scenery and action: it sets forth the basic mood from which the moods of solo characters are drawn, and it sustains the emotional keynote and ethical purpose of the composition. Sometimes it depicts the feelings of supposed participants in imaginary action; sometimes it serves a didactic purpose in propounding moral lessons; frequently it describes thrilling action for which the voice of a narrator would have proved futile.

To observe this functioning of the chorus it may prove stimulating to examine one of Handel's oratorios in detail. *Samson* was first performed in London, at Covent Garden Theatre (but as a concert work, of course), in 1743. *Samson* was one of Handel's most successful oratorios in his own day, it was frequently given in the choral hey-day of Victorian times, and it achieved the distinction (misguided, perhaps) of being produced in stage form at Covent Garden in 1958. It is a long work, with sixty-four numbers (more than those of any other oratorio) of which twenty-two are choral. Though three of these are repeats, this still leaves a greater number of separate choral pieces than in any oratorio except for *Messiah* and the unsuccessful *Deborah*.

After the Overture, Handel wrote on his autograph score: 'Act the first. Scene 1. Samson blind and in chains.

Chorus of the priests of Dagon celebrating his festivals [*sic*] at a distance.' As a matter of fact, the scene does not change at all throughout the work and the imagined action runs on continuously. Handel thus retained the conventional dramatic unity found in Milton's *Samson Agonistes*, which Newburgh Hamilton had adapted as a libretto for the oratorio. The casting of Samson as a tenor appears natural today, but it was by no means so in Handel's time, when operatic heroes were more normally sung by *castrati*.

A brief recitative for Samson leads to the joyful chorus of Philistine priests (sopranos and altos included – these were boys and men, remember). Typically, Handel sees to it that when each of the three lines of the verse is *first* sung ('Awake the trumpet's lofty sound, The joyful sacred festival comes round, When Dagon king of all the earth is crown'd'), it is sung without overlapping between parts, so that the words are heard clearly. After an air for 'a Philistine woman', the jubilant chorus is repeated in short form; and after an air by a Philistine priest the short chorus is heard again; and there is then a third air, sung by another Philistine woman. Dramatically all this is static, but the role of the chorus as emphasizing the basic mood is clearly seen.

After the three Philistine airs, three Israelite ones follow – again bringing dramatic monotony, but admirable if considered as music for the concert-hall. Each air is preceded by recitative. The first air is for Samson, the second for Micah (for which part Handel intended a contralto, not a male alto), the third for Samson again – the famous 'Total eclipse'. After it, an accompanied recitative for Micah forms a bridge to the chorus 'O first-created beam.' Nominally this represents the comment of the Israelites, Samson's people, but Handel's audience was evidently meant to feel it as *their* comment too – a splendid purposeful ambiguity characteristic of the oratorios in general. During this chorus, the words 'Let there be light!' are uttered by altos, tenors, and basses, and then *all* voices respond with 'And light was over all'. This parallels the musical technique in our Example 28a, from the Chandos Anthems;

it is also probably the model for Haydn's setting 'And there was light' in *The Creation*, a work planned by Haydn after he had been much impressed with hearing Handel's oratorios in London (see p. 167).

Samson's father, Manoa (accented by Handel on the first syllable), arrives and he sings two arias. Samson, though recognizing that his captivity and blindness are just punishment for his folly, gives vent to the air 'Why does the god of Israel sleep?' The hope that God will declare his power is then expressed by Micah, in a brief recitative, and by the fugal chorus 'Then shall they know'. The chorus once again supposedly gives the comment both of the Israelite people and of Handel's own audience.

Samson despairs, declaring that he might as well die. The drama then takes a feeble turn when Micah, instead of rallying Samson, assures him that he will find happiness in heaven. The ensuing chorus, 'Then round about the starry throne', has words which merely continue in Micah's vein. But the music of this chorus, with which Handel wishes to end the first act in a mood of nobility and confidence, is a blaze of glory. Characteristically Handel plays with an apparently commonplace musical figure of half a dozen notes (to the words 'and triumph over death') and piles it up majestically to convey an unforgettable musical experience (Example 29). Handel's skill ensures that the point of climax – the soprano's top A – is both the point of maximum discord and a point at which the sopranos are forced to intensity of utterance by the fact of singing at the top of their compass. (A comparable point, when maximum harmonic impact coincides with maximum vocal effort, is at the tenors' top A, eight bars before the end of the 'Amen' chorus in *Messiah*.)

Act Two continues the musical encounter of Samson, Micah, and Manoa. Shortly, Micah has an air 'Return, O God of hosts' which, instead of following the *da capo* convention and ending with a literal repeat of the first part, ends with a *varied* repeat of the first section in which not only Micah but the chorus take part – an example, this, of the involvement of the chorus (as Israelites) in the drama.

Ex. 29. Handel, *Samson*

Then Dalila comes. (Handel's autograph spells her variously as Dalila, Dalilah, and Delila, but the accent in singing is always on the first syllable.) She is Samson's wife (the henpecked Milton's stroke, not the Bible's), and now seeks to be reconciled with him. Dalila's pretendedly artless air, 'My faith and truth, O Samson, prove', is supported by a 'chorus of virgins' (sopranos). The only choral sopranos Handel had were boys, but, since this was a concert work and not one designed for the stage, he decided that his women soloists (even Mrs Clive, who sang Dalila) had better join in too, and his autograph score here stipulates 'tutti soprani, Mrs Clive, Signora Avolio, Miss Edwards and boys'.

Despite the repeated entreaties of Dalila and her attendants, Samson finally rejects her. A sententious chorus

'To man God's universal law gave pow'r to keep the wife in awe' (which could be sung less absurdly by boy sopranos and men altos than by sopranos and contraltos today) is of no great musical distinction. There now enters Harapha (baritone), a Philistine champion: the opposition between him and Samson (culminating in the duet 'Go, baffled coward, go') makes for some of the liveliest moments of the oratorio. Micah suggests what is virtually a contest between Dagon and the God of the Israelites – a notion which inspires the musical characteristics of much that is to follow (and which also may have suggested the similar contest in Mendelssohn's *Elijah*).

A solemn chorus of Israelites, 'Hear, Jacob's God!' displays Handel's habit of occasional borrowing: this chorus is based on material from the oratorio *Jephtha* by Carissimi (see p. 103). None the less, its measured, grave tread, quite unlike anything else in the work, is both distinctive and appropriate in this place. Shortly comes the Philistine chorus 'To song and dance we give the day', in which the dancing movement invades the orchestra as well as the voices: Handel's pagans, here as in other oratorios, are joy-loving human beings and no monsters. Israelites and Philistines are then combined in a mighty double chorus (Samson, Manoa, Dalila, and Harapha joining in). The basic pattern is simple:

> *Philistines:* Great Dagon is –
> *Israelites:* Jehovah is –
> *All:* Of gods the first and last.

– and so on; but Handel makes it flash with quick $\frac{3}{4}$ movement and with a contrast between eighth-note runs (to such words as 'the thunder roars', the kind of phrase which Handel habitually set in an illustrative manner) and emphatic, homophonic choral chords. Thus, exultantly, Act Two ends.

In Act Three the contest continues. Samson at first refuses the summons delivered by Harapha to attend the Philistine festival. The chorus (Israelites) invoke God's aid ('With thunder arm'd'). The music's dotted rhythm spells urgency; then there is a brief middle section in

smoother, longer notes, then a repeat of the first part (a
pattern unusual in Handel's choruses, though of course corresponding to the conventional *da capo* form for solo airs).
Samson changes his mind and decides to go, spurred on by
Micah and by a short homophonic chorus, 'To fame immortal go', re-using Micah's preceding musical material.
Manoa then enters. He hears the Philistine solo and chorus
'Great Dagon has subdued our foe' (which, coming from
the Philistine temple, would have to be 'off-stage' if this
were a theatrical work). As before, joy is made to strike us
as the pagan characteristic. Manoa laments at Samson's sad
state. But then comes a 'symphony of horror and confusion'.
('Symphony' at that time meant an overture or an instrumental interlude, like the 'Pastoral Symphony' in *Messiah*.)
This introduces the downfall of the Philistines, expressed
in their chorus 'Hear us, our God', based on the material
of the 'symphony'. Handel's audiences must have been
amazed to hear the way that this chorus graphically expresses catastrophe: the singers break off on the dominant
seventh chord, leaving the subdued orchestra to get back
to the tonic chord on its own.

A messenger now explains that Samson pulled down the
Philistines' temple only at the cost of sacrificing his own
life. A Requiem for him is begun by Micah and taken up
by the Chorus of Israelites ('Weep, Israel, weep'). After
a Dead March, when Samson's body is brought in, Manoa
takes the lead in a further lamentation for Samson by soloists
and chorus – a short but wonderfully varied and striking
section, including twelve unaccompanied bars for an Israelite woman, and a final chorus which has an ending reminiscent (not for the first time in this or other Handel oratorios)
of Purcell.

Here, originally, Handel planned to end his oratorio;
a tragic end. But he decided to end triumphantly instead,
and added the soprano air 'Let the bright seraphims' [*sic*],
which, once again, breaks off after what looks like a middle
section and leads straight into a chorus – 'Let their celestial
concerts all unite'. No *da capo* of 'Let the bright seraphims'
is thus called for: it is notable that the current Novello

vocal score (published 1880) is correct on this point, though in general it is a less reliable guide to Handel's intentions than the previous (1850) Novello vocal score, which gets this particular point wrong.

Handel's other English oratorios may be summarily listed. *Esther* set the precedent for other dramatic oratorios on biblical (including apocryphal) subjects or on Jewish history, all of them first performed in London. They are *Deborah* (1733), *Athalia* (1733), *Saul* (1739), *Samson* (1743), *Joseph and his Brethren* (1744), *Belshazzar* (1745), *Judas Maccabaeus* (1747), *Joshua* (1748), *Alexander Balus* (1748), *Susanna* (1749), *Solomon* (1749), and *Jephtha* (1752). At present the virtually unknown *Athalia*, based on Racine's tragedy, is perhaps the most unjustly neglected of these. The moving *Theodora* (1750) deals with a Christian martyrdom, with a rather attractive musical depiction of the pagan foe. Non-dramatic are, as we have seen, *Israel in Egypt* (London, 1739), and *Messiah* (Dublin, 1742); so is the *Occasional Oratorio* (1746), a patriotic work for which Handel lifted some numbers out of his earlier works, and from which in time he lifted numbers for his later ones. *The Triumph of Time and Truth* (London, 1757) is an allegorical work adapted from two of Handel's earlier works with Italian texts.

In a rather different class are Handel's secular choral works. The two settings of Dryden, *Alexander's Feast* (1736) and the *Ode to St Cecilia's Day* (1739) are of mixed value; *L'Allegro, il Penseroso, ed il Moderato* (adapted from Milton with additions, 1740) deserves revival: has the Italian title of this English work militated against it? *Semele* (1744) is a fine, dramatically constructed work taking a full evening. Though based (with alterations) on a text by Congreve which *was* intended for the opera stage, it was performed under Handel's direction 'after the manner of an oratorio' (that is, in concert form). But the expression 'after the manner of' indicates that it is not to be considered *as* oratorio, a term better reserved for religious (or at any rate loftily ethical) works. *Hercules* (1745) is a work of similar type. Both make considerable use of the chorus. *The Choice of Hercules* (1751) is a different, one-act work, of less importance.

English oratorio was not merely Handel's invention; it was also a form which, during his lifetime, no other composer made into a major activity. History records a few isolated examples of works such as *Abel* (1744), by Thomas Arne (see p. 185), whose more important *Judith* followed in 1761; *David's Lamentation over Saul and Jonathan* (1736) and *Solomon* (1743) by William Boyce (see p. 185); and *Judith* (1735) by the Belgian-born William Defesch (1697–1758). A work by Maurice Greene (1685–1755) called *The Song of Deborah and Barak*, which was produced in 1732 but never received the dignity of print in its own century, was brought out in a modern edition in 1956. Though the modern editor, Frank Dawes, calls it an oratorio, the contemporary manuscript in the British Museum does not use the word: and, indeed, though not without some attractive points in both the solo and choral writing, the work does not show the basically dramatic layout which we should expect in an oratorio. Handel, incidentally, disliked Greene, and possibly wrote his own *Deborah* to show the public who was top dog.

Greene, however, has his own distinction in the field of the anthem, written for church choir (boys and men), with organ accompaniment. The element of contrast comes chiefly from the alternation of solo passages with those for the full choir. (The term 'verse' is technically used to denote solo, as distinct from fully choral, passages.) A number of Greene's works are available in modern editions, and have maintained their place in cathedrals and other churches; and most of these works, it must be said, have that decorous, well-made, unemphatic quality that better suits them to such a functional purpose than to a concert performance. But some of Greene's anthems ought to be known to wider audiences, among which we may cite *Lord, let me know mine end*. It is for the usual four-part choir, from which two trebles emerge as soloists.

This anthem, appearing in 1743 in Greene's *Forty Select Anthems* and in 1938 in a good modern edition by Ernest Bullock, is in A minor. But at the words, 'He heapeth up riches and cannot tell who shall gather them', the 'foreign' notes of B flat and even E flat (for a modulation to D minor) enter with telling expression: and in the last section, B flat is again brought back with 'pathetic' significance. The setting of the English words, sometimes syncopated, is apt throughout. It is notable that Greene called on his full choir, not merely his soloists, to insert a trill at an occasional cadence. Example 30 illustrates the expressive character of the music, with its syncopations and its use of close imitation.

Ex. 30. Greene, *Lord, let me know mine end*

Senior to both Greene and Handel was William Croft (1678–1727). We have already noted that the first line of the hymn-tune *St Anne*, attributed to Croft, reappears (by accident or design) in one of Handel's Chandos Anthems. Croft was a distinguished composer of church music, bridging the gap between Purcell and Greene. Croft's setting of the words of the burial service – in a finely dignified, homophonic, measured style – has become hallowed by use in the Anglican Church. Croft's admiration for Purcell is made clear not only in his music but in his explicit refusal to re-set that part of the burial service already set by Purcell, which instead Croft printed as an appendix to his own work (in the volume *Musica Sacra*, 1724).

This volume includes two anthems with wind and string accompaniment, such as had become acceptable at the Chapel Royal after the Restoration. That these may be worth exploration is suggested by the attractive section for alto solo in the anthem *Rejoice in the Lord*: here, the voice joins in counterpoint with oboe, violins, and bass (suitable for cello and organ), and the bass-line follows a stimulating passacaglia pattern. When, in other anthems, Croft wrote an independent accompaniment for organ alone he was not always content with the bare bones: we find directions like 'Solo, cornet stop' and 'Two diapasons upon the left hand'.

Croft also wrote 'full anthems', using the organ only to double the voices. Among these is *God is gone up with a merry noise*, a lively, attractive work which awaits a good modern edition. (The Victorian edition is not quite faithful to the manuscript available in the British Museum.) In the opening section the 'merry' quality of the words is reflected in the iteration of one steady (almost dance-like) rhythm for no less than forty-one bars; and in the next section there is effective interplay between two opposing semichoruses.

There are reliable modern editions of Croft's *O rebuke me not* ('perhaps the finest of all Croft's anthems', in the view of E. H. Fellowes, a noted authority) and his *Hear my prayer, O Lord*. The latter anthem starts with a contrapuntal section for five voices (SSATB) in which plangent discords clearly portray the anguish of 'let my crying come unto thee'. Then comes a 'verse' passage in which six soloists (the altos also now being divided) are played off in threes and twos, and prominence given to 'common chords'. The voices come to rest on the dominant, and then the five-part full choir enters cumulatively with a distinct new melodic idea. Finally come nine bars marked 'Slow' by the composer, in which the choir divides into eight parts, notably matching the intensity of the prayer with the intensity of choral harmony shown in Example 31.

Ex. 31. Croft, *Hear my prayer*

(*B♮ in original)

Not even the overriding genius of Handel should be allowed to hide, as it does, the power to which lesser masters of his time could occasionally rise.

9

The Viennese Classical Period

*c.*1730–*c.*1820

ROGER FISKE

IN the 'Classical' period when the great Viennese composers were supreme in instrumental music and, less obviously, in opera, choral music was generally thought of as the servant of the Church, and only in churches or private chapels could it normally be heard. Oratorios might intrude in the theatres in Lent, and rich amateurs like Baron van Swieten might even have them performed in their own homes, but there were few public concerts of choral music until Haydn gave *The Creation* and *The Seasons* in Vienna about 1800. *The Seasons* was itself remarkable for having secular words. Though secular choral works became numerous later in the nineteenth century, they are very rare in the eighteenth. This is equally true of the smaller forms. If madrigals were ever sung in Viennese homes, it was long before our period, while the Romantic part-song was only beginning when Schubert died. Freemasonry and war produced a little vocal music (Mozart, himself a Mason, wrote masonic cantatas of indifferent quality), but of more interest in the secular field was the canon. Haydn, Mozart, Beethoven, and Cherubini all wrote numerous canons, of which Mozart's and Cherubini's are still worth singing. Mozart rivals Purcell as the greatest of all composers of canons; and though bawdy words make many of them unsuitable except for the stag-parties for which they were composed, the highly chromatic *Nascoso* ('Hidden') can be recommended as a sublime miniature fit for any company.

This chapter, then, will deal almost entirely with church music, in particular with settings of the Mass. These latter invariably enjoyed orchestral accompaniment, in spite of papal disapproval, and often were enlivened by an operatic style that is particularly apparent in coloratura arias. Austrians took their church services cheerfully, and saw no reason to disapprove of good singing, however solemn the moment or flamboyant the performance. The great Viennese composers learned nothing from the Passions and cantatas of Bach, but were much influenced by the Italians, as indeed they were in their operas and symphonies. Alessandro Scarlatti (1660–1725) may be taken as the father-figure, and he is not to be confused with his son Domenico, famous for harpsichord sonatas. Dr Burney described Alessandro as

the most voluminous and most original composer of cantatas that has ever existed in any country, to which my inquiries have reached ... I have found part of his property among the stolen goods of all the best composers of the first forty or fifty years of the present [eighteenth] century.

'Cantata' in the eighteenth century commonly indicated an extended work for only one or two singers. Scarlatti is said to have written many of his cantatas in a single day, which indicates their slightness. Nevertheless, they established the *da capo* aria throughout Europe, and were models of good vocal writing. Of Scarlatti's numerous Masses, ten survive; most of them are in the old contrapuntal style (in which instrumental accompaniment, if used, merely doubles the voices), but two have parts for string orchestra. His twenty-four oratorios were more influential, and were the prototypes of such oratorios as the great classical composers composed in the eighteenth century – for instance Haydn, before the glories of Handel burst on him in London. They are probably too lacking in variety for general consumption today, but judgement must wait on modern editions becoming available.

Scarlatti's type of church music reached the German-speaking world in various ways. The German composer Hasse (1699–1783) actually had some lessons from him before settling in Dresden, where he wrote opera and church music in a style that was almost more Italian than the Italians could achieve. Equally popular was Niccolò Jomelli (1714–74), who spent fifteen years at Stuttgart from 1753, writing operas and church music that were admired all over Europe. A more curious influence was that of Giovanni Battista Pergolesi (1710–36), whose popularity was so enhanced by early death that publishers everywhere grew fat issuing compositions as his which were not in fact by him at all. His pretty melodies and sweet style stamp him as among the first of the *galant* composers, but he was no master of counterpoint. His Masses are said to be commonplace, and in church music his reputation rests on a *Stabat Mater* (a setting of the medieval poem about the vigil of Mary by the Cross) written for two castrato soloists and string orchestra. This work is still very popular with women's choirs, the various short sections being arbitrarily divided between soloists and chorus; the best movements (it is an uneven work) will continue to give pleasure to people who neither know nor care that this is not a choral work at all.

In a Vienna where Italian was the aristocratic language and composers the servants of aristocrats, it was natural for the world of music to face south and draw its forms and colours from composers who hailed from beyond the Alps. With this in mind we can now approach Joseph Haydn (1732–1809), the first of the three great names that are the backbone of this chapter. I was myself brought up to think of Haydn as primarily an instrumental composer, and it used to save people a great deal of trouble to believe (on no evidence) that his operas and church music were not worth bothering about. In fact Haydn wrote much of his very greatest music for the church, and it is sad that uninspired symphonies from his pen receive quite frequent performances while some of his greatest choral music remains unknown even to professional musicians. I shall divide this choral music into three groups according to length, beginning with the four long works which would fill a concert on their own.

The *Applausus* Cantata (1768; about two hours in length) was probably written for the birthday celebrations of the abbot of Zwettl monastery in Lower Austria, 'Applausus' being a generic name for a cantata of this kind. It was performed by the monks, and because Haydn was not invited he had to provide copious instructions as to how the music should be interpreted. These are of enthralling interest, and they can be found in English in *The Collected Correspondence and London Notebooks of Joseph Haydn*, edited by H. C. Robbins Landon (see Bibliography). The words are in Latin, and the five soloists, representing allegorical figures such as Temperentia and Justitia, sing a series of very long *da capo* arias of quite desperate difficulty and almost uniform excellence. There is only one chorus, a fine one at the end. This splendid work has been broadcast but never published; its lack of choruses and extreme difficulty must always debar it from the normal repertory.

Haydn's first oratorio, *The Return of Tobias* (*Il Ritorno di Tobia*; about three hours) dates from 1775, a time when much of his output was rather colourless, and it does not merit attention today. The story, from the Apocrypha, moves with stupefying slowness; the first half-hour is devoted to blind Tobit and his wife being gloomy together, and it is some fifty minutes before Tobias arrives to start the plot. Again there are insufficient choruses, though Haydn added two in 1784 to bring the number up to five. There is quite a good storm chorus which can be sung separately. The oratorio is published with German and English words (but not the original Italian) in a revision of 1806, sanctioned by Haydn and made by one Neukomm.

Of far more interest is *The Creation* (1798; about two hours), which must have had more performances than all Haydn's other choral works put together. Though the original scoring is already for large orchestra, with three flutes, bassoons, and trombones, and a pair of the other wind instruments, Haydn liked to double each woodwind part whenever possible. There are three soloists (STB), no *da capo* arias, and a great many splendid choruses. It is clear that as a result of Haydn's trips to London, Handel's influence has gained ascendancy over Scarlatti's. The libretto, by Baron van Swieten, is alleged in the Eulenburg miniature score

to be based on 'Milton's *The Lost Paradise*', but it bears no
recognizable likeness to the poem nearly of that name.
Haydn's orchestration is dazzling. The opening 'Representation of Chaos' (Example 32) ends astonishingly with an

Ex. 32. Haydn, *The Creation*

anticipation of *Tristan*. Raphael's 'Now heav'n in fullest
glory shone' has an accompaniment of the most sophisticated elaboration, while the recitative 'Be fruitful all' (with
two violas and two cellos) and the Introduction to Part III
(three flutes and pizzicato strings) are scored with the
utmost originality. The duet 'Of stars the fairest pledge'
wanders through the most unexpected keys, just as do
Haydn's capriccios for piano. Haydn lays these ingenuities
alongside passages of almost excessive naïveté. It would be
priggish not to enjoy the imitations of nature (Nos. 4 and 22),
in which the composer is so optimistic as to give us the imitations (thunder, rain, 'the flexible tiger', etc.) *before* telling
us what they are meant to be. But the chorus 'A new-
created world' is surely self-consciously simple; Haydn was
by no means a naïve composer by nature. But beauties
abound, and so many of them are in the orchestral scoring

that performances with organ accompaniment should be declared illegal. I have, by the way, quoted the ancient – and now rather odd-seeming – translation; at least one more modern English version has been made.

The Seasons (1801), Haydn's last major work, does not stand up to complete performance, partly because the recitatives grow wearisome as one's indifference to the fate of Jane, Lucas, and Simon increases. But the four parts individually are a delight (about thirty-five minutes each), and choral societies might more often consider putting this work on as a serial in four consecutive concerts. The words are again by Baron van Swieten, who declared that he had based them on James Thomson's poem of the same name, happily confident that no one in Vienna would be likely to check up on this statement. It is true that Thomson's *The Seasons* is also divided into four sections, Spring, Summer, Autumn, and Winter, but it contains no Jane, Lucas, or Simon, or any other obvious link with Haydn.

In this work one can welcome the imitations of nature unreservedly, and again they precede the explanations. For instance, in the recitative that opens 'Summer', the phrase 'the lazy night retires' is sung after a curiously Berliozian phrase intended to evoke this idea. Later there is a cock-crow on the oboe. Most of the choruses (and there are plenty of them) are great fun to sing, and the solos (STB) are not too difficult. Again naïveté intrudes. The superb storm chorus 'Hark, the deep tremendous voice', with its exciting accompaniment and quiet chromaticisms at the end marks the height of sophistication, but is followed by an over-simple trio that almost jars in the context. 'Autumn' is perhaps the best of the four; the rather Handelian song about the spaniel is a winner. But 'Winter' is almost as good, with its wonderful, almost Wagnerian introduction depicting the thick fogs at the approach of winter. There is a good rustic spinning-song (are there earlier examples in music?), and countless felicities of orchestration, as indeed there are all through this engaging, if over-long work, so utterly different from anything Vienna had heard before.

Haydn's medium-length choral works, those that might fill half a concert, include two masterpieces that I shall leave for the moment, and all the best of the Masses. Excluding a *Missa Brevis* recently discovered by Robbins Landon but of doubtful authenticity, twelve Haydn Masses survive. Six of these are early works and six are very late, mature masterpieces. Of the early Masses I have space to discuss only two.

No. 3, the *St Cecilia Mass* or *Missa Sanctae Caeciliae* in C (*c.*1773; Novello No. 5, much cut), is by far the longest Mass Haydn wrote, and also the most Italian in style. The Kyrie and Gloria alone take forty-five minutes; later, things move more quickly, and an hour and a quarter covers the whole. It is scored for oboes, bassoons, clarini (high trumpets), and strings, and the solos are excessively difficult. This is a 'cantata' Mass, for concert rather than liturgical use, and Haydn follows the convention in such cases of dividing his Gloria and Credo into several separate movements. As a *tour de force* the work is remarkable, but there is too much display and too much C major for most tastes. However, the 'Benedictus' is expressive, with a spine-chilling bassoon part that doubles the top voice part even though it is at the bottom of the harmony (Example 33).

Ex. 33. Haydn, *'St Cecilia' Mass*

The 'Dona nobis pacem' has a good *presto* double fugue, and the last part of this Mass does something to dispel one's memory of endless runs and repeated-note accompaniments in the earlier movements.

No. 6, the *Mariazell Mass* or *Missa Celensis* in C (1782; Novello No. 15), was written for the monastery at Mariazell in Styria to which Haydn had made a pilgrimage as a young man. It requires the same orchestra as the *St Cecilia Mass* but makes far less demands on the soloists. The tenor solo 'Et incarnatus est' and choral 'Crucifixus' are fine; the following 'Et resurrexit' unconvincingly repeats the music that opened the Credo to give the whole some semblance to sonata form. The choral Benedictus is rather surprisingly based on an aria from Haydn's opera *The World on the Moon* (*Il mondo della luna*).

There is now a gap in Haydn's church music, occasioned by the fact that in 1783 the Emperor Joseph II put Austria in line with a great number of papal decrees and banned the use of orchestras in church. Haydn's remaining Masses date from after his second London trip, by which time the subsequent emperor, Francis II, had repealed the ban. These last six Masses follow hard on the heels of the great London symphonies; in his fruitful old age Haydn wrote little else, apart from the two great oratorios and some string quartets. Our neglect of these superb works is deplorable. All were written for the Bergkirche, the little church at Eisenstadt, for Haydn's old employers, the Esterházy family. All play for about forty-five minutes.

Of this set of Masses, No. 7 is the *Missa in Tempore Belli* (*Mass in Time of War*), also known as the *Drum Mass* (German: *Paukenmesse*) in C (1796; Novello No. 2). Napoleon was threatening Vienna at the time, and at the start of the 'Dona nobis pacem' Haydn suggests an atmosphere of war with trumpets and drums, and then dispels it; Beethoven is too often credited with the invention of this 'operatic' device. The slow introduction to the Kyrie and the cello *obbligato* in the 'Qui tollis' are especially beautiful. The scoring is normal. Four soloists are needed.

No. 8, the *Missa Sancti Bernardi von Offida* in B flat (1796;

Novello No. 1), was written in honour of a Capuchin monk
from Offida in Italy who had just been canonized. The
German name for this work, *Heiligmesse*, derives from the
Sanctus, at the start of which Haydn conceals among the
chorus altos and tenors a phrase of the old hymn *Heilig,
heilig* ('Holy, holy'). The work calls for normal classical
orchestra without flutes or horns, and six soloists, but the
latter have little to do and face no real difficulties. Again the
'Dona nobis pacem' includes trumpet and drum parts
suggestive of war. It is almost embarrassing to find that the
gentle and unforgettably lovely canon to the words 'Et
incarnatus est' makes use of music previously written for
highly amatory words.

No. 9, the *Missa in Angustiis* ('Mass in Time of Peril') in
D minor (1798; Novello No. 3), is better known as the
Nelson or *Imperial Mass*. News of Nelson's victory at
Aboukir arrived as Haydn was writing it, and Nelson and
Emma Hamilton probably heard it at Esterházy in 1800.
The scoring is curious: three clarini (high trumpets),
kettledrums, organ, and strings, but no woodwind. Unfortunately the first published edition of 1802 conventiona-
lized the scoring and much else in the Mass, and there is
still no edition which provides what Haydn wrote; one is
imminent as I write. This is Haydn's supreme masterpiece
in the choral field, terse, vigorous, and gloriously original.
Vaughan Williams said shortly before he died that hearing
this Mass was one of the most moving experiences of his old
age. There is not a weak movement, and there is plenty for
a good chorus to get its teeth into. The first section of the
Credo, a two-part canon at the fifth for full orchestra and
chorus, sounds wonderfully rugged. I wish I could quote
it all.

Next (No. 10) comes another Mass in B flat (1799;
Novello No. 16) known in German as the *Theresienmesse*,
after the Empress Maria Theresa, wife of Francis II, who
later sang the soprano solo in *The Seasons*. (She is not to be
confused with the more famous Maria Theresa, the Empress
in honour of whom Haydn's Symphony No. 48 is nick-
named.) The work is scored like the *Nelson Mass*, with the

addition of rather dull clarinet parts. The violin writing, especially in the choruses, is very inventive, except perhaps in the Benedictus where a certain flippancy intrudes. There are more trumpet and drum effects in the 'Dona nobis pacem'. This is the only Haydn Mass to be had in miniature score form, and it is a splendid work. Some of the tunes reach out towards a new age (Example 34).

Ex. 34. Haydn, *'Maria Theresa' Mass*

No. 11, the *Creation Mass* (German *Schöpfungsmesse*), is also in B flat (1801; Novello No. 4), and is so named because in it Haydn quotes from his oratorio.

Haydn's last Mass, No. 12 (in B flat, 1802; Novello No. 6), is in German called the *Harmoniemesse. Harmonie* is German for 'wind-band', and the Mass contains very elaborate woodwind writing. The music has a characteristic way of gravitating into D major, and then surprising by returning to B flat without preparation. The chromaticisms in the Hosanna make one think of the minuet in Mozart's Symphony in G minor. This Mass is another work worth the time of any choral society.

Several of these Masses (Nos. 7, 8, and 10) have their Kyrie sections designed like symphonic first movements, complete with slow introductions. But Haydn does not again make the mistake of trying to force the Credo into sonata form, as he had in No. 6 and as Schubert was sometimes to do. Nor does he attempt a musical unity in defiance of the words by repeating the Kyrie music in the final 'Dona nobis pacem', as he had done in Nos. 1 and 4, and as Mozart also did in many of his Masses. The writing for solo voices in Haydn's late Masses is much easier than in the earlier ones and avoids mere display, and he mixes solo voices and chorus with great freedom in one and the same section. His choral fugues are almost uniformly good, as indeed they had been from the first; his fugues nearly always have much more character than Mozart's. But though counterpoint came so easily to him, he increasingly saw the value of unison writing for his choir. The words 'Et in unum sanctam catholicam et apostolicam ecclesiam' ('And in one Catholic and Apostolic Church') can be symbolized by unison uniting, and are so in Nos. 8, 9, 10, and 12. There are other examples of splendidly effective unison writing, for instance the iterations of 'Miserere' ('Have mercy on us') in the Gloria of No. 8; also in the 'Qui tollis' of the *Nelson Mass* (Example 35). It will be seen that this phrase consists of a momentary departure from a basic repeated note to the one immediately above or below. This germ occurs all through the *Nelson Mass*, and helps to give it a unity: it occurs for instance (with its inversion) near the start of the Kyrie. It can also be sensed in the more virile tunes that open the Gloria and Credo.

Two other medium-length choral works remain to be noticed, and each is of the highest quality. The *Stabat Mater* in G minor (1767; about eighty minutes) was Haydn's first real masterpiece, and much the finest choral work of his earlier years. Unlike the *Applausus* Cantata of the following year, it is full of magnificent choruses, while the solo parts (S A T B) are not impossibly difficult. The contrast between this intensely felt work and the trivial music most composers were writing in the 1760s is notable. Its day will surely come.

The Seven Words (1785; about sixty minutes; called in Novello's vocal score 'Passion') had a curious history. It was commissioned by Cadiz Cathedral where, during Lent, the bishop read out the seven 'Words' or sentences spoken by our Lord on the Cross; and after each there was a pause for meditation filled with orchestral music. Haydn had to produce seven slow movements, with an Introduction at the start and a representation of the earthquake at the end; nine pieces in all. He scored them for normal classical orchestra

Ex. 35. Haydn, *'Nelson' Mass*

without clarinets. Two years later, anxious to get wider currency for some fine music, he arranged it for string quartet and also for piano solo. Returning to Vienna from London, he heard at Passau a version with choral parts added by one Friberth or Friebert, and did not much like it. Accordingly he asked Baron van Swieten in 1796 to write a new text for the new choral parts he was devising to go with the original orchestral version. (For some reason he added clarinets and trombones and removed the flutes.) He also composed a new 'Interlude' for wind alone, to be played after the fourth 'Word', and added very brief settings of the 'Words' themselves for unaccompanied voices as an introduction to each choral movement. One would not expect a work consisting of slow movements (and arrangements at that) to be successful, but the result is very moving, as for that matter is the original and almost unknown orchestral version. Haydn achieves just sufficient variety with great skill, and the third and fourth 'Words' are wonderful. Solo voices (SATB) are contrasted with the chorus in every movement except the earthquake, which is entirely choral.

I have space to mention only three of Haydn's short choral works. The late *Te Deum* in C (1799) is available in two good modern editions, needs a large orchestra but no soloists, takes under ten minutes, makes a quite overwhelming effect, and is utterly neglected. The early *Salve Regina* in G minor (twenty minutes) is much less vigorous, but wonderfully poetic and intense. It is scored for strings and solo organ, but the organ part can be played by oboes and bassoons. The four solo parts are not hard. The so-called *Madrigal: The Tempest* (1792; about ten minutes) is Haydn's only choral work to English words (by 'Peter Pindar'). In effect a *scherzo* with a calm trio section in the middle and at the end, it needs a large orchestra and is hard to bring off, for the later writing makes it almost impossible to take the opening storm music at the breakneck speed it needs. But it could be very exciting. It has never been printed with the original English words.

*

Every Haydn work mentioned above dates from the composer's maturity. But for most of the much shorter adult life of Wolfgang Amadeus Mozart (1756–91) orchestras were not allowed in church and there was no call for church music; consequently Mozart's church music is nearly all very early and a good deal less interesting than Haydn's. In any case his feelings towards Archbishop Colloredo of Salzburg were not such as to lead him to take much trouble over the music he wrote for him. The Archbishop did not like the celebration of the Mass to last for more than three-quarters of an hour, and this limited Mozart's contribution to a mere twenty minutes or so. His Masses are on a much smaller scale than most of Haydn's. Of the seventeen written at Salzburg, we may note that No. 8 in F (K. 192) features the four-note theme which Mozart later emblazoned in the Finale of the *Jupiter* Symphony (as C, D, F, E), and that this theme can also be found in the Sanctus of No. 12 in C (K. 257). Both these are above average in quality. No. 9 in D (K. 194) has a good Agnus Dei in B minor. No. 16 in C (K. 317, the *Coronation*, 1779; Novello's No. 1) is much the best, and the choruses, in particular the fugal ones, are less pedestrian than usual. Mozart does not seem to give much thought to the words, being too intent on a musical unity attempted through the recapitulation both of opening sections (in the Gloria and Credo) and of complete movements: the 'Dona nobis pacem' repeats the music of the Kyrie. Nevertheless, the whole of this is fresh, the 'Et incarnatus est . . . Crucifixus' sincere, and the Agnus Dei (the prototype of 'Dove sono' in *The Marriage of Figaro*) ravishingly beautiful. Perhaps it is still necessary to add that the work known as 'Mozart's Twelfth Mass', beloved by the Victorians, was not written by Mozart.

Amongst much other church music for Salzburg Mozart wrote four Litanies, of which the third and fourth are on a bigger scale and more interesting musically than any of the Masses yet mentioned.

The *Litaniae Lauretanae* ('Litanies of Loreto') in D, K. 195 (1774; thirty-five minutes) has a text associated with Loreto in Italy which was also set by Palestrina and others. The oboe and horn parts are dispensable, and the work might well be accompanied by strings and organ. The soprano and tenor soloists have to battle with some coloratura writing, but it does not lie high. The 'Salus' ('Salvation of the weak, refuge of sinners') is a lovely movement, and though some of the utterances of 'Miserere' ('Have mercy') at the beginning sound as though the choral singers have not got their minds on what they are singing, Mozart makes amends at the end with a celestial Agnus Dei. The *Litaniae de Venerabili Altaris Sacramento* in E flat, K. 243 (1776; forty minutes), is the best of the Salzburg church music and deserves to be better known. The text deals with the sacrament of the eucharist and is more solemn than that used for the *Litaniae Lauretanae* in D. It is scored for flutes, oboes, bassoons, horns, and strings, with some fine moments for three trombones as well. The tenor solo 'Panis vivus' ('The living bread') is difficult, not very interesting, and too long, but this is the only moment of display for its own sake, and the other movements are all good. There are plenty of fine choruses, including a double fugue to the words 'pignus futurae gloriae' ('pledge of glory to come'), which ingeniously conceals the fact that it *is* a fugue. The floating sounds of 'Miserere' in the 'Hostia' (a prayer to the Host) sound strangely modern.

We come now to two of the giants among Mozart's works, and it is sad that neither was completed. He began the Mass in C minor, K. 427, in 1782 about the time that he married Constanze von Weber. It was to be a 'cantata' Mass on a vast scale, like Haydn's *St Cecilia Mass*. It was conceived as a thank-offering, to be performed in Salzburg when he should first bring his bride to meet his parents there, and a performance did take place in Salzburg in the summer of the following year. This argues either that Mozart finished the work, parts of which later disappeared, or that he filled in the gaps by borrowing movements from his early Masses. The latter is what Alois Schmitt did when he edited the standard vocal score of 1901. The result satisfies Roman Catholic sensibilities better than musical ones, for the new music is much too good to be matched with the old.

The excellent miniature score which Robbins Landon has

recently edited gives only those sections Mozart finished or almost finished, and they add up to about an hour of superlative music. Most of the Credo and all the Agnus Dei are missing, but the repetition of the vigorous 'Osanna' after the Benedictus makes a perfectly satisfying end, at least for non-Catholics. Some of the double choruses have needed a little filling-in, and Landon does this better than Schmitt, who in any case cut several sections that he happened not to like. The result is that Schmitt's vocal score cannot be used with the full score and parts edited by Landon, and it is time that it fell out of use. The work is written for SSTB soloists, double chorus, and full Mozart orchestra including trombones. It needs considerable resources, including two really expert soprano soloists, one of whom will have to tackle the excessively difficult 'Incarnatus est'. Not every listener can take these words sung to such florid (if ravishing) music, and personally I find the Benedictus a little unyielding. But the 'Qui tollis' is tremendous, as indeed is nearly all the music. Perhaps it was the ban on orchestras in church that sapped Mozart's creative energy and caused him to leave the Mass unfinished. He later adapted some of it to an Italian oratorio text about David, *Davidde penitente*, perhaps by Da Ponte, but there is no sensible reason for performing the work in this form.

The story of how the Requiem was commissioned by a nobleman who wished to pass it off as his own has been told often enough. Mozart, ill from over-work and other undetermined causes, persuaded himself that satanic influences were behind the affair. On his death-bed he wrote what survives of the music, which is less than survives of the Mass in C minor. Only the first two movements are entirely his; and of course their repetitions much later in the work. Of the rest, Mozart completed about half in vocal score, and this was orchestrated by his friend Franz Xaver Süssmayer (1766–1803), who composed entirely the Sanctus, Benedictus, and Agnus Dei. How far he worked on sketches or ideas which Mozart played to him on the piano will never be known. Few of us would guess on internal evidence which parts of the work were his, which is another way of saying

that he did his work well. And never better than in the
Lacrymosa, of which Mozart is said to have written the
vocal parts only of the first eight bars; the completion is
miraculously good. Nevertheless, the mixed authorship gives
the work an uncomfortable feel, and there really is not
enough of it in Mozart's hand to justify the number of performances it receives. And yet as I write this sentence I
remember the very first bars for orchestra alone, some of the
most moving bars in all music (Example 36).

Ex. 36.

The basset-horn is a rare type of tenor clarinet.

Of Mozart's slighter works for chorus, the tiny *Ave verum
corpus* ('Hail the true body'), which may be sung unaccompanied, gets a world of feeling into a few bars of angelic
music.

Franz Schubert (1797–1828) wrote four Masses in his
teens for his local church in Vienna, and No. 2 in G is ideal
for small choral societies as it is short (twenty-five minutes),

easy, and scored for strings and organ only. More important, it is immensely charming. The Credo carries simplicity almost to a fault; it keeps the same tempo and style throughout, regardless of the words, and yet it comes off. There is no counterpoint of any kind. The Kyrie is equally delightful, the Gloria rather less so. But few classical works are so easy to bring off in performance and so likely to give pleasure to beginners. As in all his masses, Schubert omits the words 'Et in unam sanctam catholicam et apostolicam ecclesiam' ('and [I believe] in the one holy Catholic and Apostolic Church') from the end of the Credo, and as he cannot have done so without everyone pointing out the fact, he must have done it on purpose, from some personal conviction. His editors, not sharing this conviction, take pains to rewrite the voice parts in order to include these words.

In maturity, Schubert wrote two more Masses. No. 6 in E flat dates from the last year of his life, takes about an hour, and is a failure. The characterless fugues do much to kill it, and there are some glutinously 'Victorian' harmonic progressions, for instance at the start of the Benedictus. Its predecessor in A flat is very different. As with so many of his best works, Schubert took a long time to write it, and made numerous sketches (1819–22). The result is one of his golden dreams, ravishing the senses with its melody and its endearing harmonic twists. It plays for some fifty minutes. There is not much solo work. Schubert wrote two versions of the fugue at the end of the Gloria. The Kyrie is a wonder of supplication; the Gloria (in the remote key of E major!) stirring, the end of the Credo powerful in a Beethoven-like way, and the beginning of the Sanctus (the voices come in in F sharp minor, though the movement began in F) a quite shattering inspiration. The Osanna may be a little too like a Mendelssohn glee, but there is not much wrong elsewhere.

Schubert's shorter works for choir are numerous, but mostly hard to obtain. His setting of Psalm 23 ('The Lord is my Shepherd') for female voices and piano is delightful, while the very Handelian *Song of Miriam* (1828) for mixed voices and piano (he would surely have scored the accompaniment for orchestra had he lived) has wonderful moments to make up for the banal ones. Both these are suitable for beginners, as is the enchanting Serenade with piano accompaniment (D. 921) which can be sung by either a men's or a women's choir. For male voices there is the wonderful *Song of the Spirits over the Water* (*Gesang der Geister über den Wassern*) with accompaniment for violas, cellos, and double-bass (1823). An earlier unaccompanied setting of these words by Goethe is also well worth singing, as is *Mignon's Song* (*Nur wer die Sehnsucht kennt*, the text known in English as 'None but the weary heart') for two tenors and three basses, with its fascinating harmonic shifts (1819).

Another composer to write in the Viennese classical idiom was, rather surprisingly, an Italian, Luigi Cherubini (1760–1842). He devoted his early maturity to opera, and when in 1805 one of his operas was given in Vienna he had a number of meetings with Beethoven, from which both profited. Soon after this, Cherubini (who lived most of his life in Paris) turned to church music, writing a fine *Missa Solemnis* in D minor in 1811 which certainly influenced Beethoven's. His Requiem in C minor and Mass in C (1816) are still revived occasionally, and with reason. They contain much dexterous counterpoint, some ingenious modulations, but have moments of banality that tend to spoil them as a whole. Strangely, there is little that is Italian about them. We began this chapter with Austrian composers looking south for a style on which to lean; we end with an Italian looking north to the new cynosure of the musical world, Vienna.

10

After Handel – in Britain and America

*c.*1740–*c.*1830

RICHARD FRANKO GOLDMAN

THE century following the death of Handel cannot in all fairness be termed one of the richest or most interesting in the history of British choral music. Yet there was considerably more activity, and much more honest and attractive music-making, than it has been the fashion to recognize in recent years. It must be remembered that the tradition of choral singing maintained itself at a fairly high level, and kept English singers and public receptive to new works and in readiness to welcome the so-called Renaissance of the later nineteenth century.

The many choral festivals organized in the eighteenth century created a demand for large-scale works, after the Handelian pattern, and provided a ready stimulus for composers. The famous Three Choirs Festival, combining the cathedral choirs of Gloucester, Worcester, and Hereford, had its inception in 1724. Other great festivals were instituted at Leeds (1767), Birmingham (1768), and Norwich (1770). Many other cities held festivals, the number being especially great in the early years of the nineteenth century. Whereas a cathedral or church choir normally provided the nucleus of festival singers, it is not clear how far the supporting singers were professional and how far amateur. Women sopranos began to be used from the eighteenth century, but contraltos did not entirely displace choral male altos until well into the nineteenth.

It is true that much of the creative leadership in composition was provided by composers of the Continent. After Handel, Johann Christian Bach ('the London Bach', 1735–

82) enjoyed a phenomenal English vogue. A son of Johann Sebastian Bach, he resided in London from 1762 until his death; during this period he wrote many choral pieces, including two Odes, a Te Deum, and an oratorio, *Joash, King of Judah* (1770). Another popular and influential composer of German origin was Carl Friedrich Abel (1725–87). Towards the end of the century the dominant influence was of course that of Joseph Haydn: *The Creation* and *The Seasons* (see pp. 167–9) not only established themselves in the hearts of singers and music-lovers, but also served as models esteemed almost as highly as the masterpieces of Handel.

Spohr, somewhat later, and Mendelssohn, later still, loomed rather larger than life-size in the view of English musicians. Their influence in the area of concert music of the more ambitious sort is undeniable. William Sterndale Bennett (1816–75) is a fair example of the Mendelssohnian English composer; for all the admirable qualities of his music, it can hardly be said to have a major claim to our attention today. His anthems and his oratorio *The Woman of Samaria* (1852) indeed are weak in showing Mendelssohn's influence to an excessive degree. For English music of importance, especially vocal and choral music, we must turn to other currents in the musical life of the time.

The most typically English, and at the same time the most original, contribution to the stream of music is to be found in the catches and glees so abundant and so popular in the period, and in the continuation, by a large number of well-schooled composers, and a few gifted ones, of the highest traditions of Anglican church music. Opera and oratorio cannot be said to have shown either vigour or imagination, although both forms flourished, at least in a quantitative way, throughout the period we are considering. Opera lies outside of the province of this survey, especially since no choral excerpts from stage works of the period have made, then or later, any mark on the choral repertory. Oratorio, however, is another matter. To the very end of the eighteenth century at least, the production of oratorios continued as a thriving musical industry. Many types of lesser work were, however, dignified by the name of 'oratorio', and the decline from the grandeur of the Handelian style is all too obvious. Yet there are some few oratorios worth noting, especially those by Boyce, Arne, Samuel Arnold, and William Crotch.

William Boyce (1710–79) is one of the major English composers who, after a period of undeserved neglect, is now receiving a portion of the attention to which his work entitles him. His symphonies are again performed, and much of his cathedral music has remained in use. Boyce composed one oratorio, *David's Lamentation over Saul and Jonathan*, first performed in 1736, but his fame in the field of choral music rests primarily on his work as successor to Maurice Greene (see p. 160) as compiler and editor of the *Cathedral Music* collection of Anglican church music of the sixteenth and seventeenth centuries. Boyce took over the material gathered by his teacher, Greene, at the latter's death in 1755, and published three volumes of the collection between 1760 and 1768.

Boyce was composer to the Chapel Royal for many years and succeeded Greene as Master of the King's Music (a post then implying, as it no longer does, the superintendence of the sovereign's orchestra). He was organist at a number of London churches and was active as conductor of choral festivals throughout England. Yet despite his interest in cathedral music, and his constant activity as a performer, it cannot be said that his vocal music is either as vigorous or as original as his instrumental compositions. A few of his anthems have some distinction. The best-known is probably the five-part *O, Where Shall Wisdom Be Found?*, but the attribution of this to Boyce has been questioned by scholars. There are passages to admire also in the four-part *By the Waters of Babylon* and in the eight-part *O Give Thanks*, among others.

Thomas Arne (1710–78) was, with Boyce, one of the two most distinguished native composers of the years following Handel's death. Whereas Boyce's fame rests principally on his instrumental music and on his work as compiler, Arne is remembered chiefly for his operas, his graceful songs, and his two masques – *Comus* (1738), now restored in the *Musica*

Britannica series, and *Alfred* (1740), memorable principally as the source of *Rule, Britannia*. The masque occupies a unique place in English music, midway between the opera and the oratorio. The choral sections of *Comus* are, however, of no great dimension or strength. It is worth noting that *Rule, Britannia* occurs in *Alfred* as a solo and chorus setting, and that the original melody is stronger and more effective than the corrupt versions generally circulated during the nineteenth century.

Arne wrote nothing for the Anglican service, and was in this respect the notable exception among the composers of his generation. He did, however, produce two oratorios: *The Death of Abel* (1744) and *Judith* (1761), both of which contain pleasant and charming airs in Arne's characteristic vein. The choruses of *Judith* are an unknown quantity (not yet having been published), but it would be fair to assume that they are not too greatly to be missed. Sturdy counterpoint cannot be reckoned Arne's forte, nor are massive effects to be found elsewhere in his music. One of the most charming chroniclers of music in England during the eighteenth century* wrote thus of Arne:

His oratorios were always unfortunate, yet it would be unjust to say that they did not merit a better fate; for though the choruses were greatly inferior to those of Handel, yet the airs were frequently admirable . . . Upon the whole, though this composer had formed a new style of his own, there did not appear in his works that fertility of ideas, original grandeur of conception, or those inexhaustible resources, which are discoverable upon all occasions in the productions of his inimitable predecessor, Purcell, both for the church and stage; yet, in secular music, he is considered by many, though not by the writer of these Letters, to have surpassed him in ease, grace, and variety; which is no inconsiderable praise, when it is remembered, that from the death of Purcell to that of Arne, a period of more than fourscore years, no candidate for musical fame among our countrymen had appeared, who was equally admired by the nation at large.

The oratorios of Samuel Arnold (1740–1802) were regarded with great favour in their time. His works of this

* A. Burgh, A.M., *Anecdotes of Music ... in a series of Letters from A Gentleman to His Daughter* (3 volumes), London, 1814.

type were: *The Cure of Saul* (1767), *Abimelech* (1768), *The Resurrection* (1770), *The Prodigal Son* (1773), *Sennacherib* (1774), and *Elijah* (posthumous). Of these, only *The Prodigal Son* survived its own era. Although Arnold's reputation during his lifetime was enormous, his music does not rise above the level of the ordinary. His forty or more anthems are of much less importance musically than his continuation of the work of Boyce in collecting, editing, and publishing still more of the cathedral music of greater predecessors. Arnold's four additional volumes appeared in 1790.

Of the lesser men active in the composition of music for the church, and born before the middle of the century, we must mention William Hayes (1707–77), his son Philip Hayes (1738–97), John Alcock (1715–1806), James Nares (1715–83), William Jackson (known as 'Jackson of Exeter', 1730–1803), T. S. Dupuis (1733–96), John Jones (1732–96), Benjamin Cooke (1734–93), and Jonathan Battishill (1738–1801). Most of these composers wrote services as well as anthems, and occasional settings of metrical psalms, and a few of them composed secular odes for various occasions. Little of this music made any but a transient impression, although much of it was extravagantly admired in its time, and one reads with some wonder the fulsome praise accorded many of these composers by their contemporaries.

Jones, who was organist at St Paul's, received words of praise from no less than Haydn himself, while *Jackson in F* was for years an esteemed and favourite service. The anthems of Nares were widely sung and much admired, although they are less interesting than those of Boyce, on whose style they are modelled. Of the composers named above, Battishill is by far the most interesting. A few of his anthems are really fine, and can stand in the best traditions of English music. Battishill's counterpoint has some motion and life, and his harmony has variety and mass. Several of his anthems are available in modern editions and are still to be heard. *Call to Remembrance* and *O Lord, Look Down from Heaven* are two of the best known. The latter is an especially dignified, expressive, and moving work.

The succeeding generation brought several composers of

greater stature, of whom the two Wesleys, Samuel (1766–
1837) and his son Samuel Sebastian (1810–76), are easily
the most noteworthy. There were, however, other composers of by no means negligible gifts. Thomas Attwood
(1767–1838), pupil of Mozart and later good friend of Mendelssohn, John Christmas Beckwith (1759–1809), John
Clarke-Whitfield (1770–1836), William Crotch (1775–
1847), and John Goss (1800–80) all wrote music rising well
above mediocrity and occasionally reaching levels of originality and excellence. If it is true, as William Alex. Barrett
slyly states (see Bibliography), that composers in general at
the end of the eighteenth century 'exhibited . . . a large acquaintance with the music of Handel, and excellent memories which supplied the place of invention', then it can be said
with no less truth that a new current set in with the arrival
of new influences. Samuel Wesley's devotion to Bach and
Attwood's studies with Mozart were extremely fruitful.

Samuel Wesley was the son of Charles Wesley, the writer
of hymns, and the nephew of the founder of Methodism.
Both Samuel and his elder brother Charles (1757–1834)
were child prodigies. Charles was able, before reaching the
age of three, to improvise with correct basses on the harpsichord; he later became an excellent organist and a composer of some distinction. Samuel Wesley composed two
oratorios before he was eleven, as well as a set of lessons for
the harpsichord and an assortment of vocal and instrumental music. He became the finest organist of his time, and
was an excellent performer on the harpsichord and violin as
well. He was certainly the most versatile as well as the most
gifted English composer since the time of Boyce, and gave
evidence of the widest musical culture. He wrote in nearly
all forms except that of opera, and a revival of some of his
instrumental as well as much of his vocal music would undoubtedly have interest today.

Wesley seems to have entered the Roman Catholic
Church in about 1784, possibly because of the great attraction exercised upon him by Gregorian chant, and for that
church the greater part of his choral music was written, including five Masses and a large number of shorter works.

He returned to the Anglican Church later in life, but the music he composed for this service is smaller in amount and in importance than that which he composed for the Roman rite. In 1810, Wesley brought out, in collaboration with C. E. Horn, an edition of Bach's *Well-Tempered Clavier*; his letters to Benjamin Jacob on the subject of the introduction of Bach's work to England (published in 1878 by his daughter) make interesting reading.

Despite Wesley's great and intelligent admiration of Bach, it is not that composer of whom Wesley's best work reminds us. He was essentially an eclectic, although he had a strong individuality and a real style. He had heard many of the Italian composers of the eighteenth century; and despite his admiration for Bach, he was surely also influenced by the Handelian manner. Among his most impressive works, the motets *Tu es sacerdos* ('Thou art the priest') for six voices, *Omnia vanitas* ('All is Vanity') for five voices, and *Exultate Deo* ('Rejoice in the Lord') should be mentioned. His best-known and most admired work, the eight-part motet *In exitu Israel* ('When Israel went forth'), shows his style at its loftiest. There is something in this work that connects the greatest eighteenth-century masters with Spohr and Mendelssohn. Example 37 (to words meaning 'The sea beheld and fled') will give a clue (see p. 190).

Among Wesley's contemporaries the most important are Attwood and Crotch. At the age of sixteen Attwood attracted the attention of the Prince of Wales, later George IV, and was sent to Italy to pursue his musical studies. He remained in Italy for two years, afterwards visiting Vienna, where he became a pupil of Mozart. Mozart had 'sincere affection and esteem' for him, and told Michael Kelly that 'he [Attwood] partakes more of my style than any pupil I ever had, and I predict that he will prove a sound musician'. On his return to England Attwood received various appointments as organist and assumed a distinguished place in the musical life of his era. He became organist of St Paul's, and was one of the founders of the Philharmonic Society, appearing occasionally as conductor. He maintained most cordial relations with Mendelssohn, whose letters contain

Ex. 37. Wesley, *In Exitu Israel*

many friendly references to him. It cannot be said that Attwood is a major composer, but he is important in that his style marks a turning away from the imitation of Handel and the substitution of a kind of gentle grace for an imitation grandeur. Attwood's music is well written, and if it is not lofty it is at least not pretentious, and if it lacks forceful counterpoint it abounds in agreeable melody. Among Attwood's works are the Coronation Anthems for George IV and William IV. His death prevented the completion of his *Ode for the Coronation of Queen Victoria*.

William Crotch, like the brothers Wesley, was an infant prodigy. He played the organ at the age of two, and at four gave public concerts in London. Dr Burney, among others, was fascinated by the talents of the child, and devoted an article to him in the *Philosophical Transactions* of 1779. At the age of fourteen, Crotch composed an oratorio, *The Captivity of Judah*, performed at Cambridge in 1789. Crotch eventually became Professor of Music at Oxford, where his lectures attracted much attention, and in 1822, on the founding of the Royal Academy of Music, was named its first principal. Crotch published some of his lectures, as well as other works in musical theory. In general, his music looks back to the eighteenth century and to the grand style of Handel. It is dignified, pleasing, and written with considerable academic skill. But it lacks force and originality, and little of it has survived. Crotch's oratorio *Palestine*, with words by Bishop Heber, is, however, probably the most impressive work of its kind in the first half of the nineteenth century, and parts of it, such as the quartet 'Lo, Star-led Chiefs', have remained in the repertory. Besides *Palestine*, composed in 1812, Crotch wrote a new oratorio in 1834, on the same subject as his juvenile *Captivity of Judah*; he also composed an ode on the accession of George IV in 1820, a funeral anthem on the death of the Duke of York in 1829, and various other ceremonial works now forgotten. Of his anthems, almost all are clear and pleasant, but only a few may be called distinguished or deeply expressive.

Thomas Attwood's godson, Thomas Attwood Walmisley (1814–56), wrote a few anthems of some distinction, but like all other composers of choral music of his generation, was overshadowed by Samuel Sebastian Wesley, the one really important talent of the period. Although lacking the scope and diversity of his father, Sebastian Wesley had a personal style of genuine beauty and distinction. He composed almost exclusively for the church, and the little instrumental or secular work he did has almost no importance. But his five services and twenty-six anthems include much enduring music. Of Sebastian Wesley's music, Spohr declared that it 'is distinguished by a noble style, and by rich, well-chosen harmonies as well as by surprisingly beautiful modulations'. Wesley in his turn did not conceal his admiration for both Spohr and Mendelssohn. But there is not very much of either of these composers in his music. He inherited his father's devotion to Bach, and there is internal evidence in the anthems that he knew and revered the early masters of

English vocal music. In his time, many of Wesley's harmonies were considered daring, but we can see them now as not far removed from the beautifully voiced and expressive textures of Purcell or Greene. Wesley was in a real sense the perpetuator of the great traditions of the English school. Among his anthems may be mentioned *Ascribe Unto the Lord*, *O Lord Thou Art My God*, *Let Us Lift Up Our Hearts*, and the beautiful *Cast Me Not Away*. It is perhaps unfortunate that Wesley is remembered best by two of his earliest works, his very first anthem, *Blessed Be the God and Father*, and the celebrated anthem entitled *The Wilderness*. It is not that these do not have their beauties, but there are greater treasures in many of the works of the composer's maturity.

We must now turn to a type of choral music that is, like the music of the Anglican service, peculiarly and distinctively English. The period with which we are concerned saw the growth and decline of the glee, as well as the flourishing of all sorts of catches and canons. Many of the composers who have been named above in connexion with cathedral music also wrote glees; in addition, there were many, like Samuel Webbe (1740–1816), John Stafford Smith (1750–1836), Stephen Paxton (1735–87), William Paxton (1737–81), the Earl of Mornington (1735–81), Richard Stevens (1757–1837), J. W. Callcott (1766–1821), Reginald Spofforth (1770–1827) and William Horsley (1774–1858) who are remembered almost entirely for their contributions to this one original English form of secular music in the latter part of the eighteenth century.

The glee is essentially a work for unaccompanied men's voices, in not less than three parts. The origin of the word 'glee' is still subject to some dispute, but it is generally considered to come from an Anglo-Saxon word having the meaning simply of 'music'. In its middle and late eighteenth-century form, the glee is a distant relative of the Elizabethan madrigal. It is simpler in texture, less sophisticated in design, and is generally based on the simplest kind of diatonic harmony. Although in the best works of the glee composers there are passages of graceful and independent movement in the parts, the glee style is basically one of harmonic note-against-note writing, and the later glees are indeed hardly to be distinguished from the conventional part-song.

It is of course a question whether the glees can properly be called choral music. They were written to be sung at convivial gatherings. The Glee Club itself was founded in 1783, and was but one of numerous similar groups flourishing in London and other cities in the latter part of the eighteenth and first half of the nineteenth centuries. The Noblemen's and Gentlemen's Catch Club, founded in 1761, included in its membership several of the royal family, and there were many other clubs enjoying varying periods of popularity. One of the most important publications of the period was the *Collection of Catches, Canons, and Glees*, compiled and edited by Thomas Warren (*d.*1794), secretary of the Noblemen's and Gentlemen's Catch Club. Issued annually from 1763 to 1794, it eventually included 652 pieces. The most famous of all glees, Webbe's *Glorious Apollo*, was composed in 1790 for the Glee Club, and was used invariably to open the club's meetings. It was first sung three voices to a part, and then by the full group. As an illustration of the most accepted and popular type of glee, see Example 38.

Ex. 38. Webbe, *Glorious Apollo*

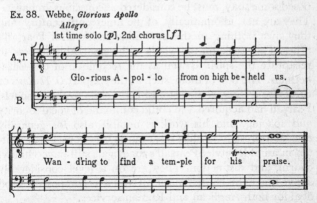

The madrigal itself enjoyed a curious renaissance in the works of a single composer, Robert Lucas Pearsall (1795–1856), whose best works of this type are not unworthy of their ancestry. Interest in the madrigal had never completely died, as witness the founding in 1741 of the Madrigal Society. But the composers of the eighteenth century added little or nothing to the great literature of the past, and it is interesting to note that in 1811, when the Madrigal Society decided to offer a prize for the best new madrigal submitted, it was apparently necessary to define the style for the contestants in the following terms:

in not less than four nor more than six parts, the upper part or parts to be for one or two treble voices . . . each part to contain a certain melody either in figure or imitation; therefore, a melody harmonized will be inadmissible.

In the early years of the nineteenth century other societies were founded, the most notable being perhaps the Bristol Madrigal Society in 1837, of which Pearsall was one of the original members. It was, in fact, largely through this society that Pearsall's interest in the madrigal was stimulated. The Society's membership was limited to thirty, so that its performances, like those of the catch and glee clubs, were in the nature of small-scale choral music.

Pearsall's madrigals and part-songs, of which he composed some sixty, must be considered as conscious archaisms. They are not, idiomatically, of the nineteenth century, and they owe nothing to the prevailing fashions of Pearsall's times. They seek, on the whole with remarkable success, to recapture the spirit as well as the technique of the Elizabethans. The best of them, such as the six-part *O Ye Roses* or *Great God of Love*, come astonishingly close to their models. Pearsall had acquired a splendid command of vocal sonority and spacing, and his work is notable also for generally excellent prosody. Unlike most music very consciously written in an older style, Pearsall's madrigals still have vitality, charm, and distinction. They are on a level considerably above that of his church music, of which he composed a good deal for both Anglican and Roman services.

In Pearsall we have the last notable composer of concerted vocal music of the early Victorian era. It cannot truly be said that the first half of the nineteenth century has left us very much English music of the highest rank, but it can at least be claimed that the vocal writing of the period does not suffer by comparison with the instrumental. To the enduring work of Pearsall and the Wesleys may be added some few of the compositions of Attwood, Crotch, and Goss, and the sum of this, if not overwhelming, is at least not negligible. The 'Renaissance' of English choral music does not occur until some time later (see Chapters 12 and 19).

We now turn to consider contemporary developments in Britain's American colonies and, later, the United States. The early history of choral music in America is almost entirely concerned with psalmody and hymns, and is, therefore, confined to a small area of what we should properly term choral music. The exception, which will be discussed below, is the music composed by the pietist Moravian settlers in the communities established about 1741 in Bethlehem, Pennsylvania, and Salem, North Carolina. It is necessary to go back to the musical usages of the dissenting sects in England to understand the development of music in New England. From the time of Calvin's dicta about the place of music in religious services, the music of most Protestant sects had been limited to the singing of metrical versions of the Psalms to simple hymn-tunes, sometimes harmonized and sometimes not. In England various metrical psalters had appeared during the sixteenth and seventeenth centuries, and it was these that the first American settlers brought with them. The two in most common use were the *Sternhold and Hopkins Psalter* (1562) used by the Pilgrims, and the *Ainsworth Psalter* (1612) in use among the Puritans.

The singing of these psalm-tunes was the only musical activity of the early New England settlers. Secular music, or art music in any form, was not regarded with favour, and in any case the rigours of life in the New World left little time for the cultivation of the amenities. It is not surprising that in a short time the old tunes themselves were almost forgotten, or at best inaccurately remembered, by most of the congregations. No new music was composed, and apparently little was brought from England by succeeding generations of colonists. There arose the practice of 'lining-

out', which meant that each line of the psalm to be sung
was read out by the minister or clerk and then repeated after
him by the congregation. This led to complete confusion,
loss of sense as well as of musical continuity, and eventually
resulted in the beginnings of pressure for reform.

The first book of importance printed in the colonies was
the *Bay Psalm Book* (Cambridge, 1640). This contained ver-
sified psalms, but no music. A second edition in 1690 contained twelve tunes. Of these traditional tunes a few, such
as *Old Hundredth*, are still in use on both sides of the Atlantic.
A more extended effort at improvement of congregational
singing was made early in the eighteenth century by John
Tufts, a minister of Newburyport, Mass., who published
some time between 1714 and 1721 *An Introduction to the
Singing of Psalm Tunes, in a plain and easy method, with a collection of tunes in three parts. . . .* Tufts's collection contained
thirty-seven tunes, using letters instead of notes but de-
ployed on the usual five-line stave, and with a system of
dots to indicate note-lengths. This type of attempt at
simplification recurs at a later date with Andrew Law
(1748–1821), and is one of the interesting phenomena in the
history of American music.

In 1721 appeared the first American tune book with
notes. This was the work of the Rev. Thomas Walter of
Roxbury (Mass.). The tunes were again in three parts, and
were taken from English collections, as were almost all of
those appearing in subsequent American publications until
the arrival on the scene of William Billings. Billings (1746–
1800) was a tanner by trade, but a self-taught musical
enthusiast. He is the first American composer in point of
originality if not of time. His first volume of music, *The New
England Psalm-Singer*, appeared in Boston in 1770. The
Urania of James Lyon (1735–94) appeared in 1761, and
Francis Hopkinson (1737–91) composed some secular songs
in 1759, but the work of Billings far overshadows these slight
efforts of his contemporaries. The influence of Billings was
enormous; in addition to composing and publishing six
volumes of tunes, he taught singing, organized choirs, and
introduced the use of the pitch-pipe, as well as of instru-

ments, to aid the singers. Most important, he created a new interest in church music and in singing which was of the greatest benefit to later generations, even to men such as Lowell Mason (see below, p. 199), who did not approve of him.

Billings's tunes are usually in four parts, and range from simple note-against-note hymns to what he denominated 'fuguing tunes'. The latter are primitive attempts at imitative counterpoint, probably based on corrupted recollections of the anthem-style. But to Billings they seemed original and powerful, and his naïvely proud descriptions of his 'fuguing pieces' make amusing reading. Billings's harmony is crude, but occasionally forceful, and he did have a genuine gift for vivacious and expressive melody. In addition to his psalm tunes, he composed some patriotic 'anthems' and topical pieces, for which he also wrote the verses. The stanzas of his *Europe*, and the opening of its 'fuguing' section (see p. 198) display Billings at his most vigorous:

> Let Whigs and Tories all subside
>> And Politicks be dumb,
> A nobler theme inspires our muse
>> And trills upon our tongue.

> O praise the Lord with one consent,
>> And in this grand design
> Let Briton and her Colinies
>> unanimously join.

So the line from a metrical psalm set by Handel – 'O praise the Lord with one consent' (see p. 150) – emerges in a new context.

Billings's work divided his contemporaries into two camps. He had many followers, among whom may be mentioned Daniel Read (1757–1836), Timothy Swan (1758–1842), and Jacob Kimball (1761–1826). But a conservative opposition found little to admire either in Billings's 'fuguing tunes' or in his vigorous ideas. This group, led by Oliver Holden (1765–1844), still remembered as the composer of the tune *Coronation*, and by Samuel Holyoke (1762–1820), forms the

Ex. 39. Billings, from *Europe*

*This is the note originally printed. It may or may not be a mistake for the expected E.

link to Lowell Mason and the subsequent development of vocal music in the United States. Billings's work survived only in remote areas, particularly in the Southern mountains, until the revival of interest in it in our own century.

The work of Andrew Law also represents the conservative opposition to Billings. Law was, unlike Billings, a man of considerable education, although his music is not very much more 'correct' than that of his forceful contemporary. Law had great influence as a teacher and organizer, travelling widely and endeavouring to establish a dignified and sober style of singing in churches and schools. In about 1803, he devised a system of 'shape-note' printing, on the theory that such notation would be more easily learned by beginners in the singing schools which he founded. The system used a note-head of a different pattern for each of the steps, 'fa–mi–sol–la', and although to a modern eye it does not seem to offer much advantage over conventional notation, it enjoyed a great vogue, especially in rural areas, where its use has continued almost until the present day. Such widely used collections as the *Southern Harmony* (1835) and the *Original Sacred Harp* (1844) employed shape-notes as late as reprintings of 1911.

'Art music' (as it may be called in distinction from hymnody and such functional music-making) entered modestly on the American scene in the late years of the eighteenth century. The first performance of Handel's *Messiah* in the New World was given under the direction of William Tuckey in New York in 1770. Tuckey (1708–81) was an English organist and composer who settled in New York in 1753 and exerted a most beneficent and constructive influence on the musical life of that community. A few of his original anthems survive, but his greatest contribution was as an organizer and teacher. He endeavoured to establish regular choral singing and public concerts, but his work did not bear fruit until a generation or so later, when the first American musical groups took shape.

Of these societies the most important was the Handel and Haydn Society, formed in Boston in 1815. Lowell Mason (1792–1872) became its president in 1827, and the Society issued Mason's first book. Mason was the most influential musician of his time in America, and his influence is still apparent in the field of hymnology and in the teaching of music in the public schools (in the American sense). Mason was an inspired and indefatigable pedagogue, organizing the Boston Academy of Music in 1832, and the Musical Convention in 1834, with the aim of teaching people to sing by note and to go out through the country as teachers. It is Mason who is usually given credit for first attempting to cultivate a taste for 'good' music among the people. Mason's own original music is confined to a number of hymns, many of which, such as *Olivet*, *Bethany*, and the hymn-tune *From Greenland's Icy Mountains*, remain in use. If many of Mason's tunes no longer seem adventurous or of the highest degree of musical inspiration, it must be remembered that Mason at least succeeded in restoring to American music some part of its connexion with the main stream of European music.

The connexion had been maintained in America, but only on a local scale, by the Moravians in Pennsylvania, and it may perhaps be counted as one of America's musical misfortunes that this activity did not spread beyond the Moravian settlements. Most of the Moravian music, composed in the eighteenth-century German tradition, remained unknown to the general musical public until very recently. Much of it is of striking quality, maintaining the highest standards of its European models, and composed with obvious professional skill. One is, in fact, astonished at this early flowering of high art on American soil, and dismayed that it produced no effect on the young nation as a whole. Instrumental as well as choral music flourished among the Moravians; indeed the only American religious compositions with orchestral accompaniment are to be found here. The chorale, the anthem, and the instrumentally accompanied aria are all represented in the works of such composers as Johannes Herbst (1735–1812), John Antes (1740–1811), John Frederick Peter (1746–1813), and David Moritz Michael (1751–1827); and the Moravian tradition continued well into the nineteenth century with the works of Peter Wolle (1792–1871) and Edward W. Leinbach (1823–1901). Many of these works are now generally available; they throw an entirely new light on early American choral music, and constitute a repertory commanding much more than local interest.

11

The French Revolution: Beethoven and Berlioz

*c.*1770–*c.*1850

J. H. ELLIOT

The French Revolution (1789) occasioned a period of quite extraordinary musical activity in France, and especially in Paris. No doubt it was the imperative need for distraction that accounted for the popularity of the theatres, of which there were about sixty in the capital. As Cherubini's wife remarked, 'In the morning the guillotine was busy, and in the evening one could not get a seat at the theatre'. Opera shared in the general artistic prosperity. But more characteristic of the special nature of the times were the vast musical festivals which the revolutionaries organized to encourage republican sentiment, and perhaps to provide 'circuses' to buoy up popular morale.

The political hysteria of the day had its effect, by no means a wholly admirable one, on composers within its orbit. The young men of the rank and file had no scruples about providing revolutionary songs on all manner of strange subjects. What was more serious, the established masters of the day, whether French by birth or by adoption, were drawn into the vortex. Men of the standing of François Joseph Gossec (1724–1839), Étienne Méhul (1763–1817), Nicolas Dalayrac (1753–1809), Charles Simon Catel (1773–1830), and Jean François Lesueur (1760–1837) found themselves virtually compelled to write choral odes to extol reason, liberty, or equality, and songs in praise of agricultural labour or anything else that the Convention (as the governing body was called) considered desirable. There were also patriotic hymns, funeral songs for popular heroes – some of dire length and tedium – and even apostrophes to

Jean-Jacques Rousseau. Cherubini himself was conscripted into the National Guard, though he was one of the few prominent musicians in Paris who at that time managed to preserve a measure of dignity and detachment.

Probably the leading composers made virtue of necessity, but it is certainly the fact that their musical conceptions became more and more grandiose. This was the heyday of massed choral music, often supported by instrumental forces no less gigantic. Gossec was the leading spirit, and indeed he already had a certain disposition towards *outré* musical effects. Before the Revolution he had written a Requiem in which the *Tuba mirum* called for two orchestras, one of which, a wind ensemble, was concealed outside the church. In his Te Deum, popular during Revolutionary days, he demanded, *inter alia*, fifty serpents (S-shaped wind instruments, now obsolete) and hordes of side-drums. Méhul became equally infected by the artistic madness of the day, and wrote for double orchestras and triple choirs. At one point he dreamed of building up a mighty chord with immense numbers of singers to each note. The gentle André Ernest Modeste Grétry (1742–1813), though he became 'Citizen Grétry' and a prominent figure of the times, had, like Cherubini, his own reservations. He was appalled by the activity of the mob and would turn aside to avoid passing the tumbrils returning from the Place de la Guillotine. It was Grétry, too, who left on record some dry and caustic comments on the bizarre inspirations of his fellow-composers.

All this vastly inflated choral music, though it had historical influence of some moment, is not undeservedly neglected today. Turning over its copious and innocuous pages, one has the impression that it was all made plain and simple 'by order'. It is almost fanatically diatonic, as though the use of accidentals had been forbidden on pain of the guillotine. A diminished seventh, cropping up in the introduction to a battle hymn (1794) by Méhul, seems like an impious stain on a page of otherwise virginal innocence, justified only by the belligerence of the subject.

It would be as tedious as it is unnecessary to pursue this

subject of Revolutionary music exhaustively. But for an example of its particular nature we may turn to the famous Festival of the Supreme Being, held in the Tuileries on 6, 7, and 8 June 1794. The political pattern of the French Revolution, as is typical of such upheavals, was complex, involving constant warring between rival factions. Robespierre, the 'incorruptible' – himself destined for the guillotine within a matter of weeks – was at the height of his power in the early summer of 1794, and had decreed that a new civic religion should be established as a counterblast to the militant atheism of other revolutionary cliques, and as a sop to the Church. The festival was designed to initiate, or to reaffirm, belief in a divinity and the immortality of the soul. The leading composers offered their co-operation, with prudence if not enthusiasm, and a spate of music followed – hymns and odes to the Supreme Being by Gossec, Dalayrac, Catel, and many others. Gossec, apart from his formal contribution, wrote a popular setting, a *larghetto* (with the direction 'very graceful and religious') in sentimental $\frac{6}{8}$, for the use of the populace at large. The whole of Paris was expected to take part, and leading musicians went out into the streets, with violin or flute, to coach the citizens for the occasion.

Some idea of the character of Revolutionary music in general may be gathered from the choral opening of Gossec's principal *Hymn to the Supreme Being*, evidently designed for experienced singers and presumably forming a special effort for a notable festival. After nineteen bars of instrumental introduction, consisting of unisons and common chords, the chorus begins (with orchestral support in similar vein) by invoking the 'Father of the universe, the supreme intelligence' (Example 40).

But the most far-reaching effects of the French Revolution, or rather the upsurging of the human spirit of which it was the most striking, spectacular, and indeed horrifying symptom, are to be found far away from the centre of the maelstrom. It is improbable that Ludwig van Beethoven (1770–1827) knew anything of this grotesque music that was being produced by his contemporaries in Paris. Nor could it have interested him, for, though at the time he was a

Ex. 40. Gossec, *Hymn to the Supreme Being*

young man at the outset of his career, his own path was laid out before him, and the whole spiritual and intellectual pattern of his art was on a far different plane, hardly of the same world. But the spirit of liberty and universal brotherhood was one of his guiding principles, and it is known that the desire to provide music for Schiller's *Ode to Joy* – which in fact was an ode to freedom, thinly disguised as a matter of political expediency – had possessed him from very early days. There is clear evidence that the idea was in his mind before he left Bonn for Vienna, in 1792. Some thirty years passed, however, before Beethoven's setting of the ode, or more accurately his own special arrangement of selected verses, became the Finale of the *Choral Symphony* – that is to say, his Symphony No. 9 in D minor.

It must not be assumed that Beethoven always intended to treat Schiller's words in this particular way. Historical record, indeed, indicates quite clearly that the conception of a symphony with a choral ending was entirely a separate issue, and may even have been fortuitous. His first proposition was to deal with the ode strophe by strophe. As for the symphony, Beethoven originally planned an instrumental Finale, but in the event diverted his sketches to the String Quartet in A minor, Op. 132.

It is impossible to say with certainty how the fusion of the two concepts came about. Beethoven's decision to produce a choral symphony may have arisen from any one of a dozen impulses. Perhaps he did indeed have a transient feeling that 'absolute' music was not adequate to his purpose. Wagner seized on this explanation and pressed it strongly, for it happened to suit his own philosophy of music particularly well. But Beethoven later came, in moments of despondency, to question the wisdom of his choral Finale, and in any event he virtually dedicated the rest of his career to absolute instrumental music in one of its purest forms, that of the string quartet.

The Ninth Symphony was completed early in 1824, and its composition seems to have occupied Beethoven intermittently since 1817. Within that period, between 1818 and early 1823, he wrote his grandest purely choral work, the great Mass in D (*Missa Solemnis*). For all his sturdy independence, Beethoven could not resist the pressure of a formidable Viennese tradition that had been shown in his earlier Mass in C (1807), a fine though unduly neglected work, written to the commission of Prince Esterházy. It is true that objections were made to the 'experimental' character of this early setting, but its style is 'Viennese classical' none the less, and traces of the accepted Viennese style survive even in the Mass in D. But in the later work these hints and suggestions (for they are hardly more) are subordinated to a conception of such power and authority as to give the Mass in D a stature of its own. Moreover, the whole organization of this work is influenced by symphonic method rather than by the precedents of choral church music. It is significant that substantial orchestral passages take their places within the scheme. Although Beethoven originally had in mind a church ceremony – albeit a spectacular one, for the installation of an archbishop – the Mass in D, as it finally emerged, is scarcely to be contained within a normal ecclesiastical framework.

It may well have been that the experience of writing this stupendous Mass in D had given Beethoven the urge to bring choral music fully within the range of his great chain of symphonies. The Mass in D, as Tovey pointed out, is not symphonic *a priori*. It derives its inner impulse always from the words of the Catholic liturgy, yet occasions some of Beethoven's 'most gigantic symphonic designs'. The Ninth

Symphony, however, is expressly and avowedly in the accepted tradition of symphony.

The idea of a choral symphony was not, in point of fact, entirely Beethoven's own, for eminent (though now virtually neglected) composers had preceded him in the field. There was, for example, Peter von Winter (1754–1825), who composed a *Battle Symphony* (1814) with a choral movement. There might even have been an element of characteristic arrogance in Beethoven's decision to compose his own choral symphony, a desire to show the smaller fry how a great man could manipulate the form. The suggestion is not put forward fancifully, and still less with any slighting intention. Beethoven undoubtedly had, if one may put it so paradoxically, an all-too-human weakness for glorying in his own strength. The astonishing *Thirty-Two Variations on a Theme of Diabelli* for piano solo formed a crushing rebuke to the minor composer and publisher who had the presumption to ask Beethoven for a single variation as a contribution to a kind of symposium by a number of composers of the day. The *Pastoral Symphony* was Beethoven's own treatment of programmatic themes underlying works by Justin Knecht (1752–1817). There was obviously no need for Beethoven to assert his towering superiority in this high-handed way, but the historical facts are beyond dispute.

The finale of the *Choral Symphony*, even more than the notoriously taxing Mass in D, demands singers of experience and no little physical stamina. It has often been suggested, with some show of reason, that the deaf Beethoven, withdrawn in his own solitary world, was writing less for fallible mortals than for some disembodied, ideal vocal ensemble. Manifestly the music is not beyond human possibility, but it is a comparatively rare experience to hear the final pages of the Ninth Symphony performed by a choir which does not betray some evidence of strain, or at any rate preoccupation with the notes to the detriment of the sublime flow of the music. A composer who asks his sopranos to sustain high A's through bar after bar – to name but one of the formidable choral difficulties – can hardly hope for a perfect result on every occasion.

The Ninth Symphony, however, is unique, utterly unique, in its spiritual range. It contains profundities, flashes of revelation, so awe-inspiring in their majesty that one could hardly bear to be confronted with them very often. It is fortunate, or rather one should say that Beethoven's percipience was such, that the work is planned as it were on a festival scale. Any other Beethoven symphony could take its place in almost any reasonably constituted 'symphony concert'. But a performance of the *Choral Symphony* must always be a special occasion.

Consideration of the Finale in isolation – however vital in the history of choral music it may be – would be inadequate, for the symphony must be seen whole. The Finale cannot be isolated from the long and tremendous orchestral pages that lead up to it. The climax must be studied in its relationship to them, and indeed to the whole of the Beethoven symphonic canon. Happily there is no lack of opportunity to do this. (A. K. Holland's extended essay on the Beethoven symphonies in the Pelican *The Symphony* is warmly recommended. See also Bibliography.) A work which has not won a place in the normal repertory, but which may in some sense be regarded as a forerunner of the Ninth, is Beethoven's Fantasia in C (1808) for piano, chorus, and orchestra. Usually known as the *Choral Fantasia*, it is a set of free variations with a text in praise of music.

The reader of the foregoing may justifiably consider Beethoven, who first brought the choral symphony into the main stream of the European musical tradition, to be far removed from the world of politically inspired massed choral music. The composer whose output, notwithstanding its own independence and originality, provided a kind of absorption of both was Hector Berlioz (1803–69).

Now Berlioz, who for long – too long – was popularly associated with wild romanticism and programme music of a peculiarly lurid character, was in fact a many-sided genius. His individuality, which even today can sometimes seem quite startling and surprisingly 'modern' in character, has often deluded commentators into treating him as though he was an entirely isolated figure in the history of music. In a sense he was, and more conspicuously than many other composers of sharply defined personality. But certain aspects of his music, notably his vast and somewhat notorious choral works, plainly owe much to the grandiose creations of the French Revolutionary period. They appear to stand alone largely because their ancestry is now almost wholly obscure.

Berlioz was born in the month Frimaire (December) of the year 12 in the Revolutionary calendar. But the Revolutionary and Napoleonic régimes had been replaced by the Bourbon régime again by the time that the composer, as a youth, went to Paris in 1821 – to study medicine, though that did not last for long. But in French music the threads of continuity had not been broken. The bent towards the colossal in music had persisted long after the tumbrils ceased to roll. Méhul and Cherubini had presided over two orchestras (not to mention a military band) which assembled in Notre-Dame for a religious celebration at Easter, 1802. Lesueur, one of the leading men of the Revolutionary musical party, was a tutor of Berlioz. So also was Anton Reicha (1770–1836), a remarkable theorist – and incidentally a former colleague of Beethoven in the Bonn orchestra – who settled in Paris in 1808 and, infected by the prevailing tendencies, planned vast outdoor works for multiple wind bands and devised many novel effects, including chords for kettledrums.

It is hardly surprising that Berlioz, an impressionable and excitable youth, should have been attracted by these apocalyptic visions. The new romantic movement, which took so many strange forms among the young artists of France, found in him a fanatical adherent. But it must be said at once, and said with emphasis, that the romanticism of Berlioz was imaginative rather than instinctive. He conceived musical works from the viewpoint of a romantic, but gave them outward shape by means of musical impulses which embraced elements of the classical, the fastidious, and the restrained. He was essentially an aristocrat in music – his adoration of Gluck is peculiarly significant – far more flamboyant in theory than in practice. There is little in Berlioz's music comparable to the 'fertilization by poetry' which makes that of Wagner so vividly identifiable with emotional states. There is nothing remarkable in the fact that these two great contemporaries never fully understood each other.

Berlioz was among the first of the prominent French musicians to realize the full stature of Weber and Beethoven, but his own artistic heritage was almost purely Gallic. His reaction to the gargantuan music of the Revolutionary and post-Revolutionary periods had a powerful, if intermittent, influence on him throughout his life. It is very evident in the grandiose plans, laid in early days, for an oratorio, *The Last Day of the World*, which was to have been written for soloists, choruses, two large orchestras, and four brass bands, and was to have concerned nothing less than the destruction of the world. The young composer actually began work on this extraordinary creation, later projected as a three-act opera and offered to the director of the Paris Opéra, who not unnaturally declined the suggestion.

Berlioz, however, outgrew such wild and impracticable ambitions. He was a far greater and more sensitive musician than his forbears of the Revolution – and, what is extremely important, he was independent. His early struggles to obtain a foothold were real and bitter, but at least he had time for reflection. Nor was he menaced by the tyrants of a former period who could not only change their policy overnight but could invoke the sinister shadow of the guillotine to strike fear into recalcitrant breasts. At a comparatively early stage in his career Berlioz discovered the basic defects in the music of the Revolution and its aftermath. He, while remaining fascinated by the colossal, created music feasible in performance as well as infinitely superior in artistic status.

'There is no such thing', said Berlioz, bursting once and for all the immense and absurd bubble, 'as outdoor music.' His musical knowledge – and few composers have been more keenly aware of the acoustical implications of musical performance – led him to realize how essential to effective sound is the provision of adequate resonators. When he did finally agree to prepare a work for an open-air ceremony, the *Funeral and Triumphal Symphony* (Paris, 1840), he not only adopted the obvious precaution (following Gossec, Méhul, and Reicha) of putting the main emphasis on wind instruments, but deliberately relied on the buildings and trees of the streets to reflect the sound. Moreover, the musicians who were expected to write criticisms of the work – Wagner, who was correspondent of a German paper at the time, was among them – were invited to a special indoor rehearsal prior to the actual occasion. Berlioz also put his finger upon another vital principle. A vast ensemble, he perceived, would reflect vastness not only in its immense sound; in addition, 'its repose [i.e., its silence] would be as majestic as the ocean'.

The famous Requiem (*Grande Messe des Morts*, Paris, 1837) is Berlioz's outstanding achievement as a rational, practical essay in the sphere of the musically gigantic. Not only did he deploy a great array of forces in an effective way, but he added other and far more subtle inflections. The Requiem has acquired a certain notoriety because of its monumental movements, primarily the *Tuba mirum* with its five orchestras – four of them, composed of brass instruments, being posted at the corners of the central body. But in fact a large proportion of the work is restrained in manner. What is extraordinary, indeed almost unique, is the constant suggestion of illimitable space by the cast of the music itself, even when it is physically restricted.

More superficial are a number of curious sound-effects, which historians have taken much trouble to emphasize. These were obviously included to conjure up illusions of a lofty ecclesiastical building, even though the place of performance might be secular and indeed lacking in special resonance. In Berlioz's Requiem some of these strange sonorities have little to do with the sung music, or even with the significance of the words. (In this work, and indeed in the choral music of the whole phase covered in this chapter, the orchestral support matched, if it did not surpass, the voices in importance.) One of the most remarkable of these sonorities, the chords for low notes on eight trombones plus three solo flutes, in the 'Hostias', was specifically claimed by the composer not only as an acoustical curiosity but also as a reinforcement of the solemnity of the pauses in the choral flow (Example 41).

Ex. 41. Berlioz, *Requiem*

The Requiem, ideally for a minimum of 210 voices and an immense orchestra, including great numbers of kettledrums (the modern instruments can effectively reduce Berlioz's original specifications) and the constituents of the four extra brass orchestras, includes some magnificent music. The opening Introit can be numbered among the greatest pages in the Berlioz canon, with its polyphonic writing which escapes the aridity that was the composer's usual defect in such essays. There is a mixture of styles in the work, but Berlioz's firm imaginative grasp of his great plan – which might be defined as a sombre pageant of ritual, influenced by contemplation of the melancholy of mortality – imposes a convincing unity on the whole creation. Contrast from the mighty cascades of sound is obtained not only by such movements as the six-part unaccompanied motet, 'Quaerens me' ('Seeking me'), but by such marvellously original conceptions as the Offertorium, wherein the orchestra gently weaves its patterns about a choral part consisting, almost to the end, of a swaying figure built on two notes lying a semitone apart. Berlioz once said that, if faced with the destruction of all his works save one, he would plead for the survival of the Requiem. It was an understandable choice. No doubt he wrote greater music, but there is nothing else in his output quite so supremely well integrated, or so magical and compelling as an example of Berlioz's unique poetry of sound.

Certainly there is not the same sensuous appeal, or a comparable evocation of a special atmosphere, in the Te Deum (Paris, 1855), though this is musically more accomplished. Moreover, it is more heavily charged with dynamic force than almost any other music of the composer. Here the relationship of choir and orchestra is reversed. The singers – there should be two choirs of 100, plus 600 children – overshadow a relatively modest orchestra of 150. (It need hardly be pointed out that satisfactory performances of Berlioz's vast works have often been given with considerable modifications of his voracious demands, and without pedantic adherence to his detailed instructions about the disposition of the performers.) The Te Deum which (as usual with Berlioz) takes liberties with the prescribed text, begins with a big double fugue and ends with the tremendously powerful 'Judex crederis' ('We believe that thou shalt come to be our judge') in which the voices take up a headlong, impelling theme a semitone higher at each entry. Among the other movements are purely instrumental ones (omitted from some editions) which imply a military background to the whole conception. Berlioz at one time formed the idea of a vast ceremonial work in honour of Napoleon I, and parts of the Te Deum are probably relics of this, just as the Requiem no doubt absorbed sketches for *The Last Day of the World*. Berlioz had an almost unparalleled flair for piecing together discarded, and sometimes quite unrelated, fragments.

If Berlioz's Te Deum may be said to mark the end of the cult of the colossal which arose out of the French Revolution and lead only into a cul-de-sac, there was another side of the composer's genius which linked him with future choral development. His admiration of Beethoven had little effect on the actual substance of his music, which is wholly original and unlike that of anyone else who is remembered today. But he took many hints from the master, and in his instrumental symphony *Harold in Italy* quite decidedly copied some of Beethoven's devices. But Berlioz also helped to establish the latter-day choral symphony, or at any rate some aspects of it.

The *Funeral and Triumphal Symphony* has a part for chorus only in the Finale, so is little more than imitative in the legitimate succession. In 1839, however, following a period of unwonted tranquillity in the life of the composer, there was performed in Paris a 'dramatic symphony with choruses', *Romeo and Juliet*. It hardly matters whether this emergence of a new kind of choral symphony was fortuitous or the result of deliberate intent. *Romeo and Juliet* is formally a strange work, and is quite extraordinarily unequal in content. Wagner's diagnosis of its quality – 'heaps of rubbish lie piled up among the most brilliant inventions' – is not entirely unjust. There are numerous orchestral movements, some of them in Berlioz's most wonderful vein, dazzling, exquisite, and touching. There are also solos, choruses (though few specially remarkable ones), and an extended Finale in quasi-operatic style. (It must be said, in passing, that the use of the chorus, and indeed soloists, is none the less quite arbitrary. The chorus is at first confined to plain recitative, and the vocal opportunities would not, in themselves, be likely to appeal to a choral society. The primary requirement is a first-rate professional orchestra.) But *Romeo and Juliet* is not opera, nor yet cantata, and if Berlioz chose to describe it as a symphony, there is a wealth of significance in the title. He saw through much of the humbug and artifice in the world of music, and no doubt realized that Beethoven, though he did not depart drastically from the traditions of classical symphonic form, had broken bonds when he wrote his Ninth Symphony. If there could be so abrupt a departure from the instrumental character of the conventional form, why not a wholesale rethinking of the nature of symphony (the 'sounding together' of the original meaning of the word)? Berlioz could well have shaken hands with Mahler, who once said that 'the symphony should be like the world' – with a place in it for any kind of manifestation of human thought and feeling. A whole new

generation of choral symphonies issued from the loins of
Berlioz's *Romeo and Juliet*.

There is yet another side of Berlioz relevant to our theme.
He wrote many choral works, some of them of considerable
size, calculated to attract the attention, and rouse the enthusiasm, of choral societies. Some of the shorter pieces,
including several composed for his own Philharmonic
Society of Paris, are perhaps better left in obscurity, though
such little things as the charming *Sarah the Bather* (*Sara la
baigneuse*, 1834) and the thoughtful *Religious Meditation*
(1831) are unjustly neglected. (Here some modification of
original demands for performers might be expedient.) The
oratorio, or sacred trilogy, *The Childhood of Christ* (*L'Enfance
du Christ*, 1850–4) reveals some of the choicest elements of the
composer's genius. The orchestral demands are not excessive, and much of the music has a charm and a tenderness
that provide the best possible correctives to the old popular
misconception of Berlioz. The work as a whole is uneven, as
is common with the composer. There are dramatic episodes,
and a few that are positively grotesque. The beautifully
chiselled central section is 'The Flight into Egypt', from
which the full trilogy grew. This has a chorus of shepherds
of such sweet simplicity that it stands alone in the music of
the composer (Example 42).

Ex. 42. Berlioz, *The Childhood of Christ*

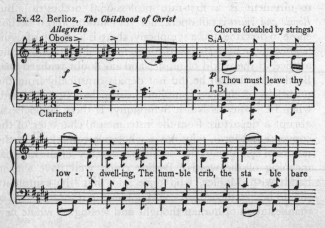

Berlioz's most familiar contribution to choral music was *The Damnation of Faust* (Paris, 1846). This work, variously described as a 'dramatic legend' and an '*opéra de concert*' – it has actually been staged, with indifferent success – was, during a comparatively recent period in the history of British choralism, almost in the same category of popularity as *Elijah*. But for some reason it has fallen from the stock repertory, along with Mendelssohn's work, and now re-emerges from time to time as something of a novelty. Berlioz's version of the Faust story, though based on Goethe – being, indeed, an expansion of an early set of eight pieces written white-hot under the stimulus of a French translation of the great poem – is very much an individual creation. The composer did not scruple to introduce incidents to suit his own needs, notably a scene on the Hungarian plains which provides an excuse for bringing in his stirring elaboration of the country's national war-march (the Rákóczi March). This is one of the fine orchestral showpieces without which a Berlioz choral work would hardly be Berliozian. But there are numerous splendid choral pages, including a rousing soldiers' chorus, and *The Damnation of Faust* as a whole gives us, so to say, Berlioz in basic form. The music has much of his piquancy and originality, but little of his occasional freakishness.

We may take leave of this strange figure in the history of music with a quotation from *The Damnation of Faust* which reveals yet another facet of his musical personality. Berlioz the satirist could not be kept entirely out of the scores of Berlioz the composer. His keen ear for what he conceived to be the pretentious and ridiculous in music sometimes tempted him to spice his own creations with tilts and gibes at conventional nonsense. He took violent exception to the traditional fugal 'Amen' chorus, with its repetitions – once, during an outburst of spleen on this subject, he spoke of Handel as 'a barrel of pork and beer'! – and in *The Damnation of Faust* set the students in Auerbach's cellar to work on a stinging parody (which, by the way, is often treated much too solemnly). Example 43 shows how it ends.

Ex. 43. Berlioz, *The Damnation of Faust*

12

The Oratorio and Cantata Market:
Britain, Germany, America

c.1830–c.1910

THEODORE M. FINNEY

In the eighteenth and early nineteenth centuries, Handel's oratorios had set a pattern followed by Haydn and numerous other composers which was to have an amazing influence until the present. Festival choirs came into existence all over Europe; and in North America (see p. 199), *Messiah* had its first performance in 1770. But several other things had to happen before nineteenth-century interest in choral singing reached a magnitude which deserved to be called a market. They were all aspects of the democratization of social and cultural life which went on so rapidly in the nineteenth century.

First, the widespread attempts to teach the rudiments of music to everybody must be noted. There had long been popular presentations of musical rudiments in the prefatory pages of psalm and hymn-tune books and other collections. The process was accelerated in the nineteenth century, with special attention to the class teaching of music and the invention of simplified systems of notation. ('Tonic solfa' dates from the 1840s: it is only one system of its kind.) At about the same time came the manufacture of cheap paper from which the 'market' was quick to profit, and the invention of rapid and much less costly methods of printing music. Choral singing as we now know it owes a debt to the very few men in London who, early in the nineteenth century, saw the possibilities of providing the broad-based popular interest in singing with well-printed, adequately edited low-priced music. The activities of Alfred Novello and Henry

Littleton (of the firm of Novello) have been described in a book entitled *A Short History of Cheap Music* (by Joseph Bennett; London, 1887). Their methods were widely imitated.

This, then, was the market: democratic societies requiring and getting music for group singing. The fact that the phenomenon is mostly to be observed in German- and English-speaking countries doubtless reflects both the rising economic status of those countries during the nineteenth century and the strength there of Protestantism as both a religious and musical heritage. We shall have occasion to note the pull exerted by Protestant England on the Catholics Gounod and Dvořák.

As we describe the works called forth by the market, we must take note of two trends. First was the ever-increasing popularity and consequent hold on public taste of Handel's *Messiah*. The piece 'clicked' from the very beginning. It has made reputations for choirs, soloists, and conductors; fortunes for editors and publishers. More than that, it has made music-lovers of millions whose normal addictions led them to other footlights. It has won the battle for the tastes of wives for two hundred years. The other trend has developed as a slowly moving antidote: the discovery, or recovery, of the choral music of Bach.

In 1837 Alfred Novello secured the English rights to Mendelssohn's *St Paul* and issued a performing edition at a greatly reduced price. This may be taken as a beginning. By 1850 the market had become international. Festivals supporting choirs, orchestras, and commissions for new works appeared from Pilsen (now Plzeň, Czechoslovakia) to Chicago, with conductors, composers, and soloists moving back and forth across the circuit. The Novello covers carry the great names of the 'market', and to some of these, beginning with Mendelssohn, we must now turn our attention.

Felix Mendelssohn (full surname Mendelssohn-Bartholdy; 1809–47) was peculiarly fitted by the circumstances of his cultural background, the quality of his genius, and the wide contacts he made with European artistic life to continue the oratorio tradition. It is worth noting that at his confirmation his grandmother gave him a hand-written copy of the score of the *St Matthew Passion* and that he edited, with revised accompaniments, such works of Handel as *Israel in Egypt* and *Solomon*. Almost one-fourth of the opus numbers by which Mendelssohn's works are identified cover choral works of one sort or another. Many of these were written at the behest of choral groups for special purposes such as anniversaries and festivals. They were facile and successful, and almost invariably met the need for music which felt familiar but which at the same time was just 'new' enough. The note from Buckingham Palace signed 'Albert' (who also composed music) lets us feel the pulse:

To the noble artist who, when surrounded by the Baal-worship of the false, has, like a second Elijah, employed his genius and his skill in the service of the true; who has weaned our ears from the senseless confusion of mere sound, and won them to the comprehension of all that is harmonious and pure – to the great master who has held in his firm control and revealed to us not only the gentle whisperings of the breeze, but also the majestic thundering of the tempest.

The oratorio *St Paul* (1836), the *Hymn of Praise* (see p. 249), and the cantata *Lauda Sion* (1846) took important places in the repertory. But the oratorio *Elijah* (Birmingham, 1846) might well be called one of the 'big three' with *Messiah* and *The Creation*. Its appeal, to performers and audience alike, was immediate, and it held on for almost a century. Even now, after the mid twentieth century, when complete performances come with diminishing frequency, such individual numbers as the quartet 'Cast thy burden upon the Lord', the chorus 'He, watching over Israel', the trio 'Lift thine eyes', and the solos, 'If with all your heart', 'O rest in the Lord', and 'Then shall the righteous' are part of the permanent church repertory. This value in the market is not hard to account for. Mendelssohn had a seemingly inexhaustible reservoir of ingratiating melody which singers generally find rather pleasant.

Let us examine the structure of *Elijah*. After three great shouts of 'Help, Lord!' the first chorus suggests in the downward chromatic progression that, without the 'help' of the shouted prayer, things will be pretty bad. The chorus, as great oratorio choruses are expected to be, is polyphonic, with two main themes. An incidental advantage in polyphonic treatment is that everyone in turn gets the tune to sing.

Other pleasures become apparent: the whole work is dramatic, moving along from one episode to another without breaks. Its religious atmosphere is enhanced by passages in the mood and style of the chorale, and its first climax is the grand storm in which the chorus is immersed in orchestral wind, rain, and thunder. Part of the preparation for this climax is a telling use of a musico-dramatic motive which first appears in the unconventional opening of the work, in which (before the first chorus) Elijah threatens God's punishment in a recitative: 'there shall not be dew nor rain . . .' (Example 44). In the second chorus

Ex. 44. Mendelssohn, *Elijah*

'the people' note that the Lord 'mocketh at us' and then give the reason (Example 45). Here the threat from the

Ex. 45. Mendelssohn, *Elijah*

opening recitative is identified musically as a 'curse'. This chorus is fugal, with three subjects, of which the 'curse' is the second. Eventually the third subject (to the words 'His wrath will pursue us') is combined with the 'curse' (Example 46).

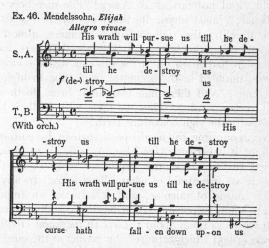

Ex. 46. Mendelssohn, *Elijah*

Part Two – it might almost be called Act Two – begins in a sombre and lyric mood which leads to the conflict between Elijah and Ahab, with the chorus finally coming to a climax in 'Let the guilty prophet perish'. A change of scene, secured by Elijah's words 'I journey hence to the wilderness', introduces the aria 'It is enough', which has made the oratorio attractive to bass soloists for a century. The music moves on through one 'hit' after another: 'Lift thine eyes' for three angels, 'He, watching over Israel' for chorus, 'O rest in the Lord' for contralto solo, 'He that shall endure' for chorus, to a climax in another storm. 'A mighty wind', 'the sea upheaved', 'the earth shaken', 'there came a fire': all these are in the grand 'descriptive' oratorio tradition, here made doubly effective by the sudden quiet interludes. These passages forecast, with considerable dramatic ingenuity, the quiet 'still small voice' to which wind, earthquake, and fire eventually subside.

The final 'scene', introduced by the short recitative 'Above Him stood the Seraphim', develops from the solemnity of the opening massing of quartet and chorus through the 'fiery chariot' ascent of Elijah – again a 'pictorial' chorus in the grand style – to the final 'all's well with the world', and last fortissimo 'Amen!' The members of the audience, almost physically lifted out of their seats time after time by the well-contrived climaxes, almost wish (remembering the history of *Messiah*) that here too the Sovereign had stood up at the obvious signal – when the chorus, doubled in the orchestra from tuba to high flute, proclaims: 'And then shall your light break forth as the light of the morning.' They too then, with all their hearts, could with the righteous shine forth!

We, in our time, can hardly participate in this enthusiasm. Perhaps it is because Mendelssohn, with his smooth, controlled surface, lacks the depth we seek. Perhaps it is because we are afraid of what Albert found. In any case, this is music of purpose, and it achieves an important stature. How important might be discerned by examining such works as Louis Spohr's *The Last Judgement* (1826) and *Calvary* (1835) which captured the market at the same time.

Robert Schumann (1810–56) belongs in this discussion partly because his music stands in such strong contrast to that of Mendelssohn. A youthful mastery of musical materials was not part of Schumann's equipment, nor was the 'classical' ease of manner which could be a result of a surefooted technique. Schumann's participation in the Romantic artistic adventures of his time involved him emotionally; finally to the detriment of his mental health. This meant that although he was of course aware of the public interest in cantata and oratorio, he could not work to the market specifications if they conflicted with his own inner urge. They always did! Thus the *Scenes from Goethe's Faust* (1844–53) wavered between opera and oratorio, was laid aside, and finally left incomplete. The one oratorio was *Paradise and the Peri*, completed in 1843. The text was adopted from Thomas Moore's *Lalla Rookh*. The work contains much beautiful music, but it has never achieved popularity. Schumann's very real claim to the attention of the music-lover is not based on his choral works.

The fact that Schumann's *Paradise and the Peri* must be

classed as a secular oratorio involves a description which might seem to indicate a contradiction in terms. It really calls attention to one aspect of the expansion of all musical forms which was characteristic of the nineteenth century. All sorts of works for chorus, soloists, and orchestra appeared on the festival programmes, and no one seriously challenged their right to be there. Liturgical, biblical but non-liturgical, legendary, secular, patriotic: all these strands in romantic culture came together in cantata and oratorio.

Franz Liszt (1811–86) was in many ways the personification of music to the nineteenth century. His influence as concert pianist, conductor, and composer was felt everywhere, and the romantic aspects of his life tended to give even the lowly choral singer a bohemian thrill. Liszt was a prolific composer of big music – big in both sound and difficulty – most of which has lost its original appeal. It seemed proper to Liszt, for instance, to 'arrange' parts of Beethoven's instrumental music for his two 'Beethoven' cantatas. In 1848 Liszt settled in Weimar where he was to remain until 1861. He was conductor of the court theatre with an excellent band of performers. During this period he composed his two oratorios, *The Legend of St Elizabeth* (1865), and *Christus* (1873). In them the attempt was made to transfer the dramatic effects of the 'music of the future' from symphonic poem and opera to the oratorio. These works were performed with great acclaim during Liszt's lifetime, but interest in them has not held up, partly, perhaps, because of what seems to be a disparity between the tenuous mysticism of Liszt's religious feelings and the size and complexity of the musical forces he used to make his sounds.

Liszt also wrote Masses and other church works up to his last years. The *Via Crucis* (a cantata on the Fourteen Stations of the Cross), written in 1879, was not performed until 1929. The use of the chorus in Liszt's symphonic music is discussed in Chapter 14.

Charles Gounod (1818–93) contributed one work which had a wide hearing, *The Redemption*, first performed at the Birmingham Festival in 1882. As a young man, Gounod vacillated between music and the priesthood. He wrote dozens of works for the Church, but these, like his music in general (even *Faust*) have steeply declined in favour in recent years. His religious strain developed in his later years into a mysticism which tended to blunt whatever critical view he had been able to bring to bear on his own work. As a result, *The Redemption* and the other works written mostly to satisfy the English and American appetite began to pall. Even those audiences found it difficult to reconcile religious mysticism with cloying lyric sweetness.

Antonín Dvořák (1841–1904) attracted the attention of the great festival choirs and audiences when his *Stabat Mater* (1880) was performed in London in 1882, and the cantata *The Spectre's Bride* was written for the 1885 Birmingham Festival. He is further discussed on pp. 245 and 286, where the connexion of his works with Czech patriotism is noted. We may observe a patriotic element also in the limited choral output of Edvard Grieg (1843–1907), notably in the cantata *Sighting Land* (for male chorus and orchestra), 1872, to words by Bjørnson.

Johannes Brahms (1833–97) contributed one of the great masterworks to the oratorio tradition. Although Brahms was a choral conductor for various short periods in his life, his interests as a composer were so strong and so broad that it is misleading to suggest that he had any very pronounced interest in writing for a market. Twice, in 1877 and again in 1892, he refused the kudos offered him by English admirers in the form of the Cambridge Mus. Doc. Perhaps he dreaded the Channel crossing, but in any case the market never persuaded him to try to say again what he had said so well in *A German Requiem* (1868). Of the smaller works the so-called *Alto Rhapsody* (the usual English name for the Rhapsody for contralto solo, male chorus, and symphony orchestra, 1870) arrests first of all by its unusual scoring. Here Brahms set words by Goethe about an unhappy young man, at odds with himself and the world: the choral entry, reserved for the final section of the work, brings the hoped-for note of consolation. Less well known are the other smaller works, *Rinaldo* (1869), the *Song of Destiny* (*Schicksalslied*, 1871), *Song of Triumph* (1872), *Dirge* (*Nänie*, 1881), and

Song of the Fates (*Gesang der Parzen*, 1883). They are not without importance, but they are overshadowed by *A German Requiem*. Brahms worked at the composition of his Requiem over a period of eleven years, completing it in 1868. As performances either of the complete work or of parts of it began to take place, Brahms's reputation suddenly grew to full stature. It is quite likely that even now many church choir singers know Brahms best as the composer of an anthem called 'How lovely is thy dwelling', sometimes without knowing that they are singing a movement of the Requiem.

A German Requiem is not liturgical, not a *missa pro defunctis*. (The late Eric Blom suggested that a proper title in English-speaking countries would be *A Protestant Requiem*.) What it says is not a dramatization of the traditional act of intercession on behalf of the soul of the departed. It is a benediction of consolation ('blessed are they that mourn') and a statement of faith ('blessed are the dead who die in the Lord'). More than that, it is Brahms saying for himself, and to all those who sing and listen, that the paradox involved in mourning and death can be reconciled. The movement of ideas in the work may be suggested by making a short paragraph of the first lines of each of the seven sections. These lines will make their own point; and the fact that the texts were selected by Brahms himself from Luther's translation of the Bible emphasizes the total intention of the work.

Blessed are they that mourn . . . For all flesh is as grass . . . Lord, show me mine end . . . How lovely is thy dwelling . . . And ye now therefore have sorrow: but I will see you again . . . For here have we no continuing city . . . Blessed are the dead . . .

The expression 'movement of ideas' occurring in the previous paragraph was used purposely. This is not the place to undertake an exposition of the 'romantic' intuition concerning the manner in which music can seem to represent an action, an event, an emotion. In this work – as in many others – Brahms selects musical expressions which in their 'gestures' suggest a true correspondence to the verbal text.

A glance at the barest possible outline of the work gives the following procession of tonal levels from part to part for the seven sections:

F–B flat–D–E flat–G–C–F

It should be noted first that this procession returns to the level of its beginning. Important to our present consideration, however, is the fact that from the end of one movement to the beginning of the next the gesture is *always* upward. The listener may not realize what has taken place, but he has been *lifted* from one movement to another.

This procession begins and ends in F. After a constantly reiterated orchestral F (pedal-point) – reiterated from the beginning except for the meaningful progression from F up to D flat then back through C to F – there is a momentary break for the first word, which is '*selig*' ('blessed') (Example 47). Here those who mourn are '*selig*'. When the whole work

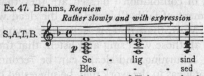

Ex. 47. Brahms, *Requiem*

is nearing its close, and the key of F is reached for the last time, the word '*selig*' reappears (not to the same music): now it is the dead who are blessed. But the reconciliation is not yet complete. It has been saved for the ending where the choir again breathes the word '*selig*' with music strongly reminiscent of the setting of the first use of the word. It should be noted that the reminiscence is modified to heighten its meaning. The third note of the soprano moves higher, the second note of the tenor is a wider leap, and the third note of the bass moves chromatically upward (Example 48).

Ex. 48. Brahms, *Requiem*

This leads to the final quiet statement on the static tonic harmony.

There is hardly a moment in the work that could not be made the subject of extended analysis and comment. It should be noted that the sombre quality of the beginning derives partly from the fact that the violins are omitted from the orchestra. Noteworthy also is an interesting reference which is lost on a non-Lutheran audience, but important as a resource to German Protestant composers. When the chorus begins to sing in the second number, the text is 'Behold, all flesh is as the grass'. The melody – in all the parts – is taken, almost note for note, from an ancient Lutheran hymn with the first line 'Who all his will to God resigneth' (Example 49). This device, also to be found in

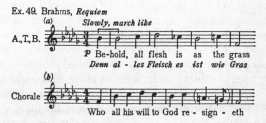

Ex. 49. Brahms, *Requiem*
(a) *Slowly, march like*

A., T., B.

p Be-hold, all flesh is   as   the grass
Denn al - les Fleisch es   ist   wie Gras

(b)

Chorale

Who all his will to God re - sign - eth

English ballad operas, yields the possibility of deploying two supplementary ideas simultaneously. The reader will have already noted from Chapters 4 and 7 the practice of earlier German composers of quoting chorales in a way similarly evocative to the envisaged audience. After comparing these two melodies, and noticing that Brahms does not use the upward leap (F to B flat) which began the chorale tune, the reader might turn in the score to the junction between this movement and its predecessor to see the use that is made of those two notes.

Our discussion may well close with only a reference to the two great fugal passages, one in the third section and the other in the sixth. Each of these comes not at the beginning but as a climax of its section. In each the polyphonic texture of the chorus is complemented by the orchestra; in section three by almost another fugue. It is a mistake to understand these passages only as references to the traditional choral-religious polyphony of Bach and Handel. Their function here is supremely expressive.

We turn now from the Continental composers whose music was so affectionately accepted by English and American audiences to composers who themselves represented the English-speaking peoples. Among many, the following deserve something beyond the attention of the antiquarian: Arthur Sullivan (1842–1900), C. H. H. Parry (1848–1918), Charles Villiers Stanford (1852–1924), George W. Chadwick (1854–1931), and Horatio Parker (1863–1919).

Sullivan and Parry were English; Stanford, born in Dublin, made his career in England (see Chapter 15). Chadwick and Parker were Americans, living and working in New England. All five studied in Germany. This may in part account for the fact that at a decade past the middle of the twentieth century we are a little surprised at the vogue they had. Until nationalism began to seem slightly artificial and shop-worn, England and the United States worked pretty hard at finding an indigenous music that could carry the right label, even to the extent of sending composers abroad and importing performers. As a result there was a 'renaissance' in England and a 'flowering' in New England. Now we are not certain just how this music should be listened to: mostly we solve the problem by leaving it to whatever musicologists may be around in the year 2100.

If we insist that everything our own English-speaking musical grandparents believed in was wrong we cannot listen to their music. If we can hear them even partly in their own terms we may discover that some of them were not without merit. Certainly they were welcomed by their own audiences!

Sullivan's oratorios and cantatas stand in the shadow of his theatre music, and probably rightly so. *The Prodigal Son* (1869) and *The Light of the World* (1873) went the rounds of the great festivals, and the cantatas *On Shore and Sea* (1871) and *The Golden Legend* (1886) had numerous performances. Revivals would not convince us that they were more than Victorian. Parry was versatile in quite another way than

Sullivan: his books probably stand on more shelves than do any of his odes and oratorios. Some of the music might well be heard again. He was praised for his mastery of textual accentuation and his ability to produce powerful climaxes. The *Ode at a Solemn Music* (1887) – a setting of lines by Milton 'Blest pair of Sirens' – and the oratorios *Judith* (1888) and *Job* (1892), out of a long list of similar works, probably represent Parry at his best. Stanford was a versatile and prolific composer but his work was uneven: it is discussed on p. 266. Another Victorian composer, Sir John Stainer (1840–91), achieved many performances and record sales with *The Crucifixion* (1887).

On the other side of the Atlantic Ocean a choral festival atmosphere existed where even the names of some of the festivals would have had a familiar look – if not sound – to the English visitor. The Handel and Haydn Society of Boston, the Worcester (Mass.) Festival, the New York Festival Choir were characteristic. George Whitfield Chadwick (1854–1931), who lived in Boston, was for a time conductor of the Worcester Festival. His *Viking's Last Voyage* (1881), *Noel* (1888), and *Phoenix expirans* (1892) were at least performed, while the thick scores of many of his American contemporaries gathered dust. His too now gather dust.

The present writer, as an American, must be forgiven for suggesting that perhaps with Horatio Parker we arrive at a minor climax. Performances at the Three Choirs Festival and at the Festivals at Chester, Hereford, Bristol, and Norwich, climaxed by the honour of a Mus.Doc. from Cambridge, seems pretty shiny! A large part of Parker's total output consisted of choral works. Among these the oratorios *Hora Novissima* (1893) and *The Legend of St Christopher* (1898) achieved the distinction of those Novello covers between which appeared the great majority of the works which formed the staple English choral diet. The last oratorio, *Morven and the Grail*, was written for the hundredth anniversary of the Boston Handel and Haydn Society (1915). *Hora Novissima* is a work that will bear rehearing, and it was revived in New York in 1937. The text was translated from a twelfth-century Latin poem entitled *De contemptu mundi* ('On Contempt of the World') written by Bernard de Morlaix of Cluny. The music was composed by a man who approached his work with no doubts concerning the expressive efficacy of the musical conventions of his own time. Within those conventions he created a minor masterpiece, deeply felt and completely realized. It has qualities of genuine sincerity, even eloquence, which may carry it through the cult of prejudice against works of its form, time, and place.

The market for new works has tapered off, or composers have lost interest in it, or two wars have taken the profit out of it, or more recent forms of mass entertainment have replaced it. But thousands of choirs still do parts or all of the *Messiah* every year. Do they never look at the vast literature produced for the market between *St Paul* and *Hora Novissima*?

13

The Mass – from Rossini to Dvořák

*c.*1835–1900

MOSCO CARNER

THEORISTS have often discussed whether there exists in
reality such a thing as a musical style which is definitely
ecclesiastical, or whether it is not a mere question of convention and the association of ideas. The problem is not an easy
one to decide. During the nineteenth century most composers of the front rank devoted themselves – with the
exception of Bruckner, and he only during his earlier period
– to secular music and only occasionally wrote a work for
the church. Symphony and opera, concerto and chamber
music – these were the principal fields in which such musicians worked; if they turned their attention to a Mass or a
Requiem, it was wholly natural that they should treat these
works in a style closely related to, if not indeed identical
with, their customary manner, except that counterpoint
played a more conspicuous part.

Of course the nature of the text asked for emotional restraint, for the replacement of subjective romantic feelings
by a more impersonal objective attitude; but in France and
Italy this was the case more in theory than in actual practice. Berlioz's Requiem (see p. 210) can certainly not be
held up as a paragon of how to write in an ecclesiastical
style. Rossini's Mass (*Petite Messe Solennelle*) and Verdi's
Requiem admittedly contain sections where a comparative
restraint has been practised, but it is evident that the two
masters approached the text from a quasi-operatic angle,
treating it with a dramatic conception that goes beyond what
listeners in northern Europe and America may find appropriate to the setting of a religious work. But it is just as well

to remind ourselves of the fact that it has always been the custom of southern peoples to dramatize their religion, and the Roman Catholic Church in these countries is giving true expression to national tendencies in surrounding its services with the glamour and sensuality of dramatic effect. In other words, it is the prerogative of the composer of opera in those lands to make his offering to God in his own kind.

In dealing with Gioachino Rossini (1792–1868) some words will not be found amiss on his *Stabat Mater* of 1842, one of the many settings by composers of the Latin poem about the vigil of Mary by the Cross. This work had a curious history. It was begun in Spain at the request of the Spanish prelate Varela, but on his return to Paris Rossini was seized with a severe attack of lumbago after the composition of the first six numbers. Being continually pestered to deliver the work, he entrusted the remainder to Tadolini, the conductor of the Théâtre Italien in Paris. In 1837 Varela died and his heirs decided to sell the publication rights to a French publisher, Aulagnier. Rossini, however, informed the latter with the utmost firmness that he would do everything in his power to prevent this, since he alone possessed these rights and sold them to his own publisher, Troupenas. He also revised and completed the work himself. The final fugue was written some time in the summer or autumn of 1841. By then eleven years had passed since Rossini had composed his last opera, *William Tell* (1829).

Rossini modelled his *Stabat Mater* on Pergolesi's (see p. 166). If we approach it as a religious work we shall be disappointed, for it is more secular in spirit than Verdi's Requiem, and in parts unashamedly theatrical. But if it is taken as music pure and simple, then not much fault can be found with it. Admittedly the last four numbers are superior, but there are also delightful things to be found in the first six. The introductory 'Stabat Mater' is perhaps the best of these – an expressive quartet for soli and chorus in G minor which Rossini repeated in the final number. Except for an unfortunate passage in $\frac{6}{8}$, the succeeding 'Eia Mater' has an eloquent chorus, and there is much harmonic variety in the ensuing 'Sancta Mater'. But the next number, 'Cuius animam', is a facile operatic aria for the tenor, and the following duet, 'Quis est homo', abounds in sentimental florid writing. Of the last four numbers every one recommends itself. There is much tender grace in the *cavatina* 'Fac ut portem', and the 'Inflammatus' impresses by the dramatic cut of the soprano solo which is set against a vivid chorus and reaches up to top C. As for 'Quando corpus morietur', recognized by Rossini himself as one of his most felicitous inspirations and much admired by Wagner, it is a splendid example of unaccompanied four-part writing. Perhaps the most successful number is the final double fugue, with two subjects in complementary rhythm; the first, 'In sempiterna saecula, Amen', has a boldly rising line which is freely imitated by the second fugue, on the word 'Amen'. There are several expositions and *stretto* sections, separated by episodes. Then, after the interpolated repetition of the first number, a mainly chordal coda brings the fugue to its impressive end. The first public performance of the *Stabat Mater* took place at the Salle Ventadour in Paris in January 1842, when it was an unqualified success.

More than twenty years later Rossini wrote the most successful of his sacred works – the *Petite Messe Solennelle*, which in an inscription to God he described as 'the last mortal sin of my old age'. He added: 'Have I written music that is blessed, or just some blessed music? I was born for *opera buffa*, well Thou knowest! Little knowledge and a little heart is all here. Be blest and grant me Paradise.' The idea of writing the work was not, as usually stated, due to a performance of Liszt's Mass in the Church of St Eustache, in Paris. The work had been contemplated by Rossini for some time before, and work on it made him, apparently, moody and irritable. Far from being '*petite*', it is longer than most Masses. The word must either have been a jest or must have referred to its original form, in which the four solo voices and small mixed chorus were given an accompaniment only of two pianos and an harmonium. Rossini later scored it for full orchestra, so as to prevent someone else doing it after his death, but he himself preferred it in the original version.

The Mass is far less operatic in style than the *Stabat Mater* and, although Rossini professed indifference to scholastic ingenuity, it contains contrapuntal sections of masterly skill which can easily stand comparison with Cherubini's Masses (see p. 182). Rossini told his friend, Michotte, that his main ambition in it was to leave a final legacy which might serve as an example of how to write for the voice. Beauty and originality of melody, and audacity of harmony are other characteristics, though the latter is, in Rossini's own words, 'often coated with sugar'.

The Kyrie, in A, contains some of the best ecclesiastical counterpoint – notably in the 'Christe eleison', in C minor, where, at one bar's distance, the choral voices are linked in pairs, bass with alto and tenor with soprano. The Gloria, in F, opens in a jubilant manner, but from 'Et in terra pax', which is chiefly for the four soloists, the mood is subdued. The ensuing 'Gratias agimus tibi' is a tenderly moving trio; the tenor aria in D, 'Domine Deus', smacks perhaps too much of opera but is remarkable for its modulations to distant keys. In the following 'Qui tollis peccata mundi' the two women soloists are given music of noble tragedy to sing; the piece begins in F minor and ends in F major. 'Quoniam tu solus sanctus' is an extended aria in A for the bass soloist, rich in melodic and harmonic beauties. One of the finest things in this Mass is the double fugue 'Cum sancto spiritu' (Example 50).

Not only is the subject full of character and variety, but the treatment, if somewhat lengthy, is most varied, containing a *smorzando* section, in which counterpoint yields to effective homophonic contrast, and a most imaginative coda.

The Credo derives its great impact from the combination of the voices with an *ostinato* figure for the piano which is first one bar and then half a bar long. The piece modulates from E through various keys to A flat in which key the soprano solo intones the 'Crucifixus'. Then, after the repeat of the Credo music, there follows the powerful double fugue, 'Et vitam venturi'. With the ensuing 'Religious Prelude' Rossini gave proof that his subscription to the

Ex. 50. Rossini, *Mass*

complete works of Bach had not been without its practical use; the piece, which is for organ or piano, is an admirable essay in intricate four-part writing. The Sanctus and Benedictus, which follow each other without interruption, are set for unaccompanied chorus. Rossini then breaks with the authorized text of the Mass by inserting the Latin hymn 'O salutaris hostia' ('O saving victim') which he sets as a contralto aria, notable both for the beauty and length of its phrases and for its modulations. Equally noteworthy is the final chorus with contralto solo in which, combined with an *ostinato*, the Agnus Dei is thrice uttered to the identical melody but different harmony. This is followed by a new and more contrapuntal section, which in the last bars turns to the key of E major.

The Mass was first performed in 1864 at the house of the Countess Pillet-Will in Paris. Leading artists of the Théâtre Italien sang the solo parts, and the chorus was selected by Auber from the best students of the Paris Conservatory.

It was the death of Rossini in 1868 that gave Giuseppe Verdi (1813–1901) the idea of proposing that a Requiem Mass should be written by leading Italian composers in collaboration to be performed on the next anniversary of

Rossini's death in the church of San Petronio at Bologna (the town where Rossini had spent his boyhood). The scheme came to nothing – in Verdi's view, because of lack of collaboration on the part of his friend Angelo Mariani, the famous conductor, whom he suspected of resentment because he had not been included among the composers, and, more certainly, because of hostility on the part of Scalaberni, the impresario of the Teatro Comunale at Bologna, who refused to permit his singers and orchestra to take part. The net result was that Verdi was left with his own contribution to the collective Requiem, the 'Libera me' for solo soprano and chorus. Then, in 1873, occurred the death of Alessandro Manzoni, author of the classic Italian novel *I Promessi Sposi* (*The Betrothed*) and one of the very few human beings before whom Verdi bowed his head. Verdi proposed to the Mayor of Milan that he should write a Requiem to be performed in the following year, and incorporated in it his contribution to the abortive work in memory of Rossini.

To the smart judgement that the Requiem is 'Verdi's finest opera', the best answer is to be found in what the composer's widow said when commenting on certain adverse criticisms that had been made of the work. Giuseppina Verdi wrote:

They talk a lot about the more or less religious spirit of Mozart, Cherubini, and others. I say that a man like Verdi must write like Verdi, that is, according to his own feeling and interpreting of the text. The religious spirit and the way in which it is given expression must bear the stamp of its period and its author's personality. I would deny the authorship of a Mass by Verdi that was modelled on the manner of A, B, or C.

We cannot indeed expect Verdi to have shed his personality in writing the Requiem. If here and there we are reminded that opera was after all his *métier*, we note on the other hand that while most of his operatic ensembles portray a conflict of emotion in the personalities on the stage, in the Requiem such conflict within ensembles is non-existent. Superficially, the fiercest contrasts reign between

its seven sections, but they are merely different manifestations of a unity that lies in the prayer for the dead soul's
peace.

Melody and harmony in the opening 'Requiem aeternam' are given to the muted strings, the four-part chorus
only whispering the prayer in more or less broken declamation until the beautiful fugal section, 'Te decet hymnus',
brings the first agitation for the unaccompanied voices.
With 'Kyrie eleison' begins a new section in which the four
solos and, presently, the chorus share the melody with the
orchestra. The longest section is a setting of the 'Dies irae',
a text depicting the Last Judgement. Its great orchestral
chords, with the bass drum marking the unaccented beats,
its rushing of strings, and its partly chromatic choral shouts,
suggest a mood of darkness and despair. This is unquestionably the most dramatic part of the Requiem.

Then trumpets, both in the orchestra and placed at a distance, suitably reproduce the sound of the 'last trumpet' in
the choral 'Tuba mirum'. The bass solo, as if terrified,
declaims the 'Mors stupebit' ('Death will be aghast').
This is followed by an extended dramatic section for the
mezzo-soprano, while the chorus mutter from time to time
their 'Dies irae'. The wide compass of this solo — from B
below the stave up to high A flat — is noteworthy. After
the repeat of the choral 'Dies irae', clarinets and bassoons
introduce the moving trio in $\frac{6}{8}$, 'Quid sum miser', which is
sung by the two women and the tenor soloists. In 'Rex
tremendae majestatis' the choral basses are entrusted with
a majestic motive while the remaining parts of the chorus
and the soli execute counterpoints on 'Salva me, fons pietatis'.

A lyrical duet for soprano and mezzo-soprano, 'Record-
are, Jesu pie', leads to an extended tenor solo accompanied
by expressive orchestral triplets; and finally a bass solo
declaims, in virile tones, the 'Confutatis maledictis'. These
last three sections, all for the soloists, are rounded off by
the choral 'Dies irae'. Now begins once more, 'with great
expression', the 'Lacrymosa', whose simple, almost child-
like melody might have come from one of Verdi's early
operatic ensembles. The mezzo-soprano opens with it,

and then combines with oboe and clarinet into a lamenting counterpoint while simultaneously the bass solo repeats the melody. Out of this a choral movement of solemn beauty and musical complexity is engendered (Example 51). The soloists now intone, unaccompanied and in a style of great ecclesiastical purity, the final prayer to Jesus; the chorus takes the text up to the original melody ('Lacrymosa'); and the whole movement would seem about to expire – when, on the word 'Amen', there occurs an unexpected and, in the harmonic context, magical modulation from B flat major to G major which is supported by a *crescendo* to *forte* and a *diminuendo* again to *pianissimo*. The close of the movement, for the orchestra alone, is in B flat, the relative major of G minor, in which key the movement had begun. Into a mere six bars Verdi concentrated the expression of a poetic idea and the musical rounding-off of a vast movement.

The Offertorium does not invite such dramatic treatment. It is only at the words 'sed signifer sanctus Michael' ('But the holy standard-bearer Michael') that the soprano solo indulges in something like operatic behaviour. 'Quam olim Abrahae' makes a feint at a fugue but soon settles down to secure homophony, and this is followed by the peaceful strain 'Hostias et preces' for the four soloists. The Sanctus, after being ushered in by trumpet fanfares and three choral shouts, takes the form of a double fugue for two choruses. Pedants may frown upon it, but for others its two themes and the handling of them are most felicitous. The fugue is brought to a glorious close by augmentations to the word 'Pleni sunt coeli' and 'Hosanna'. The Agnus Dei, the shortest piece, opens with the two women soloists singing, in octaves and unaccompanied, a broad peaceful melody which shows a perfect compromise between Verdi's individual melodic style and liturgical tradition. There follows the 'Lux aeterna', which takes the form of a trio for mezzosoprano, tenor, and bass, and begins in uncertain tonality. It is a solemn and, in parts, sombre movement.

And so we arrive at 'Libera me', surviving from the original Requiem intended for Rossini. Here at last it is the soprano solo who is given the lead. In a recitative (marked

Ex. 51. Verdi, *Requiem*

senza misura, that is, 'in free rhythm' in the first bar) she
prays for deliverance from the pains of hell, and her prayer
is repeated by the chorus. Then the 'Dies irae' returns from
the earlier movement; then the soprano and unaccompanied chorus recall the opening 'Requiem aeternam',
after which the introductory recitative is repeated. The
ensuing fugue cannot be faulted from the technical point
of view, but it is its character – cheerful to the point of
jauntiness – that unfits it to be the coping-stone of this great
edifice. Not until the soprano solo joins in with an aug-
mentation of the theme does the piece approach the grandeur and tragic nobility of the rest of the Requiem. The
first performance of the work took place at St Mark's
Church, Milan, in 1874, under Verdi's direction.

Verdi also composed four *Sacred Pieces* (*Pezzi sacri*).
The *Ave Maria* for unaccompanied chorus and the *Stabat
Mater* for chorus and orchestra were written shortly before
his last opera, *Falstaff* (1893); the *Te Deum* for chorus and
orchestra, and the *Laudi* (Praises in honour of the Virgin
Mary, to a text of Dante) for unaccompanied chorus were
his last works. In the *Stabat Mater*, Verdi repeats not a
single word in his setting of the text, and the sombre opening given out by the chorus in unison sets the appropriate
atmosphere at once. This miniature, which shows a most
individual harmonic style and is admirably scored, deserves
to be mentioned in almost the same breath as the Requiem.

The most considerable of the four *Sacred Pieces* is the *Te
Deum*, which uses a large orchestra including an English
horn. Verdi did not use the text ('We praise thee, O God')
as the majority of composers do – to celebrate occasions of
public rejoicing – but concentrated on the basic thought of
this canticle, which is a prayer for deliverance from the
wrath to come and the avowal of trust in God's mercy.
The setting is very dramatic and is based upon two themes
of liturgical character and provenance. The first theme
opens the work, providing the subject for the subsequent
chorus, and the second occurs on the trumpets before the
words 'Tu rex gloriae' and is then treated in complex
eight-part writing. The orchestral handling is as vivid as

it is elaborate. The four *Sacred Pieces* were performed for the first time in Paris in Holy Week, 1898, and then in Italy at the Turin Exhibition that year under the young Arturo Toscanini.

Verdi did not associate himself with the Church as such. But Bruckner's almost fanatical attachment to the Roman Catholic faith not only determined his entire outlook on life but was also the chief inspiration of his art. Of the Austrian composers of the nineteenth century, Anton Bruckner (1824–96) was the most religious. Though in determining his general position in the history of music his symphonies are more important, the best of his church music raises him to the front rank of nineteenth- and twentieth-century composers for the Catholic Church. There is no fundamental difference between the style of his symphonies and that of his religious works; the former are to a large extent the continuation in instrumental terms of the latter. In the Masses in D minor and F minor, the orchestra takes a considerable share in the general texture of the music, and is given themes of its own independently from the choral material. These themes are subjected to elaboration in a truly symphonic manner. Moreover, there are many thematic similarities to be found between the Masses and the symphonies, similarities which spring from characteristic fingerprints of Bruckner's general style, as Example 52 (p. 242) shows.

It was while he was a cathedral organist at Linz, up till 1868, that Bruckner wrote his Masses. Thereafter, living in Vienna (where he wrote eight of his nine numbered symphonies), he wrote only two major works of a devotional character, the *Te Deum* and his setting of Psalm 150, neither of which was intended for religious service. (For the former, see also p. 254.) But no less than seven Masses are extant from his early period; and of these the Masses in D minor, E minor, and F minor, are masterpieces, each representing a different solution of the composer's problem of setting the text of the Mass. The first and the third are orchestral or festival Masses; characteristic of them is their symphonic form and texture. Haydn, Mozart, Beethoven (Mass in

Ex. 52. Bruckner, *Mass in F minor*

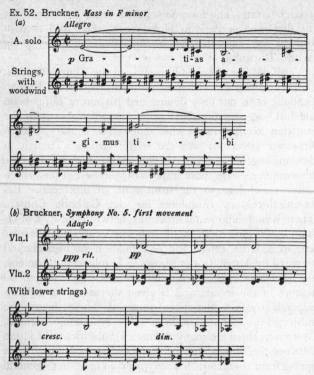

D), and Schubert are here the chief models, but Bruckner goes also further back to Gregorian plainsong and the polyphony of the Palestrina period; at the same time, the melodic and harmonic novelties of his own romantic age, especially those indebted to Wagner, are not ignored. It was the symphonic grandeur of the Masses in D minor and F minor which aroused the hostility of the purists in the Roman Catholic Church – the Cecilians – a hostility which, ultimately, drove the composer into the camp of their opponents.

Yet, aware of the antagonism that divided the Church in the matter of musical settings of the Mass, he had attempted a pacification in writing, in 1866, the Mass in E minor, which is an eight-part vocal work with wind accompaniment. The work was intended to conform more closely to the pattern of what was regarded as 'official' church music. Apart from being much simpler than the other two Masses, it shows a certain bridge between the old modes and modern tonality. This Mass was repeatedly revised (mainly as to the instrumental parts) and not published till 1890.

The Mass in F minor, which is Bruckner's largest choral work, was written in 1867–8 at the end of his Linz period, and its composition was partly overshadowed by his serious breakdown of 1867. Its first performance took place in 1872 at St Augustine's Church in Vienna under the composer's direction. Brahms, who attended, was deeply moved by it, as were Hellmesberger, Herbeck, Hanslick, Dessof, and many others of Vienna's musical notabilities. Bruckner subjected the work to repeated revisions in 1872, 1876, 1881, and 1883. In a final version undertaken shortly before publication in 1894, the number of horns was increased from two to four.

The Kyrie is dominated by a step-wise descending motive of four notes which gives expression to a feeling of contrition. (It shows a curious resemblance to the opening figure in Verdi's Requiem.) The 'Christe eleison', beginning in A flat and modulating to D and G flat, operates through a new figure of wide steps (fifth and octave), and the addition of solo passages to the chorus introduces a more subjective feeling. The third part returns to the opening but interpolates an unaccompanied 'Kyrie eleison' of great intensity before closing in an abject mood. The Gloria in C opens with a theme of jubilation. Twice in its later course it is given to the solo, and finally comes to rest in the key of D minor. 'Qui tollis peccata mundi' is set in a contrapuntal manner, with a marked symphonic treatment of the orchestra. After the next section has repeated the 'Gloria' theme in the fashion of a sonata recapitulation, a double fugue of majestic proportions follows whose festive march character is emphasized by the instrumental accompaniment.

The Credo is the most extensive movement and the

centre of the Mass, having connexions with both the preceding and succeeding movements. The first part in C is largely a unison, with a Gregorian theme for its main idea. In the 'Incarnatus' and 'Crucifixus', the tenor and bass soloists combine with the chorus against a throbbing orchestra, the pace being slow. The 'Et resurrexit' is dealt with in a mainly chordal *allegro*, with a slightly broader coda on the words 'cuius regnum'. After a reprise of the opening of the movement, to which the words 'Et in spiritum sanctum' are now set, a new section in G ensues, with a *fugato* for the four soloists. The climax of the movement is reached in the breathtaking double fugue 'Et vitam venturi' where of particular interest is the shape of the subject, based on the Credo theme: its harmonized version is tacked on as counter-subject, and this provides regular chordal interruptions in the majestic flow of choral polyphony (Example 53).

Ex. 53. Bruckner, *Mass in F minor*

The Sanctus is the shortest of the movements. In its first part (*moderato*) it reverts to the 'Christe eleison' theme of the Kyrie; the second part (*allegro*) begins in Gregorian style but then continues in a manner more typically Bruckner's own.

The Benedictus opens (*andante*) with a tender eight-bar orchestral prelude which anticipates the first of the two choral themes. This is a melody which moves by steps and is announced by the alto solo, and repeated, at a bar's distance, by the soprano and then the tenor solo. The second melody, a wide-ranging theme (which Bruckner employed again in the *Adagio* of his Symphony No. 2) is given to the bass solo and freely repeated by the women's chorus. These two melodies are twice reiterated, but each time with extensions and other modifications. An instrumental epilogue leads to an Allegro which repeats the corresponding section of the Sanctus.

In the Agnus Dei, which returns to F minor, a short orchestral prelude announces a tragic theme that forms a counterpoint to the ensuing ideas put forward by chorus and soloists. At 'Dona nobis pacem', minor changes to major, the step-wise descending fourth and the choral octave of the opening Kyrie makes a brief appearance, and shortly before the end Bruckner recalls the fugal subject from the Gloria and the first of the themes of the Credo.

For Bruckner's Czech contemporary, Antonin Dvořák (1841–1904), religious music represented not much more than a side-line in his prolific output. But for sheer beauty of invention and sincerity of expression, some of his religious works can bear comparison with the finest of his instrumental music. The place of such works as the *Stabat Mater* (Prague, 1880) and the Requiem (Birmingham, 1891), both for four soloists, chorus, and orchestra, is not on the shelves of a music library but in the live atmosphere of the concert-hall. So also with the *Te Deum* (New York, 1892) for soprano and bass solos, chorus, and orchestra. From 1877, when he worked on the *Stabat Mater*, to 1894, the date of the *Biblical Songs* for voice and piano, we count altogether eight compositions of a religious nature – a proof that, even if some were written as pieces demanded by a particular occasion, the setting of the religious music signified for Dvořák more than a mere convention to which almost every nineteenth-century composer was expected to pay his tribute. It is true that he was at heart an instrumental composer, and felt generally hampered rather than inspired by words. All the same, he succeeded in expressing the meaning and feeling of the liturgical text in an effective manner.

Broadly speaking, Dvořák may be said to be at his most inspired when setting those sections that give expression to grief, pathos, suffering, drama, and exaltation – in the movingly expressive lyricism of the *Stabat Mater*, for instance, or the dramatic climaxes of the Requiem, the Mass (1881), and the *Te Deum*. On the other hand, those sections in which the text is in a meditative vein, inviting contemplation, show in the setting a falling-off of the melodic invention and do not escape the charge of conventionality.

In his formal division of the text Dvořák follows the tradition as he found it in classical church music, though in details he goes his own way. In the musical treatment he successfully observes balance, contrast, and emotional weight. But where the 'absolute' musician in Dvořák tends to go astray is in the thematic handling of the individual numbers. He frequently resorts to the device of splitting up a vocal melody into its constituent motives, with which he operates in the manner of an instrumental development. That the musical texture gains thereby cannot be denied, but the defects of this method in a predominantly vocal composition are only too evident. This quasi-instrumental handling leads to unnecessary length, and entails consequently the stretching of the text to fit the music. The result is tedious word-repetition. In constructing 'symphonic' texture Dvořák also fails to pay much attention to a detailed musical characterization of word-pictures. Yet this does not mean that these works lack the sense of characterization altogether. A splendid example is found, for instance, in the leading-motive of the Requiem, which symbolizes the idea of death and mourning and which pervades the entire work, thus giving it spiritual and thematic unity.

A few words may not be amiss on the various influences to which Dvořák was subjected. Reared as he was in the classical tradition, he saw his chief models in the church music of Beethoven, Schubert, and – this was due to his frequent visits to England – Handel. It was above all Han-

del's vigorous, majestic choral style that left its mark on
Dvořák's choruses. It is Bach, however, with whom Dvořák
shows affinity in his *Te Deum*, particularly in the vital
rhythm of the first movement. Cast in the form of a miniature choral symphony, it is also full of imaginative touches
in the orchestra. The *Te Deum* is a strikingly original work –
perhaps the most felicitous contribution Dvořák made to
religious music. Also not without influence on Dvořák were
such composers of the romantic period as Berlioz, Mendelssohn, and Liszt. The principal motive in the 'Quis est homo'
of Dvořák's *Stabat Mater* is almost identical with a figure in
the 'Lacrymosa' of Berlioz's Requiem (see p. 210). Wagner's
influence, which was strongest in Dvořák's early and very
late periods, manifests itself chiefly in certain harmonic
predilections, notably in progressions of secondary sevenths.
The Verdi of the Requiem also left his mark, as may be
seen in the typically Italianate character of certain melodies
in Dvořák's own Requiem – for instance, the 'Rex tremendae majestatis' and the 'Confutatis maledictis'.

A different kind of influence went very deep with Dvořák:
the national element of Czech folk music. Generally speaking, the broadness and straightforwardness of his melodic
style and the melancholy that informs many lyrical passages of the *Stabat Mater*, the Requiem, and the Mass are
of a general Slavonic heritage. But there are numerous other
passages in these works of a more tangible form of musical
nationalism, such as the influence of medieval Czech hymns,
pentatonic turns in the melody and certain rhythmic patterns which derive from Slavonic dances. The 'folk' influence is also evident in Dvořák's part-songs for mixed
voices and men's voices. These, and Dvořák's longer
secular choral works, are dealt with in Chapter 17.

14

Chorus and Symphony: Liszt, Mahler, and After

from c.1850

DERYCK COOKE

THIS chapter concerns an anomalous but extremely important aspect of choral music – its assimilation into the symphony, an assimilation which was an innovation of the romantic movement.

The sudden triumph of humanism, achieved by the French Revolution after centuries of struggle, resulted in a changed attitude to life. The classical conception of man, as the servant of a static civilization governed by church and state authority, yielded to the romantic conception of the dynamic free individual, working in brotherhood with his fellows towards full self-realization in a perfect society created by himself. And the new conception found expression in music, as in the other arts: the artisan-composer, using traditional forms to provide liturgical music for the church and entertainment music for aristocratic patrons, was superseded by the free artist, expressing his own mystical or social ideals in forms of his own devising.

This new attitude naturally affected the most human element in music – the voice, solo and *en masse*. Before 1800, composers wrote choral music in accepted forms for the forces to hand, and, with few exceptions, wrote within the capabilities of their singers. But after 1800, composers felt entitled to introduce a chorus into any work, according to expressive need, and to write for it as they pleased, regardless of technical difficulty.

Among great composers, Beethoven was the pioneer of this, as of other romantic innovations. Composers who had abandoned orthodox religious beliefs found the traditional religious choral forms, such as the liturgical Mass, inadequate to express man's new aspirations; humanism demanded new forms, and the first was the symphony – as refashioned by Beethoven. In the *Eroica* and the Fifth, he voiced magnificently man's struggle against fate and his victory over it. But his final representation of this struggle – the Ninth Symphony (1824) – was on so tremendous a scale that he felt the need of something more than the customary orchestral 'triumph-finale'. Man himself must be called in – and men and women in the mass – to proclaim human aspiration, both political and mystical, in unambiguous verbal form. (See p. 205.) Beethoven's novel conception had a considerable influence: it not only permitted direct expression of the composer's idea, but it solved the 'finale problem'. With the growing size and intensity of symphonic compositions, composers found it hard to build a finale powerful enough to crown a big work; but the Ninth Symphony showed the way to a successful apotheosis, complete with those elements of the programmatic, the visionary, the theatrical, and the colossal, which were all part of the romantic conception of man's elevation to the status of Superman.

The first 'choral symphony' after Beethoven's – Berlioz's *Romeo and Juliet* of 1839 – was hardly in the direct line of succession. (See p. 213.) Mendelssohn's Symphony No. 2 – the *Hymn of Praise* (*Lobgesang*) of 1840 – might seem a more legitimate successor to Beethoven's Ninth, since it comprises three orchestral movements with choral Finale; but there is a crucial difference. The orchestral part is not, like Beethoven's, a big symphonic drama creating instrumental tension which cries out for choral release, but a modest three-part introduction to a large self-sufficient cantata. And this cantata is an orthodox Protestant one, clothing biblical texts traditionally in conventional types of recitative, aria, chorale, and choral fugue.

Only with the second wave of revolutionary romanticism did a composer appear who adapted Beethoven's conception to his own ends – Franz Liszt (1811–86). His oratorios have already been mentioned. (See p. 223.) We are here concerned with the *Faust Symphony* and *Dante Symphony*. These are admittedly illustrative works, no less than Berlioz's *Romeo and Juliet*, but they are true symphonies, and the programmes are of a different kind. The literary models express man's mystical aspirations, and Liszt chose them for this reason: in each case, the orchestral part presents a conflict between good and evil, which is resolved into a mystical vision by the choral ending. Nevertheless, three important features differentiate these works from Beethoven's conception. The choral section does not practically monopolize the Finale, but is a brief epilogue; the chorus is not a large one of 'triumphant humanity' but a small one of 'redemptive divinity'; and the choral writing is extremely simple.

The legend of Faust, as told in Goethe's great poetic drama (part I, 1808; part II, 1831), inspired nearly all the romantics, and it impelled Liszt to compose what is probably his masterpiece. Faust, like Don Juan, Manfred, and the Devil himself, was one of those mythical figures in whom the romantics saw an image of their own quest: he personified the dangerous dynamic instincts of man, which, long held in check by the classical civilization, were now being released in the interests of human self-realization. Goethe's *Faust* contains three of these elements, each potent for good or evil – man's search for more than human knowledge and power (Faust himself), the sexual instinct (the Gretchen episode), and the restless demonic urge which spurs men on to new discoveries but threatens them with destruction (Mephistopheles). Liszt had much of both Faust and Mephistopheles in his temperament, and had loved many a Gretchen, so he was well qualified to compose *A Faust Symphony in Three Character Portraits*.

The first movement, portraying Faust, is a turbulent Allegro with slow introduction, built out of themes representing Faust's thirst for knowledge, his suffering, his yearning for love, and his will to triumph. Gretchen is portrayed in a beautifully delicate, if slightly sentimental Andante, into which Faust's 'suffering' and 'yearning' themes intrude violently. Mephistopheles appears in a diabolical Scherzo, laughing Faust's ideals to scorn, parodying his themes and

juggling with them cynically. And here, when he composed
the work in 1854, Liszt left it, with a brief coda alluding to
Gretchen and to Faust's 'will to triumph'. But he soon
realized that this left Mephistopheles victorious; something
more was needed to exorcise the spell of that long and magnificent Scherzo. Liszt's temperament demanded a resolution of humanistic striving in terms of religion. And so the
choral Finale was forced on him, as on Beethoven – but for
different reasons: Faust (and mankind) must be redeemed,
as in Goethe. In 1857, he composed a new coda – a short
setting for tenor and men's chorus of the famous Chorus
Mysticus which concludes Goethe's drama:

All that is transient is only a symbol; the unattainable is here
attained; the unimaginable is here achieved; the Eternal-Womanly
[Goethe's untranslatable conception, *Das Ewig-Weibliche*] leads
us onwards.

Liszt integrated his choral coda beautifully with the whole
work: the new choral theme takes up the rhythm of the
symphony's opening (Faust's 'search for knowledge' theme),
and converts its eerie melodic augmented triads into a bold
major one (Example 54). The choral coda begins as a simple
rhythmic chanting in unison, and this simplicity is

Ex. 54. Liszt, *Faust Symphony*

maintained to the end – unison giving way to octaves and
finally to block chords. It is entirely appropriate to the beatific
resolution of humanity's spiritual conflict; choral complexity – imitation and fugue – would be quite unsuitable.
The sense of being led onward is conveyed by the almost
operatic line of the tenor soloist, soaring above the chorus
and leading the symphony to an affirmative *fortissimo* conclusion.

The *Dante Symphony* (1855–6) is similar in conception –
a journey through states of good and evil to a transcendent
choral epilogue – but here the vision belongs to the world
of Roman Catholicism (which attracted Liszt so strongly
that he eventually took lay orders). When he began his
Symphony to Dante's Divine Comedy, he intended three movements – 'Inferno', 'Purgatorio', and 'Paradiso'; but unfortunately Wagner persuaded him that no human being could
portray the joys of heaven, and thereby probably robbed us
of a full-blown choral finale. Liszt contented himself with
two movements – 'Inferno' and 'Purgatorio' – concluding
the latter with a setting of the *Magnificat* for women's (or
boys') choir, to suggest a distant vision of heaven.

The 'Inferno' movement has a slow introduction, in which
baleful trombones intone a theme based on the rhythm of
the motto over Dante's hell-gate: '*lasciate ogni speranza, voi
ch'entrate*' ('Abandon all hope, ye who enter here'). The
main Allegro represents Hell itself:

I heard sighing, crying and wailing in the starless air . . . diverse
tongues, terrible ravings, shrieks of grief and screams of rage.

Again, as in the *Faust Symphony*, the equivocal sexual
element appears, in a pathetic central episode depicting
the two lovers Paolo and Francesca, eternally damned for
their illicit carnal passion; after which the uproar of Hell
resumes and concludes the movement.

The 'Purgatorio' movement is a broad Andante, opening
with murmurous strings and harp ('the sweet colour of sap-
phire in the eastern sky gladdened my eyes as I emerged
from the dead air of Hell'). The central section expresses
the pangs of repentant sinners in a truly purgatorial fugue

on a *lamentoso* subject; then the string and harp murmurings
return, and woodwind phrases foreshadow the theme of the
choral epilogue. Liszt uses the theatrical potentialities
inherent in the long-delayed entry of the voices, directing
that his choir shall be invisible, or, if that is impossible,
placed well above the orchestra. The setting of the *Magnificat*, like that of the 'Chorus Mysticus' in the *Faust Symphony*, is appropriately simple: Liszt avoided any suggestion
of tastelessness by writing a serenely joyful melody in
plainsong style, and presenting it in unison or two-part
medieval-type counterpoint, and occasionally in basic chord-
progressions. The work ends with high *pianissimo* chords for
woodwind, strings, and harp; the alternative *fortissimo*
conclusion, which Liszt provided to please Princess Sayn-
Wittgenstein, is quite unthinkable as the climax of a
distant beatific vision.

After this, no important choral symphony appeared for
forty years – the humanistic ideal found other musical out-
lets, notably in the dramatic solo voices of Wagner's
music-dramas – but two works claim brief attention. César
Franck (1822–90) composed *Psyche* (1886–8) which has
been called 'a choral symphony of love', but has less claim
to this title than Berlioz's *Romeo and Juliet*. It is, in fact, a
large symphonic poem in six sections, dramatizing the old
Greek legend of Eros and Psyche, the last four sections
introducing two soloists and mixed chorus. Franck used the
subject as a vehicle for his own personal Catholic conception of divine love. This fascinating work deserves a full
performance (only the orchestral sections are ever heard);
but it is in no sense a choral symphony.

The First Symphony (1889) of Alexander Skryabin
(1872–1915) is, on the other hand, the genuine article. An
orchestral Prologue is followed by the usual four symphonic
movements (Allegro, Lento, Scherzo, and Vivace); after
which the final sixth movement is a large-scale setting, for
mezzo-soprano, tenor, and mixed chorus, of a 'Hymn to
Art' by the composer himself (glorifying the civilizing power
of Harmony, like the text of Beethoven's *Choral Fantasia*).
Unfortunately, the choral Finale is quite unmotivated – it

seems merely tacked on – and the whole symphony is of negligible value. A youthful work, composed when Skryabin was a student at the Moscow Conservatory, it shows remarkable fluency and promise, but gives no indication of his later mastery in the field of free chromaticism; the concluding choral fugue is a pure examination-piece.

At this point, we may consider why Bruckner (1824–96) never wrote a choral symphony – a feat for which he was singularly well equipped. The reason is that he had no humanistic interest in glorifying art, progress, or personal concepts of religion; the transcendental longings of his peasant soul were fully satisfied by the liturgy of the Roman Catholic Church, for which he composed three great Masses (see p. 241). When, in the Finale of his huge Fifth Symphony (1876), he borrowed from Beethoven's *Choral* the device of parading themes from previous movements and dismissing them, it was only to clear the air for a magnificent orchestral solution of the 'finale problem' – a vast structure combining sonata, fugue, and brass chorale. And when, on his deathbed in 1896, realizing that he would never complete the purely orchestral finale of his Ninth Symphony, he suggested that his great choral *Te Deum* might serve instead, it was a mere counsel of despair: the Symphony is in D minor, the *Te Deum* in C, and they are entirely separate works.

It was the last wave of revolutionary romanticism which threw up the true inheritor of Beethoven's conception. Gustav Mahler (1860–1911) was full of the same divine unrest and humanistic aspiration as Beethoven; but being a characteristic figure of the self-doubting late-romantic period, he sensed more keenly the terrible difficulty which stood in the way of humanistic perfectionism – the weakness of humanity. If he lacked Beethoven's supreme symphonic mastery and classical balance, he nevertheless charted more comprehensively the whole battlefield of the human spirit, exploring the furthermost poles of despair and exultation. It may well have been his special awareness of the danger of spiritual defeat (expressed with great cogency in his instrumental works) that impelled him to reach out for a religious assurance – to erect defiantly his gigantic choral and orchestral structures, involving a much-expanded orchestra, chorus, and time-scale.

His Symphony No. 2 (The 'Resurrection' Symphony, 1887–94) demands a large orchestra, with off-stage brass band and organ; as in Berlioz's *Fantastic Symphony*, there are five movements, and as in Beethoven's Ninth, the Finale employs soloists (soprano and contralto) and chorus. The first movement, a lengthy *Allegro maestoso*, Mahler originally entitled 'Ceremony for the Dead'. Basically a funeral march of great tragic power, it generates a tension akin to that of the equivalent movement in Beethoven's Ninth: it poses, according to Mahler's programme, 'the great question – Why did you live? Why did you die? Is it all nothing but a huge, frightful joke?' The next two movements form an interlude – a wistful *Ländler* evoking 'a long-past hour of bliss', and a sardonic Scherzo portraying 'the never-resting, never-comprehensible bustle of life'. Then follows a complete innovation – a movement for solo voice and orchestra. The contralto steals in straight away, dispelling the restless nagging of the Scherzo with a rapt, hymn-like setting of the old religious folk-poem *Urlicht* (*Primordial Light*): 'I am from God, and to God will return.'

Like Beethoven, Mahler had reached the point where he needed – in his own words – to 'bring in the word to convey the musical idea'; but he still had finale trouble. Three years passed before he found the solution: at von Bülow's funeral in 1894, the choir sang a setting of the *Resurrection Ode* by the German poet Klopstock (1724–1803), and Mahler realized that this was the text he had been seeking.* His enormous Finale resumes the unresolved argument of his first movement with a long and lurid orchestral portrayal of the Day of Judgement: 'The dead arise and stream on in endless procession [the off-stage band is first heard here]; the cry for mercy strikes fearfully upon our ears.' Finally the distant last trumpet is heard, and the chorus emerges

* A fascinating psychological explanation of the reason for Mahler's delay and his final decision can be found in the book by Theodor Reik listed in the Bibliography.

magically out of silence, with the spell-binding effect of massed voices murmuring unaccompanied. Together with the soprano soloist, they sing Mahler's setting of Klopstock's *Resurrection Ode* – 'Thou shalt rise again, my dust, after a short rest' (Example 55). Like Liszt, Mahler begins

Ex. 55. Mahler, *Symphony No. 2*

simply – with a theme of the German chorale type, in block harmony – and for a time he maintains this simplicity, the soprano soloist occasionally rising *pianissimo* out of the choral mass with exquisite effect. But soon, as in Beethoven's Ninth, the music quickens to complex life: the voices take over the remaining half of the Finale, to words added by Mahler himself, which answer the questions of his first movement. After a pleading contralto solo – 'O believe, my heart, you did not live in vain, suffer in vain!' – male voices proclaim the certainty of resurrection, and the two soloists soar in urgent imitative passages, defying despair and death. Then the chorus takes up the words 'On new-won wings I shall soar on high' in a quasi-fugal development, and the work ends with a triumphant *fortissimo* statement, by chorus and orchestra, of the *Resurrection* chorale.

In his Symphony No. 3 (1893–6), Mahler again used a chorus, but in a much more reticent way. The Third is not a choral symphony, but an anomalous work, like Berlioz's *Romeo and Juliet*, hardly referable to the true symphonic tradition – a vast programmatic affair, presenting a Dionysiac vision of life as a great chain of being, extending from elemental nature to the love of God. Part I is an out-size sonata-movement representing the primeval force of nature burgeoning out of winter into summer. Part II comprises five shorter movements, balancing Part I in combined weight: a 'flower' minuet; a 'birds and beasts' scherzo; a nocturne concerned with the questionings of humanity (contralto solo); a choral movement portraying the joy of angels (women's and boys' voices); and an orchestral Adagio-Finale hymning the love of God. The 'angel' movement – a setting of the old folk-poem 'Three angels were singing' ('*Es sungen drei Engel*') – has a carol-like simplicity and charm. To a light accompaniment of woodwind, horns, glockenspiel, bells, two harps, and strings without violins, the women sing a gay folk-like melody, while the boys imitate the sound of bells to the syllables 'Bimm-Bamm'. The piece would make a delight-ful effect if performed on its own, with the accompaniment arranged for organ.

In his colossal Symphony No. 8 (1906–7), Mahler carried Beethoven's conception to its logical conclusion by writing the first fully choral symphony. Known as 'The Symphony of a Thousand', the work calls for eight soloists, two large mixed choirs, boys' choir, a very large orchestra, and organ. Such size may awaken suspicions of megalomania, but to consider the problem Mahler faced is to realize that he was compelled to use such huge forces by sheer necessity.

For his text he chose two poems which express man's spiritual longings from complementary points of view – the medieval Latin hymn *Veni Creator Spiritus* ('Come, Spirit that Creates'), which states the orthodox religious view; and the closing scene of Goethe's *Faust* (not merely the final *Chorus Mysticus*, like Liszt), which presents the questing humanistic conception. The two texts coincide in stressing humanity's need for creative inspiration, wis-dom, power, and love; and Mahler set out to affirm man's

aspiration towards complete possession of these qualities,
and the assurance that he must attain it.

The symphony is in two parts. Part I – *Veni Creator* –
is a taut sonata-Allegro; Part II – the *Faust* scene – comprises Adagio, Scherzo, and Finale in one continuous
whole. The work is genuinely symphonic throughout,
soloists and chorus stating and developing the main themes
in conjunction with the orchestra. As in Beethoven's
Ninth, the universality of the conception inspired themes
of a peculiarly direct quality; Hans Redlich aptly describes
them as 'projectiles capable of piercing the hearts of the
most distant listeners'. And again as in Beethoven's Ninth,
the demands made on the chorus are extreme.

Mahler decided on a double choir for antiphonal purposes
with a separate boys' choir singing independently in unison
for the most part (a similar kind of lay-out to that in the
opening movement of Bach's *St Matthew Passion*), and here
the problem arose. The weight of the nineteenth-century
affirmative style required very large choruses, and against
these the normal romantic orchestra and four soloists
would have been powerless – as they usually are in big
choral works of this period; so Mahler used eight soloists
and enlarged the orchestra. With his lifetime's experience
of clarifying the thick sound of the romantic orchestra, he
knew exactly what was needed. The strings, so often submerged, he doubled in strength; the weakest section of all
– the woodwind and horns – he augmented considerably,
using quintuple wind and eight horns. But to the strongest
section – the heavy brass – he added only one trumpet and
one trombone; he did use a separate group of four trumpets
and three trombones, 'placed apart', but only for a short
peroration at the end of each part of the symphony. The
result is that, instead of the confused sound of the typical
romantic choral work, we have a clear, hard texture, with
every contrapuntal part standing out vividly.

Part I, a sonata movement enclosing a double fugue, does
not so much entreat for salvation as imperiously demand
it; the Mahlerian shadows of doubt do intrude, but are
forcibly dispelled. The movement is basically a great

triumphal march (a conception derived from lines like 'Our
leader, go before'), and it uses the traditional methods of
choral affirmation – passages of block chords in antiphony,
both choirs in shattering unison, and fugal development –
but with the greatest originality. Some idea of Mahler's
mastery of choral and orchestral polyphony can be gained
from this passage in the double fugue, where three themes
are presented in conjunction, to words addressed to the
Holy Spirit, meaning 'Grant that through thee we may
know the Father and the Son' (Example 56). As can be
seen, Mahler uses his vast army, not for an orgy of counterpoint in umpteen 'real parts', but to make his 'projectile-
like' themes stand out starkly, by means of every kind of
doubling. He is not out to amaze – or to deafen – but to
communicate clearly.

The quieter, more warmly romantic Part II is dominated
for long periods by the soloists, but the chorus is used

Ex. 56. Mahler, *Symphony No.8.*

intermittently with brilliant imagination. In the Adagio section, the mysterious utterances of Goethe's anchorites are whispered by male voices, *staccato* and *pianissimo*, merging beautifully with *pizzicato* cellos and basses; in the Scherzo section, women's and boys' voices take over with carol-like unisons and thirds, representing the angels who bear Faust's redeemed soul heavenwards. The Finale, as in the *Resurrection Symphony*, sums up with a murmured chorale – the *Chorus Mysticus* (Example 57). This swells to

Ex. 57. Mahler, *Symphony No. 8*

a mighty *fortissimo* peroration, which is finally crowned by the extra brass.

The first fully choral symphony had successors – notably Vaughan Williams's *Sea Symphony* (1910; see p. 282), which continued the humanistic tradition by treating the sea as a symbol of man's boundless potentialities; but this work, though tremendously inspiriting, is largely immature. Stravinsky's orthodox Roman Catholic *Symphony of Psalms* (1930; see p. 310) and Holst's purely poetic *Choral Symphony* to texts by Keats (1934) are not in the true symphonic tradition. Mahler's Eighth was the last great humanistic choral symphony.

Or perhaps not. The original Beethovenian conception of an orchestral symphony with choral finale found one final exponent – in Havergal Brian (*b*.1876). This Staffordshire composer came briefly to the fore around 1907, but has since suffered a shameful neglect which has only begun to be remedied by performances of several of the more recent of his nineteen symphonies on the BBC Third Programme. It was no doubt Brian's isolation from public musical life that led him to compose the most colossal of all choral symphonies in the 1920s, when the romantic humanistic ideal was being widely rejected in the interests of a new classicism. His Second Symphony – the *Gothic* (1919–22) – lasts for two hours, and calls for the following gargantuan forces: thirty-one woodwind, twenty-three brass, and much percussion; four separate groups of brass and kettledrums raising the total brass to fifty-five and the number of kettledrummers to six (playing twenty-two drums!); strings; four soloists; four large mixed choirs; children's choir; and organ.

The work is continuous. The three orchestral movements are a violent Allegro, a grim, cortège-like Lento, and a strange fanfare-Scherzo, which together play for about forty minutes. The choral finale, lasting nearly an hour and a half, is a Latin setting of the Te Deum, in three sections – Te Deum, Judex, and Te Ergo. This gigantic choral apotheosis was motivated by the old romantic 'finale problem', and was connected with that favourite inspiration of romantic choral symphonists, Goethe's *Faust* – as one of Brian's letters makes clear.

The composition of the *Gothic Symphony* presented no problems beyond the usual vexatious one of the Finale – should it be instrumental or choral? As the first part was largely coloured by Goethe's *Faust* (Part II), I had an idea of setting to a choral finale a large portion of the last act. But the Te Deum had never been out of my mind . . . It pushed itself forward as the only possible Finale for a Gothic Symphony . . .

Although both Sir Hamilton Harty and Sir Eugene Goossens wanted to mount the symphony, financial considerations prevented them. The first performance was eventually given in London, conducted by Bryan Fairfax, in July 1961. Any attempt to assess the work on a single hearing would be idle: it suffices to say that the music reveals the mind of a truly visionary genius. The fantastic 'Gothic' element, manifest in the strange, granite-like style of the orchestral movements, breaks out, in the Finale, into a dithyrambic paean of complex neo-medieval counterpoint like nothing else in music. It culminates in an apocalyptic vision of judgement – a ferocious assault by the extra brass and kettledrums, and a cry of terror from the choruses to the Latin equivalent of 'Let me never be confounded' – after which a *pianissimo*, unaccompanied murmur of the same words brings the symphony to a dramatically subdued conclusion. But perhaps the best idea of Brian's boldly original choral writing can be given by quoting the opening of the Judex ('Judge') section (Example 58), where chords of D minor, E minor, G major, and A minor are sung simultaneously. (This is no mere 'effect'; the rising figure D–E–G–A is one of the unifying elements of the *Te Deum*.)

Meanwhile, the first 'choral' piano concerto had been composed. It seems fitting that such an extraordinary conception should have been realized by Ferruccio Busoni (1866–1924), since he was one of the most extraordinary figures in musical history, combining within himself the conflicting temperaments of an Italian and a German, and the conflicting geniuses of a profound thinker, a great

Ex. 58. Brian, *Gothic Symphony*

virtuoso pianist, and a revolutionary composer. Busoni had no sympathy with the romantic humanistic ideal – he was one of the pioneers of the new twentieth-century classicism – but he was a characteristic romantic in one respect: his music, like Liszt's, evokes his private mystical experience. Busoni's esoteric vision was founded on a belief in the necromantic; inexplicable in words, it radiates from his strange music, composed in a style like that of no other composer.

His Piano Concerto (1903–4) is a huge five-movement work, as much a symphony as a concerto. Like Brahms's piano concertos, it is deeply serious and shuns mere virtuosity: the piano part, though of phenomenal difficulty, merges with the orchestra in a weighty symphonic structure. The work is symmetrical in shape: the first, third, and fifth movements are massive, majestic, and darkly glowing, presenting Busoni's German side; the second and fourth are swift, glittering, Italianate scherzos, which make oddly sinister use of popular Neapolitan-type melodies.

It was no doubt this conflict between Germanism and Italianism, as well as the curiously supernatural flavour of the whole work, that led Busoni to bring in a chorus for a mystical apotheosis. Although his formal precedent was Beethoven's *Choral Fantasia*, he did not follow that work in allowing the chorus to monopolize the Finale, but adopted the more reticent procedure of Liszt's *Faust* and *Dante* symphonies. In the Finale, the orchestra sets up a quiet, swaying accompaniment, against which a male chorus, off-stage eventually enters with a hymn-like theme in block chords (recalled from the first movement). With his usual esoteric taste, Busoni chose for text a 'Hymn to Allah' from the play *Aladdin* by the Danish dramatist Oehlenschläger (1779–1850), using a German translation (an English version by Walter M. Clement is available). But the theological implications are irrelevant: what must have appealed to Busoni was the poem's pantheistic aspiration towards absorption into the infinite, where all human conflicts are resolved. The chorus remains in the background throughout; even though the quiet chordal texture swells to an affirmative *fortissimo* unison, it is still in the distance, and the piano and orchestra clinch the work with a brief but brilliant coda.

The only noteworthy inheritor of Busoni's conception stands at the opposite spiritual pole. Alan Bush (*b*.1900), in the Finale of his Piano Concerto (1937), called in a baritone soloist and male chorus – on-stage – to voice the creed of communism. His three preceding orchestral movements reflect the uneasy mood of the pre-war period: a strenuous toccata-like *Con moto moderato*, with ominous side-drum interjections and angry fugato passages for piano and brass; a swift, malicious Scherzo; and a dark, brooding *Grave*. The latter rises to a powerful climax, and the Finale begins straight away as a joyous Allegro. Although the tension has been considerable, a choral finale hardly seems motivated; but the joy of the Allegro clouds over, a violent climax is reached, and the chorus strikes in didactically from outside the music, as it were. For his conception, Bush has used an even more startling procedure than Beethoven in the *Choral Symphony*: the chorus enters, not singing, but speaking the first line of the text, against a militant kettledrum-roll: 'Friends, we would speak a little of this performance.'

As in Beethoven's *Choral Fantasia* and *Choral Symphony*, the voices dominate the rest of the Finale (but with the pianist still prominent). To a simple rhythmic chanting in two parts, interrupted at times by the baritone, the chorus sings the praises of music – not as a divine gift, however, but as 'the mind-changer'. The great humanistic concepts – man free and triumphant, knowledge, power, and love – are all glorified, but with a particular emphasis. The humanistic ideal has become an ideological slogan: 'Come, there can be no more sides than two: war and waste for the privilege of a few, or a share for all in all men make or do.' The work ends with a *fortissimo* choral exhortation – 'Man's future is to be fought for in our time' – and a brief triumphant coda for piano and orchestra.

Bush's Finale is hardly an artistic success; in fact, it spoils an otherwise impressive concerto, since the choral section is by far the least satisfactory as music, rising to no convincing melodic statement at all. But the work is significant as a portent: it points to the final division of the humanistic ideal into two irreconcilable concepts. Beethoven brought the chorus into the symphony to voice man's aspiration in its twin aspects – political and religious. Liszt, Mahler, and Busoni, all, to a greater or less extent, concentrated on the purely religious ideal, ignoring the implications of Beethoven's 'all men shall be brothers'; but Alan Bush has pursued the purely political ideal, rejecting the implications of Beethoven's 'Seek your Creator above the starry firmament.' Thus choral-symphonic music has come to the parting of the ways, mirroring the disastrous cleavage in the human mind which Arthur Koestler has defined as the conflict between 'the Yogi and the Commissar.'

May some later Beethoven arise and proclaim their reunion in a new Choral Symphony!

15

Britain from Stanford to Vaughan Williams

*c.*1880–1939

CHARLES REID

THE period with which this chapter is concerned carries us from the apogee of organized English choralism, through a period of disastrous decline occasioned both by the First World War and by the development of the gramophone and radio, to what appeared to be a permanent state of subservience, with orchestral music (formerly a train-bearer merely) as musical overlord.

Between Stanford's early opus numbers in the 1870s and Vaughan Williams's *Sea Symphony* (1910) some 200 choral pieces were expressly written by English composers for the Three Choirs, Birmingham, Norwich, Sheffield, Cardiff, Hanley, Leeds Triennial, and similar great festivals. Of these works very few survive in today's repertory. There is only one undoubted masterpiece among them: *The Dream of Gerontius* (Birmingham Festival, 1900), by Edward Elgar. This, ironically, is an oratorio. It dates from the hey-day of Darwinian rationalism. Around the turn of the century, rationalists took the view that the oratorio form was as obsolete as the belief it adorned. *The Dream of Gerontius* has handsomely confuted them.

Choral taste in the first part of our period – the 1870s and 1880s – was still dominated by Handel and Mendelssohn. Bach and Beethoven were well down the performance lists. In 1886–7 Stanford, according to a census of contemporary programmes, was performed three or four times oftener than either. Let us take a closer look at this formidable pedagogue and compiler of cantatas. Sir Charles Villiers Stanford (1852–1924), an Irish Protestant from

Dublin, identified himself with prevalent English musical tastes more skilfully and copiously than any composer of his generation. The knighthood that was conferred upon him in 1901 confirmed his status as one of the nation's unofficial laureates. Among legions of amateur choralists it gave the same kind of pleasure as is given to a somewhat wider public by cricketing knighthoods today.

In the course of an assiduous life, much of it devoted to conducting as well as teaching (Cambridge University and the Royal College of Music), Stanford published 177 opus numbers. Of these some fifty were choral works, his range being from oratorios, masses, motets, anthems, and Anglican services to secular odes, ballads, cantatas, and such topicalities as the *Welcome Song for the Opening of the Franco-British Exhibition*, 1908, to words by the Duke of Argyll. Listening nowadays to samples of Stanford's liturgical music, one notes the fluent craftsmanship, the ready flow of ideas, the technical evocations and mood-echoes of Schubert, Mendelssohn, Beethoven, Wagner, Brahms, and Sullivan. Vaughan Williams, once Stanford's pupil, singled out the Requiem (Birmingham, 1897) and the *Stabat Mater* (Leeds, 1907) for special praise. These scores, he said, typified Stanford 'thinking his own beautiful thoughts in his own beautiful way'.

Certain other commendations were more sweeping. Writing as late as the mid-1930s, Sir Edward Bairstow (1874–1946), a leading authority on Anglican service music, said:

I must have heard some of Stanford's church services . . . many hundreds of times; but there are as fresh to me now as on the day when I first heard them . . . It is only great music that can wear like this . . . His Services in B flat, A, G, and C are far and away the most perfect settings since Tudor times.

Overpraise of this kind gave a parochial air to English choralism in Victorian and later days. No gulf could be greater than that which separates Stanford's facile eclecticism from the grave, gleaming purity of Byrd and his peers.

Sometimes the eclectic method was discarded for direct
personal utterance with happy results. What could be more
charming than Stanford's part-song *The Blue Bird* (1910)?
As a rounded and perfect miniature, it is to be classed
with the best, in equivalent fields, of Mendelssohn, Sullivan, and Schumann. This setting of words by Mary
Coleridge, with its final note suspended, as it were, in mid-
air, has a unique and delicate nostalgia. Its end is given in
Example 59.

Ex. 59. Stanford, *The Blue Bird*

The Revenge, a choral ballad, which came out in 1886, is
still occasionally sung by local choral societies. Going
through the score nowadays, however, one may be put
off as much by the glibness of the music as by Tennyson's
bluff chauvinism. Of Stanford's *Songs of the Fleet*, for baritone and chorus, with words by Henry Newbolt (Leeds
Festival, 1910), Vaughan Williams used to say that Stanford could adopt the technique of any composer he chose.
He singled out one movement in particular – *The Middle
Watch* – as 'beating Delius at his own game'. Is not this
another case of fraternal hyperbole? *The Middle Watch*
is a marvellously skilled piece of nocturnal tone-painting,
but I fail to detect in it any phrase or sequence that could
be called unmistakably Delian.

When it came to post-Wagnerian techniques, Stanford
was uncertain of touch and intemperate of tongue. He lamented the influence of Debussy and would mock consecutive
fifths by putting both his hands to his nose, with fingers
spread in a double snook. Tchaikovsky he found 'inherently
superficial' and agreed with the proposition of his friend
Lord Leighton, P.R.A., that the *Pathetic Symphony*, although
it might impress greatly at a first hearing, wore through at

the third. The greatest of his phobias, however, concerned Richard Strauss. *Elektra* and *Salome* he dismissed as pornographic rubbish. According to his biographer, Harry Plunket Greene, Strauss was the target he had in mind when composing, in 1914, his musical squib:

Ode to Discord, A Chimerical Bombination in Four Bursts by Charles L. Graves, set to Music(?) for Solo, Chorus, and Orchestra (Organ and Hydrophone ad lib.) by Charles Villiers Stanford, Hop 1, dedicated (without permission) to the Amalgamated Society of Boiler Makers.

Graves's skit originally appeared in the *Spectator*. 'Hence, loathèd Melody', it begins. There are heavy-handed salutes to 'divine Cacophony', 'percussion's stimulating aid', 'the reign of Sturm und Drang' and so on. The *Ode* delighted Stanford who, after reading it, sat down and began setting it to music at once. Playing through the score nearly half a century after its sole performance, one is faintly beguiled by progressions of the kind which Stanford, when he found them in student contexts, denounced as 'damned ugly, me boy'. There is nothing conspicuously Straussian about them, however. The most easily identifiable parody is of Debussyan whole-tone procedures which accompany the chorus's invocation:

> ... Ye trumpets, blare
> In unrelated keys and rend the affrighted air!

With Stanford is usually paired Sir Hubert Parry (Charles Hubert Hastings Parry, 1848–1918). His oratorios have already been commented on (see p. 229), but his best-known choral works are his unison song *Jerusalem* and his cantata *Blest Pair of Sirens*. First performed in 1916, with orchestration by Elgar, *Jerusalem* became, through the force of its melody and of Blake's words ('And did those feet in ancient time'), almost a supplementary British national anthem. When *Blest Pair of Sirens* (on Milton's text, *At A Solemn Music*) was first performed, in 1887, the massive diatonic discords in its orchestral introduction must have recalled the prelude to *The Mastersingers*, an opera which had reached the London stage only five years before.

No anti-Wagnerite, Parry had drawn the reproof of an elder English musician, George Macfarren (1813–87), for visiting Bayreuth: 'An earthquake would be good that would swallow up the spot and everybody on it.' But Parry himself lived to be somewhat baffled, apparently, by a later type of 'advanced' music. His singular comment on Schoenberg's *Five Orchestral Pieces*, given in London under Sir Henry Wood in 1912, was: 'I can stand this fellow when he is loud. It is when he's soft that he is so obscene.'

After Parry's and Stanford's works, those of Frederick Hymen Cowen (1852–1935) were reckoned sufficient novelty for any healthy taste. Between 1870 and the close of the reign of Edward VII in 1910, Cowen, a celebrated conductor of northern choirs and orchestras, composed over a score of oratorios, cantatas, choral odes, and the like, from *The Deluge* (1878) and *The Transfiguration* (1898) to *The Water Lily* (1893) and *John Gilpin* (1904). Such compositions, as Cowen's obituary notice in the *Musical Times* observed, 'were born of fashion and the invitation of festival committees. They stand not for the artist but for the English musical worthy and his duty to society.' English choralism is to be congratulated on having freed itself from such conventions and obligations in our own day.

Sometimes a masterpiece was received ambiguously. Stanford's attitude to *The Dream of Gerontius* is a case in point. Plunket Greene testifies that the oratorio was 'antagonistic to his inherent Protestantism' – as if theology had any conclusive bearing on aesthetic merit. According to other witnesses he complained that the music 'stank of incense'. Yet we have Herbert Howells's testimony that, hearing it played on the piano, Stanford confessed, 'I would have given my head to have written Part I of *Gerontius*.' This self-contradiction is of a piece with the oratorio's early reception and fate. As we shall see, England sensed a work of genius and at the same time was puzzled and faintly repelled by it.

Before this, Sir Edward Elgar (1857–1934) had written many part-songs, accompanied and unaccompanied, as well as much liturgical music for the Roman Catholic rite

during his struggling early phase as a West Country organist, choirmaster, bandmaster, music teacher, and violinist in
the Three Choirs Festival and other orchestras. Neither this
output nor his early choral festival pieces – *The Black
Knight* (1893), *The Light of Life* (1896), *King Olaf* (1896),
The Banner of St George (1897), and *Caractacus* (1898) – need
detain us for more than a sentence or two. All were works of
self-training and probation. Of *The Light of Life* Elgar once
remarked in mock apology to Delius that the oratorio form
was part of the penalty of his English environment. Of a
fugal movement in it, he added, 'I thought a fugue would be
expected of me. The British public would hardly tolerate an
oratorio without a fugue.' With its romantic tale of conflict
between the Christian hero and the old Nordic gods, *King
Olaf* had much currency among provincial choral societies
for thirty years or more but is not much heard now. The
first performance was at Hanley, Staffs., a choral stronghold
of high repute and enterprise. 'It was', comments Diana
McVeagh, whose book proclaims her an acute analyst of
Elgar's works, 'exactly the kind of music the people of the
Potteries understood.'

A different matter was *The Dream of Gerontius*, Elgar's
seventh substantial choral score. 'This', as he wrote on the
last page of the manuscript, 'is the best of me.' Pondered
over for eleven years, Cardinal Newman's poem released in
Elgar a sureness of musical touch, vision, and style which,
except for the *Enigma Variations* of 1899, are unparalleled in
his previous output and unexcelled by anything he wrote
later. Constructed in a closely integrated way, with a debt
that few would deny to Wagner's principle of 'leading-
motives', *The Dream of Gerontius* showed itself a thoroughly
modern work, with none of the narrow musical parochial-
ism that had been almost the badge of English oratorio.
Nowhere was Elgar's touch more striking than in the
massive and expressive orchestral writing.

Certitude that he was achieving something momentous
and enduring was with him throughout the time of gestation
and setting down. In a letter to a friend he quoted the
mighty sunburst of tone on the opening line of Newman's

hymn (Example 60) – and exulted: 'The trees are singing my music – or have I sung theirs?' 'Praise to the Holiest' is quintessential Elgar in its limitations as well as its strength. As often happens with Elgar, a superb tune of individual colour and high emotional tension finds no complementary or balancing theme that can be regarded as really valid. The hymn resolves itself into an amiable $\frac{6}{4}$ romp for mixed chorus which could have come from various other hands of the period. The miracle is that the bars quoted above and the three bars that follow give pulse and incandescence to the entire score.

Ex. 60. Elgar, *The Dream of Gerontius*

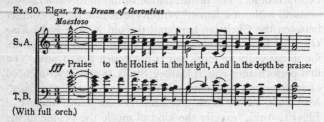

(With full orch.)

The idiom of *The Dream of Gerontius* has now for decades seemed simplicity itself. To a generation aware of *Parsifal*, César Franck, and certain aspects of Tchaikovsky, the work should not have presented much difficulty even in 1900. But evidently the public originally found *The Dream of Gerontius* a hard nut to crack. Professional musicians seem to have been in little better case. Even the great Hans Richter, who conducted the first performance, had difficulty with what was currently described as Elgar's 'novel idiom'. After the first rehearsal with the Birmingham choir, he is said to have spent half the night pacing his hotel bedroom, with the score propped up over the fireplace, in a belated effort to memorize and master it.

The première was almost a fiasco. The chorus-master, as an ardent nonconformist, had been openly unsympathetic to the work, the chorus were not given time enough in which to prepare it, and some of the choralists (notably the basses) refused to take the music seriously and were guilty of buffoonery. There was some appallingly flat singing, and discrepancies between the baritone soloist (Harry Plunket Greene) and the choir. The result of this mischance and incompetence was that Elgar had to contend for years with the notion that *The Dream of Gerontius* was too difficult to perform. It was only after the oratorio had made its mark in Germany – notably at the Lower Rhine Festival of 1902, when Richard Strauss raised his glass to 'the first English progressivist musician, Meister Elgar' – that the work really began to make headway in its native land.

Already Elgar was at work on other oratorio projects. With a text compiled by himself from the Bible and the Apocrypha, *The Apostles* opens with Christ's prayer in the mountain and ends with the Ascension. It was first sung – with much greater artistic success than *The Dream of Gerontius* – at the Birmingham Festival of 1903. Next (1906) came *The Kingdom*, which deals with the Church in Jerusalem, the descent of the Holy Spirit, and the scriptural events that followed.

It may be wondered whether either of these oratorios is ever likely to find a permanent niche in the repertory. Both are generally acknowledged to contain some of Elgar's most glowingly and dramatically imagined pages. One or the other score has, however, been assailed for imperfect structure or proportion, occasional lapses into bombast, fussy quasi-Wagnerian leading-motive technique, and voice parts pinned almost as an afterthought on to what basically are symphonic stretches. The great handicap of *The Apostles* and *The Kingdom*, however, is that they invite comparison with the incomparable *Gerontius*.

There was to have been a third oratorio (completing a trilogy), dealing with after-life and the Church of God. But by this time Elgar was disillusioned. The returns of oratorio-writing were meagre. He concluded that, for the sake of his dependants he must not waste more time in attempting to write 'high-felt' music. To a correspondent he confided: 'When I write a big, serious work, e.g. *Gerontius*, we have had to starve and go without fires for twelve months as a reward.' After *The Kingdom*, Elgar concentrated on orchestral and concerted works. His only other pieces of note for

voices were *The Music Makers* (1912), a setting of a poem by
Arthur O'Shaughnessy which includes quotations from
half a dozen earlier scores, starting with the *Enigma Variations*; and a patriotic triptych, *The Spirit of England*, com-
prising *The Fourth of August, To Women,* and *For the Fallen*
(texts by Laurence Binyon), which came out during the
First World War.

The extent to which Elgar amassed official recognition –
knighthood (1904), a shower of honorary degrees, the O.M.
(1911), the post of Master of the King's Music (1924), and
baronetcy (1931) – is to be noted. Edward VII is said to
have had a genuine personal regard for his music. The virtually automatic conferring of knighthood on eminent composers from late-Victorian times betokened, it is true, an
enhanced official standing for the art of music, but may be
said to have depreciated the value of the honour itself. Take,
by contrast, the position of Elgar's great continuator, Ralph
Vaughan Williams. By the time of his death (1958) his income from performing rights and publications is said to have
been comparable with that of a well-placed surgeon or a
tolerably fashionable Q.C. But Vaughan Williams was
conspicuous in *not* becoming 'Sir'. (He is said to have declined the honour.) In 1935 he received the Order of Merit,
a decoration which – though Elgar himself had worn it – at
once took on new lustre in all men's eyes.

Just as Elgar's other choral works suffer by comparison
with *The Dream of Gerontius*, so the great handicap of all
other choral pieces of Delius is that they invite comparison
with the unique *Mass of Life*. Frederick Delius (1862–1934)
was born in the Yorkshire mill town of Bradford, and lived
for long terms a withdrawn life, almost that of a recluse, in
the wilds of Florida or the social isolation of a French village.
Towards the end blindness and paralysis, borne with stub-
born equanimity, further sealed off a romantic and ego-
centric soul which was proof against almost all outer
musical influences and, especially in the case of traditional
ones, harshly disdainful of them. From the *Appalachia*
('Variations on an Old Slave Song for baritone, chorus, and
orchestra') of 1902 to the *Songs of Farewell* for chorus and

orchestra (to words by Whitman, 1930–2), Delius composed choral pieces of widely differing techniques. Among them is a handful of unaccompanied numbers – *The Midsummer Song*, *The Wanderer's Song*, *On Craig Dhu*, *To be sung of a summer night on the water*, and *The Splendour Falls*. Listening to the generality of his output one reflects that, with Delius, choral tone and feature were never an end in themselves but rather a colour adjunct or partner whose uses were determined as much by orchestral blendings and contrasts as by their own nature and laws.

One feels this strongly in the choral epilogue to *Appalachia*, 'O honey, I am going down the river in the morning.' Here the chorus is as much an extension of the tonal paint-box as a vehicle for words and sentiment. With differences of emphasis and of pictorial or literary emphasis, much the same aesthetic approach is shown in *Sea Drift* for baritone, chorus, and orchestra, to words by Whitman (1903), *Songs of Sunset* for soloists, chorus, and orchestra, to words by Arthur Symons (1906–7), and *A Song of the High Hills*, for orchestra and wordless chorus (1911–12). Often the voices are there merely to add their own strands to a Delian colour scheme, which allots equal importance to the string, brass, and woodwind choirs, the whole forming a sort of aural tapestry against which the solo voices take most of the emotional floodlight. Delius was never reluctant to deprive the chorus of words altogether. The ah-ings and oh-ings of the chorus in *A Song of the High Hills*, like the maidenly (and interminable) la-la-la-ings and tra-la-la-ings of *A Mass of Life*, are an evasion of the voice's grand function, whether in speech or song, namely, to articulate thought, or at any rate, sentiment.

As a vehicle for sentiment, the music of *Sea Drift* is conspicuous in the Delius canon. Whitman's tale of mating sea-birds and their sundering is narrated now by the choir, now by the baritone soloist, with an accompanying beauty of texture and phrase-pattern that is shot with an anguish wholly typical of Delius and wholly delectable. This was one of the many Delius works conspicuously championed by the young Thomas Beecham, whose prompt and easy mastery of a disturbingly innovatory piece staggered all observers. He conducted his first *Sea Drift* at Hanley in 1908. Between the last rehearsal and the performance the full score disappeared. Philip Heseltine, Delius's first biographer, hinted that it was stolen by some enemy of the composer or the conductor. Not in the least put out, Beecham gave as fine a rendering of the work as he ever gave with the score in front of him.

Delius's Requiem (so-called) was composed in 1914–16, 'dedicated to the memory of all young soldiers fallen in the war', and derives its text, a railingly sceptical one, from Nietzsche. One of the libretto's more aggressive pages is a divided chorus during which the Christian section shouts 'Hallelujah' against fervent reiterations of '*La il Allah*' from the Mohammedan section. In a personal apologia the composer explained, a little needlessly, that his Requiem was not a religious work.

Its underlying belief is that of a pantheism that insists on the reality of life. It preaches that human life is like a day in the existence of the world, subject to the laws of All-Being. . . . Independence and self-reliance are the marks of a man who is great and free. He will look forward to his death with high courage in his soul, in proud solitude, in harmony with nature and the ever-recurrent, sonorous rhythm of death.

The concert-goer of average sensitivity, whatever his private philosophical convictions, will tolerate doctrine as nebulous and bleak even as this, provided the musical setting has beauty and power. In the case of the Requiem this condition is not, by common consent, met. Leading champions of Delius are agreed that the music fails.

A Mass of Life, too, is based on Nietzsche ('Thus spake Zoroaster' – *Also sprach Zarathustra*); but here the 'philosophy of denial', instead of being crudely pressed, is transmuted into a twilit poetry with only enough gall in it to enhance the prevalent honey and rapture. The work was composed in 1904–5. One can well imagine the startled ecstasy which such outbursts as that in Example 61 (from the opening invocation, 'O Thou, my will!') aroused in

Ex. 61. Delius, *Mass of Life*

understanding ears at the historic London performance
under Beecham in 1909.

What Beecham always maintained is utterly true. The
note was new. It was a note of high beauty. It was beauty
from a complete and hitherto unsuspected world. The mind
that gave birth to that world was lofty, after its fashion, and
had few affinities among other minds of its day. Even those
(and they are many) who find themselves temperamentally
averse from Delius's art would go most of the way with
Beecham's assessment. The quarrel begins when praise
wildly overreaches itself. Thus Philip Heseltine described
A Mass of Life as 'without doubt the greatest musical achievement since Wagner, a Mass worthy to rank beside the great
Mass of Sebastian Bach . . . in the fullest sense of the word, a
deeply religious work . . . .'

Valid arguments against the comparison of Delius with
Bach are not far to seek. Employed as Bach employed them
– with broad aesthetic vision, profound yet widely ranging
emotion and keen overriding intellect – the polyphonic arts
of the seventeenth and eighteenth centuries, supported by a
newly perfected harmonic system, are better adapted in
themselves to grandeur and variety of achievement than the
extremely limited technical procedures of Frederick Delius.
Bach achieved more than Delius because he had more – and
better – tools. Consider one of Delius's typical limitations –
over-addiction to harmonic slithers. These are a perfect
symbol of Nietzschean pessimism, but Delius by no means
confined them to his Nietzsche settings; he imposes them
equally on the buoyantly sanguine platitudes of Walt Whitman. A final limitation in the case of *A Mass of Life* is the
text. For all its proud gesture and brazen colour, Nietzsche's
philosophical poetry makes little purchase on the human
mind and heart as compared with the immemorial text set
by Bach. The one text is a waning intellectual fashion. The
other spans the ages.

Now to Gustav Holst (1874–1934). Many of us in Britain
were first gripped by Holst, considered as a choral composer,
by hearing *The Planets* at the Proms or elsewhere. Nearly all
this long work (first performed complete in 1920) is for

orchestra alone. But at the end of the final movement, 'Neptune', a hidden chorus of women's voices wordlessly reiterates the disturbing and iridescent sequence quoted below, which becomes fainter and fainter until all sound and, it would seem, all life evanesce amid interstellar space (Example 62).

Ex. 62. Holst, *The Planets*

In relation to the suite as a whole, this wordless vocalization takes up little time and room. Yet, as with the 'Praise to the Holiest' tune in *The Dream of Gerontius*, it colours in retrospect the score as a whole. One may go further. It is a symbol of Holst's entire mind, talent, and output. It points to a central value; to something rarefied and lonely, with hints of forbidding bleakness beyond. From his earliest days of self-realization, Holst was a visionary who seemed subject to sways and pulls unknown to most mortals. Listening in Worcester Cathedral as a youth to Bach's Mass in B minor, he found himself clutching the arms of his chair during the *Sanctus*. Bach's sublime music made him feel he was floating on air, and he feared (literally, it seems) lest he should find his head bumping against the groined roof.

The Planets, his first success, followed miscellaneous choral essays, including four groups of hymns from the *Rig Veda* hymns (1908–12), whose composition involved Sanskrit studies and immersion in Eastern philosophy. (Group I is for mixed voices and orchestra, II for female voices and orchestra, III for female voices and harp, IV for male voices and orchestra.) At the height of the First World War, Holst settled down in a sound-proof study to write *The Hymn of Jesus* to a text which he had himself prepared, with some expert assistance, from the Apocryphal Gospels. The profound impression it made on its first performance (London,

1920) under the composer's baton has inevitably dwindled;
but even forty years later it is impossible to rehear such
passages as the opening chorus (Example 63) without salut-
ing the Miltonic scale and earnestness of Holst's conception
at its best. Just what the apocryphal text meant to him it is
hard to say. The most anybody extracted from him on his
metaphysical beliefs was this:

> I believe most thoroughly in comradeship in all shapes as being
> the ideal of this world. And, as regards the future, I am Hindu
> enough to believe that comradeship becomes transmuted into
> Unity, only this is a matter that lies beyond all words.

Ex. 63. Holst, *Hymn of Jesus*

For cloudiness this beats Delius on the inner meaning of
his Requiem. But cloudiness never obtruded on Holst's
art. Like the rest of his output, *The Hymn of Jesus* is, for better
or worse, uncompromisingly concrete in musical purport.
The 1920 première swept men of grave and seasoned judgement off their feet. 'It could not', wrote Sir Donald Tovey,
'have been done before . . . and it can't be done again. It
is a blessed, abiding fact; and not a matter of taste at all. If
anybody doesn't like *The Hymn of Jesus* he doesn't like life.'
Vaughan Williams, a lifelong friend of Holst, said the
music made him 'want to get up and embrace everybody
and then get drunk'.

Listening to *The Hymn of Jesus* today one is aware that certain of its harmonic devices and schemes of instrumentation belong, in a derivative way, to their period, a period dominated by Debussy, Ravel, Stravinsky, and (let us add) Puccini, rather than to posterity. But the opinion of Imogen Holst, who is the composer's daughter and the most eminent of Holst scholars (see Bibliography), is that 'the music is great enough to withstand most of its weaknesses'. In this opinion most critics will concur.

During the ten years which followed, Holst wrote two other choral scores of wide scope – the *Choral Symphony*, a setting of an arbitrary collection of poems by Keats (Leeds Festival, 1925), and the *Choral Fantasia*, a setting of Robert Bridges's *Ode to Music*, written for the Three Choirs Festival (1931). Of these two pieces, the *Choral Fantasia*, although much neglected, is generally conceded to have the greater merit; the *Choral Symphony* to have higher pretensions. The latter has had few admirers. Its shortcomings, which are those of *The Hymn of Jesus* aggravated and multiplied, have been laid bare by Imogen Holst. She reproaches her father especially for his mannerism of 'too easy fourths and fifths', both consecutive and melodic, and speaks of the 'embarrassing platitudes' of the Finale. After the first performance Vaughan Williams wrote to the composer reluctantly confessing that all he had felt was 'cold admiration'. Holst himself who treated, or affected to treat, success, failure, and his own brain-children with amused detachment, wrote back: 'I am not sure that the Keats Symphony is good at all. Just at present I believe I like it, which is more than I can say about most of my things.'

If Vaughan Williams did not care for Holst's *Choral Symphony* Holst did not quite know what to make of Vaughan Williams's *Flos Campi* ('The Flower of the Field', a reference to the Song of Solomon). This, too, came out in 1925, and pits a small orchestra and solo viola against a small chorus with nothing but 'ahs' and 'ohs' to sing. The two composers remained, however, on terms of the most intimate musical friendship. We may now turn to consider in some detail the choral works of Ralph Vaughan Williams (1872–1958) himself.

After a tame, probationary setting (1905) of Walt Whitman's *Towards the Unknown Region* for chorus and orchestra, he made a name for himself five years later with a more protracted and elaborate setting of Whitman, *A Sea Symphony*. Among those who assiduously attended the rehearsals for the first performance (Leeds Festival, 1910) was Vaughan Williams's former teacher, Charles Villiers Stanford. It was reverently noted that, aided only by a vocal score, Stanford detected missing accidentals in quick-moving inner orchestral parts during complex ensembles and corrected these mistakes on the spot. His former pupil's idiom might be daring and disagreeable at times, but the old man's ear wasn't to be foxed! Another veteran pedagogue and composer heard *A Sea Symphony*: Hubert Parry. 'Big stuff,' pronounced Parry, 'but full of impertinence as well as noble moments.'

Rehearing the *Sea Symphony*, after half a century, one reflects that there was something, after all, in what Parry said. The opening blare of brass and the chorus's proud cry, 'Behold, the sea itself!', with much that follows, impress by sheer, heaving bulk and genial breadth. For the first time since the rise of Romanticism, to which the *Sea Symphony* clearly belongs, an English composer was broaching an epic subject in the epic vein. Stylistically there is much in the symphony's four movements which falls wide of the modal harmony and accompanying traits which were later seen to be essentials of Vaughan Williams's art. The composer himself later avowed that *A Sea Symphony* derives in part from *The Mystic Trumpeter* of Holst and, as to the Finale especially, from two Elgar scores, the *Enigma Variations* and *The Dream of Gerontius*, on which he had spent hours of study in the British Museum. But one highly personal element asserted itself in 1910 which persisted on and off in Vaughan Williams's music to the end. I refer to the facile and jocose 'hornpipy' strains which occur between the opening chorus and the soprano's 'Flaunt out, O sea'; and to the related jollities of the Scherzo. The late Hubert Foss, the leading authority of his day on Vaughan Williams and his music, rejoiced in the master's 'galumphings', as he called his scherzo manner. When they recurred fifteen years later in *Flos Campi*, he praised their 'riotous, boisterous, ancient, broad, un-puritanized humour'. It seems unlikely that this aspect of Vaughan Williams is going to wear well. It is obvious, not conspicuously beautiful, and conspicuously mannered.

In all, Vaughan Williams composed, like Stanford, some fifty choral works. The unaccompanied Mass in G minor (Birmingham, 1923) is an absorbing exercise in Vaughan Williams's matured style, which assimilates folk-song patterns, certain harmonic features that are related to 'Debussyism', and polyphonic values that spring from the Tudor masters. The question disturbingly arises whether a musical method of such various provenance is ideally suited to liturgical ends. My own feeling is that the Mass in G minor defeats itself by its inner diversity of style. The *Sancta Civitas* for tenor, bass, chorus, and orchestra (Oxford, 1926) is again characteristic of its composer in that the text (compiled by himself) insouciantly draws on disparate sources, including the Book of Revelation, the Roman Missal, and the *Phaedo* of Plato – all, however, translated into English. (The title of the work means 'The Holy City'.) *Dona Nobis Pacem*, also in English despite the title ('Give us peace'), offers an even more striking example of collation. First heard at Huddersfield in 1936, it has a text which assembles poems of Walt Whitman, John Bright's 'Angel of Death' speech, Latin liturgical prayer, and passages from eight books of the Old and New Testaments. *Five Tudor Portraits* (Norwich Festival, 1936), a choral suite based on salty poems by John Skelton (1460–1529), is regarded by adherents of Vaughan Williams as representing the high summer of his craftsmanship and artistic fulfilment. Certainly, the choir, whether rioting and soaring in the foreground or providing a backcloth for the baritone and contralto solos, is handled with humorous and flashing virtuosity. Why, then, do I feel frustrated at the end of it? Partly, I suppose, because Skelton is so exceedingly wordy. His words are vivid and droll as well as numerous. That is precisely the trouble. The voice-parts tend to become a word-vehicle rather than beautiful and revealing in their own right. Jane Scroop's lament for Philip, a sparrow, killed by Gib, a cat, drags in lines from the Requiem Mass, the 'Dies irae' and all. The language has few more charming examples of quaint and satirical fancy. But the triumph is, and remains, Skelton's.

Three other composers of this period made much stir in their day but have little, it would seem, to say to ours. Of the score or so choral works, most of them lengthy and complex, which Granville Bantock (1869–1946) brought out during his thirty most active years, two are talked of still by veteran choral singers. His *Omar Khayyám* is a three-part setting of Fitzgerald's famous translation of the *Rubáiyát*. The first and principal portion converted into solo and choral music 54 out of Fitzgerald's 101 quatrains. The original (1906) audience were rather bewildered, not so much by Bantock's musical idiom, which was assimilable enough in an opulent, modish way, but by the mass of words, notions, and literary images they were required to swallow. *Atalanta in Corydon* (1912), described as a 'choral symphony,' was a setting of four odes by Swinburne for an unaccompanied choir, divided into three main sections. The first choir (six parts, mixed) is said to have corresponded to the strings of an orchestra, the second choir (three parts, mixed) to the woodwind, the third choir (male, four parts) to the brass. Described, with reason, as the stiffest job ever presented to English choralists, *Atalanta in Corydon* was much honoured in print as a tonal experiment, but, after a few intensively rehearsed performances, remained unsung.

Sir Henry Walford Davies (1869–1941), who succeeded Elgar as Master of the King's Music in 1924, began his career with an oratorio, *The Temple*, which was produced without success at the Three Choirs Festival (Worcester) in 1902. But his *Everyman*, after the medieval 'morality', was greatly relished at the Leeds Festival in 1904 and for the next few seasons was sung by every progressive choral society in the land. By 1911, however, the *Everyman* vogue was over. Davies continued with persevering pen. Between *Everyman* and 1925 he wrote ten other choral pieces. None of them found favour. Had it not been for his highly successful radio talks on music (plus, one may add, his sentimental *Solemn*

Melody and his R.A.F. March), his name would have been entirely forgotten by a later generation.

Dame Ethel Smyth (1858–1944) is another who survives through her prose writing and ancillary fame rather than through her compositions. Yet her Mass in D (1891) was published at the expense of the Empress Eugénie, sung by the Royal Choral Society through the intervention of Queen Victoria, and praised in the 1930s by Bernard Shaw (a former music critic): 'The originality and beauty of the voice-parts are as striking today as they were thirty years ago, and the rest will stand up in the biggest company.' Among other choral pieces by Dame Ethel, *The March of the Women*, based on a tune she heard while holidaying in the Abruzzi, became the official ditty of the pre-1914 Suffragette movement and, though technically difficult for amateurs, was required singing at many suffragist rallies. A much later work for chorus and orchestra, *The Prison* (1930), with text by the composer (based on the doctrines of her philosopher friend W. H. Brewster), was conducted in London to mark her seventy-fifth birthday by no less a personage than Sir Thomas Beecham, who had championed Dame Ethel's music from Edwardian times.

Apart from *The Dream of Gerontius*, *A Mass of Life*, *Sea Drift*, and *A Sea Symphony*, the only choral works dating from the turn of the century or its early years which have given solid and continuing satisfaction are of a much less pretentious kind. I refer to the trilogy, *The Song of Hiawatha*, by Samuel Coleridge-Taylor (1875–1912). The choral writing and narrative skill of the first section in particular, 'Hiawatha's Wedding Feast' (1898), have a sturdy warmth and individuality which lift the piece far above mere facility. At twenty-three, Coleridge-Taylor was a supremely ready and professional composer with a vein very much his own. The fate of half a dozen other works in cantata or oratorio form which he wrote between 1900 and his early death suggest that after the *Hiawatha* series he had little left to say. The best of his output, modest in aim though it be, reasserted formal values which, in an age of choral innovation and rebellious experiment, were too often ignored or spurned.

16

Slavonic Nationalism from Dvořák to the Soviets

from *c.*1870

GERALD SEAMAN

It was not till the second half of the nineteenth century that a national school of composers began to appear in what we now call Czechoslovakia (covering the Moravian as well as Czech and Slovak peoples). There were several reasons for this late start. The region had for many years been under Austro-Hungarian dominion, and national musical life had been stifled. There had admittedly been many talented Czech composers, but they were not musically conscious of their nationality. But two events of major importance for the future development of Czech music were the organization of the Prague choral society 'Hlahol' in 1860, and the building of the Provisional Theatre in Prague in 1862.

The two great names in Czech music of the period are Bedrich Smetana (1824–84) and Antonin Dvořák (1841–1904). Although Smetana was responsible for a number of works for male-voice choir making use of the folk idiom, as well as several larger compositions such as *Czech Song* for mixed chorus and orchestra (1868, revised 1878), his prime importance lies in the field of orchestral and operatic music. Dvořák, on the other hand, wrote a whole series of cantatas, folk-song arrangements, and other choral works. Outstanding among his larger choral works (if we omit those to religious texts, discussed on pp. 245–7) is the cantata *The Spectre's Bride* (1884) for solo voices, chorus, and orchestra. This is the accepted English title for what in Czech is called *The Wedding Shift*, on a narrative poem of the same name by Karel Jaromír Erben (1811–70), a distinguished historian and collector of folk-lore. The rather gruesome plot of *The*

Spectre's Bride describes how a young girl prays for the return of her lost lover. There is a knock at the door and his phantom appears. Beckoning her to follow it, the spectre leads her over many weary miles of country where she eventually reaches a country churchyard. Here fresh horrors await her, and she is saved from perdition only by invoking celestial aid. The cantata was conducted by Dvořák both at its first performance by Hlahol at Plzeň (then known as Pilsen) in 1885 and at its first English performance at the Birmingham Festival in the same year. Musically, the language is rich and dramatic, abounding in Romantic harmonies typical of the composer. The vocal writing is effortless and eminently singable. Some idea of the general style may be gained from Example 64 (p. 288).

Among Dvořák's other secular choral works may be mentioned the patriotic hymn *The Heirs of the White Mountain*, for chorus and orchestra (1872, revised 1880); the cantata *The American Flag* (1892), written shortly before the composer's visit to the United States; the beautiful song-cycle *Amid Nature*, for mixed chorus (1882), to words by Halek; and the *Hymn in Praise of Czech Life* for mixed chorus and orchestra (1885), to words by Karel Pippich. We may also mention Dvořák's excellent arrangement of *Three Slovak Folk-Songs* (1877) for male voice choir and piano duet and his other choral songs – one of which, *I am a fiddler*, yielded the melody on which Dvořák based his own *Symphonic Variations* for orchestra (1877).

Dvořák's most outstanding contemporary and successor was Leoš Janáček (1854–1928). Receiving his first musical training in the Augustinian monastery at Brno (the capital of Moravia) under Father Pavel Křížkovsky, himself a composer of some standing, he later collected folk-songs in collaboration with František Bartoš, the distinguished ethnographer. Janáček is essentially a national composer whose music stems directly from Moravian folk-song, which differs to some degree from Czech. All his life he did much to encourage national music by encouraging musical organizations, conducting choirs, and propagating the works of Dvořák, Smetana, and his contemporaries. An important

Ex. 64. Dvořák, *The Spectre's Bride*

part is played in his work by inflections derived from speech, which he studied and noted down. With regard to this, he made the following interesting statement:

After having studied the musical side of the language, I am certain that all melodic and rhythmical mysteries of music in general are to be explained solely from rhythmical and melodic points of view on the basis of the melodic curves of speech. No one can become an opera composer who has not studied living speech.

As a composer, Janáček is extremely uneven. When he is at his best, as in the *Glagolitic Mass* (1926), he is truly great, but sometimes, for example in *Songs of Hradčany* (1916) for women's voices, his music is repetitive and unrewarding. His output is vast and ranges from simple folk-song arrangements to large works such as *Amarus* (1897) for tenor, chorus, and orchestra and *The Eternal Gospel* (1914) for soloists, chorus, and orchestra, both of which are settings of poems by Jaroslav Vrchlický, one of his favourite poets. Janáček's most representative choral works are the three settings for unaccompanied male chorus of poems by the nationalist writer Petr Bezruč – *Kantor Halfar* (1906), *Maryčka Magdanova* (1906–7), and *The Seventy Thousand* (1909), together with the *Glagolitic Mass*.

One of Janáček's most outstanding qualities was his humanitarianism and his understanding of the trials and sufferings of the common man. These sentiments are well revealed in *Kantor Halfar* (i.e. Halfar the teacher) which concerns the life of a poor village schoolmaster. Remarkable in this piece are the repetition of certain words and phrases by the chorus, which brilliantly suggest crowd psychology. An example of this occurs at the moment when the teacher is found hanging from an apple tree and the tenors murmur 'Schoolmaster?', 'Schoolmaster?' followed by the basses. The music, which is in rondo form, stems from a single theme and has alternating sections of ever-changing tempo. Much use is made of sustained pedal notes, together with lively rhythms and warm lyricism. His *Maryčka Magdanova* makes similar use of speech rhythms and choral effects and is intensely dramatic. Musically it is written in an almost instrumental style, with short concise motives peculiar to each voice. Of exceptionally wide range, it allows the greatest freedom in performance while making no small demands on the musicianship of the singers. In *The Seventy Thousand*, by far the easiest of the three, a solo quartet alternates with the rest of the choir. This too is highly effective, single words such as 'pain' being given exceptional prominence. It possesses a real Slavonic feeling.

Janáček's best-known choral work is his *Glagolitic Mass*,

proof of his complete mastery of choral composition. ('Glagolitic' refers to an old Slavonic alphabet.) Like much of his music, the separate sections of the Mass are made up of short fragments, sometimes of a lyrical nature, but more often reminiscent of folk-song. The Mass is divided into eight movements, three of which are purely instrumental. The largest and most important section is the Credo, during which episodes from the life of Jesus are made into an orchestral interlude – Jesus praying in the desert, Jesus blessing the multitude, and lastly, the Passion, which takes the form of a turbulent organ solo. The presence of purely instrumental numbers, such as the Introduction and the final 'Intrada', results from an old Bohemian custom in which the Mass itself was often framed by dignified or triumphal music marking the entry and departure of the clergy. Despite Janáček's almost pantheistic philosophy, the Mass is a fervent expression of a simple faith. The music, which is quite unique, follows closely the spoken word and alternates between passages of pure lyricism and astringent harmonies. Example 65 (the beginning of the Agnus Dei) is a good illustration of his dramatic and harmonic gifts, in which the sinister (and remarkably orchestrated) opening, representing the powers of darkness, is contrasted with the simplicity of the people's plea for peace (see p. 292).

The closing years of the nineteenth century and the first decades of the twentieth saw the appearance of a whole host of national composers such as Joseph Bohuslav Foerster (1859–1951), Vitežslav Novák (1870–1949), Rudolf Karel (1880–1945), Jaroslav Křička (b.1882), Bohuslav Martinů (1890–1959), Karel Jirák (b.1891), Otakar Jeremiáš (b. 1892), Zdeněk Folprecht (b.1900), and Iša Krejčí (b. 1904), all of whom paid attention to choral composition. Of these, two composers are outstanding.

Foerster is a recognized master of choral music and his works cover a wide field ranging from ecclesiastical compositions, unaccompanied choral music (frequently settings of poems by the poet J. V. Sládek), to large-scale works such as the cantata *Mortuis fratribus* (*To Dead Brothers*, 1918). His harmony is piquant and not seldom makes use of

Ex. 65. Janáček, *Glagolitic Mass*

accumulated masses of sound. Foerster's music is comparatively unknown outside his own country, but his choruses, which vary considerably in difficulty, are fascinating to perform and well worth the effort involved.

A controversial figure is presented by Bohuslav Martinů (1890–1959), who, as most biographers are not slow to tell us, gained immortality by being born in a superior position – a church tower. A pupil of Suk and Roussel, he later became resident in the United States. Martinů's musical style is complex and shows the influence of Stravinsky, of the old Flemish masters such as Josquin des Prez, of Lassus, and of Palestrina, but especially that of Moravian Slovakia, a district unique for its folk music. Martinů wrote several choral compositions including *Czech Rhapsody*, for large orchestra, chorus, soloists, and organ (1918); *Songs of Mary*, for women's chorus, based on folk texts (1936); *Madrigals for Six Voices* (Czech folk legends) (1938); and the *Field Mass*, for male chorus, baritone solo, and orchestra (1939).

Of these, the best known are his *Czech Rhapsody*, which is of a patriotic nature something in the manner of Smetana, being written to celebrate the liberation of Czechoslovakia, and his *Field Mass* – a soldier's prayer for safe deliverance and victory over the enemy – which is dedicated to the Czech Army volunteers. According to the composer, 'the *Field Mass* was written to be performed out of doors – under the sky and clouds that unite us with the soldiers at the front as well as with our compatriots at home', and this patriotic feeling permeates the whole work, which is not a liturgical one. The words, which are by Jiří Mucha, show the influence of folk poetry, but draw in part on the psalms. The Mass is scored for two piccolos, two clarinets, three trumpets, two trombones, piano, harmonium, and a battery of percussion. In style it shows the influence of Stravinsky in the constantly changing time-signatures, the dotted rhythms and the harsh discords alternating with lyrical passages (a beautiful moment is at the words 'From foreign shores, O Lord, I call'). The choral writing is varied, though, contrary to Martinů's usual practice, counterpoint is conspicuously absent. Particularly effective are the final passages for un-accompanied chorus.

We turn now to Russia, where long-standing choral traditions are manifest both in folk-music and the music of the Orthodox Church.

Much of Russian folk-music is polyphonic, though hardly comparable with polyphony in our sense of the word. Russian Orthodox Church music is purely vocal, instruments being forbidden. The first Russian choir (that of the Imperial Chapel) was founded by Peter the Great in 1713. Its directors have included Sarti, Bortnyansky, Glinka, and Balakirev. It has now been renamed the U.S.S.R. State Choir.

But choral music in the concert-hall has always been

overshadowed in Russia by its close relative, opera. However, both genres share a common descent from the monumental choruses of Mikhail Glinka (1804–57) – who borrowed much from the contrapuntal technique of Handel, and from the works of Giuseppe Sarti (1729–1802), an Italian who worked in Russia – and Dmitri Bortnyansky (1752–1825). Choral societies in Russia were slow to appear, and it was not till the opening of the St Petersburg Conservatory in 1862, and of its Moscow rival, the Free School of Music, in the same year that choral music began to be widely practised. Russian music during the nineteenth century, like Russian art in general, is marked by a dichotomy between Slavophils – believers in purely native art – and Westerners – who favoured imitation of West-European ideals. The choral music of the Slavophils is best represented by Modest Mussorgsky (1839–81), Nikolai Rimsky-Korsakov (1844–1908), and Pyotr Tchaikovsky (1840–93), though choral music was also written by César Cui (1853–1918), Anatoly Lyadov (1855–1914), Sergei Taneyev (1856–1915), Alexander Grechaninov (1864–1956), and Anton Arensky (1861–1906).

Mussorgsky's two chief choral compositions, if hardly among his most inspired, are *The Defeat of Sennacherib* and *Joshua*. *The Defeat of Sennacherib*, which is written for mixed voice chorus and orchestra (or piano) and is taken from a translation of Byron's *Hebrew Melodies*, exists in two versions (1867 and 1874). The latter version preserves only the poem's main outline, the words being completely rewritten. In comparison with Mussorgsky's major compositions, it is of little value and yields in drama and musical technique to its companion piece, *Joshua* (1874–7). According to an inscription on the score, this is founded on Jewish melodies, besides making use of fragments from Mussorgsky's unfinished opera *Salammbô*. Of interest on account of their truly national flavour are the four short *Russian Folk-songs* for unaccompanied male voice chorus (1880). The third and fourth of these are particularly beautiful and certainly deserve an occasional performance. Example 66 shows the opening of No. 4 – 'Rise, red sun'.

Ex. 66. Mussorgsky, *Russian Folk-Songs*

The choral compositions of Rimsky-Korsakov are of interest in that they anticipate many of the essential characteristics of the modern Soviet cantata and oratorio, with their emphasis on melody, the use of the Russian epic style frequently united with patriotic themes, and the employment of large orchestral forces. Among his four cantatas, *Verses about Alexei the Godly Man* (1878), *Svitezyanka* (1897), *The Song of the Prophet Oleg* (1899), and *From Homer* (1901), the second and third are outstanding. *Svitezyanka*, which is written for soprano, tenor, chorus, and orchestra, is reflective in mood and is distinguished by its simplicity. *The Song of the Prophet Oleg*, on the other hand, for two solo male voices, male chorus, and orchestra, is a more animated work in which an intensely chromatic language vies with the Russian heroic style. Some pages are of extreme lyrical beauty. As in much of Rimsky-Korsakov's vocal work, the principal fault of the cantatas is the unimaginativeness of the choral writing, which is eclipsed by the virtuosity of the orchestral parts.

Mention must also be made of Rimsky-Korsakov's numerous unaccompanied choruses, many of which were performed at concerts of the Free School of Music. His Op. 19 (*Russian Folk-songs Arranged in Folk Harmony*, for female, male, and mixed voices, 1879), Op. 23 (*Four 3-part Choruses*, for men's voices, 1876), and his *Two Choruses for Children's Voices* (1884) are, for the most part, beautifully written and completely Russian in spirit, besides being very entertaining. They would certainly make a pleasant addition to the normal repertory.

Tchaikovsky's choral compositions may be divided into three categories – church music, cantatas with soloists and orchestral accompaniment written for specific occasions, and a number of choruses either unaccompanied or with piano. Probably the best of his short choruses is the unaccompanied arrangement (1889) of his *Legend* ('The Christ-child had a garden'), written originally for voice and piano. However, his religious music, all of which dates from 1878–85, is of greater importance. Although possessing little religious feeling, Tchaikovsky was fascinated by the pageantry and symbolism of the Orthodox Church. Besides editing the complete ecclesiastical works of Bortnyansky, he composed a *Vesper Service* (1881), *Three Cherubic Hymns* (1884), *Six Church Songs* (1885), and a number of other works. His church compositions have been criticized on technical grounds such as the inaccuracy of his verbal accents, and the inconsistency of his modal harmonies. However, Russian music owes him a debt in that his efforts aroused interest in ecclesiastical music and marked the beginnings of an artistic revival.

The three above-mentioned composers represent Slavophil tendencies. The 'Westerners', whose productions were for the most part inferior to their rivals, were represented by A. N. Serov (1820–71), Anton Rubinstein (1829–94), founder of the St Petersburg Conservatory in 1862, and, at a later date, Sergei Rakhmaninov (1873–1943). The fact that they favoured Western ideals by no means precluded their incorporation of Russian material in their compositions. Indeed, in all three composers the national idiom figures strongly. Serov's choral works, which include a *Stabat Mater*, are of little importance, while those of Anton Rubinstein, although enjoying phenomenal popularity in their day (particularly in London) are remarkable for their aesthetic aims rather than their musical content. Aware of the incongruities of oratorio, Rubinstein sought to create an intermediary genre entitled 'Sacred Opera', his theories taking concrete form in *The Tower of Babel* (1870), *Sulamith* (1883), and other works.

Far more important is Rakhmaninov, whose choral works range from groups of part-songs to a choral symphony, *The Bells* (1910). His ecclesiastical music consists of a *Liturgy of St John Chrysostom* (1910) – to all extents and appearances a preparation for his *Vesper Mass* (1915) – and several cantatas and oratorios. Undoubtedly his finest work is the choral symphony, *The Bells*, which was based on Balmont's Russian adaptation of Edgar Allan Poe (Balmont's version being virtually a fresh poem). Its four sections may be compared with the movements of a symphony. Scored for solo tenor, soprano, and baritone, mixed chorus and large orchestra, *The Bells* is a remarkable work whose musical content ranges from dissonance to moments of poignant lyrical beauty. It is a difficult work to perform.

A special place in Russian music is held by Alexander Nikolayevich Skryabin (1872–1915), whose use of the chorus in his Symphony No. 1 (1889) is mentioned on p. 253.

Choral music in the Soviet era plays a significant part in everyday life, its two most important genres being those of 'mass song' and of Soviet cantata and oratorio. Other forms such as part-songs, children's songs, and the ubiquitous folk-song arrangements are also common. Choral music also frequently appears in intermediary forms such as the choral symphony and the symphonic cantata.

'Art must belong to the people,' wrote Lenin, and this succinctly sums up the Soviet attitude to music in general. Music must be comprehensible to the masses, must serve a social purpose; it must edify but not dictate, must show adherence to the traditions of the Russian past, but not necessarily imitate; it must show originality but not eccentricity.

In a word, it must be communistic. As is well known, Soviet composers have often found it difficult to fulfil these rather vague but exacting requirements. From time to time the Communist Party has found it necessary to issue directives (as in 1936 and 1948) to 'correct' composers' divergences from the paths of truth. However, despite the many-sidedness of Soviet music over the last forty years, a pattern clearly emerges.

The first choral works to appear after the Revolution were mass songs which either followed the form of well-known Revolutionary songs such as the *International*, *Dubinushka*, and the *Marseillaise*, or were arrangements of folk-songs. The principal themes of songs of this period were the struggle for freedom and self-sacrifice for the Motherland. This led to the rise of the *chastushka* – a popular song sometimes with a satirical flavour. Realizing the deficiencies of their choral music, the Soviet authorities did their utmost to create a choral repertory, the principal composers being Alexander Kastalsky (1856–1926), Mikhail Ippolitov-Ivanov (1859–1935), Grigori Lobachev (1888–1953), and A. V. Aleksandrov (1883–1946). The latter is best known through his work with the Red Army Ensemble, his compositions taking the form of lively arrangements of popular folk-songs. Example 67 is based on the Ukrainian song *Through the Valleys* (*Po dolinam*). Typical of all these songs is the strong rhythm, the patriotic subject-matter and the familiar and effective technique of gradual approach, climax, and departure. Mention must be made of the work of the Pyatnitsky Russian Folk Choir, long under the direction of V. G. Zakharov (1901–56), who was also a composer.

With the advent of the thirties, a new form of mass song arose. The most famous song of these early days was the march from the score written by Isaak Dunayevsky (1900–55) to the film *The Happy Children* (1934), whose outstanding features were tunefulness, cheerfulness, lucidity, and comprehensibility. The subject-matter of the songs of this period often dealt with the Communist Party and its leaders, the Soviet State, the new life on the collective farms, the Soviet

Ex. 67. Aleksandrov, *Through the Valleys*

Army and Soviet youth. The second half of the thirties saw the appearance of Dunayevsky's best work, most of which was connected with films, particularly the piece *Song of Our Country* from the film *The Circus*.

This period was also marked by an accent on children's songs, outstanding being the composer Mikhail Starokadomsky (*b.* 1901). Typical of this genre is a short opening phrase which then breaks into two-part harmony. It is incidentally to be noted that children's music, as indeed all forms of youthful art, is rated highly in the Soviet Union, and leading composers such as Shostakovich, Prokofiev, Kabalevsky, and Koval have not considered it beneath their dignity to write many pieces suitable for juvenile performance. Similarly, much work has been done on children's films, a typical title being *Ah, But It's Good to Live in the Soviet*. The U.S.S.R. Children's Choir was founded in 1936.

The entry of the Soviet Union into the Second World War brought forth a spate of patriotic songs ranging from praises of the Soviet Army and its generals, and of the might of the Russian land, to human emotions such as the parting of the Russian soldier from his wife and family. Among the leading choral composers were Anatoly Novikov (b.1896), the brothers Daniil Pokrass (1905–54) and Dimitrif Pokrass (b.1899), and Matvei Blanter (b.1903). Also popular throughout the war years were the age-old folk-songs such as *Down by Mother Volga*, which continued to appear in ever-varying arrangements.

With the close of the Second World War, as the Soviet spokesmen put it, 'certain unhealthy tendencies received reflection in the world of music' and these matters came to a head with the celebrated Zhdanov decree of 1948, calling even masters such as Prokofiev and Shostakovich to heel. Since that year, Soviet mass song has dealt with themes such as the struggle for peace, the international solidarity of the working masses, and the hope for a brighter future. The leading choral institutions, such as the Red Banner Song and Dance Ensemble of the Red Army and the Pyatnitsky Russian Folk Choir, together with many regional choirs, continue to perform the traditional songs. New choral compositions such as Shostakovich's *Ten Poems* for unaccompanied chorus to words of Revolutionary poets (1951) are constantly appearing, and each year sees the founding of fresh choral institutions such as the Russian Choral Society in Moscow in 1957.

The second principal genre of Russian choral music is that of Soviet oratorio and cantata. Although the terms have no religious significance (save only that Communism is a religion in itself), formally they adhere to the traditions of the past – particularly Handel, Glinka, and Mussorgsky – the accent being for the most part on monumental forces, both instrumental and vocal, and patriotic subject matter of a dramatic, spiritually uplifting content. The distinction of writing the first large-scale Soviet works of this nature belongs to A. D. Kastalsky (1856–1926) whose choral compositions *Lenin*, *To the Proletariat*, and the cantata *The Year 1905* achieved widespread popularity. These first efforts had many imitators, among whom may be mentioned D.

Vasilev-Buglai (1888–1956) and A. A. Davidenko (1899–1934), the latter being chiefly remembered for a dramatic piece entitled *Burlaki* (the name given to the so-called *Song of the Volga Boatmen*). The success of Davidenko's music led to the composition of a collective oratorio *The October Path* (1927) for soloists, chorus, orchestra, and reciters, which was written by a group of no less than nine students from the Moscow Conservatory, of whom Davidenko was one. Generally speaking, however, the whole of this early period may be criticized for its unevenness and lack of homogeneity. Most of the works were difficult to perform, and only those which drew their inspiration from folk-song, as in the case of Kastalsky and Davidenko, achieved any measure of success.

The next period – from 1934 to 1941 – represents the high-water mark of Soviet oratorio and cantata, outstanding being the compositions of Sergey Prokofiev (1891–1953) and Yuri Shaporin (*b.*1887). If Prokofiev's works up to and during his stay abroad (1918–33) are notable for their iconoclasm and revolutionary nature, the music written on his return shows a desire for simplicity and melodiousness. Such is the case with the symphonic cantata *Alexander Nevsky*, which was first written in 1938 as incidental music to Eisenstein's memorable film of the same name. The story describes the decisive victory of the Russians, led by Alexander Nevsky, over the Teutonic knights at the battle of Lake Chudskoye in 1242. The music, which was subsequently arranged as a suite, is divided into seven sections and includes pure lyricism in the manner of Russian 'protracted' folk-song (No. 6 – 'The Field of the Dead'), scenes of lively festivity (No. 7 – 'The Entry of Alexander Nevsky into Pskov'), and episodes of vivid realism in which one hears the clash of swords and the groans of the ice labouring under the impact of the two mighty armies (No. 5 – 'The Battle on the Ice'). The whole work is permeated by a spirit of ardent patriotism, and although Prokofiev represents the aggressors by means of a pseudo-plainchant, the overall feeling is essentially Russian. Example 68, from the fourth movement – 'Arise, ye Russian People' – gives some idea of the cantata's musical style with its poignant and unusual harmonies, sturdy melodies, and rhythmic vitality. *Alexander Nevsky* has acquired universal renown. In its obvious connexions with the Russian classical opera of the nineteenth century, its use of folk-music, the patriotic subject-matter, and the freshness and accessibility of the music, it is regarded in the Soviet Union as the perfect example of its kind.

Ex. 68. Prokofiev, *Alexander Nevsky*

Yuri Shaporin's great work *On the Field of Kulikovo* is called a symphony-cantata, a title which is explained by the monumental size of the work. It is scored for mezzo-soprano, tenor and bass, mixed chorus, and large orchestra and falls into eight sections. Although it was planned originally in the early 1920s, it was not completed till 1938. Like *Alexander Nevsky*, Shaporin's symphony-cantata makes use of a historical subject, in this case the defeat by Dmitri Donskoy of the Tartar hordes, led by Khan Mamai, at Kulikovo on the River Don in 1380. Shaporin himself said of the work: 'Its theme is the immortal idea of folk heroism, the infinite all-conquering patriotic love of the people for their native land.' The music is lyrical in content, though less adventurous than Prokofiev, showing greater affinity with nineteenth-century Russian composers, particularly Rimsky-Korsakov and Borodin.

Yet another work of some importance is the oratorio *Emelyan Pugachev* by Marian Koval (born 1907) written in 1939. This deals with the peasant uprising of 1773–75 in the time of Catherine II – a theme immortalized in Pushkin's novel *The Captain's Daughter*.

The Second World War marked the appearance of a whole stream of patriotic compositions, among which may be mentioned *Kirov is With Us* (1943) by Nikolai Myaskovsky (1881–1958), Shaporin's *Story of the Battle for the Russian Land* (1943–4), and the choral orchestral suite *People's Avengers* (1942) by Dmitri Kabalevsky (*b.* 1904). However, after the Zhdanov decree of 1948, a change was discernible in the approach to choral music, most representative of the new attitude being the *Song of the Forests* (1949) by Dmitri Shostakovich (*b.* 1906), which is dedicated to the theme of re-afforestation. The music makes much use of mass song.

Within the last fifteen years or so, there has been a constant stream of new works by Russian and Soviet composers. In Armenia the *Cantata of the Motherland* (1948–9) by Alexander Arutyunian (*b.* 1920) has been received with great success, while in Georgia *The Heart of Kartli* (1952) by Archil Chimakadze (*b.* 1919) and *My Country's Day* (1954) by Alexei Machavariani (*b.* 1913) are regarded as masterpieces of their kind. In each case the composer has succeeded in combining folk inflections with the generally accepted West European harmonic language.

In Russia itself important contributions have also been made by Prokofiev, whose oratorio *On Guard for Peace* was written in 1951, and Shostakovich in his *Over Our Native Land Shines the Sun* (1952). A gifted young composer is Alfred Shnitke (*b.* 1934), whose cantata *Nagasaki* (1959) also shows signs of considerable originality.

However, there is little doubt that at present the musical scene (from the point of view of oratorio at least) is dominated by the figure of Georgi Sviridov (*b.* 1915). Sviridov has two major choral compositions to his credit – *Poem in Memory of Sergei Yesenin* (1956) and the *Pathetic Oratorio* (1959). The latter is written for reciter, soloists, chorus, orchestra and organ: its title refers to the 'pathetic' (that is, tragic) content of the words. Both works are essentially Soviet in their concept and, apart from the fact that they make use of words by Soviet poets (Yesenin and Mayakovsky respectively), employ all the favourite ingredients of Soviet musical art – massive choruses, vast orchestral forces, a declamatory style of recitative and patriotic subject matter. The music itself is dramatic, melodious and easy to listen to, its principal sources being Ravel, Carl Orff, Mussorgsky, and the Russian folk element. The *Pathetic Oratorio* was awarded a Lenin Prize in 1960 and has since been referred to constantly in the Soviet musical press. It seems highly probable, therefore, that it will serve, like *Alexander Nevsky* in the forties and fifties, as the model for many years to come.

17

Four Revolutionaries

c.1900–60

DIKA NEWLIN

MANY amateurs of choral music may not be aware of the somewhat extensive contributions to their field made by four of the twentieth century's most renowned composers. We give this chapter the title *Four Revolutionaries*, for Schoenberg, Stravinsky, Hindemith, and Bartók have all, from time to time, been associated with musical concepts considered revolutionary. Yet a closer examination of each composer's work might reveal varying degrees of evolution, revolution, or even reaction. Let us now apply this process to representative choral works by each of them.

First Arnold Schoenberg (1874–1951), who liked to say 'I am a conservative who was forced to become a radical'. As so often, the composer's verbal paradox betrayed a keen realization of his historical position. Reared in the shadow of conservative Viennese classicism, yet under the spell of Wagner, he might well have become merely another follower of Wagner or of Brahms. Instead, courageously accepting the possible consequences of his actions, he relentlessly fulfilled the prophecies which he found in the works of his forebears.

The young Schoenberg had early practical experience of the technical demands of choral writing, for one of his first musical jobs was as choral director of a metal-workers' choral society in Stockerau, some twenty miles from Vienna. It was, in part, the inspiration gained from this activity which stimulated him to write the magnificent choruses of the *Songs of Gurra* (*Gurre-Lieder*, 1900–1, orchestration completed 1911). This broodingly romantic cantata is based on

Jens Peter Jacobsen's verses (in the German translation of Robert Franz Arnold) drawn from Danish history, and legend. The work precedes Mahler's *Symphony of a Thousand* (see p. 257) in conception, and virtually equals it in terms of resources demanded. Six soloists, including a reciter, are called for; and choral participation is on a grand scale, for the composer requested three four-part male choruses and an eight-part mixed chorus. It is this last-named group which proclaims the work's triumphant climax:

> Behold the Sun! See how her glowing morning dream greets us from the East! Smiling she rises from the floods of night; freely flows from her bright brow the glory of her gleaming locks.

As to the orchestration, it is, as might be expected, in the monumental post-Wagnerian tradition; one need only mention such items as eight flutes, five oboes, ten horns, six trumpets, four Wagner tubas, and a veritable percussion orchestra including a brace of heavy iron chains! It is, as we see, a work best suited to grandiose festival occasions.

Another, briefer work, this time exploiting the possibilities of unaccompanied voices (from four to eight parts), was still completed during the composer's 'first' (tonal) period. This is *Peace on Earth* (*Friede auf Erden*, 1907) to a Christmas text by the Swiss poet C. F. Meyer. However, it is not until after the First World War that we find a notable increase in Schoenberg's production of choral works or of works in which the chorus is prominent. In the 1920s there are the *Four Pieces* for mixed chorus (sometimes accompanied by small instrumental group), Op. 27 (1925), based on texts by the composer and on adaptations from the Chinese by Hans Bethge; the *Three Satires*, Op. 28 (also 1925), which we shall examine in more detail below; and the *Six Pieces for Male Chorus* (four-part, unaccompanied, 1929–30), again based on the composer's own texts and dealing with subjects such as 'Restraint', 'The Law, ' 'Happiness', and 'Obligation'.

Later, after Schoenberg had to leave Germany in 1933, he tended increasingly to concern himself with subjects relating to Jewish religious themes, or to the persecutions inflicted upon the Chosen People. In this category belong the *Kol Nidre*, for reciter (rabbi), mixed chorus, and orchestra, Op. 39 (1938); the *Prelude to 'Genesis'* for orchestra and (wordless) mixed chorus, Op. 44 (1945); *A Survivor from Warsaw*, for reciter, male chorus, and orchestra, Op. 46 (1947); *Thrice a Thousand Years (Dreimal tausend Jahre)*, for unaccompanied mixed chorus, Op. 50 A(1949); and *Out of the Depths* (the Hebrew text of Psalm 130) for unaccompanied mixed chorus, Op. 50 B. We shall have more to say of another work – in no way sectarian, but, rather, the testament of a dying man's most personal approach to 'the last things': the incomplete setting of one of the composer's many 'Modern Psalm' texts in German, for mixed chorus, reciter, and orchestra, Op. 50 C (1950). And we should also not fail to mention the extremely important spoken and sung choral portions of the great unfinished opera *Moses and Aaron* (composition begun in 1930). In these, Schoenberg has, perhaps, reached his highest degree of unity between note and word; this is shown by his skilful use of alliteration in the text and of onomatopoeia in both text and music. While this work was, of course, written for the stage, it has proved to be eminently suitable as well for production in concert or radio form.

In all of the above-mentioned works, written in or after 1925, we may see the fruits of Schoenberg's search for a new way in music. He was no longer satisfied with the complete freedom offered by 'atonality', the lack of a tonal centre – a freedom which in its turn imposed new responsibilities. He, therefore, tried to find new laws to control the wealth of material liberated by what he liked to call 'the emancipation of the dissonance' (i.e. the elimination of the concept that certain intervals had perforce to resolve to certain other intervals, or that only certain combinations of notes formed suitable points of rest). Thus was born the famed, oft-misunderstood 'method of composition with twelve notes related only to one another' (twelve-note method, system, or technique). Though this cannot be elaborated here, we may mention that each twelve-note composition is founded on a *note-row* (also called series or basic set). This is made up of the twelve notes of our chromatic scale in a certain chosen order. Acquaintance with the note-row of the piece he is performing is most valuable to the choralist in a twelve-note composition. In practice, it has been found that to acquaint singers with the note-row improves their intonation materially and makes it much easier for them to learn the complex melodic lines. This should be kept in mind by the choral conductor wishing to perform one of Schoenberg's twelve-note choral works.

The *Three Satires* for mixed chorus, Op. 28 (1925), show a side of Schoenberg which is not his most pleasant but which is essential to his personality. In a polemic preface, he lashes out against all those who seek the middle way (the only one, according to him, that does not lead to Rome!), against all those who travel under the banner 'Back to . . .', and against all exponents of folklorism and every other kind of 'ism'. The *Satires* (the texts of which are also by the composer' then carry on in this spirit. *At the Crossroads (Am Scheideweg)* depicts wittily the dilemma of a composer who cannot decide whether to be 'tonal' or 'atonal' (Example 69).

Ex. 69. Schoenberg, *At the Crossroads*

The theme of the clever canon sums up his plight perfectly, for it begins with an uncompromising C major triad and then wanders into more distant regions.

The second Satire *Many-Sidedness (Vielseitigkeit)*, lives up to its name, for it may be read in the usual manner or upside-down and backwards with identical results. The text pokes fun at one noisy little 'Modernsky' (obviously Stravinsky in a transparent disguise) whose 'genuine false hair' makes him think that he looks exactly like 'Papa Bach'. Schoenberg, however, would show us by his mastery of counterpoint that *he* is more deserving of such a designation – at least, one might read such an implication into the almost arrogant skill of this music.

Finally, we have an ambitious and effective little cantata, *The New Classicism* (*Der neue Klassizismus*), which adds to the mixed chorus an accompaniment of viola, cello, and piano. Here, Schoenberg is tilting at those who loudly proclaim their intention to renounce the fleshpots of Romanticism and to write thenceforth in purest classical style. In a twelve-note burlesque of a fugue (which ends triumphantly on a unison middle C sung *fortissimo* on all voices) the chorus announces the comfortably ambiguous creed of the neo-classicists. We give a translation:

> Classical perfection,
> Strict in each direction—
> It comes from where it may—
> I really couldn't say;
> It wanders where it will—
> That is the newest style!

A very different atmosphere is found in Schoenberg's last, unfinished choral work. In 1950, he began to work on a series of *Modern Psalms*. Unfortunately, he lived to compose only part of one of these poems. The fragment is, however, quite performable. Its first hearing took place on 29 May 1956, in Cologne.

We turn now to Igor Stravinsky (*b*.1882) who at one time was considered as the 'anti-pope' to Schoenberg. Indeed, it was not merely the disciples of these composers who treated them as rival standard-bearers, but the composers themselves also seemed to maintain such an attitude. We have already noted the bitterness of Schoenberg's little satire on 'Modernsky'. We might also mention that, though for many years Schoenberg and Stravinsky lived but a few miles apart in different fashionable suburbs of Los Angeles, they virtually ignored each other during that period. But today, Stravinsky, stimulated by his contact with the music of Schoenberg's disciple Anton Webern – a relatively little-appreciated figure in his own lifetime, but one whose delicate, personal music has truly come into its own since his death* – feels that the twelve-note, serial method is the hope

* See p. 362.

of present and future generations of composers. He has remarked (see the book *Conversations with Igor Stravinsky*, by
Stravinsky and Robert Craft):

> A masterpiece is more likely to happen to the composer with the
> most highly developed language. This language is serial at present,
> and though our contemporary development of it could be tan-
> gential to an evolution we do not yet see, for us this doesn't matter.
> ... Masterpieces aside, it seems to me the new music will be
> serial.

Is this latest transformation of Stravinsky a deep-seated one
or is it but another in his series of 'masks', like folklorism,
barbarism, neo-classicism, neo-medievalism? Hard to say –
but, meanwhile, we may observe with interest the bright
array of his successive musical costumes. Many of these
costumes come to light in his choral works. Thus, early ties
to Romanticism as represented in the person of his distinguished mentor are reflected in the *Lament on the Death of
Rimsky-Korsakov* for chorus and orchestra (1908); mysticism
in the difficult, seldom-performed *King of the Stars* (also
sometimes called the *Star-Faced One*; 1911) for male chorus
and orchestra; interest in Russian folklore and local colour
in *Saucers*, four Russian songs for female voices (1914–17).

The same interest is revealed in an important stage work,
also most suitable for concert performance: *The Wedding*
(1923), a stylized treatment of Russian wedding customs,
for four soloists, chorus, and percussion orchestra in which
four pianos play a dominant role. (The original words are
Russian, so there is no good reason for the use of the title
Les Noces in English-speaking countries.) The objectivity
and impersonality of the Latin language as a medium for
musical setting has often attracted the neo-classic (or neo-
medieval) Stravinsky. Smaller works such as *Pater Noster*
(1926) and *Ave Maria* (1934) show this trend, as it were, in
miniature. It is 'monumentalized', however, in more significant compositions – the 'opera-oratorio' *Oedipus Rex* (1927–
8), the oft-performed *Symphony of Psalms*, for chorus and
orchestra (1930), and the Mass (1951) for double wind
quintet (two oboes, English horn, two bassoons, two trum-

pets, and three trombones) and men's and children's voices, a work often showing strangely Machaut-like sonorities. In such works, Stravinsky is concerned to avoid the obvious sensual instrumental and vocal effects which a Romantic composer might have used. Contrast, for example, Bruckner's triumphant, glowing setting of Psalm 150 (see p. 241), with its festal opening wherein the full orchestra and chorus sound forth the praise of God *fortissimo* and its sensuous violin solo, with Stravinsky's austere *piano* opening for the same psalm (Finale of the *Symphony of Psalms*). Throughout this work, the upper strings are avoided, only the more sombre colours of the cellos and basses being heard. (Like Bruckner before him, Stravinsky does not succumb to the temptation of using the cymbals to illustrate the line, 'Praise Him upon the high-sounding cymbals'!)

Tendencies towards orchestral asceticism culminate in the instrumental restraint of the *Cantata* (1952) for soprano, tenor, and female chorus on anonymous fifteenth- and sixteenth-century English lyrics; this is accompanied only by two flutes, two oboes (English horn alternating with the second) and cello. Similar tendencies – flavoured, in Stravinsky's typically eclectic way, by many other stylistic elements – may also be seen in the twelve-note works of the composer's recent period, among them the *Sacred Canticle* (*Canticum Sacrum*, 1955) and the *Lamentations of Jeremiah* (*Threni, id est Lamentationes Jeremiae prophetae*, 1957–8). Of these two works with Latin texts, it is the first which, as a representative example of his approach to twelve-note composition, we shall now discuss in further detail.

This work first came before the public during the 1956 Festival of Contemporary Music in Venice. In fact, it became the dominating work of this festival in spite of its relatively brief duration – about seventeen minutes. Stravinsky is restrained not only in length but also in the avoidance of sensuous sound. Through the use of the 'dead' Latin language, he gains a sense of impersonality; through his orchestration, he achieves a severe, harsh sound. The ensemble includes a flute, two oboes and English horn, two bassoons and double-bassoon, four trumpets, four trombones, harp, violas, and double-basses. Note the absence of the upper strings! The upper wind instruments, too, are often silent, as in the work's first major movement. The vocal ensemble consists of tenor and baritone solos with four-part mixed chorus.

As the work is divided into five distinct movements plus an introduction, it is well to discuss these sections individually.

Dedication. This nine-bar introduction presents, in medieval fashion, the work's 'motto' – the dedication 'To the City of Venice, in praise of its Patron Saint, the Blessed Mark, Apostle'. The Latin words are intoned by the soloists against a sparse background of trombones. Vocal and instrumental lines alike suggest the turns of Gregorian chant – one might speak here of Stravinsky's 'neo-medieval' manner. To combine such devices with the use of twelve-note rows – as happens later – is, of course, completely characteristic of Stravinsky's eclecticism.

1. *Go ye into all the world (Euntes in mundum).* This is the first movement of a symmetrical arrangement which is intended to correspond to the pattern of the five domes of St Mark's in Venice. As we shall see, the first movement corresponds to the fifth, and the second to the fourth, while the third is divided into three sections of which the outer two are symmetrical. The 'St Mark' theme is carried out in the text, which is chosen from his Gospel: 'Go ye into all the world, and preach the gospel to every creature.' The five-sectional division of the entire work is mirrored in miniature here, for this movement is divided into five subsections. These alternate between sections for chorus and orchestra and interludes for organ with bassoons. In the choral sections, an *ostinato*-like figure predominates in the lower instruments; it includes the notes B flat, G, and D flat. The possible implications of the key of B flat minor are, however, contradicted by nervous figures of repeated sixteenth-notes in the trumpets which include B natural and D natural. Quite possibly this sort of simultaneous clash is a carry-over from Stravinsky's earlier polytonal practices

(one remembers the famed *Petrushka* chord with its bold superposition of C major and F sharp major). Thus a hint of polytonality (that is, of the simultaneous use of two or more keys) becomes but one more element in the stylistic mixture of this work.

2. *Awake, O north wind (Surge, aquilo)*. With the passionate words from *The Song of Songs*, a new note enters the music. The solo tenor sings an intensive, melismatic line based on a twelve-note row. Example 70 shows the row (Row A), the melody based on it with words meaning 'Awake, O north wind, and come, thou south', and a later row-form (Row

Ex. 70. Stravinsky, *Sacred Canticle*
(a) ♩ = 92
T. solo
mf
Surge, a-qui-lo,— et ve - - ni, ve - - ni, auster;

(b) Row A (basis of the above) and Row B

m2 = minor second, half tone
M2 = major second, whole tone

B) of which we shall have more to say. Only double-basses, harp, flute, and English horn are used in this section; the chorus takes no part. The use of a small specialized group of instruments, the transparent texture with many rests, and the frequent leaps of a ninth or a seventh suggest some of the ways in which Stravinsky has utilized his gleanings from Webern's scores. The 'old' Stravinsky of *The Rite of Spring* still lurks, however, behind the irregular time-signatures frequently changed ($\frac{7}{16}$, $\frac{5}{16}$, $\frac{8}{16}$, $\frac{6}{16}$, and $\frac{7}{16}$ again occur within a space of ten bars).

3. *Exhortations to the Three Virtues: Charity, Hope, Faith (Ad Tres Virtutes Hortationes: Caritas, Spes, Fides)*. Twelve-note row B (see Example 70 above) is used in this movement. First announced in its original form, in octaves, by the

organ, it is subsequently used in various retrograde, inverted, and transposed forms. Our diagram in Example 70 shows the points of resemblance between Row A and Row B. (Stravinsky, though, does not follow Schoenberg's classical practice of using the *same* row or its most nearly related variants for all twelve-note sections of a composition.) As in Schoenberg's twelve-note choruses, the demands made on the singers in terms of intonation are considerable. Stravinsky has even provided for optional support of the chorus by the viola section, should problems of intonation arise.

4. *Brief Movement in Cantilena (Brevis Motus Cantilenae)*. In this and the final movement, Stravinsky returns to the Gospel of St Mark. The moving words here chosen are these: 'Jesus said unto him, If thou canst believe, all things are possible to him that believeth. And straightway the father of the child cried out, and said with tears, Lord, I believe; help thou my unbelief.' Again we hear, as in the second movement, a melismatic solo vocal line – this time sung by the baritone; it is based on Row B. The chorus plays a prominent role in this movement. First we hear it is as a quiet echo of the soloist's agitated exclamations; later, it enters into an energetic imitative passage depicting the cries of the father. Finally, it disappears, leaving the baritone voice alone to plead for faith. The orchestra fades away gradually too – wispy motives in oboe and bassoons blend into a soft organ chord; *pizzicato* notes in double-basses and violas provide the final resonance.

5. *And they went forth (Illi autem profecti)*. We have come full circle. The proclamation of the beginning has reached its fulfilment: 'And they went forth, and preached everywhere, the Lord working with them, and confirming the word with signs following. Amen.' The music, too, comes full circle, for this movement is basically a retrograde version of the first. Thus Stravinsky, ever aware of classic design, has preserved the desired symmetry till the very close of his *Sacred Canticle*.

In 1962 was first heard *A Sermon, a Narrative, and a Prayer*, for speaker, contralto, tenor, and chorus, in which Stravinsky set a New Testament text in English. The composer has said that he regards this as a companion-piece to the *Lamentations of Jeremiah*.

The versatile Paul Hindemith (*b*.1895) – conductor, theoretician, player of nearly every orchestral instrument, and composer of solo music for most of them – has also, not surprisingly, made a noteworthy and sizeable contribution to choral literature. In stressing the 'useful' aspect of this contribution, it is not meant to minimize the importance of Hindemith's less immediately 'practical' works. None the less, it may well be that his Utility Music (*Gebrauchsmusik*), will survive longer – for instance in the repertory of professional, semi-professional, or amateur choirs – than some of his more pretentious creations.

This concept of Utility Music or Music for Use is, indeed, a symbol of the composer's easy adaptability; for throughout his career we find him choosing texts with a good deal of thought as to the spirit of the time and of the country in which he was writing. The 1920s brought forth much choral music for amateurs to sing and play (one example of which, *In Praise of Music*, we shall analyse below). Convivial, pleasant texts are often chosen by Hindemith for this purpose, and the joys of making music together informally are emphasized. Thus, in his preface to the jolly *St Martin's Song*, Hindemith admonishes the performers:

> Singers and players of this *Martinslied*! Please try to perform this music lightly and joyously – be of good will. Do not use this piece as an excuse to argue about contemporary tendencies and technical problems; it isn't important enough.

But in the restless Germany of 1929–30, social satire, too, found its place in Hindemith's music. In his *Five Choruses for Male Voices* (1929–30) we find texts by Bert Brecht and Gottfried Benn; one of the latter's poems, *Prince Strength* (*Fürst Kraft*) is a devastating memorial to a dead tycoon, set by Hindemith with full appreciation of its heroic irony. Later, as an emigrant to America, where he was for many years Professor of Composition at Yale University, he seems to have made some effort (not altogether successful) to come to terms with American tradition. This effort is best documented, perhaps, by his really moving 'American Requiem' for chorus and orchestra entitled *When Lilacs Last in the Dooryard Bloom'd* (1946), to the beloved text of Walt Whitman. However, Hindemith's subsequent return to Europe and his spirited if often inaccurate criticisms of the American scene seem somehow contradictory of the emotions expressed in the work.

A continuing concern of this composer has been the creation of a true *Gemeinschaftsmusik* – that is, music for the community, which could be participated in with a minimum of rehearsal not only by amateur performing groups but even by the audience that came to hear them. Thus he came to compose *In Praise of Music* (*Frau Musica*; 1928, revised 1943). In this work, written to text by Martin Luther, Hindemith pays his fullest tribute to the idea of 'music for use'; therefore I have chosen it as a representative example of this philosophy. The composer's preface to the revised edition is well worth quoting as a clear description of the work's intent:

This work was not written for the concert-hall or for professional musicians. It is intended to provide interesting twentieth-century material for practice by those who like to sing and play for their own pleasure, and perhaps for the pleasure of a small group of like-minded listeners. In keeping with this intention, no very great technical demands are made on the singers and players. The *tutti* string-players need hardly go above the first position, and the solo and choral voice parts consist so far as possible of easy and singable melodic lines. At the same time, no one will expect that a piece of music written in these times and for our present needs should be instantly playable at sight by one and all. The amateur is provided with a few nuts to crack.

The opening and closing choruses may well be sung by everyone present – performers and 'listeners' alike. For this purpose, song-sheets are available from the publishers at a nominal price. A brief rehearsal immediately before the performance will suffice.

The piece can be performed with any instrumental combination from four strings up. A flute would be valuable, but its part may be played by a violin. Other wind instruments are used mainly to reinforce the voices in the opening and closing choruses. The four 'string' parts include added lines providing for all the common orchestral instruments, and including transpositions where necessary.

Suggested instrumental possibilities include: flutes, oboes, clarinets, trumpets, or soprano saxophones (to play with the first violins), alto saxophones or alto horns (with the seconds), French horns or English horns (with the violas), and bassoons, bass clarinets, tenor saxophones, tenor horns or trombones (with the cellos and basses). By 'alto horns' and 'tenor horns' Hindemith presumably refers to those of the saxhorn and related families, as used in brass and other bands.

The work is organized as a small four-movement cantata, as follows:

1. *Moderately fast*. Everybody (audience included), reinforced by as many instruments as possible, sings a spirited simple melody in transposed Dorian mode (Example 71).

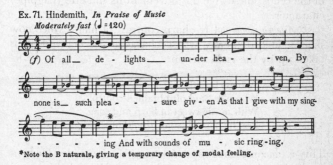

Ex. 71. Hindemith, *In Praise of Music*
Moderately fast ($\quarternote$ = 120)

(*f*) Of all__ de - lights__ un-der hea - - ven, By none is__ such plea - - sure giv - en As that I give with my sing - - - - - ing And with sounds of mu - sic ring - ing.

*Note the B naturals, giving a temporary change of modal feeling.

The four string parts, also doubled by as many instruments as possible, join in with lively, not too demanding counterpoint. After a forceful instrumental interlude whose basic theme is characterized by the trenchant opening leap of a fourth, the basses (later imitated by the tenors) proclaim a strain beginning:

> No evil thing can ever be,
> Where good friends join in melody.

(Translated by Harvey Officer and W. Strunk.)

Once more, all instruments present the forceful theme; a sudden, one-measure *ritardando* prepares for the next movement.

2. *Pastorale-Musette*. Gentle sonorities of two solo violins and a group of cellos accompany a woman's solo voice. The second violin, centring about the note B, constantly alternates between the thirds D and D sharp, while the first violin fluctuates between E, G, and G sharp. Similarly, the seventh note of the scale of E on which the vocal line is based appears sometimes as D sharp, sometimes as D. This changeability lends the melody a piquant air of flexibility and freedom which fits well to the section's opening words:

> And one and all to sing are free,
> Since in this joy no sin can be.

The section closes quietly over drone-like fifths and fourths in the cellos; these give the movement its 'musette' (bagpipe) character.

3. *Allegro moderato*. In sharp contrast, a man's voice now sings a jagged theme, whose characteristic octave-leap is taken up by the viola section:

> Witness David, that kingly soul,
> Who o'er Saul oft obtained control
> With music sweet of harp and song,
> Lest he commit some dreadful wrong.

This is accompanied by the string section only. Next, a woman's voice takes over, beginning softly and rising to a full climax accompanied by *fortissimo* quadruple-stops in the plucked strings – vividly depictive of the sound of the harp by which 'wise Elisha required . . . to be inspired'. These chords are counterpointed by the jagged 'David' theme.

4. *Trio*. A solo flute (for which a solo violin *may* be substituted, though Hindemith definitely prefers the flute here) joins with two solo violins in this sprightly instrumental interlude. Smoothly, it blends into a mixed vocal duet; the voices sing, in canon, a variation of the Trio's merry theme,

praising the spring and the song of little birds. Of these, the loveliest is the nightingale; we must be grateful to her,

> Or rather we the Lord must hail,
> For He hath made the nightingale.

Now at last, the entire chorus (joined, in this final climax, by everyone present) sings a full-throated song of praise.

Hindemith has here created a work which certainly has the qualities that he sought to give. It is relatively simple and could surely be played, sung, and enjoyed by amateurs without too high a level of performing technique. What, one may ask, is so 'revolutionary' about this? Yet, in a way, this twentieth-century concern with music for home use is a revolution too. One senses in it a turning away from the nineteenth-century idealization of the virtuoso in favour of a 'do-it-yourself' approach to music.

Unlike Schoenberg, Stravinsky, and Hindemith, Bela Bartók (1881–1945) may be characterized as consistently a nationalist composer. As is well known, he was a pioneer in the discovery and preservation of authentic Hungarian folk-music as opposed to the 'salon-gipsy' variety perpetrated and perpetuated by Liszt. For him, this discovery was a means to the realization of his own artistic personality; through his self-identification with this music, he was enabled to transcend the late-Romantic influences which dominated his early works, and to develop his own style. He utilized folk material in three different ways: (1) in scholarly editions of the unaltered folk-tunes; (2) in free transcriptions for instruments or voices; (3) as inspiration for free compositions wherein no actual folk-tune may be cited, but into the texture of which Bartók has completely assimilated his knowledge of the scales and rhythms on which such tunes are based.

Many of Bartók's choral works belong under the second of the headings. We might mention the *Four Old Hungarian Folksongs* for men's chorus (1912), the *Two Rumanian Folksongs* (unpublished) for four-part women's chorus (1915), *Four Slovak Folksongs* for mixed chorus and piano (1917), *Five Slovak Folksongs* for men's chorus (1917), *Three Village*

Scenes, based on traditional Slovakian material, for four or eight female voices and chamber orchestra (1926; arranged from Nos. 3, 4, and 5 of *Five Village Scenes*, songs of 1924), *Six Székely Folksongs* for men's chorus (1932), *Twenty-Seven Choruses* for two and three equal voices (1935; Nos. 1, 2, 7, 11, and 12 of this set were also provided with an accompaniment for small orchestra by the composer, 1935–6), and *From the Past*, three choruses for three-part men's choir, with traditional text arranged by the composer (1935–6).

Much of this material is arranged in extremely simple homophonic style, with fidelity to the characteristic metric shifts of the composer's models. However, Bartók also utilized folklore for works of more ambitious scope. Such a one is the *Cantata Profana* (1930), or, as we may call it from the content of its text, *The Giant Stags*. It is for double mixed chorus, tenor and baritone solos, and large orchestra. Unlike the brief choruses mentioned above, this work has a duration of sixteen to seventeen minutes. It seems, then, that Bartók was striving to present an idea of some importance to him. That this is even more true than the *ostensible* subject-matter of the work might suggest will appear in the course of our description.

After a brooding orchestral introduction, emphasizing the scale D–E–F–G–A flat–B flat, we hear the voices of both choruses entering gradually, each on a different tone so that harsh 'note-clusters' are formed (Example 72). The tale unfolds: 'Once there was an old man who treasured nine sons fair and sturdy, seed of his own body.' The sons were taught nothing of work by their father – neither trade nor farming; instead, they learned only 'hill and vale to wander, hunting the noble stag'.

The hunting episode next heard (*Allegro molto*) is ushered in by a vigorous rhythmic orchestral passage based on the chord E flat–B flat–F. An inner pedal-point on D links up with the tonality of the preceding section, based on the key of D. An energetic theme, in which both choruses now join (the voices entering successively in fugue-like fashion), is well suited to tell the story of the nine sons' wild hunt. Wandering ever further into the forest, they suddenly

Ex. 72. Bartók, *The Giant Stags (Cantata Profana)*

come to a haunted bridge – evocatively depicted in chords of parallel sixths sung softly by sopranos and altos of both choruses, spiced with dissonances produced by the contrary motion of the basses. Again, a sustained note – this time A in the tenors – tends somewhat to restrain the 'floating' harmonies. The tracks of magic stags have crossed the bridge. Heedless of what may befall them, the young men follow.

The music becomes ever slower and softer. A series of shifting metres ($\frac{9}{4}$, $\frac{5}{4}$, $\frac{6}{4}$) announces the mysterious transformation of the nine youths. 'All were changed to stags there in the forest shadows.' Now begins the work's

second major portion. There is a *pianissimo* orchestral introduction; again, the 'floating' harmonies, with contrary
motion between upper and lower parts, are heard. The
tenors and basses sing imitatively a motive opening with a
diminished fifth (or augmented fourth). The tonal vague-
ness of this interval expresses perfectly the restless waiting of
the father. Eventually he sets forth to look for his nine sons.
Finding the bridge and the traces of magic stags, he finally
arrives at a clear fountain. There he sees nine stags standing. Kneeling, he takes aim at the largest one, but to his
amazement it calls out with a human voice. Now, against
tremolando harmonies punctuated by brief violent orchestral
interjections, the tenor sings an agitated solo. 'Dearest,
loving father, aim not at thy children! Or surely our antlers must pierce thee and pin thee . . .' The father (baritone solo) pleads anxiously with his sons: 'Oh, my dearest
loved ones . . . come home now, your sweet mother waits.'
His motive is taken up by the altos, tenors, and basses of
both choruses. He interrupts with an even more urgent
plea – but all in vain. The favourite eldest son, once more
singing in an intensive rhythmically free style, begs his
father to go back home; he, and the rest of the sons, can
never go back. The two choruses underline his refusal with
their restless, irregular $\frac{5}{8}$ rhythm.' 'Our antlers cannot pass
thy doorway,' the son explains; 'our slender bodies cannot
wear clothes, but only the wind and the sun.' The light
feet of the stags must be free to run on the forest moss, not
confined to the hearth; their mouths may no longer drink
from crystal glasses, but only from clear streams.

Now, the choruses bring a final varied recapitulation
of the opening narrative. This closing portion of the work
combines solo, choral, and orchestral elements into a unifying reprise. The tonality of D, too, recurs in altered form;
instead of the scale of the opening (minor-like, restless,
unresolved in character) we find D–E–F sharp–G sharp–
A–B–C (major-like, reaching a final resolution in a D major
triad).

What was the special appeal of this subject for Bartók?
As indicated above, we may suspect that there is more be-

hind the seemingly simple legend than meets the eye. In the passionate statements of the young stag, we discern the plea for freedom. The sons, once having escaped into the outer world, are no longer able to return to conditions of greater restriction; their antlers have grown too wide for the door. Thus, in the guise of a folk-tale (we have quoted Robert Shaw's translation), Bartók may express his impatience with political restrictions and persecutions – an impatience which was eventually to drive him from his native land, and to American shores.

Whenever it may be performed, *The Giant Stags* will always have a message to impart to freedom-loving peoples. Thus – as every great work of art must – Bartók's cantata has succeeded in transcending the purely personal and national.

18

France from the Age of Fauré and Debussy

from c.1900

ROLLO H. MYERS

CHORAL music in France has never been widely cultivated or indulged in by 'the masses' as a form of relaxation or distraction. Regional folk-music exists, of course; but in neither the country nor the town has choral singing ever been a favourite workers' pastime as it has been, and still is, in other continental European countries, for example Germany or Russia. French music has always been predominantly aristocratic in its higher manifestations, and owes less than that of most other countries to 'popular' sources of inspiration. The arts in France have always been a matter for the expert, the professional, rather than for the man in the street, and have in consequence been marked by a high degree of sophistication. In the fact that music has been a product of the court, rather than of the marketplace, we may discern one of the reasons why the ruder and more uncultivated forms of art, such as communal singing, have never flourished in France as much as in other countries where music is nearer to the hearts of the people, and singing therefore felt to be a natural form of expression. This does not mean, of course, that choral singing as an art has not been brought to a high degree of perfection in France. Men like Pérotin, Machaut, and Dufay (see Chapter 1) in the thirteenth and fourteenth centuries helped to lay the foundations of a fine tradition which has continued to the present day.

This brings us to an examination of the contribution made to this particular branch of music by French composers born about the middle of the nineteenth century and after. The main contribution of Charles Gounod (1818–93) and César Franck (1822–90) to choral music had been in the form of oratorios and cantatas on religious themes (see p. 223). Thereafter, church music had been more or less neglected by nineteenth-century French composers until Gabriel Fauré (1845–1924) at the age of forty-two composed a Requiem in memory of his father which has won for itself a rather special place. The Requiem, which is scored for soprano and baritone solos, chorus, organ, and orchestra, had its first performance at the church of the Madeleine in Paris in 1888, since when it has been more or less continuously in the repertory of choral societies both in France and abroad. Simplicity is the keynote of the Requiem. The composer has deliberately eschewed any attempt at dramatization, even in the *Dies irae* section, concentrating rather on the creation of an atmosphere of serenity and spiritual contemplation. It is an affirmation of faith expressed in the simplest musical terms – a risky formula where religious music is concerned; but the danger of lapsing into banality (to which a composer not possessed of Fauré's instinctive good taste and natural tendency to understatement would inevitably be exposed) is here miraculously avoided. Apart from the Requiem, the only other choral works of any importance from Fauré's pen are the choruses in *Prometheus* (1900) and *Penelope* (1913), his only operatic works, and the *ad lib*. choral section of the *Pavane* (1887) for orchestra, which is sometimes dispensed with in performance.

Another notable but little-known Requiem of about the same period is that of Alfred Bruneau (1857–1934). It might seem surprising that Bruneau, who was a friend of Zola's, many of whose works he set to music in operatic form, should have written any religious music at all; but in this Requiem (1889), which seems to have been his only excursion into this field, he shows considerable proficiency in the handling of choral masses – although his treatment and approach, unlike Fauré's, are definitely inclined to be operatic, if not theatrical. The choral writing is homophonic rather than strictly polyphonic, and the harmonic progres-

sions often distinctly bold for the period. Bruneau's fondness for abrupt modulations is exemplified, for instance, by
a sudden and most effective transition in the first few bars
from the key of E flat minor to C major, repeated whenever
the same words occur later in the work as a kind of leading-
motive. The work is a full-scale Requiem Mass in nine
parts, and is scored for solos, chorus, organ, orchestra, and
an additional choir of children's voices. In the *Dies irae*
the composer, taking (as one cannot help feeling) a leaf
out of Berlioz's book, divides his trumpets into two groups
placed to the right and left of the main orchestra. Though
practically unknown in this country today, Bruneau's
Requiem somewhat surprisingly was performed by the
Bach Choir in London under the direction of Sir Charles
Stanford in 1896. Choral societies today might find it well
worth reviving.

With the advent of the twentieth century it might be said
that the attitude towards choral music in France had undergone a change. In the first place if must not be forgotten
that to the new generation of composers who were then
coming into prominence, with Claude Debussy (1862–1918)
and Maurice Ravel (1875–1937) at their head, vocal music
was slightly suspect. This was no doubt one of the results of
the reaction that had set in against contemporary Italian
opera and its imitators in France, and a result also of the
hostility in *avant-garde* circles to the popularity of composers
like Massenet and Saint-Saëns. Facile vocal 'effects' from
now on were taboo, and the tendency among composers of
the modern school, if they wrote for the voice at all, was to
treat it as an instrument supplying a characteristic tone-
colour in an ensemble, not as a vehicle for coloratura display. Hence the practice which became common at that
time of adding a wordless chorus to such symphonic works
as *Sirens* (the third of Debussy's *Nocturnes*, 1898), Ravel's
ballet *Daphnis and Chloe* (1912), and Roussel's *Evocations*
(1912), to name only a few instances. Darius Milhaud in his
Choephori, as we shall see later, makes his chorus whistle and
hiss and shout.

Both in the opera-ballet *Padmâvatî* (Paris, 1923) and

Evocations (inspired by his travels to Cochin-China and India when an officer in the French Navy) Albert Roussel (1869–1937) mingles voices with the orchestra. In the third part of the latter work, 'On the shore of the sacred river', he employs not only a tenor, baritone, and contralto as soloists, but two choirs, one large and the other small, and a large orchestra (which should include, he directs, 'a few double-basses with five strings'). The choruses are largely wordless, often accompanying the soloists on a simple vowel sound, such as 'A' or 'O'. Roussel also introduces a chorus in his ballet *Aeneas* (Brussels, 1935). But there is no doubt that his master-work in this field is his fine setting of Psalm 80 (1928). He composed it originally on the English text of the psalm, although a French adaptation was made later. An examination of the score reveals no faults in English prosody or accentuation – in itself a remarkable feat. Dedicated to the Queen of the Belgians and scored for tenor solo, chorus, and orchestra, the psalm is a magnificent piece of choral writing that deserves to be better known and might well prove rewarding to an English choir adventurous enough to add it to their repertory.

More famous is the setting by Florent Schmitt (1870–1959) of Psalm 47, scored for soprano solo, mixed chorus, large orchestra, and organ. The text is from the French translation of the Vulgate (where the psalm is numbered 46; Schmitt's work is consequently known in Roman Catholic countries as Psalm 46). This is an impressive work in its way – conceived and executed on a large scale, big and full-blooded, with the somewhat thick and turgid orchestration characteristic of the composer. It was written in 1904 as a 'Message from Rome' when Schmitt, after winning the French Prix de Rome (Rome Prize) for composition, was an inmate of the French Institute's foundation in Rome, the Villa Medici. It was not, however, heard in Paris until 1910 when it was performed in public for the first time. Other notable choral works by Schmitt are his *Festival of Light* (*Fête de la Lumière*) for soprano, chorus, and orchestra written for the Paris Exhibition in 1937, and some half-dozen unaccompanied works composed between 1896 and 1943.

All the composers mentioned so far were more or less conformist in their style of choral writing, continuing the classical or late Romantic tradition, and respecting the accepted canons of polyphonic vocal composition – although Roussel already seems to be experimenting with a freer, more 'modern' technique in his handling of the vocal masses. It was left to Charles Koechlin (1867–1951) and one or two of his contemporaries, such as Bourgault-Ducoudray (1840–1910), Roger-Ducasse (1873–1954), and Maurice Emmanuel (1862–1938) to develop choral singing along less orthodox lines by injecting it with a massive dose on the one hand of Gregorian chant, and on the other of 'folk' and popular song.

The model character of so much of Koechlin's music is nowhere better exemplified than in his choral compositions. Among his very numerous works in this field, one of the most important is *The Abbey* (*L'Abbaye*) for solo voices, chorus, organ, and orchestra, a cantata or 'religious suite' as he called it. It is in two parts, the first dating from 1899 to 1902, and the second from 1906 to 1908. The key to the mood which inspired the work is supplied in the following quotation (source unnamed) with which the score is prefaced:

The old abbey disappears, buried under the new forest. But very often, near these ruins, Man sits dreaming of the past – dreaming of voices – naïve, trustful, and faithful voices, sincere, fervent, and solemn voices speaking the language of the true faith, the song of the ancient cloisters, voices primitive and pure . . .

The work is planned on a large scale. Part I consists of: Prelude; Ave Maria; Kyrie; Requiem; Interlude for organ; O salutaris; and Benedictus. Part II consists of: Prelude (organ and orchestra); Benedictus; Ave verum corpus; O salutaris; Interludes for six trombones; Interlude for organ; Ave Maria; Requiem (without words) for four solo singers and organ; 'Bells at Evening'; Finale (two versions, one without chorus). The limpid, modal harmonies create an impression of freshness and unforced, spontaneous, and entirely unconventional religious feeling. There is little contrapuntal writing, the voices for the most part moving together homophonically over sustained chords in organ and orchestra, with long chant-like figures in Koechlin's characteristic manner.

In the same serious, but wholly unpompous, vein is Koechlin's moving and expressive *Funeral Song in Memory of Young Women* (Requiem) for double chorus, organ, and orchestra, the chorus consisting of twenty voices in the first choir and twelve in the second. Though written between 1902 and 1907, the *Funeral Song* is still unpublished, like so much of Koechlin's work, and exists in manuscript only – although public performances in recent years suggest that parts must be available. Among his other numerous choral writings mention should be made of the religious choruses in modal style, unaccompanied (1935).

Koechlin was a prolific composer in almost every field. He had an eclectic taste and took a great interest in every aspect of the contemporary scene, and his *Seven Stars Symphony* (1933) celebrates film stars by name. His admiration for Rudyard Kipling led him to compose orchestral suites inspired by *The Jungle Book*, as well as to set (1899–1910) three of the poems occurring in that book – *The Seal's Lullaby*, for mezzo-soprano solo and women's chorus; *Night Song of the Jungle*, for contralto, bass, and women's chorus; *Song of Kala Nag* for tenor solo and chorus of tenors. It was Koechlin's great merit to have revivified choral music in France by breaking away from the conventional nineteenth-century idiom and reintroducing modal harmonies and a style of writing which, though recalling in some ways earlier centuries, was resolutely 'modern' in its freedom of form and often bold harmonic innovations.

We have mentioned the name of the composer Bourgault-Ducoudray. He was a late nineteenth-century pioneer in the treatment of popular, or 'folk' music. His modal harmonizations of folk-tunes of different countries, including Greece, Brittany, Scotland, and Wales, are models of their kind. Others who followed in his footsteps were Maurice Emmanuel for Burgundian songs, Vincent d'Indy (1851–1931) for songs of the Vivarais region, and Charles Bordes (1863–

1909) in his harmonization of Basque tunes. The work of
these pioneers introduced a new element into French choral
music and set a fashion which was followed by a whole new
school of 'regional' composers such as Paul Ladmirault
(1877–1944), Jean Huré (1877–1930), and Guy Ropartz
(1864–1955) for Brittany; Joseph Canteloube (b.1879) for
Auvergne; and Déodat de Sévérac (1873–1921) for Pro-
vence. This is to mention only a few of those who, in bringing to light a considerable body of hitherto unknown
regional folk-music, thereby enriched the repertory of choral
societies and singers all over the country.

Even Maurice Ravel, though by no means a composer
with a dominant interest in folk-music or any kind of
regionalism, yet made his contribution to the 'folk' vocal
repertory in his harmonization of *Five Greek Songs* (1907) and
of seven popular songs of different nations (Spanish, French,
Italian, Hebrew, Scottish, Flemish, and Russian) in 1910.
To these may be added his own brilliant pastiches – for so
they might be called – of the 'folk' style published in 1916
under the title of *Three Songs* (*Trois chansons*) – for mixed
unaccompanied chorus, of which he wrote the words. The
wordless choruses in *Daphnis and Chloe* and animals' chorus in
his opera *The Child and the Spells* (*L'Enfant et les Sortilèges*) are
the only other examples of Ravel's choral writing, but they
are enough to show that his technique in the handling of
vocal ensembles was as flawless as in every other branch of
his art.

One does not think of Debussy as being, any more than
Ravel, a composer of choral music of special importance,
and yet we have to remember not only his Prix de Rome
cantata *The Prodigal Son* and the early setting of Rossetti's
The Blessed Damozel (in French translation) in which the
choral writing is already accomplished and distinctive, but
such memorable examples of his skill in handling voices as
the female chorus in *Sirens* (the third of the orchestral
Nocturnes), the delightful unaccompanied *Three chansons by
Charles d'Orléans* and above all the masterly choruses in *The
Martyrdom of St Sebastian* (a stage work, 1911, on D'Annun-
zio's play). All these seem perfectly to fulfil Debussy's own

ideal of 'a style of choral writing which is extremely simple but extremely flexible', of which the following extract from the angels' chorus ('Take six wings of angels') in *The Martyrdom of St Sebastian* is a fair example (Example 73).

Ex. 73. Debussy, *The Martyrdom of St. Sebastian*

Among Debussy's immediate contemporaries it would be unjust not to mention André Caplet (1878–1925) whose *Mirror of Jesus* for voices, string quartet, and harp, and also certain unaccompanied choruses show a natural feeling for the niceties of choral writing, besides being of intrinsic musical interest; Vincent d'Indy, whose *Song of the Bell* and *Legend of St Christopher* are fine examples of choral writing on an ample scale; and Gabriel Pierné (1863–1937) who carried on the Franck tradition in his oratorios *The Children's Crusade*, *The Children at Bethlehem*, and *St Francis of Assisi*.

The interregnum between the two world wars was a period of unrest and fermentation in the arts, especially music, and inevitably produced a violent reaction against the aesthetic ideals of the pre-war generation of composers.

In France it was the group of young composers known as the 'Six' who led the revolution: Georges Auric (*b*.1899), Louis Durey (*b*.1888), Arthur Honegger (1892–1955), Darius Milhaud (*b*.1892), Francis Poulenc (*b*.1899), and Germaine Tailleferre (*b*.1892). For a time it looked as if their deliberate cult of frivolity and merciless debunking of former idols was going to be the hallmark of the new music. As time went on, however, each member of the group began to assert his or her individuality, and it soon became clear that the resemblances between them were only superficial.

One of the first to break away was Arthur Honegger, who had never really been in sympathy with the group's avowed and widely advertised aims, but was bound to them by ties of friendship only. He was also the first to achieve world-wide celebrity, as early as 1921, with his 'dramatic oratorio' *King David* – for mixed chorus, woodwind, brass, double-bass, piano, harmonium, and percussion which was first performed at Mézières in Switzerland. (Though born in France, Honegger was of German-Swiss parentage.) It was an immediate success, and today still holds its place in the international choral repertory as firmly as Walton's *Belshazzar's Feast*, which is constructed on very much the same lines. *King David* is in twenty-seven episodes, some of them extremely brief, which explode one after another, projecting a vivid, almost cinematographic image on the mind. The writing is forceful and concise, crude in places and frequently polytonal. One of the most effective episodes is the wailing chorus (wordless) for women's voices (soprano and contralto) in *The Lamentations of Gilboa*, on which the voice of David, *parlando*, is superimposed. Example 74 is from the last choral bars, which the orchestra then (not quoted) rounds off quietly. Other important choral works by Honegger are *Judith* (1926), *Joan of Arc at the Stake* (1934–5), *The Dance of Death*, on a text by Claudel (1938), and his *Christmas Cantata* (1953).

Choral music likewise occupies an important and varied place in the enormous output of Darius Milhaud. His first important essay in this field was the incidental music he wrote for Claudel's adaptation of the *Choephori* (the second part of the *Oresteia* of Aeschylus) at the age of twenty-three. Already in this vivid score his powerful musical personality and unconventional approach to the problems of composition assert themselves in a manner that at the time was con-

Ex. 74. Honegger, *King David*

sidered revolutionary. Here he makes his chorus whistle and
shout and hiss, much of the vocal writing being nothing but
pitchless declamation. Since then Milhaud has composed
more than thirty choral works, the most important being
(apart from the full-length operas *Christopher Columbus*, 1928,
Bolivar, 1943, *Maximilian*, 1930, and *David*, 1953,) the cantatas *In Praise of the Lord* (1928), *Pan and Syrinx* (1934), *War
Cantata* (1940), and *The Birth of Venus* (unaccompanied,
1949), as well as a number of Jewish liturgical works.

Choral music has also always had a great attraction for
Francis Poulenc, many of his compositions in this field
being of a religious nature. Especially noteworthy are the
deeply felt *Litanies to the Black Virgin of Rocamadour* for mixed
chorus unaccompanied (1936), the Mass, also unaccompanied (1937) and the *Stabat Mater* (1951) for soprano solo,
chorus, and orchestra. In this last-named important work,
setting the famous medieval devotional poem, Poulenc has
given free expression to a naturally religious temperament
without falling into any of the pitfalls with which the path
of a composer of religious music is inevitably strewn. A kind
of joyful spirituality pervades the work which, from a purely
musical point of view, is both solidly constructed and intensely appealing. The vocal writing, as often with Poulenc,
is homophonic rather than contrapuntal, and the various

entries of the solo voice are most effectively contrived. An equally important and no less striking *Gloria* for the same combination (1959) was commissioned by the Koussevitzky Foundation and first performed under Charles Munch in January 1961.

Of Poulenc's secular choral compositions the most important are *Seven Songs* (unaccompanied, 1936); the cantata *Drought* (*Sécheresses*) on a text by Edward James (1937); and the very striking setting of Paul Éluard's *The Human Face* (*La Figure Humaine*) for unaccompanied double chorus (1943), which was written during the war as a kind of hymn to Liberty and was given its first performance – after the liberation of France – by the B B C in 1945.

The Human Face is, to begin with, unusual in form, for there are not many instances, in French music at any rate, of large-scale choral works scored for a double mixed chorus, unaccompanied. Poulenc excels in writing for the voice, and he seems here to have been especially inspired by Éluard's moving, though somewhat cryptic verses, extolling liberty at a time when France was temporarily in bondage. There are eight poems expressing a passionate conviction that the nightmare will pass and human values triumph in the end. The music is alternately fierce and tender, and reveals the composer in what must have seemed an unfamiliar light to those who had hitherto looked upon him as nothing more than a charming *petit maître*, with an unusual gift for melody, but incurably frivolous and the very epitome of Parisian wit and elegance. There is a toughness and tenseness in this impassioned hymn to liberty and a sense of burning conviction that compel our admiration; while the actual choral writing is immensely effective and shows a real mastery of the medium. Often, by the use of the simplest means, an effect of extraordinary poignancy is obtained, difficult to demonstrate in a necessarily brief quotation; but Example 75 is an example of how, in one of the more subdued episodes, the limpidity and transparency of the texture enhances the emotional impact of the words.

I have left to the last, in this necessarily very condensed

Ex. 75. Poulenc, *The Human Face*

survey, one of the most prolific and original modern French composers, and one whose large output, unlike that of most of his contemporaries, has been principally in the form of large-scale cantatas and oratorios and other works for choral ensembles of various kinds – Georges Migot (*b*.1891). On account of his aloofness from any of the cliques and coteries so common in music today, Migot is sometimes referred to as 'The Group of One'. From the first his endeavour has always been to write music firmly established in the French tradition, taking as his models Gregorian chant, the troubadours, the great polyphonic masters of the Middle Ages and the Renaissance, the lutenists, François Couperin, Rameau, Berlioz, and Debussy. For him line is all-important, and a polyphony based on free counterpoint. Since he is of a

deeply religious nature, it is not surprising that a great
many of his choral works are on biblical subjects. He has
in fact composed a complete cycle of spiritual oratorios
on the life of Christ consisting of an *Annunciation* (1946),
The Nativity of Our Lord (1954), *The Sermon on the Mount*
(1936), *The Passion* (1939–45), *The Entombment* (1949), and
The Resurrection (1953). In addition to settings of Psalms
19 and 118 (1927 and 1952) his other most important
religious compositions are the oratorio *Saint Germain
d'Auxerre*, called a '*chanson de geste*' (a title originally applied
to a medieval French epic poem) for three mixed choirs and
soloists, unaccompanied (1947); *The Little Gospel* (1952),
episodes in the life of Jesus, and a Requiem (1956) both
for unaccompanied chorus.

Had space permitted, more than a passing reference could
have been made to other contemporary French composers
who have enriched the choral repertory in different ways.
We may mention *Three Little Liturgies of the Divine Presence*
(1944) and *Cinq Rechants* (1949) by Olivier Messiaen (*b.*
1908); *The Apocalypse*, by Jean Françaix (*b.* 1912); *The
Truth about Joan of Arc*, by André Jolivet (*b.* 1905); *Joan of
Arc at Orleans*, by Tony Aubin (*b.* 1907); *St Francis of Assisi*,
by Manuel Rosenthal (*b.* 1904); *The Mystery of the Holy
Innocents*, by Henri Barraud (*b.* 1900); *Joan of Arc*, by
Roland-Manuel (*b.* 1891), and *Five French Songs for four
mixed voices*, by Georges Auric. The record, though still
incomplete, shows nevertheless that choral music has by no
means been neglected by modern French composers.

We may conclude with a note on the organization of
choral singing in France. The nineteenth century witnessed
a revival of choral activities of all kinds there. As early as
1828 Habeneck founded the Société des Concerts du Con-
servatoire in Paris, endowing it with a professional mixed
chorus; in 1835 the Paris Municipal Council voted that
singing should be taught in all communal schools, and in
1838 this was extended to the universities. But what probably did more to popularize choral singing in France than
anything else was the foundation in the 1840s of the
Orphéon, an association of amateur male voice choirs

which spread throughout the provinces, two of the oldest being the Cercle Choral of Aix-en-Provence (1842) and the Union des Orphéonistes of Lille (1846). In Paris the Union Chorale and Les Enfants de Lutèce came into being in 1848, and in 1853 there was founded the École Niedermeyer specializing in the choral masterpieces of the Renaissance. The reorganization of the teaching of music in schools dates from about 1890; the composer Gabriel Pierné (1863–1937) was appointed inspector of choral singing in French *lycées*, and wrote a number of part-songs expressly for these schools.

Choral societies exist in most of the French universities, and special mention should be made of the Chorale des Jeunesses Musicales de France under the direction of Louis Martini. In Paris, the choirs of the French Radio-Television and the Elisabeth Brasseur Chorale play a great part today in the interpretation of new music.

19

Modern British Composers

from *c.*1925

ERNEST BRADBURY

A SINGLE choral work would seem to be the starting point for this particular chapter – *Belshazzar's Feast* by William Walton (*b.*1902). When this dramatic cantata was first produced at the Leeds Festival in 1931 it was generally agreed that nothing like it had been heard before in English choral music. Beside its seeming difficulties the fancied enormities of Elgar's *The Dream of Gerontius* – before which a Birmingham Festival choir had quailed only thirty years earlier – appeared old-fashioned and almost insignificant. Now, in the sixties, we can see the romance that lies at the heart of Walton's mighty score, though indeed the work has lost none of its vigour or splendour. Choralists have learned to take it more or less for granted, and it was amusing to observe that, at a recent Viennese Festival, when British choralism itself was on show, the men of the Huddersfield Choral Society sang the fierce opening prophecy confidently and accurately without so much as glancing at their copies.

Yet in some respects, for all its surface modernity, *Belshazzar's Feast* does not so drastically challenge the traditional concept of oratorio as did *The Dream of Gerontius*, where Elgar did for oratorio what Wagner had done for opera. Sir Osbert Sitwell showed a sound instinct when he returned – against the general trend of modern oratorio – to a full-blooded biblical text in furnishing Walton with his libretto. Our Victorian forefathers would hardly have understood Walton's musical treatment of the words; but they would have understood the words themselves, *qua* oratorio, better than those employed by Elgar, and they would have responded instinctively.

None the less, Walton breaks new ground since he has modern resources – and a modern technique – at his command. He needs no second invitation to invoke the gods of Iron, Stone, Wood, and the rest: these pictures stir the adventurer in him. Nor is he afraid, when opportunity offers, to make a joyful noise unto the God of Jacob, and blow up the trumpet in the new moon – with the aid of two added groups of brass instruments, if available. These again are surface qualities, immediately recognizable and immediately overwhelming. But they no longer leave us, as apparently they left that first audience, with a sense of insecurity, or bewilderment. It is the essential Walton that, in thirty years or so, has fallen into some sort of perspective. His noisy moments, we find, are as fundamentally romantic as his quiet ones, while his chromatically inflected harmonies, though pungent and ascetic still, no longer have the power to terrify the choralist.

Belshazzar's Feast undeniably had a liberating effect on other British composers. Unable to hide from the explosive effects of this work of 1931 some of them responded with that sincerest form of flattery – imitation. Thus for the Worcester Festival of 1935 George Dyson (*b.*1883) turned to the story of another King of Babylon in *Nebuchadnezzar*. Less extreme in expression, this score yet shows some striking parallels, in method and construction, with *Belshazzar's Feast*. Its climax is the song of praise of the Three Holy Children who withstood the burning fiery furnace; the long setting of the *Benedicite* is skilfully worked out. Here, too, an unaccompanied soloist has a singular narration, telling not of 'gold and silver, of precious stones, of pearls, of fine linen . . .' as in Walton's work, but of the sound of 'the cornet, flute, harp, sackbut, psaltery, dulcimer, and all kinds of music . . .'. Then, to continue this curious creative leap-frogging, Walton, two years later (again for Leeds), took a poem already set by Dyson in 1928, William Dunbar's *In Honour of the City of London*, setting it, like Dyson, for mixed choir and orchestra without soloists. A comparison of the openings of the two works serves to show, in miniature, something of the musical character of both composers, Dyson on the whole being more obviously 'melodic', finding freshness in his harmonies by a simple flattened seventh, forming a G major triad within his basic E major (Example 76).

Ex. 76. Dyson, *In Honour of the City*

Walton, on the other hand, immediately explosive, virile, and compelling (Example 77, page 342).

Walton renewed his association with the Huddersfield Choral Society when he wrote his *Gloria* for its 125th anniversary in 1961, using contralto, tenor and bass soloists as well as large chorus and orchestra. Previously his *Coronation Te Deum*, written for the Coronation of Queen Elizabeth II and first performed during the Abbey ceremony on 2 June 1953, showing that familiar tricks could still be put to new use. This eight-minute work calls for a large orchestra, with organ, double chorus, and semi-chorus.

Dyson has been more prolific. Before *Nebuchadnezzar* he

Ex. 77. Walton, *In Honour of the City*

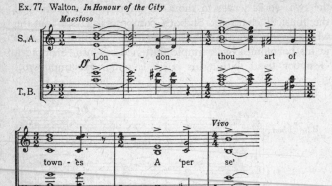

had produced (perhaps not entirely uninfluenced by Walton) the unjustly neglected *St Paul's Voyage to Melita* (1933), a vivid musical account of storm and shipwreck, and the somewhat clamorous *The Blacksmiths* (Leeds, 1934). The two parts of *Quo Vadis?* (settings of words from many sources) were first heard at the Three Choirs Festivals of 1939 and 1947 respectively. But British choralists in general have taken to their hearts a work earlier and in many respects surer than any of these – *The Canterbury Pilgrims*, first performed at Winchester in 1931, when Dyson was director of music at the College there. This unquestionable masterpiece among modern British choral works remains the best thing that Dyson has done and gives free rein to his true lyrical, melodic, and harmonic qualities. This musical tapestry of knight and squire, ecclesiastics, carpenter, franklin, and doctor of physic appears as colourful, as rich in humour, and as observant as Chaucer's. Dyson catches the singular attitudes of these characters from the famous Prologue, and provides for them deft touches of orchestration. Thus we have the scholarly fugue for the Clerk of Oxenford 'that unto logic long had gone'; the solemn *pizzicato* chords that depict the haberdasher and his fraternity; the rolling sea-music for the shipman and the grinding discords of nasty medicine that accompany the doctor! There is untold charm in the music, not only in the transparent April freshness of the unaccompanied opening chorus but also through all the varied portraits until 'the condition of each of them' being told, they ride away into the distance to the first strains of the Knight's Tale.

Of two other composers who came to manhood about the time of the First World War, Herbert Howells (b.1892) has become more familiar to choralists than Sir Arthur Bliss (b.1891). Bliss, indeed, has done little in the choral field. His *Pastoral* ('Lie strewn the white flocks'), for chorus, mezzo-soprano, flute, drums, and strings, appeared in 1928, a setting of seven bucolic poems ranging from Theocritus to Robert Nichols. It is difficult now to understand early criticisms of the work on the grounds of the composer's use of such combined texts, particularly since the device has been used by several later composers, notably Benjamin Britten. Bliss's *Pastoral* has been particularly welcomed by smaller choral societies who wish to have a modern work in their repertory, for it calls on only a few dozen voices to support the chamber texture of the instrumentation.

In 1930, for *Morning Heroes*, described as a Symphony for Orator, Chorus, and Orchestra, Bliss again went to various sources for his text – the *Iliad*, the Chinese poet Li T'ai-po, Walt Whitman, and the two 'war poets' Wilfred Owen and Robert Nichols. This is a vaster work, heroic and ceremonial, and requires a large orchestra with greater (besides more skilful) choral resources. It was written in memory of the composer's brother and other comrades killed in the First World War, and is occasionally revived by larger societies at Armistice-tide in November, 'the month of requiems'. Today there seems to be an Elgarian influence behind this music, which is strongly coloured and rich in ensemble, but free from excessive difficulty. In 1954, as Master of the Queen's Music, Bliss wrote a third choral work for the home-coming of Queen Elizabeth II, *A Song of Welcome* (words by C. Day Lewis) for soprano, baritone, chorus, and orchestra. It is a characteristically joyous *pièce d'occasion*. The Coventry Cathedral Festival of 1962 brought forth *The Beatitudes*, a large-scale work for soprano, tenor, chorus, and orchestra.

Excessive difficulty has sometimes seemed a stumbling-block to a full appreciation of the choral music of Herbert Howells, of which there is a large quantity. Howells is performed regularly in English cathedrals and large churches where good musical establishments are maintained, for he has written much church music of incontestable merit, including sets of Evening Canticles for specific cathedrals with their particular acoustical properties in mind. In his larger works what has sometimes been taken for mere note-spinning or unnecessary complication may really be seen as the product of an acute and brilliant, but poetically sensitive, mind that almost seems unaware of technical difficulties. This skill is apparent in all Howells's published works, which cover a wide field of musical endeavour. Many of the choral pieces are of small dimension, such as the exquisite unaccompanied carol-anthem *A Spotless Rose* (1919), with its fragrant, shifting harmonies produced by parallel fourths between the soprano-alto and tenor-bass parts, or the similar *Sing Lullaby* of the following year. A good example of Howells's more robust choral style will be found in the ballad *Sir Patrick Spens* (1918), for baritone, chorus, and orchestra, and the equally racy *A Kent Yeoman's Wooing Song* (1935).

But it was as recently as 1950, with *Hymnus Paradisi* (in English, despite its Latin title), that Howells at last won a wider regard as a composer of choral music. Both technically and spiritually the *Hymnus* was undoubtedly Howells's finest achievement up to that time. It is based on an eclectic requiem-text, like Brahms's *German Requiem*, the sources being either biblical or liturgical. (The score is inscribed 'To my son, Michael Kendrick Howells, in remembrance'.) It is, figuratively and literally, a work of light, the composer elaborating the word *lux* in a musical tissue of extraordinary beauty and incandescence, with a dazzling Sanctus and a radiant final section depicting the eternal 'home of unfailing splendour'. Since its first performance at the Gloucester Three Choirs Festival of 1950, the *Hymnus* has been taken up

rewardingly by many of the larger choral societies. Moreover, the new sources of inspiration which Howells discovered in the *Hymnus*, and the new floods of choral sound
he then released, seemed to be even more firmly realized
and directed in the *Missa Sabrinensis* (literally 'Severn Mass':
the text is again in English, despite the title), given at
Worcester in 1954. The writing is again complex, and has
fewer points of repose than the *Hymnus*, but it is not laboured,
it has unity, and the sense of exhilaration it imparts is very
strong.

Another West Country composer of the senior generation
may be mentioned here, Julius Harrison (*b*.1885), chiefly
for two notable choral works of fairly recent origin. The
Mass in C (Hanley, 1948) – also a memorial work, for the
composer's daughter – is inspired by the deepest feeling
expressed with craftsmanship of the highest order that also
takes into account the limitations of choral singers. His
instinct for the capabilities and limitations of the human
voice (elsewhere I have suggested that choralists enjoy
Harrison's music as orchestral players enjoy Elgar's)
is further shown in the even more impressive *Requiem Mass*,
first heard at the Worcester Festival of 1957.

In this Harrison openly acknowledged the model of Verdi,
at least in some of the dramatic moments of the *Dies irae*
(there is of course no actual musical resemblance) and even
declared himself 'content to follow the beaten track of
well-tried consonance' – which might be interpreted as
meaning that Harrison is not afraid of obtaining beautiful
effects by means which a superficial age might label old-
fashioned. But this is rather an understatement, for the
older vocabulary does in fact seem refreshingly new in this
fine Requiem Mass which is actually constructed on Elgarian
lines, with many motives correlated throughout the work to
emphasize or illustrate the meaning of the words. The work
has its complexities, though the choral writing is never so
tortuous as that of Howells in the *Missa Sabrinensis*. At the
end the 'Lux aeterna' seems bathed in celestial light;
and like Fauré in this Requiem, Harrison ends with the
antiphon 'In paradisum', where a silver web of sound is

suspended, as it were, in the air, with a trio for women's voices and a solo soprano adding poignancy to the music before the final lovely key-change – an inspired touch.

Most of the music considered so far in this chapter represents an extension of what we might call the Parry/Stanford revival. The competence expressed in British music by these great teachers has come to flower in the work of these younger men whose music again has virility, ingenuity, melodic and harmonic distinction, and – not least – a constantly progressing contrapuntal mastery. These qualities seem self-sufficient for a period; it is in the music of those composers born in the next decade that we first detect newer, and sometimes 'outside', influences, even though undeniable 'Englishry' (a quality rather more easy to recognize than to define) remains. Thus we may find Tudor, French, or jazz influences respectively in the choral works of Edmund Rubbra (b.1901), Lennox Berkeley (b.1903), and Constant Lambert (1905–51), added to the solid gains mentioned above in the work of the senior composers.

Rubbra's work covers a wide range of instrumental, vocal, and choral music, but he seems chiefly a symphonist. He is a natural contrapuntist whose musical ideas germinate in a form that invites such treatment, and his work shows a distinct affinity with the Tudor composers, perhaps best revealed in the *Five Motets* (1934), in which canonic writing predominates, to poems by Herrick, Donne, Henry Vaughan, and Richard Crashaw. Works with orchestra, such as *The Dark Night of the Soul* (1935), a richly chromatic setting of a passage from St John of the Cross, and *The Morning Watch* (1941), from a poem by Henry Vaughan, are on a smaller scale. The fact that both these poets were mystics is also not without relevance to Rubbra's habits of mind. A larger work, for double choir and (in the Credo only) organ, is the *Missa Cantuariensis*, the Service of Holy Communion with text from the English Rites of 1662 and 1928, set for the choir of Canterbury Cathedral in 1945. Here Rubbra's harmonic simplicity and contrapuntal ingenuity may be seen at their best, notably in the Sanctus, Benedictus, and Agnus Dei.

Neither Berkeley nor Lambert have been quite so prolific as Rubbra in the choral field, and when Lambert's untimely death occurred, two days before his forty-sixth birthday, he was doubtless better known as a conductor of ballet than as a composer. His talents were also exerted in the field of criticism, his book *Music Ho!* (1934) ranking as one of the most controversial books of its time. None the less, he wrote two choral works of more than passing interest in *The Rio Grande* (1927) and *Summer's Last Will and Testament* (1935). The former, for the unusual combination of solo pianoforte, chorus, and orchestra, which uses a poem by Sacheverell Sitwell, is a vigorous, satirical, and intellectually penetrating work in a jazzy idiom. *Summer's Last Will and Testament*, Lambert's largest work, is described as a Masque for orchestra, chorus, and baritone solo, and is chiefly based on the 'pleasant comedy' of the same name by Thomas Nashe (1593). It paints a grimly realistic picture of the Elizabethan age, with drunken revelry, ebullient town life and (drawing also on Edgar Allan Poe's story *King Pest*) the horrors of the plague, and the dreadful consequences thereof. Then the work concludes with a touching and beautiful saraband, 'Adieu, farewell earth's bliss'. It is a sad fact that one of Lambert's last appearances in London was to conduct this work.

Lennox Berkeley worked in Paris from 1927 to 1933 as a pupil of Nadia Boulanger, and thus stands rather apart from the English academic traditions outlined earlier, expressing his individual voice in the more markedly French qualities of elegance, a spicy sense of harmony (in the earlier works) and economy. His oratorio *Jonah* (1935) did not find favour with the Leeds Festival of 1937, partly because of its aggressive, somewhat 'instrumental' style of vocal writing, though it is difficult at this date to understand why the melodic beauty of the tenor aria 'When my soul' or the choral sonority of 'I am cast out of Thy sight' did not impress a choir and audience already familiar with Walton. Perhaps the very lack of English 'roots' in Berkeley's idiom was partly the reason; but *Jonah* might well be now revived again. In later works a greater consideration for singers and a general broadening of lyricism in expression have worked more in Berkeley's favour, and undoubtedly his best work in this genre is the *Stabat Mater* on the medieval devotional poem – set for six solo voices and twelve instruments, and written for the English Opera Group in 1946. His other few works for full chorus, all on the same scale, are mostly part-songs and anthems.

With the noticeable decline of the bigger choral festival in our own day and the general shift of public interest from the choral to the orchestral concert, to opera, and to some extent to chamber music, later composers have not been stirred (as their forefathers were) to the writing of larger cantatas and oratorios except by invitation or for some special occasion. Delius's sarcastic remark that Parry 'would have set the whole Bible to music if he had lived long enough' could never have been prompted by the activities of the later generation, finding for itself a new (mainly instrumental) kind of expression based on new techniques of composition. Thus, just as several modern composers have attempted only one or two symphonies, one or two operas (rarely making it three or four), so it has been with larger-scale choral works. Some incentive has been wanting, while choralists, for their part, have appeared unable or unwilling to keep pace with the forward-looking methods of the composers.

Michael Tippett (*b.* 1905) is a case in point. He has written two operas, two symphonies (separated by a thirteen-year interval), and one oratorio, *A Child of Our Time* (1941). The early *A Song of Liberty* (1937), for chorus and orchestra (words by William Blake) and to some extent the later unaccompanied *The Weeping Babe* (1944), to words by Edith Sitwell, are chorally less effective than we might expect, where the (often doubled) part-writing seems unenterprising. The unaccompanied eight-part *Plebs Angelica* (1944), an English anthem written, like Rubbra's *Missa Cantuariensis*, for the choir of Canterbury Cathedral, is more resourceful. Its harmonic asperities and its freedom in accent build up a powerful invocation to the angelic host, though there is little actual eight-part writing, most of the work being for one four-part choir answering the other.

With *A Child of Our Time*, however, Tippett touched new depths with a libretto of his own composition that reveals both his humanism and his social sincerity. The oratorio, a compassionate cry against man's inhumanity to man, is (like Menotti's opera *The Consul*) that rare thing, a work of social significance that is also a work of art. It was based ostensibly on the Nazi persecutions of the Jews, but its libretto is sufficiently removed from specific time or place to have no mere temporal value, while the score is one that transcends a narrow interpretation of the words, so that ultimately it is by the music alone that Tippett moves us to a like compassion, as well as to an admiration for his own skill in organization and presentation. The insertion of Negro spirituals at several points, after the manner of Bach's use of chorales in his cantatas and Passions, is a case in point. Tippett is often a complex composer, but here an unusual and telling simplicity prevails, and the arrangements of the familiar tunes make their full effect without trace of sentimentality. The work is evenly divided between four soloists and the choir, and the chorus parts are often short, sometimes only a few bars of comment or observation, again after the manner of Bach. The première of *A Child of Our Time*, in 1944 (when Tippett was thirty-nine), served the wider purpose of drawing the attention of the general musical public to Tippett's works for the first time, and this oratorio is now in the repertory of many choral societies.

By contrast Benjamin Britten (*b*.1913) came to wide public notice as early as his twenty-first year through a broadcast of his brilliant set of choral variations *A Boy was Born*. This ingenious and original score, begun in November 1932 (and revised by the composer in 1955), is an astonishing *tour de force* that has not in any way been eclipsed by the composer's considerable later achievements. Written for unaccompanied choir of men's, women's, and boys' voices (the later version has an *ad libitum* part for organ, mainly provided to assist the singers and hold the parts together) it consists of a theme ('A Boy was Born') built from a four-note figure (D, E, G, E) to which these words are set, and six variations, each a setting of another carol, generally one from the fifteenth century, the only later writer represented being Christina Rossetti, with 'In the bleak midwinter'.

After this remarkable début in the choral world Britten added two part-songs, *I Lov'd a Lass* and the humorous *Lift Boy* (1933), to his output, as well as a *Te Deum* in C (1935), for choir and organ, while continuing active in other branches of composition and notably in the field of solo vocal music. Then, shortly before his visit to America in 1939, Britten produced two choral works with as much political as musical interest, an *a cappella* chorus for mixed voices *Advance Democracy* (words by Randall Swingler) and the more ambitious *Ballad of Heroes*, for high voice, chorus, and orchestra (words by W. H. Auden and Randall Swingler), neither of which have become widely known. The existence of these two works reminds us that Britten, no less than Tippett, is a composer with a strong humanitarian sense. Both are pacifists, and in the *Ballad of Heroes* Britten commemorates the men of the International Brigade's British battalion killed in the Spanish Civil War.

Britten remained in America until 1942, and it is said that his next two choral works (1942), the *Hymn to St Cecilia* for unaccompanied mixed voices (words by Auden), and the *Ceremony of Carols* for treble voices and harp, were written as he crossed the war-time Atlantic in a Swedish cargo boat. These quickly became popular works – especially the *Ceremony of Carols* – from the moment of their first performances, when it was evident that Britten's art had found a new maturity and some new spell-binding qualities – consummate ease of expression, musical invention of immediate attractiveness, and a way with words that seemed indeed to be a true extension of their power, rather than a mere musical addition to it. In the *Hymn to St Cecilia*, towards the end, Britten requires soloists to imitate instruments suggested by the poet. The violin is suggested by contralto solo on the fifths of the violin's open strings, against a held chord from the other singers (Example 78). The drum is suggested by a bass solo, drumming a rhythmic sequence on the note

Ex. 78. Britten, *Hymn to St Cecilia*

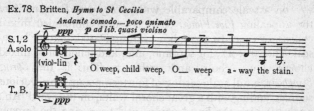

Ex. 79. Britten, *Hymn to St Cecilia*

C, a flute by a soprano, and a trumpet by a fanfare-like figure for solo tenor (Example 79).

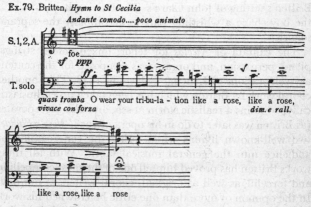

Such freedom and ingenuity, governed at the same time by creative discipline and absolute sureness of touch, quite literally sounded a new note in British choral music, and from now on there began a surge of interest in Britten's work which has never slackened, since the genius of the composer was acknowledged on all sides with the triumphant production of the opera *Peter Grimes* at Sadler's Wells Theatre in 1945, when the composer was thirty-one.

The individual character of Britten's personal idiom is continued in two other smallish works of the period, the festival cantata *Rejoice in the Lamb* (words by Christopher Smart) of 1943, and the *Festival Te Deum*, for choir and organ, of 1945, which represents not so much an advance on the *Te Deum* of a decade earlier as a guide to Britten's characteristic rhythmical freedom. None of these works, however, was on a scale comparable with *A Boy was Born*, nor are the appealing *Five Flower Songs*, for unaccompanied mixed chorus, of 1950. In 1949, however, appeared another large-scale choral work, for soprano, alto, and tenor solos, mixed chorus, boys' choir, and orchestra. This is the *Spring Symphony*, a full-scale setting of fourteen poems from various sources, ending with a great choral waltz, on the word 'Ah', against which the boys' voices, in $\frac{3}{4}$ time, sing the famous thirteenth-century English song *Sumer is icumen in*. Another bright feature in this splendid and significant score is Britten's setting of John Clare's 'The Driving Boy', in which the boys have a whistling part to accompany the soprano soloist.

The cantata *St Nicolas* for tenor, mixed voices, strings, piano, percussion, and organ, was composed for the centenary celebrations of Lancing College in 1948. This, another choral work by Britten which has been taken up enthusiastically, contains a realistic storm at sea, and also incorporates (as Britten was later to do in his opera of 1958, *Noye's Fludde*) two well-known hymns which bring the congregation or audience into the general musical fabric. With all these works Britten has proved himself one of the most compelling and forceful, as well as original, choral writers of our day. In the opinion of more than one critic he crowned his work with *A War Requiem* (Coventry Cathedral Festival, 1962) which juxtaposes the words of the Latin Requiem Mass and anti-war poems of Wilfred Owen. Soprano, tenor, and baritone soloists are used with large chorus and orchestra.

In 1958 the Leeds Triennial Festival celebrated its centenary, and for that occasion – perhaps hoping to repeat the success of *Belshazzar's Feast* – a large-scale choral work, *The Vision of Judgement*, was commissioned from Peter Racine Fricker (*b.*1920). Until that time Fricker had written few choral works, and all of them at the level of chamber music. The romantically modern *Rollant et Oliver*, three exquisite miniatures for unaccompanied voices, are good examples of his vocal style, which is exploited with great power in *The Vision of Judgement*. This exciting work, which completely fulfilled Leeds's expectations, has a text adapted from the eighth-century poem *Christ*, by Cynewulf. Fricker's apocalyptic vision is balanced, like *Belshazzar's Feast*, between two great and opposing choruses, one of doom and the other of joy. Also like Walton, Fricker writes for an enormous orchestra, demanding additional brass (trumpets and trombones) consisting 'of as many players as possible'. (Walton was content with seven players in each band!)

Fricker's work, however, has more points of sheer repose than Walton's, while an effective contrast is made with the central Latin part of the work where the writing is for choral forces alone. Fricker writes for two soloists (soprano and tenor) as against Walton's one (baritone).

The boldness and economy of the choral writing is plain. (Example 80).

Ex. 80. Fricker, *Vision of Judgement*

Since 1958 *The Vision of Judgement* has been given a second time in Leeds and also elsewhere, but so far it has no successor, which indicates again that large-scale choral works do not primarily interest composers today unless they have actually been commissioned for performance. Another composer prompted by special invitation to enter the field was Alexander Goehr (*b.* 1932) whose large-scale choral-and-orchestral *Sutter's Gold* was given at the Leeds Festival of 1961.

But there is one composer who proves the exception to this rule, Anthony Milner (*b.* 1925), whose output has been predominantly choral with words on religious subjects. *The City of Desolation* (Worcester, 1957) was commissioned by the Dartington Summer School in 1955, where it was performed, and takes some of its text from Ronald Knox's

translation of the Bible – the first occasion on which this has
been used by a composer. This work made a fine impression
at its first public performance at Worcester. 'The opening
notes, D sharp and E', wrote the composer at that time,
'present an opposition of tonalities which pervades the
entire musical organization and determines much of the
form, melody, and harmony.' But for all that, Milner's musical language is tonal and, by modern standards, not difficult to assimilate, yet never less than strongly personal and
effective.

In *St Francis* (1956) Milner's rhythmical and contrapuntal ingenuities are even more cleverly displayed. But
again the music is appealing and, in the best sense, 'singable'; and perhaps Milner will be one of the composers to
effect a reconciliation between 'modern music' as such
and the habits of mind of the choralists who are asked to
perform it. For these, generally speaking, and especially in
the larger industrial centres, are amateurs who attend rehearsals for relaxation, as a hobby. They are conservative
in taste, suspicious of change, and sometimes hostile to the
more extreme manifestations of musical writing, at least
when they first encounter it, having for the most part neither
the knowledge, technique, nor sight-reading ability of
today's orchestral musicians.

One may wonder, for instance, how many choirs could
master the prodigious difficulties of the cycle of three
unaccompanied Latin motets, collectively called *Pro Pace*
(1955–8) by John Joubert (*b.*1927). These have a magnificent technical assurance and emotional power. A remark
printed with the music suggests that the title (literally
'For Peace') carries the present-day political implication
of disarmament, though the poems themselves are medieval.
Whether the linking of political aspirations and Latin
motets will seem odder to politicians or choralists is an
open question.

The uneasy relation today between the genuinely modern
composer, the choralist, and the listener is thus sharply
illuminated. That choirs may, by careful wooing, be eventually won over to new works – and can enjoy performing

them – has been successfully demonstrated on several occasions. But that a cross-roads has been reached in British choral music none can deny.

[The distinctive contributions to choral music of Havergal Brian and Alan Bush are discussed by Deryck Cooke in Chapter 14.]

20

A Mixed Modern Group

from *c.*1920

PETER J. PIRIE

In considering certain other European composers of the twentieth century, it would be useless to impose a pattern where none exists. Very broadly, nevertheless, the field may be divided into serialists and the followers of traditional (in the sense of non-serialist) methods. We will deal with the traditionalists first.

Ernst Bloch (1880–1959) was born in Switzerland, and died in America, but considered himself a Jewish composer. His *Avodath Hakodesh*, or *Sacred Service* (1932–4), for baritone solo, chorus, and orchestra, is a setting of the Jewish Sabbath Morning Service, according to the Union Prayer Book of America; but its spirit transcends purely sectarian bounds. It may be described as the most considerable of Bloch's specifically Jewish works, although *Shelomo* (1915) for cello and orchestra is possibly a more perfect, self-contained whole. The style of the *Sacred Service* is simple, and quite plain; the harmony grave, traditional, and modally inflected. Thus it differs from Bloch's instrumental works, with their luxuriant harmonic and instrumental colouring and occasional orientalism. The baritone solo takes the part of the Cantor in the Jewish rite, and very occasionally the vocal line breaks out into a melisma of oriental inspiration, but is in the main a grave recitative, allied to chanting, on which the chorus meditates. The Service is in the traditional five parts, and each part is further subdivided, these smaller divisions having Hebrew titles. The first and third parts are prefaced by an instrumental prelude for the orchestra or organ accompanying the work; part two is called

'Kedusha' ('Sanctification') and the last and longest part, 'Epilogue'. Its effect is cumulative; the solemn chanting of the soloist, and the meditations of the choir move towards the last section, in which the soloist (as the Minister) intones in a quasi-speaking voice a long and moving prayer for the establishment of God's kingdom on earth, and for the fellowship of all men. The work (which lasts about fifty minutes) ends with an elaborate song of praise, and a short benediction.

Example 81 is from Part 3 ('Silent Devotion and Response'). It illustrates the way soloist and chorus are dovetailed in together, and the simplicity of writing for both vocal and instrumental parts; also the occasional slight orientalism (the semitone grace-note on the word 'heads'). The figure D–E–G in the bass is a Bloch 'fingerprint' and is thematic in this work.

This is Bloch's only choral work (if we except the opera *Macbeth*, 1909), and was the result of a commission from Gerald Warburg of New York in 1930.

The name of Zoltan Kodály (*b*.1881) is united historically with that of Bartók (see p. 319). Both were pupils of Hans Koessler at the University of Budapest. Together they collected Magyar folk-songs, and both generally participated in the Hungarian nationalist movement that chafed under Austrian political and cultural domination. Kodály's music is full of Hungarian folk and nationalist material, and in its liberal but not radical temper has been compared with that of Vaughan Williams. It is, however, much more accomplished technically than Vaughan Williams's, while less rugged in personal idiom. Kodály has written in every form – opera, orchestral music, chamber music, piano music, and songs; and his choral work is of paramount importance. There is a vast quantity of music for unaccompanied chorus (much of it based on folk material), some liturgical music with organ, and important works for chorus and orchestra. The unaccompanied pieces are often written with amateurs in mind, and there are a number of sets for children; the idiomatic writing and the sympathy with which these works are written makes them valuable

Ex. 81. Bloch, *Sacred Service*

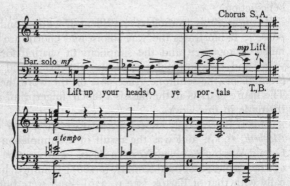

material for such choirs. For children there are, among other things, the *Bicinia Hungarica* (Latin for 'Hungarian duets'), sixty two-part settings (1937), and some more of the same kind of things dating from 1938. The pieces for mixed choir are varied in difficulty, but always skilfully written for voices; the attractive *Jesus and the Traders* (1934) may be mentioned.

But it is among his works for chorus and orchestra that his most important music is to be found; indeed, the best of these, the *Psalmus Hungaricus* (1923), has a good claim to be considered his masterpiece. There is also the powerful *Te Deum* for chorus, soloists, and orchestra. The style of the latter works is plainer than that of the *Psalmus Hungaricus;* and indeed, all Kodály's work becomes less florid, more sober and plain, with advancing years. The *Missa Brevis* in particular has this certain solemnity. The original version (which Kodály himself conducted at the Three Choirs Festival in 1948) used an organ accompaniment, and this has coloured the orchestral version of 1951. The successive sections of the Mass are clearly defined, and the work is based on a polyphony deriving from ancient usage. This, however, is coloured by Kodály's Hungarian nationalism, as is the scoring of the orchestral version, which, although betraying its origin as organ music, takes on in places the high colouring of such things as the opera *Háry János* (1926); the writing for the solo parts, both singly and in combination, is very effective.

The *Psalmus Hungaricus* is a colourful and dramatic setting of words by the sixteenth-century Hungarian poet Michael Veg, who was born in Kecskemet, Kodály's birthplace. The words are a passionate outburst of indignation at betrayal, with a fervent calling on the Lord of Hosts for support. It was written in celebration of the fifteenth anniversary of the union of the cities of Buda and Pest, and was commissioned by the city of Budapest. It has travelled all over the world, and has carried Kodály's name with it; next to the orchestral suite from the opera *Háry János* it is his best-known work. It opens in a mood of passionate lamentation (Example 82), and ends in one of fierce exultation. There is a brilliant solo for tenor, couched in passionate declamation; the very individual swaying rhythm, seen in the extract below, pervades the work, and contributes much to its character. The orchestration is brilliant, with a certain barbaric edge (this is the young Kodály) and

Ex. 82. Kodály, *Psalmus Hungaricus*

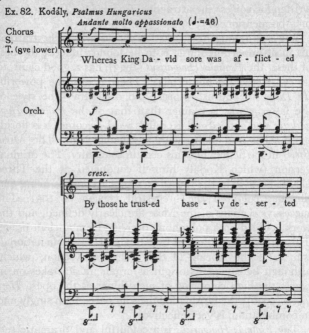

the choral writing fierce and strong. It makes a tremendous effect wherever the necessary forces, a standard symphony orchestra, good choir, and proficient soloist, of professional or very good amateur quality, are available to do it justice. Modern Hungarian music, of the generation of Kodály's pupils, has come under the specific demands of a Communist régime, and as a consequence tends to be pallidly conservative; in practice, a faint copy of Kodály, without his individuality and brilliance.

Switzerland, international in its very structure, has stood outside the struggle that has torn Europe for fifty years. Besides Bloch, who was, as we have seen, primarily a Jewish composer, Switzerland numbers among her composers Frank Martin (*b*.1890), Robert Oboussier (1900–57), and Willy Burkhardt (1900–55). Swiss music tends to be eclectic and mildly traditional; none of the above has attempted the more rarefied flights of twentieth-century serial composition. Burkhardt's choral music shows a certain conscious archaism, wedded to an outlook that remained modern in spirit, as can be seen in his most important work, the Protestant oratorio *The Vision of Isaiah (Das Gesicht Jesajas)* (1933–5). The use of the pentatonic scale (the scale represented by the black keys on the piano) often with the addition of harmonic seconds to the archaic-sounding chords (built of octaves, fifths, and fourths) gives his early and middle-period works their distinctive flavour of the primitive and the elemental. Into this texture, as time went on, Burkhardt gradually introduced his own variety of chromaticism, until his rigid harmonies had quite softened. During this process his later choral works appeared; *The Four Seasons (Das Jahr,* 1942) and the Mass (1950–1). Among his earlier works is a setting of Psalm 12 (1934) and he wrote a great many unaccompanied compositions. Frank Martin sometimes employs a series of all the twelve notes in succession but retains tonal harmony, and his is therefore not 'twelve-note music' in Schoenberg's sense. Martin's principal choral compositions are the oratorio *Golgotha* (1945–8) and *The Mystery of the Nativity* (1959), which is based on an old French mystery play and may be performed as opera or oratorio.

There is a gulf between the foregoing composers and those now to be dealt with, over whom hangs the shadow of Arnold Schoenberg (see p. 305) and his 'serialist' revolution. This revolution is fraught with problems and difficulties for the choral composer, but is also full of the possibilities of new effects. Schoenberg himself felt the need for a new approach when he evolved the principle of 'speech-song' (*Sprechgesang*). In the music of Vladimir Rudolfovich Vogel (*b.*1896) choral song indeed spills over into actual speech. His choral declamation has been said to achieve an intense, nerve-wracking effect. His *Thyl Claes* (1937–45) is a secular oratorio for two reciters, soprano, speaking chorus, and orchestra. It lasts for about four hours, and vividly depicts the suffering of the Netherlands under tyrannical Spanish occupation. In another secular oratorio, *Wagadu's Descent*

into Vanity (*Wagadus Untergang durch die Eitelkeit*, 1930),
Vogel uses soloists, chorus, and five saxophones. Vogel, who
had a German father, was born in Moscow and studied with
Tiessen and Busoni, coming under the influence of Schoenberg in the years immediately after the First World War.

We now turn to Webern himself, the most radical of our
group of serialists. The music of Webern shrinks into an
ever-increasing reticence, intimacy, and understatement.
Apart from some small things, he composed three important
choral works – *The Light of the Eyes* (*Das Augenlicht*, 1935),
the Cantata No. 1 (1940), and Cantata No. 2 (1943). The
words of all three, in German, are by Hildegarde Jone
(whose correspondence with Webern has recently been
published), and are of a symbolist nature; English versions
for performance are available.

Webern's relationship to serialism in general and Schoenberg especially is that of an alchemist and refiner, detecting
the very essence of a thing, and removing all impurities,
until the logical implications are revealed, and the developments implicit in the original are crystallized.

It has been said that there is no detectable difference
between his pre-serial work and those later pieces that he
wrote with meticulous and almost fanatical regard to the
letter and spirit of twelve-note technique. The sound is
transparent, note succeeds note with meticulous placing,
each note sounding as in a vacuum; phrasing confines itself
to terse and gnomic statements of a few notes each. Given
this texture and the vocal line inherent in serial music
(augmented and diminished intervals, leaps of more than
an octave, and so on) it is obvious that this music is difficult
to sing; and to argue against this that it has been sung is
disingenuous. It would be painful to hear an amateur choir
of average abilities trying to sing it, and most performances
heard of it are inadequate; one of the few exceptions is the
excellent recording that has been made of Webern's complete works, where the vocal music is performed in exemplary manner. This music should not be tackled except by a
choir of outstanding ability who are prepared to give it
adequate rehearsal time. This advice is almost superfluous;

one glance at a score should be enough. That said, it may be remarked that Webern tends, more than Schoenberg does, to write for voices with due regard to vocal style; some of Schoenberg's vocal lines are more forbidding.

These three late works of Webern, then, are written in a concentrated serial style, are terse and brief in duration, and demand the study of an individual aesthetic. *The Light of the Eyes* (*Das Augenlicht*) is scored for chorus and a chamber orchestra that includes alto saxophone and mandolin; it lasts for ten minutes. The Cantata No. 1, for soprano solo, chorus, and similar but not identical orchestra, lasts twenty minutes, which is long for a Webern work. The Cantata No. 2, for soprano and bass soloists, chorus, and a somewhat larger orchestra, lasts sixteen minutes and is in six sections.

In this Cantata No. 2, a curious feature of the last section (curious for serial music) is that it is in strophic form, the music being repeated three times to different verses. The first five parts share the usual Webern texture of disparate notes of different character forming an oddly mosaic-like pattern; the sixth part bears a very strong resemblance to the chorale with which a traditional cantata might be expected to end. The second part of this cantata may be considered as typifying the composer's method. The first note heard is a D flat on the harp, a solitary note. Following immediately on this the bass soloist exposes a twelve-note row beginning on the same note. From then on the row and its derivatives are distributed round the instruments and the soloist (this has begun to happen even during the exposition of the row), until at the end its salient shape is broadly hinted at once more. The composer's characteristic style is also seen in Example 83, from the fifth part of the cantata. (The words mean: 'Then you know it: it hurts you deeper far than death when a dark cloud comes.')

Here the process is not so easy to discover; but the C sharp to A natural and from G sharp to E natural and C natural are clearly visible as Webern manipulates his row. The complex chromatic writing, and need for rock-steady intonation, are also obvious. Webern's is a still, concentrated,

Ex. 83. Webern, *Cantata No. 2*

passionate, miniscule world, well compared to the haunted claustrophobia of the last tragic works of Paul Klee; tension is here, rather than tragedy, and needle-sharp beauty of a limited kind rather than Klee's closing twilight, but the comparison has often been made, and is most apt.

Schoenberg and Webern, and serialism in general, were denounced in Nazi Germany, but their influence has overwhelmingly pervaded post-war West German music. (In Communist East Germany, official theory still opposes serialism.) But the best-known modern West German composer is one who stands quite on his own and has been performed alike in Moscow and in the West: Carl Orff (*b.* 1895). His music reveals an extreme reaction against textural and intellectual complexity. His preoccupation with rhythm gives him a slight link with that other German individualist, Boris Blacher (*b*.1903). Orff's liking for medieval texts for his music goes with a suggestion, in his sheer sound, of such twelfth-century composers as Pérotin.

In total effect, however, his scores sound like no one else's, old or new. Huge batteries of percussion instruments, including pianos in the plural, are used to create a rhythmic pattern of hypnotic insistence, over which voices chant tunes of primitive simplicity which occasionally break out into short-lived florid phrases. His best-known work is *Carmina Burana* (1936), a setting of texts (mainly in medieval Latin) found in the monastery of Benedictbeuern in Upper Bavaria. The work is really designed for stage performance, dancers miming the action, but has been frequently and successfully given by choral societies – who will need soprano, tenor, and baritone solos, and a large modern orchestra with multifarious percussion.

Carmina Burana is in three parts: 'Spring', 'The Tavern', and 'Love'. Both choral and orchestral writing are of extreme harmonic simplicity, completely eschewing counterpoint, and the main attraction of the work is its sheer dynamic impact, a sense of athletic freshness very much in keeping with the nature of the words. Helen Waddell, who has translated some other Benedictbeuern lyrics, points out that this is possibly the only poetry in existence that gives one a sense of youth and joy unmixed with the regret and wistfulness associated with the most sophisticated treatment of the subject – by Keats and Shelley, for instance.

Carmina Burana is probably Orff's masterpiece. Later, in a similar style, he wrote *Catulli Carmina* (*Songs of Catullus*, 1943) and *Triumphs of Aphrodite* (1952), as well as other stage works. In 1930–3 he wrote an educational method, *School-work* (*Schulwerk*), in which his interest in rhythmic schemes is also demonstrated.

We now turn to Italy, where notable contributions have been made to the choral repertory by Goffredo Petrassi (*b*.1904) and Luigi Dallapiccola (*b*.1904). Of these two Petrassi is more eclectic, Dallapiccola more completely

Italian. Which is not altogether to be expected, since Petrassi was born in the heart of Italy, at Zagarola in the Roman *campagna* (and entered Rome for the first time on top of a wine-cask, aged seven), while Dallapiccola was actually born an Austrian subject, and today his birthplace (Pisino, Istria) is in Yugoslavia. Dallapiccola is a true child of this time, therefore; and if, typically, his birth-place is no-man's-land, part of the famous political empire of cloud-cuckoodom, he has made up for this with the spirit of a true artist, by being utterly Italian.

Bartók, Stravinsky, and even Richard Strauss seem to have presided over Petrassi's musical christening, and the paternal spirit of Hindemith hovered over his early work. He began his musical career as a choirboy, and studied at the Santa Cecilia Academy in Rome. His music is cast in every form. His principal choral works are: *Psalm 9* for chorus, strings, brass, two pianos, and percussion (1934–6), *Magnificat* for soprano, chorus, and orchestra (1939–40), *Chorus of the Dead* (*Coro di Morti*) to words by Leopardi, for male voices, three pianos, brass, and percussion (1940–1), *The Dark Night of the Soul* (*Noche Oscura*, 1950), to words by St John of the Cross, for mixed chorus and orchestra; and *Nonsense* (1952), some settings of Edward Lear (in Italian) for unaccompanied chorus.

Petrassi's setting of the Latin text of Psalm 9 is strongly influenced by plainsong in the treatment of the declamatory passages. Lyrical elements are woven in when the words seem to demand them, making a texture in which these two styles are mixed, rather than alternate. The vocal writing tends to simplicity, while the writing for orchestra is sophisticated; both polyphonic and rather bare harmonic devices are used, and the work generally turns to account a certain duality of means and mood.

Chorus of the Dead, to words by the dark and pessimistic poet Leopardi, was written under the impact of the outbreak of the Second World War; in this work serial elements – of a fragmentary and transient nature – appear for the first time in Petrassi's work. It is described as a 'dramatic madrigal'. There are three choral sections, alternating with orchestral scherzos. It is natural in such a work, a setting of almost nihilistic poetry, that the music should be of a corresponding dark and brooding character.

The form of *The Dark Night of the Soul* is largely moulded on the stanzas of the poem, with orchestral interludes; the style is varied, with the composer's usual mixture of polyphonic and harmonic methods. Once more, serial elements are present, but are very freely used; more, one might say, as a method of organizing incidental chromaticisms than as a thoroughgoing discipline in composition. The poem is one of incandescent mysticism, and this conditions the mood of the setting, in which many of the twentieth century's musical discoveries and methods are called into play for expressive purposes, and Petrassi's own past works quoted. The orchestra needed is a large one, with triple woodwind and quadruple brass.

Dallapiccola is an eminent practitioner of serial methods in his own individual way. He grew into this technique, so to speak, half-way through his career and its method has obviously come into head-on collision with an Italian's gift for flowing, vocal, and, ultimately, diatonic melody. His times have also contributed to his tensions. Deliberately choosing Italian nationality out of several possibilities, he came into conflict with Fascism, and rejoiced at its fall – but not at the agony of mankind incidental to that fall. The distinction is the man. This concern with man's plight has deeply marked his work. His first important work for chorus and orchestra is *Songs of Prison* (1938–41), the three prisoners concerned being Mary Stuart, Boethius, and Savonarola. There are three sections, each one a setting of the testament of the prisoner concerned, and these parts are held together by the pervading use of the *Dies irae*, and by serial elements. The orchestration is for two pianos, two harps, six drums, xylophone, vibraphone, bells, and other percussion. The evanescent effect of this accompaniment, heard against the firm texture of the chorus, is an effect typical of Dallapiccola.

And yet the fundamental impression one derives of the work is of darkness; the introduction to the 'Mary Stuart' section is impressive in the extreme, and the whole work is imbued with that fundamentally humanist attitude that makes Dallapiccola such a striking figure in our age. Here is a deep emotionalism far removed, as Roman Vlad remarks in his excellent study of the composer, from 'the desperate, half-crazed desolation which permeates the emotional world of Schoenberg' and also removed from the world of Webern. In many ways this work is linked with Dallapiccola's later opera, *The Prisoner* (1949).

Songs of Prison was concerned with the situation just before, and during the first years of, the Second World War; *Songs of Liberation* (1955) celebrates, a little wryly, the liberation of Italy from Fascism. Dallapiccola can never forget the human suffering underlying any situation. The work is in three parts, once more, and the texts are from a letter by Sebastiano Castellio (1515–63), from Exodus, and from the Confessions of St Augustine. The opening phrase (Latin for 'O brother, if our faith had been firm') may be quoted as typical of Dallapiccola's outlook (Example 84). This great sweeping vocal phrase is a twelve-note row; but it is intensely lyrical, quite vocal, and ends with the uncompro-

Ex. 84. Dallapicola, *Canti di liberazione*
Molto lento; flessibile (♩=72)

mising statement of the triad of C minor; the characteristic percussion accompaniment should also be noted. This theme is also related to piano music he wrote to celebrate the eighth birthday of his daughter, Annalibera. The *Songs of Liberation* make constant references to tonality, in spite of the work's definitely serial construction. The last of the three sections has extraordinarily imaginative and mysterious scoring. From time to time speech is used by the chorus. The work demands a large orchestra, with saxophones and a huge percussion section as well as the usual full forces.

In *Job* – called a *Sacra Rappresentazione*, the exact Italian equivalent of the English medieval 'mystery play' – the chorus speaks, and on occasion sings, the words of God and Satan; the parts of Job, messengers, and friends are taken by soloists. The percussion effect of the spoken chorus is most striking, and relates to that of Vogel – but with very different effect, since the effect of *Job* in performance is largely one of a glittering and percussive brilliance. The drama of this direct but far from simple attempt to deal with the whole problem of human suffering is taken without modification from the book of Job, and its climax is the splendour of God's answer from the whirlwind, with its invocation of an infinitely mysterious and ineffably beautiful cosmos. Like *Songs of Liberation*, the work is scored for a large orchestra, in which the multi-voiced percussion section plays a big part. Here, then, even in this anti-humanist age we have a religious work by a profound humanist, and moreover, one that makes the age-old claim for the artist that his is the redemptive work of his Creator; and it is a composition that glorifies the singing voice. We have come full cycle, and perhaps the answer rests with Dallapiccola – that a fine artist may in his work still uphold the ancient dignity of man, and may make his peace, however uneasy, between the old technique and the new.

21

Twentieth-Century Americans

ROBERT SABin

The United States has come of age, musically speaking, in the twentieth century, and nowhere can one see this more clearly than in its choral music. Of fascinating diversity, ranging from solid tradition through creative modernity to wild experimentation, this music reveals men who have acquired a technique and a language of their own. Over much of it might be written the prophetic words of Walt Whitman, who has inspired more American choral composers, probably, than any other poet:

> Of Life immense in passion, pulse, and power,
> Cheerful, for freest action form'd under the laws divine,
> The Modern Man I sing.

Certainly this is true of William Schuman (*b.*1910), Norman Dello Joio (*b.*1913), and the others of their generation. These men have brought a stinging freshness of ideas and conceptions into their music and have shaped new forms to convey it. To understand how bracing this is, it might be well to take a backward glance at American choral music at the turn of the century – the era of the potted palm, the overstuffed drawing-room and eight-course dinner, and of the overstuffed, eight-course oratorio.

Nineteenth-century American composers had been prolific producers of oratorios and cantatas on such themes as *The Voyage of Columbus* (Dudley Buck, 1839–1909), *The Culprit Fay* (Frederick Grant Gleason, 1848–1903), *The Wreck of the Hesperus* (Arthur W. Foote, 1853–1937), and *The Uplifted Gates* (William Wallace Gilchrist, 1846–1916). Many of them leaned heavily upon Wagner. Gleason's *Culprit Fay*, for instance, boasted a 'mystery motive', a 'water sprites' motive', a 'night on the Hudson motive', and a 'sylphid queen's love motive'. Even a work of such dignity and careful craftsmanship as the *Hora Novissima* (see p. 229) of Horatio Parker (1863–1919) was still in the genteel tradition. Philip Hale, a distinguished Boston music critic, wrote that it was a work to which 'an acknowledged master of composition in Europe would gladly sign his name'. To which the best reply is that made by Gilbert Chase in his admirable history, *America's Music*: 'But what we really needed was some American music to which no European master of composition could sign his name and get away with it.'

There was one man in the nineteenth century who was writing such music – Charles Ives (1874–1954).

This amazing and unique composer really belongs to the twentieth century. In fact he is still ahead of our time in the imaginative boldness and fearless experimentation of his music. A glance at the passage quoted from his brief *Sixty-Seventh Psalm* (Example 85) will show what I mean.

Although this work was composed in 1898, we find Ives blithely writing for sopranos and altos in C and for tenors and basses in B flat. As a matter of fact, this is very mild for Ives. When he went to Yale University in 1894 and studied with Horatio Parker, he submitted for inspection two fugues with the theme in four different keys! The composer of the *Hora Novissima* 'would just look at a measure or so, hand it back with a smile, or joke about "hogging all the keys at one meal", and then talk about something else', Ives tells us.

One of Ives's most powerful choral works is the *Harvest Home Chorales* (1898–1912), for mixed chorus, brass, double-bass, and organ. These three relatively short pieces with their strange vocal lines combining semitones and leaps of a seventh, their free rhythms, their fantastic dissonances and harmonic combinations, are like all of Ives's music – so powerfully expressive that one forgets their idiosyncrasies. There is something almost pagan and pantheistic about them, and one senses the splendour and profusion of nature in these hymns of thankfulness.

What might be called the elder generation of our leading

Ex. 85. Ives, *67th Psalm*

twentieth-century choral composers splits rather neatly into the more or less conservative and romantic wing and the most or less radical and venturesome wing. To the former belong such men as Howard Hanson (*b*.1896), Randall Thompson (*b*.1899), Vittorio Giannini (*b*.1903), Leo Sowerby (*b*.1895), and (to a lesser degree) Roy Harris (*b*.1898). To the latter category belong Roger Sessions (*b*.1896), Walter Piston (*b*.1894), Wallingford Riegger (1885–1961), Henry Cowell (*b*.1897), and (again, to a lesser degree) Virgil Thomson (*b*.1896). It is impossible and undesirable, of course, to separate composers into rigid categories. Thomson, for instance, although he is extremely modern and technically adventurous in spirit, is essentially a Romantic (although he would probably die rather than admit it). And Riegger, who has used the twelve-note idiom and has always kept abreast of the times, is none the less closer to Hanson and Harris in spirit than he is to Sessions.

When Howard Hanson composed his Second Symphony in 1930, he called it his *Romantic Symphony*, and in a statement made at the time of its première he said:

Much contemporary music seems to me to be showing a tendency to become entirely too cerebral. I do not believe that music is primarily a matter of intellect, but rather a manifestation of the emotions.

As a matter of fact, the *Romantic Symphony* was a bit too lush, repetitive, and sentimental for most of us, and in his later works Hanson has achieved a better balance of mind and emotion in his music. But five years earlier, in 1925, he had composed a work that represented romanticism at its best and that has worn singularly well with the critics as well as the American public – the *Lament for Beowulf*, for chorus and orchestra.

In this extended work, with its powerful, insistent rhythm, its sombre masses of sonority, and its cumulative excitement, the young composer had fully reached his creative stride. The bars which I quote (Example 86) illustrate

Ex. 86. Hanson, *Lament for Beowulf*

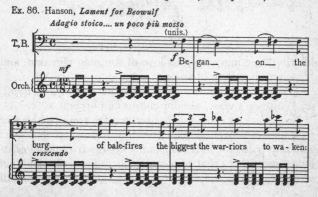

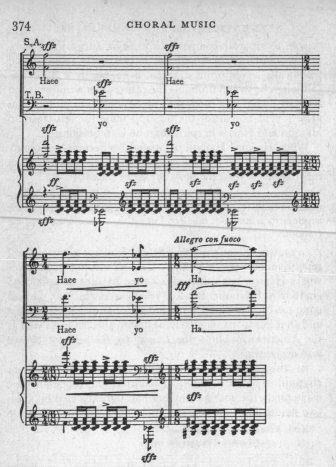

his rhythmic ingenuity, his love of stunning climaxes, and his canny handling of voices.

These same qualities are evident in his *Drum Taps* (1935), on Whitman's verse, also for chorus and orchestra.

No American composer has written for voices with more ease and effectiveness than Randall Thompson. His brief *Alleluia* (1940) for unaccompanied chorus is a model of its kind, and proves that one can be a traditionalist and still write fresh, powerful, inspiring music. An extended work of great charm, skill, and originality is *The Peaceable Kingdom* (1936), also for unaccompanied chorus, with texts from Isaiah. The title refers to a delightful painting by the early nineteenth-century American artist Edward Hicks, which inspired the composer. Hicks was a Quaker preacher, and his painting radiates loving-kindness. Thompson's scheme is more varied and dramatic. He contrasts the reward of the righteous with the torment of the wicked. Notable is the double chorus with antiphony, 'Howl Ye', which leads to a finale in which the righteous are reassured by the prophet. Thompson is also endowed with a salty, typically American sense of humour in music. His compact *Americana* consists of five choruses on texts from the *American Mercury* which deal in merciless fashion with five features of American life: fundamentalism, spiritualism, temperance, capital punishment, and optimism.

A lesser talent, Leo Sowerby has nevertheless made solid contributions to the choral repertory. Typical of his abundantly melodic, richly orchestrated, and effectively written choral music is the *Canticle of the Sun*, a full-length cantata for mixed chorus and orchestra (or piano). A high eclectic composer who pours out grateful melodies and who never fails to write effectively, if a bit conventionally, is Vittorio Giannini. Typical of his choral output is *A Canticle of Christmas*, with its well-wrought texture, almost operatic climaxes, and familiar tunes, all in a small space.

Roy Harris published a sort of credo in 1933 called *Problems of American Composers*. In it he wrote:

> Musical literature never has been and never will be valuable to society as a whole until it is created as an authentic and characteristic culture of and from the people it expresses. History reveals that the great music has been produced only by staunch individuals who sank their roots deeply into the social soil which they accepted as their own.

Harris's Fourth Symphony, the *Folk Song Symphony* (1940) for chorus and orchestra, was written to carry out the intentions of his credo in a very practical way by bringing about 'a cultural cooperation and understanding between the

high school, college, and community choruses of our cities
with their symphonic orchestras'. It is made up of five
choral sections and two instrumental interludes using folk-
tunes taken from the collections of John and Alan Lomax
and Carl Sandburg.

Now the basic idea of this work is excellent, for, just as
the community chorus (or local choral society, as it would be
termed in Britain) was the core of musical life in the United
States in the nineteenth century, so the symphony orchestra
has become the core in the twentieth. But to use folk materials directly in a symphonic context is a perilous business.
Both in this symphony and in his *Folk Fantasy for Festivals*
(1937), which calls for double mixed chorus and men's
and women's choruses, Harris has had his troubles. Perhaps it is fair to say that he has captured the folk spirit more
successfully in his deeply moving purely orchestral symphonies – particularly the Third, Fifth, and Seventh. But,
even if his folk settings become too literal and 'arranged',
they are marked by a great love of the material and an
acute sense of vocal effectiveness.

A glance at the bass (Example 87) from Aaron Copland's
compact work entitled *In the Beginning*, for unaccompanied
chorus (1947), will dispel any illusions that he invariably
writes for chorus in a 'folksy' style.

Yet he has none the less been profoundly influenced by
folk-music. It so happens that this work belongs to another
style, in which he drew away from the folk themes which
had been so memorably and beautifully used in the ballet
scores, *Billy the Kid* (1938), *Rodeo* (1942), and *Appalachian
Spring* (1944), and were to recur in the opera *The Tender
Land* (1954).

Copland (*b*.1900) is one of the few American composers
outside the jazz field who have taken jazz seriously in their
own work. He is an artist to whom line, rhythm, and
structural stress have always been supremely important.
The somewhat frightening complexity on paper of the passage I have quoted makes beautiful sense in performance.
It is a sort of mosaic of rhythmic phrases which dovetail,
beautifully in larger sentences. Like Ives, Thomson, Cowell,

Ex. 87. Copland, *In the Beginning*

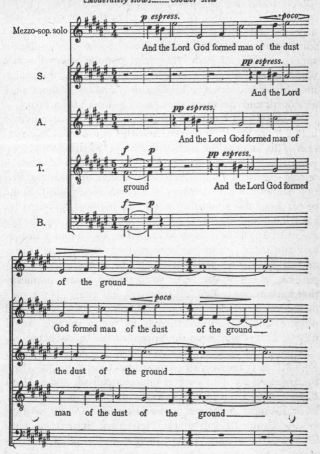

and many other American composers, Copland has always had a great affection for the wonderfully original early hymns and other religious music of the United States. The bracing harmonies of this music with its unabashed fourths and fifths and free rhythmic patterns and stresses seem curiously 'modern' today.

That Copland can write in a folk style with mastery is shown in the choruses from *The Tender Land*. The haunting quintet 'The Promise of Living' from the opera has been arranged for mixed chorus, as has the exuberant choral square-dance 'Stomp Your Feet'. Some of Copland's superb settings of early American popular songs for solo voice have also been arranged for chorus. His fine craftsmanship reveals itself in his *Canticle of Freedom*, a short work for chorus and orchestra, performed in New York in 1955.

No American composer knows or loves the early hymns better than Virgil Thomson, and this is a partial explanation of the fact that he is always at his best writing for voices. Even when he was living in Paris in the 1920s (scarcely a setting evocative of the American hymn), he incorporated two of them in his *Symphony on a Hymn Tune* (1928). Some of his best choral writing occurs in his operas, based on zany Gertrude Stein texts that are always marvellously singable. In his *Four Saints in Three Acts*, which had a Broadway run in 1934 and has been revived several times since, and in *The Mother of Us All* (1947) he writes with a transparence, a faultless sense of word setting, and a piquancy that have added something new to choral music. Thomson's deliberate simplicity and naïveté, his square-cut musical phrases and homespun themes by some miracle avoid mere cuteness and have the appeal of the vernacular.

Among his smaller choral works are *Three Antiphonal Psalms* (1924) for women's voices unaccompanied, a *Missa Brevis* (1925) for men's voices unaccompanied, and a *Missa Brevis* (1936) for women's voices with percussion. A newer work, his most ambitious, is the *Missa Pro Defunctis*, written for the Crane Chorus of the New York State University College of Education. It had its first performance in Potsdam, N.Y., on 14 May 1960, and made a profound impression on those who heard it, among whom I was unfortunately not numbered.

For the average listener the music of Roger Sessions is a tough nut to crack. Sessions writes in a highly dissonant, intellectual, and uncompromisingly logical style. But, once its forbidding exterior has been accepted and understood, it will be found to contain a great deal of personality and expressiveness. Sessions's setting of *Turn, O Libertad* (1944), to Whitman's verse, for chorus accompanied by piano duet, is a good example of his choral writing with its great compactness and impact. Of equally high intellectual quality, the music of Walter Piston (*b*.1894) is much less 'tough' than that of Sessions. Piston, who is noted as an admirable teacher and the author of admirable texts on harmony, counterpoint, and orchestration, has not written as much choral as instrumental music, but he is at home in it.

Henry Cowell is an extremely diversified talent. Despite his experiments with note-clusters and other new musical forms and ideas, his choral writing is relatively simple and sometimes frankly popular, as in the brief *Lilting Fancy* (*Nickelty Nockelty*) for unaccompanied chorus (1949). Cowell has used the early American hymn style with its modes, its open fifths, and its unusual prosody, in his settings of passages from Stephen Vincent Benét's *John Brown's Body* for two-part women's chorus, *American Muse* (1943).

Like Cowell, Wallingford Riegger is less venturesome in his choral writing than in his instrumental works. He is a unique figure in his blending of lyricism and romanticism with extremely advanced and intricate techniques of composition. Bernard Rogers (*b*.1893) is also thoroughly contemporary in technique, but a romanticist at heart. His oratorio *The Passion* (1944) and his ambitious cantatas *The Raising of Lazarus* (1931) and *The Exodus* (1932) are solid, proclamatory works that command respect, if not great enthusiasm.

If one were asked point-blank to name the most original and forceful of twentieth-century American choral composers thus far, the choice would fall inevitably upon William Schuman. For he has revolutionized the style and technique of choral writing not merely for professionals but for amateurs, and his choral music is unmistakably American in spirit and texture. Like Emerson's essays, like Whitman's poetry, Schuman's music reveals the ideas and conceptions and visions and experiences that make the United States what it is. But his America is the land of jazz, skyscrapers, and jet planes, as well as of prairies, mountains, and great rivers. Schuman combines many seemingly contradictory qualities. He is salty and down-to-earth, yet no one can write in a loftier and more intellectually concentrated style. He is very much of the people; he has written popular songs; and he knows the musical vernacular in all its forms, from Broadway to the back hills. Yet he writes with far less direct reference to these influences than many of his colleagues. He is enormously practical in his thinking as well as in his life, but he is a visionary and an idealist. When I first heard his magnificent Symphony No. 6, I called it a requiem for the twentieth century.

It was not by accident that Schuman won the first Pulitzer Prize in music in 1942 with his compact secular Cantata No. 2, *A Free Song*, inspired by Whitman. He had enjoyed an ideal practical opportunity to experiment with choral writing at Sarah Lawrence College for women (New York), where he joined the teaching staff in 1935 and in 1938 became director of the college chorus which won national fame under his dynamic leadership. The students were excited by the challenges which his music offered to them, and an editorial in the college newspaper declared that 'the chorus is the football team of Sarah Lawrence'.

The comparison was a happy one, for there is something athletic and out-of-doors about much of Schuman's choral music. It is terrifically alive in rhythm, prevailingly linear despite its often rich sonorities, and fearless in its harmonic treatment. Vincent Persichetti (see Bibliography) has pointed out that:

Schuman does not use tonality for structural purposes. Nevertheless, it is strongly felt in his music, even though there is no key signature . . . He covers the wide gamut of scales bestowed upon Occidental civilization, and needs the elbow room afforded by the freedom of shifting modes, twelve-note melodies if he chooses, but always a tonality . . . Some of his harmony is misunderstood. The much mentioned polytonality in Schuman is not polytonality but polyharmony. Triads of kindred tonalities joining to form one resonant five- or six-note chord result in a harmony enriched by overtones and belonging to one key.

In a tribute to Martha Graham, the great American modern dancer, Schuman once said that he had always been able to love and understand her work, because he had 'been brought up on the consonance of the angle and the dissonance of the curve'. There is jutting strength as well as soaring power in his succinct settings of Whitman's *Pioneers!* (1937), for eight-part unaccompanied chorus and of Genevieve Taggard's *This Is Our Time* (1940), his Secular Cantata No. 1, for chorus and orchestra. An admirable introduction to his choral style is afforded by the relatively brief *Choral Étude* (1937) for unaccompanied chorus, composed while he was still at Sarah Lawrence College, before he left to become president of the Juilliard School of Music in New York. Schuman, incidentally, is another admirer of early American choral music, and in his *William Billings Overture* (1943) he pays tribute to the sturdy and independent eighteenth-century Boston tanner whose 'fuguing tunes' delight modern listeners more than they did Billings's staid contemporaries (see p. 196).

Another outstanding figure in American choral composition is Norman Dello Joio (*b.*1913). Although Dello Joio has always proudly proclaimed his Italianate love of melody and opera, he had the good fortune to study with Paul Hindemith, who put some iron into his musical veins and encouraged the neo-classical tendencies that he has always had. At its best, Dello Joio's music is exciting, tender, soaringly lyrical, and at the same time structurally impressive. Less daring and adventurous than Schuman's, it has the same abounding energy and immediacy. Small wonder that Dello Joio, too, has been inspired by Whitman. *The Mystic Trumpeter* (1943), a well-developed work for soprano, tenor, and baritone solos, chorus, and French horn (or piano) won him a wide reputation. Another characteristic work is the *Song of Affirmation* (1944), a symphonic cantata for mixed chorus, narrator, soprano solo, and orchestra. This setting of verses from Stephen Vincent Benét's *Western Star* has a vigorous, sprawling swing to it that well suits this tribute to the American pioneers: 'Let the forgotten wounds of those first sowers of wild seed burn in us again.' But Dello Joio is not always a reliable self-critic, as the melodic clichés and padded climaxes of his *A Psalm of David* (1950) for chorus and orchestra reveal all too clearly.

Samuel Barber (*b.*1910), on the other hand, is extremely self-critical, and the little choral music he has written exhibits the same finish and fastidious workmanship that his songs for solo voice and other works do. There are two early works for chorus: *The Virgin Martyrs* (1935), for four-part women's chorus, and *Let Down the Bars, O Death* (1936), for four-part mixed chorus. But it was in his longer setting of Stephen Spender's *A Stopwatch and an Ordnance Map* (1940), for men's chorus and three kettledrums (with an optional addition of four horns, three trombones, and tuba), that he made his mark as a choral composer. Every element in this profoundly dramatic yet contained score – rhythm, harmony, melody, and tone-colour – is subtly used to enhance the poignant text. The more ambitious *Prayers of Kierkegaard* (1954), for solo voices, chorus, and orchestra is a masterfully wrought score, but it fails to make the prayers seem very profound or emotionally searching.

Paul Creston (original name Joseph Guttoveggio, *b.*1906) has achieved wide popularity through the tunefulness and luxuriance of his scores. At times his music sounds almost as if Mascagni were writing in the manner of Reger. But, at his best, he achieves dignity as well as abundant power. His *Three Chorales from Tagore* (1936), unaccompanied, is one of his few larger choral works. Another composer who presents no problems of comprehension to the listener is Elie Siegmeister (*b.*1909). Siegmeister has made his major contribution in his arrangements of American folk-music, and it was fitting that the firm of Presser should choose him to edit its American Folk Song Series for chorus in 1953. He has called upon many distinguished composers to contribute to it. He has frequently based his original choral works upon American themes, as in his setting of Vachel Lindsay's *Abraham Lincoln Walks at Midnight* (1937); it was recently performed in New York at a concert which also included a setting of the same poem for chorus and orchestra by Robert Palmer (*b.*1915). Palmer, a conservative romantic, has written some eloquent and solidly constructed music.

Notable alike for original and challenging musical thinking and for emotional depth are the choral works of Lukas Foss (*b.* Berlin, 1922), who settled in the United States at the age of fifteen. Foss won his spurs in choral composition with *The Prairie*, a lengthy work with text by Carl Sandburg, written when he was only nineteen. But his masterpiece is *A Parable of Death* (1952), for narrator, tenor solo, chorus, and orchestra. This extended setting of excerpts from Rainer Maria Rilke is fully worthy of the poetry, and can bear comparison with the settings of Rilke of Foss's teacher Hindemith. Foss composed the work to the original German, but used simultaneously a metrical English version by Anthony Hecht.

One of the most popular composers in the United States today is the prolific and unique Alan Hovhaness (*b.*1911), whose innate lyricism always shines through, even in his most rhythmically complex and exotic music. The son of an Armenian father, Hovhaness developed a keen interest in the ancient chants of the Armenian Church and in oriental music in general. Sometimes he writes modally; and he combines intricate counterpoint with an oriental cast of melody. Some of his music is completely oriental in style, eschewing development in the Western sense and creating ever new patterns as it goes along. He has visited the Far East and in India worked with native artists. His Magnificat (1959), for four solo voices, mixed chorus, and orchestra is a striking example of his fascinating writing for chorus. At several points in the work there are sections marked *senza misura* (in free rhythm) in which the voices or instruments repeat a rhythmic pattern rapidly but not together, rising from a *pianissimo* to a colossal *fortissimo* and subsiding to the most evanescent *pianissimo*. This marvellous effect is not used for its own sake but to enhance the mysticism of the text. An enchanting work is *Thirtieth Ode of Solomon* (1949), a cantata for baritone solo, mixed chorus, trumpet, trombone, and string orchestra. The cantillations of the solo voice and instruments and the gorgeous tone-colours of the piece have made it an American favourite.

Two composers who have little of Hovhaness's popular appeal but who are notable for their intelligence and sheer musical invention are Halsey Stevens (b.1908) and Elliot Carter (b.1908). The major influence upon Stevens has been the music of Béla Bartók, but, like that great master, he can write in a disarmingly lyric and transparent manner, as in his *Four Carols* (1951) for male voices unaccompanied. These lovely little pieces are notable for their rhythmical and metrical freedom and rich but spontaneous imitation in part-writing. Stevens escapes the tyranny of the bar-line completely, yet his music never becomes loose. A larger work is *A Testament of Life* (1959), for tenor and bass solo, chorus, and orchestra. Carter's music tends to become laboured, as in *The Defence of Corinth* (1941), a short work for men's voices and piano duet, with a text by Rabelais, and *The Harmony of Morning* (1944), for women's voices and chamber orchestra; but there is no denying the solidity and power of this music. And he has a lighter touch in some of his unaccompanied choruses.

Some startling experiments have been made by Henry Brant (born in Canada, 1913). Typical is the sprawling *December* (1954), commissioned by the famous Collegiate Chorale founded by Robert Shaw, which has been a tremendous stimulus to choral writing in the United States. The text includes excerpts from the *Old Farmers' Almanac*, the *Family Almanac and Moon Book for 1954*, and *The Golden Bough*, as well as satirical poems by Maeve Olen about the dubious charms of modern Decembers. The work calls for a huge apparatus – a large and a small chorus; two oboes, two clarinets, saxophone, four horns, trumpet, trombone, organ, and seven drums; soprano and tenor soloists placed out in the hall; three muted trumpets and three trombones; and a 'bell sonority group' including vibraphone and chimes. The chorus often sings isolated syllables, first in unison, then in two, four, and eight parts, and then in a 'kind of free multiple polyphony'. Brant likes to scatter his performers through the hall, to obtain novel acoustical effects, and he is positively surrealistic at times in his handling of text and scoring. But his music has genuine fascination; one never knows what he will do next.

A gentler and more lyrical temperament, Lou Harrison (b.1917) has also been boldly adventurous. He has rebelled against the tempered scale and written works in what he calls 'Strict Style' and 'Free Style'. In the Strict Style the instruments employ the 'pure' intervals that were in use in European music up to the sixteenth century. In the Free Style Harrison notates the exact intervals as mathematical fractions. His *Four Strict Songs* (1956) are scored for eight baritones, strings, trombones, maracas, and retuned piano; his sensitive Mass is for chorus, trumpet, harp, and strings. This is one of the many works championed by Margaret Hillis and her New York Concert Choir and Orchestra, which have exerted a potent influence on composers. Miss Hillis conducted the first performance (1959) of the oratorio *For the Time Being*, after Auden, by the talented young Marvin Levy (b.1932). This work, for narrator, two sopranos, contralto, tenor, baritone, and bass, soloists, chorus, and orchestra, is eclectic and uneven, but none the less brilliantly imaginative.

Two promising talents of the younger generation are Ned Rorem (b.1923) and William Flanagan (b.1926). Rorem has been a prolific and skilful song writer, and it is not surprising that his setting of seven anonymous sixteenth-century lyrics for unaccompanied chorus, *From an Unknown Past*, should reveal admirable vocal writing as well as a rich harmonic texture and sensitive reflection of mood. Flanagan, a disciple of Copland, is less fluent than Rorem, but he tends to dig deeper. His *Billy in the Darbies* (1949), a setting of Melville, for mixed chorus with piano is involved but searchingly eloquent. It portrays Billy Budd before he is hanged. ('Darbies' are handcuffs.) The ending is haunting:

Sentry are you there? Just ease these darbies at the wrist and roll me over fair. I am sleepy and the oozy weeds about me twist.

I have not room to give detailed attention to a host of other American choral composers but I can assure the reader

that the following are worth attention: Harrison Kerr
(*b*.1899), Robert Ward (*b*.1917), Philip James (*b*.1891),
Ulysses Kay (*b*.1917), Peter Mennin (*b*.1923), Vincent
Persichetti (*b*.1915), Harold Shapero (*b*.1920), Irving Fine
(*b*.1914), Herbert Haufrecht (*b*.1909), Charles Mills
(*b*.1914), Ben Weber (*b*.1916), Ernst Bacon (*b*.1898), Gail
Kubik (*b*.1914), Robert Moevs (*b*.1920), and William Bergs-
ma (*b*.1921), not to mention many other talented men
and women and the purveyors of popular and standard
choral fare in schools, churches, and concert halls.

Several American composers have shown themselves
adept in the madrigal. Madrigals specially composed for the
David Randolph Singers include the exquisite *Like As the
Culver on the Bared Bough* by Halsey Stevens and works by
Charles Mills (*b*.1914), Daniel Pinkham (*b*.1923), and
Ulysses Kay (*b*.1917).

I should also give brief attention at least to some of our
leading composers 'by adoption'. Besides Schoenberg and
Hindemith (see Chapter 17), and Bloch (see Chapter 20),
the names of Ernst Křenek (born in Austria, 1900) and
Kurt Weill (born in Germany, 1900) are to be noted.

Křenek settled in the United States in 1938. Among the
works he has written here are *The Santa Fe Time Table* (1945),
for unaccompanied chorus, of which the text consists of the
names of the railway stops between Albuquerque and Los
Angeles; the *Cantata for Wartime* (1943); and *Five Prayers of
John Donne* (1944), for women's voices unaccompanied.
Kurt Weill also sought refuge in the United States from the
plague of Nazism. From his earliest days he had proved a
skilful writer for voices, and the choruses in his Broadway
shows (such as *Street Scene*, 1947) as well as the separate
pieces he wrote are eminently singable, if rather between-
worlds in style.

It will be seen that twentieth-century American choral
music is enormous in bulk, widely varied in style and content, and very much a part of our musical life. Whether any
of it will last through the ages or not, it has unquestionably
enriched the music of our time.

22

Postscript

ARTHUR JACOBS

As the foregoing pages show, the choral repertory is both older and broader than that of the symphony orchestra or opera house. For most purposes we date the modern symphonic repertory from Haydn, the modern operatic repertory from Gluck. But two centuries before Gluck's *Orpheus* (1787), Palestrina in Rome and Byrd in London were composing their masterpieces. Three centuries earlier still, an English monk wrote for choral performance the round which we know as *Sumer is icumen in*. A continuity of seven centuries was shown when the melody of this round was incorporated in Benjamin Britten's *Spring Symphony* (1949). It was incorporated chorally, the medieval melody cutting in on boys' voices through Britten's own polyphonic web. The idea of thus combining disparate musical strands, one of them not the composer's own, would not have surprised Machaut, Palestrina, Bach, Haydn, or Mahler. I name only five of Britten's predecessors among the great masters of choral writing.

The choralist's repertory, then, covers a huge span in time. It has also a remarkable range in depth, in the varying relationship of the performer to the music. Singing in a Mahler symphony, the choralist is like the member of a symphony orchestra. In a Bach cantata (if the performance is on Bach's own restricted scale) he is like a chamber-orchestral musician. Singing a madrigal by Monteverdi or Morley, with only one or two voices to each part, he may compare himself to the player in a string quartet by Beethoven or an octet by Schubert. The delights of 'vocal chamber music', as we may call it, should not be forgotten under the pressure exerted in our musical life towards the big-scale performance and the grand sound. Many a large choir might happily increase the variety of fare at its concerts by including madrigals or other works sung by a small choir formed from some of its own members. Some jazz concerts might here be taken as a model.

Thus the most massive and most delicate effects, the most ancient and the most modern of musical expressions are open to an enterprising choral body according to its nature and size. Limitless, indeed, seem the possibilities in choral music for performers, listeners, and composers. Yet in fact choral music has dropped in relative importance in musical life in Britain, America, and elsewhere. The period 1875–1900 perhaps marked the peak of choral activity in Britain. It was then that, when the famous French conductor, Pasdeloup, came to London, his host was able to take him to a choral concert in one part of London or another every night of the week. This is recalled in Percy Scholes's book *The Mirror of Music* (London, 1947) – where, incidentally, the reader may find an illumination of the changing character of British choral activity between 1844 and 1944, as revealed through the pages of the *Musical Times*.

No foreign conductor visiting London now could be regaled as Pasdeloup was. Choral music has yielded first place in popular consumption to the music of the symphony orchestra, which the twentieth century has (for the first time) made very widely accessible to the musical public, both in live and mechanically reproduced form. Moreover, within the symphony orchestra's repertory, public favour has been mainly bestowed on the period that may be summed up as Beethoven to Rakhmaninov – and this is a period in which choral music, despite not a few masterpieces, cannot hope to compete generally with the richness and power of the orchestral repertory.

The increased interest in opera in English-speaking countries has also probably contributed to the lessened interest in choral concerts. Bernard Shaw, in his days as a splendidly forthright music critic, unerringly characterized certain Victorian cantatas as 'unstaged operettas on scriptural

themes'. Their composers seemingly laboured to induce a
dramatic experience to be savoured without the morally
dubious associations of the theatre. We may recall that Sullivan in the score of *The Golden Legend*, produced at the
Leeds Festival in 1886, went as far as to give the imaginary
stage direction, 'Struggles at the door, but cannot open it'.
This type of narrative cantata now seems quite dead.
Indeed, a complete reversal in public taste appears to have
taken place. Sir Charles Hallé (the founder of the Hallé
Orchestra) managed in 1861 to introduce Manchester and
London audiences to Gluck's opera *Iphigenia in Tauris* by
the expedient of performing it in oratorio form. At the
Leeds Festival in 1958, and afterwards in London, the way
chosen to revive Handel's *Samson* (a true oratorio, not
planned by its composer as a stage work at all) was by
making an opera of it.

Nineteenth-century oratorios and cantatas followed each
other as the night the day (and, mostly, disappeared no less
irrevocably). But in the 1960s the incentive given to a composer to write a major choral work is not a quarter of what
would have been given a century before. Vanished today
are many former important choral festivals, and those that
survive sometimes wear an anachronistic air. (Walton's
Belshazzar's Feast, the outstanding successful British choral
work of this century, was until 1957 never given at the
Three Choirs Festival, presumably because the work's
merely secular approach to the events narrated offends the
ecclesiastical conscience.) New festivals beckon, nationally
and internationally, where the audiences flock primarily
to the opera house and the symphony concert. There,
choirs may participate, but they do not dominate. Signi-
ficantly, the conductor of a choral society in a mining district of South Wales publicly lamented, early in 1961, that
his was the sole society surviving out of a dozen formerly
existing in the area.

In the general conservatism of their repertory, it might
almost be suspected that choral societies have accepted
without a struggle their relegation to a second-class power
in the world of music. In the last century, choirs vied to

perform new music by such current overseas celebrities as
Dvořák and Gounod; today, however, one notices no comparable scramble for Stravinsky. Indeed, when choral
societies do try occasionally to slake their consciences and
extend their repertory, they too often turn not to the great
modern masters but to some figure of no conceivable significance in the wider world of music. It is not certain who is
deceiving whom by this process. But it is certain that a huge
gap frequently stretches between a choral society's choice
of a classical repertory (normally grounded in a selection,
albeit narrow, from the greatest practitioners of the art)
and its choice of a modern repertory, which often takes
deliberate refuge in mere local and ephemeral works.

Not all the blame for present difficulties, however, is to
be laid at the door of the choralists themselves. We have
here a special aspect of today's general gap between public
taste and radically modern music. (That a gap of some sort
should exist is reasonable; that it should be such a broad
gap as at present is disquieting.) It might be validly argued
that certain composers today appear to have withdrawn
into purely esoteric types of artistic creation which issue no
invitation to the intelligent lay listener of the composer's
own time. On the other hand, the great majority of today's
leading composers *have* written choral music deliberately
suited to actual capabilities of performance, and (as is
pointed out in the foregoing chapters) many works written
to foreign-language texts also have English performing
versions available.

Part of the general backwardness of choral activity today
is due, paradoxically, to something which is the particular
traditional glory of that activity: its close connexion with
amateur performance and with social custom and ritual.
Choral singing, in our west-European musical sense, is an
art rooted in the Church. For well over a thousand years the
Church has maintained the chief establishments of choral
singing – maintained them at an economic cost in order to
carry out a well-defined social function. This function links
the most diversified activities: Monteverdi composing for
St Mark's in Venice, Bach supplying choirs for five churches

in Leipzig, a mid-twentieth-century English schoolmistress acting as village church organist for a few shillings each Sunday. All these social contexts imply an ordered relation between choral music, its performers, and its listeners; all of them imply an ordered choral repertory fitted to prevailing social conditions and prevailing musical skills. The difference is obvious between this and the modern organization of a symphony orchestra's programmes or an opera season, which may be considered economically almost as belonging to the 'entertainment business'.

The other pillar of choral activity, besides the Church, has been the amateur choral society of the mixed-voice type firmly established in the nineteenth century (particularly in Britain, Germany, and America, where Protestantism had already encouraged congregational singing). This type of choral society commandingly adapted an earlier repertory to its own needs, and in addition called forth an extensive new repertory of its own. An older type of choral society – intimate, male, and convivial, as in the English glee clubs – lingered on with some local strength, and still does; but it soon yielded in importance to the nineteenth-century mixed-voice type, just as glees yielded to cantatas.

The amateur mixed-voice choral society, though not strictly 'functional' in the sense that the word can be applied to a church choir, resembled it in being tailored to answer a definite social need. In England, the connexion of the rise of choralism with other musical and social developments (sight-singing methods, publication of cheap music, the brass band movement), all as part of the growth of leisure facilities in the new industrial towns, has been perspicaciously noted by Mr Reginald Nettel.* As a basis for this choral activity there already existed the habit of massed singing, encouraged as part of religious (especially Wesleyan) revivalism. From this, some radical political propagandists tried to go further: thus Thomas Cooper, one of the leaders of the Chartist Movement of the 1840s, wrote 'revolutionary' verses to the familiar psalm-tune known as the *Old Hundredth*.

* See particularly his book *The Englishman Makes Music*, London, 1952.

But choralism, in the sense of the establishment of regularly constituted choral performances before the public, was anything but revolutionary in its social aspect. It was, on the contrary, anti-radical and conservative, a manifestation of the idea that ordinary people could be led to moral improvement within the existing society by the ennobling cultivation of the arts. Choral singing, practically the one artistic activity for which sufficient basic material lay immediately to hand, was thus encouraged with what we should regard as genuinely moral fervour. In 1850 the great singing-teacher Joseph Mainzer, having been in Manchester only six months, conducted a public concert there with 2,000 amateur singers whom he had taught in classes from scratch. (His fee varied, but in some towns was as little as a penny per person per weekly lesson.) The significance of the occasion was not lost on the Bishop and the Mayor of Manchester, both of whom addressed the company and lauded the philanthropic aspect of Mainzer's work. The anti-radical aspect of choralism is amusingly illustrated by the provision in the early rules of the Huddersfield Choral Society (founded 1836) that:

No person shall be a member of this Society, who frequents the 'Hall of Science' or any of the 'Socialist Meetings', nor shall the Librarian be allowed to lend any copies of music (knowingly) belonging to this Society to any Socialist, upon pain of expulsion.

Because of the strength of the Protestant tradition, and because religion in Victorian England was emphatically a bulwark of the established social order, it was natural enough that the Bible should form the great source of texts for the music supplied to these amateur choirs. Mendelssohn's *Elijah* (1846) occupied the pinnacle of success; innumerable foothills with such inviting names as *Joash* and *Bartimeus* surrounded it. Cantatas not on biblical subjects often had, none the less, a text more or less of a religious nature (far more often than Sunday occurs in a week). Such was the strength of this convention that Parry, in private an unbeliever, but none the less a pillar of the established order, numbered a substantial quota of oratorios, anthems, and so forth among his compositions.

Nor did Victorian choral societies lack works celebrating (with pious adjurations) topical festive events: a military victory, a royal jubilee, an exhibition. Not only British composers supplied such works. Verdi's *Hymn of the Nations* was written for, though in the event not performed at, an international exhibition held in London in 1862. Such a work as Stanford's *The Revenge* (1886) may be regarded as reflecting current patriotic pride by extolling patriotic deeds of the past. The social importance of choral performance is to be gauged from such a manifestation as the periodic Handel Festivals at the Crystal Palace in the London suburb of Norwood. At the first festival in 1857 nearly 3,000 choralists and 400 instrumentalists participated; the audiences for the three concerts exceeded a total of 40,000. No wonder that, in the words of a report of the opening concert, 'the "Hallelujah Chorus" could be distinctly heard nearly half a mile from Norwood.' No wonder that Queen Victoria turned up for the second concert.

We may smile. We may reasonably think Handel better served otherwise. But our distance from such manifestations is also our distance from the hey-day of choralism. The roots of choralism in society have weakened. The churches maintain their choral establishments, but the churches themselves no longer command their former strength of allegiance. (One may recall that S. S. Wesley's hymn *The Church's One Foundation* and Sullivan's *Onward, Christian Soldiers* became as widely known as any tunes in Victorian England; today no hymn could, through church use, attain a popular circulation at all.) Secular choral societies are no longer called on to reflect the nation's mood. The topical or patriotic work is (surely unfairly) held to be suspect. It was no mean or purely local event, but such a victory of the human spirit as the conclusion of the Second World War which inspired Vaughan Williams's cantata, *Thanksgiving for Victory*. Yet soon afterwards this honourable title was apparently found embarrassing and was emasculated to *A Song of Thanksgiving*.

If a composer today, recognizing that choralists may constitute a lessened force but do not constitute a spent one, wishes to compose a choral work of substantial size to what text shall he write? A work with a religious text, if presented by a twentieth-century composer to a twentieth-century audience, no longer has the certainty of basic communication which such a work might in the past have assumed. Is there then some way of using, instead of a religious text, one that is broadly ethical and humanistic but free from dogma? It is remarkable that only one work of this kind has firmly established itself, and that a work more than 125 years old: Beethoven's *Choral Symphony*. The problem of the text, form, and manner of the modern choral work remains difficult. Britten's choice of a 'symphonic' form, and a lyrical rather than didactic or ethical content (in the *Spring Symphony*), is a happy solution, but one cannot say an all-conquering one.

We have discussed the weakening of the social roots of choral singing. This is illustrated by a curious incidental phenomenon: the increasing number in Britain of performances of Bach in German. In the last century it was opera which ranked, in general, as the remote, foreign-language activity; choral music was linked to the vernacular tongue. The reason in those days for extensively translating Bach's texts into English was not only so that the British amateur choralist would find the works easier to perform but so that he could associate them with the sentiments and even actual phrases of the cherished English Bible, Prayer Book, and hymnals. Today, instead, we have regular performances in London of something called the *Matthäus-Passion*; we have the BBC performing *Ich hatte viel Bekümmernis* (and not *My spirit was in heaviness*) at the Festival Hall. The musical merits of the procedure are, perhaps, defensible. But socially the phenomenon points to an alienation of choral music from the associations which formerly nourished it.

Indeed, if we set aside such 'closed' social groups as schools and colleges, it would seem that only one choral activity is still deeply part of our society and would be widely missed if it disappeared. I refer to the performances of Handel's *Messiah*, and of carols, at Christmas time. The one festival of the Christian year which has broadened itself into an important secular festival has carried over the originally Christian choral celebration into the new context. (That Handel did not actually intend *Messiah* as a Christmas work is not the point.) There is an eloquent moral in the fact that leading choral societies habitually base their financial plans on the certainty that performances of *Messiah* and Christmas carols will yield enough profits to offset substantially the loss expected on almost everything else.

If choral music, with its inescapable and noble suggestions of a deeply human utterance, can still respond to the seasonal need of Christmas, can it not then serve on other occasions of popular emotion? To speak only of Britain, why have no modern choral works been found to express the spirit roused by the Trooping of the Colour, the Durham Miners' Gala, the Aldermaston marches, the annual switching-on of the Blackpool illuminations? If a composer gifted with the broad touch of an Elgar could seize one of these occasions chorally, it would be a hundredfold more significant an augury for choral music than the composition of yet another anachronistic anthem or cosy cantata. Alas, the miners are left to their brass bands, the Aldermaston marchers to their strolling guitarists.

The Soviet attempt to make a new choral form out of the 'mass song' may bring our superior smiles, particularly when we are faced with the banality of the accompanying words as they are usually translated. But the idea is not nonsensical. If the English 'mass song' is that of the type of Parry's *Jerusalem*, then we could do with more. But if such a national choral song *should* again come to birth, then perhaps it may come from a musician engaged in composing for West End or Broadway musicals – and may even be born in one of those shows, not through the midwifery of our middle-class-minded, *Messiah*-bound choral societies at all. This would not be to torpedo choral activity, but to give it a tonic. The Cornell University Glee Club, visiting London early in 1961, jumped happily from classical polyphony to an excerpt from *West Side Story*. A portent, perhaps!

Meanwhile these pages leave our choral societies, and our church choirs too, in an anomalous position. They are the possessors of a magnificent repertory; but, as to status, they occupy a grandstand commanding a splendid view of a procession that is no longer there. Milton's 'sphere-born harmonious sisters, Voice and Verse' (words set unforgettably by Parry in *Blest Pair of Sirens*) look out on a changing world. Lovers of choral music, mindful of the extent of changes of the past, need not succumb to the facile pessimism of supposing that the changes of the future must necessarily be for the worse.

APPENDIX I: *The Mass*

'MASS, the principal service of the Roman Catholic Church; High Mass is sung, Low Mass said. The musical setting of the "Proper" of the Mass, varying with the occasion, has normally been left to the traditional plainsong – except for the Requiem Mass, to which new settings have been frequently composed. The unvarying part, called the "Ordinary" or "Common" of the Mass and consisting of five sections (Kyrie, Gloria, Credo, Sanctus with Benedictus, and Agnus Dei), has been frequently set.'

The above is reproduced from *A New Dictionary of Music* by Arthur Jacobs (Penguin Books). For detailed musical consideration of the liturgy see *The Pelican History of Music*, vol. I, edited by Alec Robertson and Denis Stevens, p. 160 ff.

It should be further noted that the items of the 'Proper' and 'Ordinary' are intermingled in their order, so that the time-interval elapsing between sections of the 'Ordinary' (set by a composer) as actually performed in church may be considerable, creating a different effect from when the work is performed uninterruptedly in the concert-hall. Some composers (see for example the remarks on Schubert on p. 181) have altered or re-arranged the text for personal or musical reasons.

The text of the five sections mentioned above is as follows:

Kyrie eleison
Christe eleison
Kyrie eleison

Lord, have mercy.
Christ, have mercy.
Lord, have mercy.

Gloria in excelsis Deo; in terra pax hominibus bonae voluntatis. Laudamus te; benedicimus te; adoramus te; glorificamus te. Gratias agimus tibi propter magnam gloriam tuam, Domine Deus, Rex coelestis, Deus Pater omnipotens. Domine Fili unigenite Jesu Christe; Domine Deus, Agnus Dei, Filius Patris, qui tollis peccata mundi, miserere nobis; qui tollis peccata mundi, suscipe deprecationem nostram: qui sedes ad dexteram Patris, miserere nobis. Quoniam tu solus sanctus: tu solus Dominus: tu solus altissimus, Jesu Christe, cum Sancto Spiritu, in gloria Dei Patris. Amen.

Glory be to God on high, and on earth peace to men of good will. We praise thee; we bless thee; we adore thee; we glorify thee. We give thee thanks for thy great glory, O Lord God, heavenly king, God the Father Almighty. O Lord Jesus Christ, the only-begotten Son: O Lord God, Lamb of God, Son of the Father, who takest away the sins of the world, have mercy on us: thou who takest away the sins of the world, receive our prayers: thou who sittest at the right hand of the Father, have mercy on us. For only thou art holy: thou only art the Lord: thou only, O Jesus Christ, with the Holy Ghost, art most high in the glory of God the Father. Amen.

Credo in unum Deum, Patrem omni-potentem, Factorem coeli et terrae, visi-bilium omnium et invisibilium. Et in unum Dominum Jesum Christum, Filium Dei unigenitum, et ex Patre natum ante omnia saecula. Deum de Deo; Lumen de Lumine; Deum verum de Deo vero; genitum non factum; consubstantialem Patri, per quem omnia facta sunt. Qui propter nos homines, et propter nostram salutem, descendit de coelis, et incarnatus est de Spiritu Sancto, ex Maria Virgine: et homo factus est. Crucifixus etiam pro nobis: sub Pontio Pilato passus et sepultus est. Et resurrexit tertia die secundum Scripturas; et ascendit in coelum, sedet ad dexteram Patris: et iterum venturus est cum gloria judicare vivos et mortuos: cujus regni non erit finis. Et in spiritum Sanctum Dominum et vivificantem, qui ex patre filioque procedit. Qui cum patre et Filio simul adoratur et conglorificatur; qui locutus est per Prophetas; et in unam sanctam catholicam et apostolicam Ecclesiam. Confiteor unum baptisma in remissionem peccatorum. Et exspecto resurrectionem mortuorum; et vitam venturi saeculi. Amen.

I believe in one God, the Father almighty, Maker of heaven and earth, and of all things visible and invisible. And in one Lord Jesus Christ, the only-begotten Son of God, born of the Father before all ages. God of God; Light of Light; true God of true God; begotten not made; consubstantial with the Father, by whom all things were made. Who for us men, and for our salvation, came down from heaven and was incarnate by the Holy Ghost of the Virgin Mary; and was made man. He was cruci-fied also for us, suffered under Pontius Pilate and was buried. The third day he rose again accord-ing to the Scriptures; and ascended into heaven and sitteth at the right hand of the Father: and he shall come again with glory to judge both the living and the dead: of whose kingdom there shall be no end. And I believe in the Holy Ghost, the Lord and Giver of life. Who proceedeth from the Father and from the Son; who together with the Father and the Son is adored and glorified; who spake by the Prophets. And in one holy Catho-lic and Apostolic Church. I con-fess one baptism for the remission of sins, and I look for the resurrec-tion of the dead; and the life of the world to come. Amen.

Sanctus, sanctus, sanctus, Dominus Deus Sabaoth. Pleni sunt coeli et terra gloria tua. Hosanna in excelsis. Bene-dictus qui venit in nomine Domini. Hosanna in excelsis.

Holy, holy, holy, Lord God of Sabaoth. Heaven and earth are full of thy glory. Hosanna in the highest. Blessed is he that cometh in the name of the Lord. Hosanna in the highest.

Agnus Dei, qui tollis peccata mundi, miserere nobis. Agnus Dei, qui tollis peccata mundi, miserere nobis. Agnus Dei, qui tollis peccata mundi, dona nobis pacem.

Lamb of God, who takest away the sins of the world, have mercy upon us. Lamb of God, who takest away the sins of the world, have mercy upon us. Lamb of God, who takest away the sins of the world, grant us thy peace.

The Requiem Mass, so named from its first word (*requiem*, rest), is also called Mass for the Dead (*Missa Pro Defunctis*). It varies the text of the Mass as given above, notably by omitting the Gloria and Credo (as being inappropriately joyful texts) and by including the words of the thirteenth-century Latin hymn, *Dies irae*, about the terrors of the Day of Judgement. The text of the Requiem as frequently set by composers is, therefore:

INTROIT

Requiem aeternam dona eis Domine; et lux perpetua luceat eis. Te decet hymnus Deus in Sion; et tibi reddetur votum in Jerusalem: exaudi orationem meam; ad te omnis caro veniet. Requiem aeternam dona eis Domine; et lux perpetua luceat eis.

Eternal rest give to them, O Lord; and let perpetual light shine upon them. A hymn, O Lord, becometh thee in Sion; and a vow shall be paid to thee in Jerusalem: hear my prayer; all flesh shall come to thee. Eternal rest give to them, O Lord; and let perpetual light shine upon them.

KYRIE

Kyrie eleison

Christe eleison

Kyrie eleison

Lord, have mercy,

Christ, have mercy.

Lord, have mercy,

SEQUENCE

Dies irae, dies illa
Solvet saeclum in favilla,
Teste David cum Sibylla.

Day of wrath, that day
shall dissolve the world in ashes,
as David and the Sibyl testify.

Quantus tremor est futurus,
Quando Judex est venturus,
Cuncta stricte discussurus!

What a trembling there will be
when the Judge shall come
to try all things truly.

Tuba mirum spargens sonum
Per sepulchra regionum,
Coget omnes ante thronum.

A trumpet, spreading wondrous sound
throughout the graves of all kingdoms,
shall drive all men before the throne.

Mors stupebit et natura,	Death and nature shall be astonished
Cum resurget creatura,	when creation rises again
Judicanti responsura.	to make answer before the Judge.
Liber scriptus proferetur,	A book of writings shall be brought forth
In quo totum continetur,	in which shall be contained everything
Unde mundus judicetur.	for which the world shall be judged.
Judex ergo cum sedebit,	And so, when the Judge sits,
Quidquid latet apparebit:	whatsoever is hidden shall be made manifest,
Nil inultum remanebit.	and nothing shall go unavenged.
Quid sum miser tunc dicturus?	What will I say then, wretched as I am?
Quem patronum rogaturus,	Whose advocacy beg,
Cum vix justus sit securus?	when even the righteous may hardly be carefree?
Rex tremendae majestatis,	O King of dread majesty
Qui salvandos salvas gratis,	who freely savest the redeemed,
Salva me fons pietatis.	save me, O fountain of goodness.
Recordare Jesu pie,	Remember, dear Jesus,
Quod sum causa tuae viae,	that I am the cause of Thy journey;
Ne me perdas illa die.	do not lose me in that day.
Quaerens me sedisti lassus,	Seeking me Thou didst sit down weary,
Redemisti crucem passus;	didst suffer the Cross to redeem me;
Tantus labor non sit cassus.	let not so great a toil be in vain.
Juste Judex ultionis,	O righteous Judge of vengeance,
Donum fac remissionis	grant the gift of remission
Ante diem rationis.	before that day of reckoning.
Ingemisco tanquam reus,	I groan as one guilty,
Culpa rubet vultus meus,	my countenance blushes for guilt;
Supplicanti parce Deus.	spare a supplicant, O God.
Qui Mariam absolvisti,	Thou who didst absolve Mary Magdalene
Et latronem exaudisti,	and gavest ear to the robber,
Mihi quoque spem dedisti.	hast given hope to me also.
Preces meae non sunt dignae:	My prayers are not worthy;
Sed tu bonus fac benigne,	but, in Thy goodness, grant a boon
Ne perenni cremer igne.	that I burn not in everlasting fire.

Inter oves locum praesta,	Grant me a place among Thy
Et ab hoedis me sequestra,	sheep,
Statuens in parte dextra.	and separate me from the goats,
	setting me upon Thy right hand.
Confutatis maledictis,	When the accursed are con-
Flammis acribus addictis,	founded,
Voca me cum benedictis.	and consigned to the fierce flames,
	call me among the blessed.
Oro supplex et acclinis,	Kneeling, a suppliant, I pray;
Cor contritum quasi cinis:	my heart is contrite as ashes;
Gere curam mei finis.	take Thou charge of my end.
Lacrymosa dies illa,	Sorrowful that day
Qua resurget ex favilla	when from the dust will arise
Judicandus homo reus.	guilty man to be judged.
Huic ergo parce Deus.	Spare him, therefore, O God.
Pie Jesu Domine	Good Lord Jesu,
Dona eis requiem.	Grant them rest.

SANCTUS

Sanctus, sanctus, sanctus, Dominus Deus Sabaoth. Pleni sunt coeli et terra gloria tua. Hosanna in excelsis. Benedictus qui venit in nomine Domini. Hosanna in excelsis.	Holy, holy, holy, Lord God of Sabaoth. Heaven and earth are full of thy glory. Hosanna in the highest. Blessed is he that cometh in the name of the Lord. Hosanna in the highest.

OFFERTORY

Domine Jesu Christe, Rex gloriae, libera animas omnium fidelium defunctorum de poenis inferni, et de profundo lacu: libera eas de ore leonis, ne absorbeat eas tartarus, ne cadant in obscurum; sed signifer sanctus Michael repraesentet eas in lucem sanctam, quam olim Abrahae promisisti, et semini eius.	O Lord Jesus Christ, King of glory, deliver the souls of all the faithful departed from the pains of hell and from the deep pit: deliver them from the mouth of the lion, that hell may not swallow them up, and they may not fall into darkness, but may the holy standard-bearer Michael introduce them to the holy light; which thou didst promise of old to Abraham and to his seed.

AGNUS DEI

Agnus Dei, qui tollis peccata mundi, dona eis requiem. Agnus Dei, qui tollis peccata mundi, dona eis requiem. Agnus Dei, qui tollis peccata mundi, dona eis requiem sempiternam.	Lamb of God, who takest away the sins of the world, grant them rest. Lamb of God, who takest away the sins of the world, grant them rest. Lamb of God, who takest away the sins of the world, grant them rest everlastingly.

Hostias et preces tibi Domine, laudis offerimus; tu suscipe pro animabus illis, quarem hodie memoriam facimus: fac eas Domine transire ad vitam. Quam olim Abrahae promisisti et semini eius.

We offer to thee, O Lord, sacrifices and prayer; do thou receive them on behalf of those whom we commemorate this day. Grant them, O Lord, to pass from death to that life which thou didst promise of old to Abraham and to his seed.

COMMUNION

Lux aeterna luceat eis Domine. Cum sanctis tuis in aeternum, quia pius es. Requiem aeternam dona eis Domine; et lux perpetua luceat eis.

May light eternal shine upon them, O Lord. With thy saints for ever, because thou art merciful. Eternal rest give to them, O Lord, and let perpetual light shine upon them.

On certain occasions the following is sung (not an integral part of the Requiem but incorporated, notably, in Verdi's setting):

RESPONSORY

Libera me, Domine, de morte aeterna in die illa tremenda, quando coeli movendi sunt et terra, dum veneris judicare saeculum per ignem.
Tremens factus sum ego et timeo, dum discussio venerit atque ventura ira. Quando coeli movendi sunt et terra.
Dies illa, dies irae, calamitatis et miseriae, dies magna et amara valde. Dum veneris judicare saeculum per ignem.

Deliver me, O Lord, from everlasting death in that dreadful day, when the heaven and the earth shall quake, when thou shalt come to judge the world by fire. I tremble and am sore afraid for the judgement and the wrath to come. When the heaven and the earth shall quake. O that day, that day of wrath, of woe and of tribulation! a great day and exceeding bitter, when thou shalt come to judge the world by fire.

Requiem aeternam dona eis, Domine, et lux perpetua luceat eis.

Eternal rest give to them, O Lord; and let perpetual light shine upon them.

APPENDIX II: *The Continuo*

CONTINUO

(It., abbr. of *basso continuo*): a type of bass-line which was written (particularly about 1650–1750) for a keyboard instrument playing an accompaniment or taking part in an ensemble, and which required a special interpretation. Given only a single bass-note, the player had to work out for himself the correct harmonies to play above this note: he was commonly, but not always, helped by figures giving a kind of short-hand indication of the harmonies required (figured bass). To play the continuo, therefore, is not to play a particular kind of instrument; it is to play on any keyboard instrument from this particular kind of bass. It was customary for the actual bass-notes, though not the harmonies above, to be sounded also by, e.g., cello and double-bass. The historic English equivalent for continuo is 'thorough-bass', i.e. 'through-bass'; but 'continuo' has now acquired standard usage in English.

Extract from *A New Dictionary of Music*
by Arthur Jacobs (Penguin Books)

RECOMMENDED BOOKS

Books for further reading are here listed for Chapters 1–21 in the following order – general books relevant to the chapter, in alphabetical order of author, and then books on particular composers, in alphabetical order of composer. All (except*) are in English.

1. *Choir and People in the Later Middle Ages*

Bukofzer, Manfred, *Studies in Medieval and Renaissance Music*, Norton, New York, 1950; Dent, London, 1951.

Harrison, Frank Ll., *Music in Medieval Britain*, Routledge, London, 1958; Dover, New York, 1959.

Harman, Alec, *Man and his Music*, vol. 1, *Medieval and Early Renaissance Music*, Rockliff, London; O.U.P., New York, 1958. Also in *Man and his Music*, one-vol. edn, Barrie & Rockliff, London; O.U.P., New York, 1962.

Hughes, Dom Anselm, ed., *The New Oxford History of Music*, vol. 2, *Early Medieval Music up to 1300*, O.U.P., London and New York, 1954.

Hughes, Dom Anselm, and Abraham, Gerald, eds., *The New Oxford History of Music*, vol. 3, *Ars Nova and the Renaissance, 1300–1540*, O.U.P., London and New York, 1960.

Reese, Gustave, *Music in the Middle Ages*, Norton, New York, 1940; Dent, London, 1941.

Robertson, A., and Stevens, D., eds., *Pelican History of Music*, vol. 1, *Ancient Forms to Polyphony*, Penguin Books, Harmondsworth, 1960.

Waite, William G., *The Rhythm of 12th-century Polyphony*, O.U.P., London; Yale University Press, New Haven, 1954.

2. *From Ockeghem to Palestrina*

Dart, Thurston, *The Interpretation of Music*, Hutchinson, London; Longmans, New York, 1954.

Harman, Alec, *Man and his Music*, vol. 1, *Medieval and Early Renaissance Music*, Rockliff, London; O.U.P., New York, 1958.

Harman, Alec, and Milner, Anthony, *Man and his Music*, vol. 2, *Late Renaissance and Baroque Music*, Barrie & Rockliff, London, 1959; O.U.P., New York, 1960. Also in *Man and his Music*, one-vol. edn, Barrie & Rockliff, London; O.U.P., New York, 1962.

Reese, Gustave, *Music in the Renaissance*, Dent, London, 1954; revised edn, Norton, New York, 1959.

Robertson, A., and Stevens, D., eds., *Pelican History of Music*, vol. 1, *Ancient Forms to Polyphony*, Penguin Books, Harmondsworth, 1960.

Castiglione, Baldasar, *The Book of the Courtier* (1516), Doubleday, New York, 1959. (This book gives a contemporary view of aristocratic Renaissance life.)

3. *Tudor England and After*

Colles, Henry C., *Voice and Verse*, O.U.P., London and New York, 1928.

Fellowes, Edmund H., *English Cathedral Music*, 4th edn, Methuen, London, 1948; British Book Centre, New York, 1952.
    The English Madrigal, O.U.P., London and New York, 1925.

Morley, Thomas (ed. Alec Harman), *A Plain and Easy Introduction to Practical Music*, Dent, London; Norton, New York, 1952.

Nicholson, Sydney H., *Quires and Places where They Sing*, Bell, London, 1932.

Pattison, Bruce, *Music and Poetry of the English Renaissance*, Methuen, London, 1948.

Phillips, C. Henry, *The Singing Church*, Faber, London; Ryerson Press, Toronto, 1945.

Fellowes, E. H., *William Byrd*, 2nd edn, O.U.P., London and Toronto, 1948.

Stevens, Denis, *Tudor Church Music* [with an EP record] Faber, London; Norton, New York, 1961.

Stevens, John, *Music and Poetry in the Early Tudor Court*, Methuen, London; Ryerson Press, Toronto, 1961.
    Thomas Tomkins 1572–1656, Macmillan, London; St Martin's Press, New York, 1957.

4. *Germany and Northern Europe, before Bach*

Bukofzer, Manfred, *Music in the Baroque Era*, Norton, New York, 1947; Dent, London, 1948.

Harman, Alec, and Milner, Anthony, *Man and his Music*, vol. 2, *Late Renaissance and Baroque Music*, Barrie & Rockliff, London, 1959; O.U.P., New York, 1960. Also in *Man and his Music*, one-vol. edn, Barrie & Rockliff, London; O.U.P., New York, 1962.

Liemohn, Edwin, *The Chorale*, Muhlenberg Press, Philadelphia, 1953.

Reese, Gustave, *Music in the Renaissance*, Dent, London, 1954; revised edn, Norton, New York, 1959.

Smallman, Basil, *The Background of Passion Music*, S.C.M. Press, London; Ryerson Press, Toronto, 1957.

Moser, Hans, *Heinrich Schütz: his Life and Work*, Concordia, St Louis, 1959.

5. *At the Courts of Italy and France*

Bukofzer, Manfred, *Music in the Baroque Era*, Norton, New York, 1947; Dent, London, 1948.

Harman, Alec, and Milner, Anthony, *Man and his Music*, vol. 2, *Late Renaissance and Baroque Music*, Barrie & Rockliff, London, 1959; O.U.P., New York, 1960. Also in *Man and his Music*, one-vol. edn, Barrie & Rockliff, London; O.U.P., New York, 1962.

Mellers, Wilfrid, *François Couperin and the French Classical Tradition*, Dobson, London, 1950; Roy Publications, New York, 1951.

Gray, Cecil, and Heseltine, Philip, *Carlo Gesualdo, Prince of Venosa: Musician and Murderer*, Paul, London; Dial Press, New York, 1926.

Redlich, Hans F., *Claudio Monteverdi*, O.U.P., London and New York, 1952.

Schrade, Leo, *Monteverdi: Creator of Modern Music*, Norton, New York, 1950; Gollancz, London, 1951.

Pincherle, Marc, *Vivaldi: Genius of the Baroque*, Norton, New York, 1957; Gollancz, London, 1958.

6. Church and State in England

Fellowes, Edmund H., *English Cathedral Music*, 4th edn, Methuen, London, 1948; British Book Centre, New York, 1952.

Husk, W. H., *An Account of the Musical Celebrations on St Cecilia's Day*, Bell & Daldy, London, 1857.

Walker, Ernest, *A History of Music in England*, 3rd edn, by J. A. Westrup, O.U.P., London and New York, 1952.

Wesley, S. S., *A Few Words on Cathedral Music* [reprint of the original edition of 1849], Hinrichsen, London and New York, 1961.

Holland, A. K., *Henry Purcell: The English Musical Tradition*, 2nd edn, Penguin Books, London, 1948.

Westrup, J. A., *Purcell*, 4th edn, Dent, London; Farrar, Straus, New York, 1960.

7. Bach and his Time

Liemohn, Edwin, *The Chorale*, Muhlenberg Press, Philadelphia, 1953.

Bach, C. P. E., *Essay on the True Art of Playing Keyboard Instruments*, Cassell, London, 1951; Norton, New York, 1949.

North, Roger (ed. John Wilson), *Roger North on Music*, Novello, London, 1959.

Smallman, Basil, *The Background of Passion Music*, S.C.M. Press, London; Ryerson Press, Toronto, 1957.

Boult, Adrian, and Emery, Walter, *The St Matthew Passion, its Preparation and Performance*, Novello, London, 1949.

Day, James, *The Literary Background to Bach's Cantatas*, Dobson, London; McClelland, Toronto, 1961.

Geiringer, Karl, *The Bach Family*, Allen, London; O.U.P., New York, 1954.

Schweitzer, Albert, *J. S. Bach* (2 vols.), Black, London; Macmillan, New York, 1923.

Terry, Charles S., *Bach: a Biography*, 2nd ed., O.U.P., London and New York, 1933.

The Passions (2 vols.), O.U.P., London and New York, 1926.

Terry, Charles S., *The Mass in B minor*, O.U.P., London and New York, 1924.

Whittaker, William G., *Fugitive Notes on Certain Cantatas and the Motets of J. S. Bach*, O.U.P., London and New York, 1924.

  The Cantatas of J. S. Bach (2 vols.), O.U.P., London and New York, 1959.

8. *England in the Age of Handel*

Fellowes, Edmund H., *English Cathedral Music*, 4th edn, Methuen, London, 1948; British Book Centre, New York, 1952.

Walker, Ernest, *A History of Music in England*, 3rd edn, by J. A. Westrup, O.U.P., London and New York, 1952.

Abraham, Gerald, ed., *Handel: a Symposium*, O.U.P., London and New York, 1954.

Dean, Winton, *Handel's Dramatic Oratorios and Masques*, O.U.P., London and New York, 1954.

Myers, Robert M., *Handel's Messiah: a Touchstone of Taste*, Macmillan, New York, 1948.

Sadie, Stanley, *Handel*, Calder, London, 1962.

9. *The Viennese Classical Period*

Geiringer, Karl, *Haydn: a Creative Life in Music*, Norton, New York, 1946; Allen, London, 1947.

Haydn, Joseph, ed. H. C. Robbins Landon, *Collected Correspondence and London Notebooks*, Barrie & Rockliff, London; O.U.P., New York, 1959.

Blom, Eric, *Mozart*, Dent, London; Dutton, New York, 1935.

Einstein, Alfred, *Mozart: his Character, his Work*, O.U.P., New York, 1945; Cassell, London, 1946.

Brown, Maurice J. E., *Schubert: A Critical Biography*, Macmillan, London; St Martin's Press, New York, 1958.

Einstein, Alfred, *Schubert*, O.U.P., New York; Cassell, London, 1951.

10. *After Handel – in Britain and America*

Barrett, W. A., and Beard, G. H., *English Church Composers*, Low, London, 1910; Scribner, New York, 1911.

Blom, Eric, *Music in England*, Penguin Books, London and New York, 1942.

Walker, Ernest, *A History of Music in England*, 3rd edn by J. A. Westrup, O.U.P., London and New York, 1952.

Langley, Hubert, *Doctor Arne*, Cambridge University Press; Macmillan, New York, 1938.

Chase, Gilbert, *America's Music from the Pilgrims the the Present*, McGraw-Hill, New York, 1955.

Goldman, R. F., and Smith, R., *Landmarks of Early American Music*, Schirmer, New York, 1943.

Howard, John Tasker, *Our American Music*, revised edn, Crowell, New York, 1939.

Metcalf, Frank J., *American Writers and Compilers of Sacred Music*, Abingdon Press, New York, 1925.

Barbour, James M., *The Church Music of William Billings*, Michigan State University Press, 1960.

11. *The French Revolution: Beethoven and Berlioz*

Tovey, Donald F., *Essays in Musical Analysis*, vol. 2, O.U.P., London and New York, 1935. (This contains a lengthy essay on Beethoven's *Choral Symphony*, followed by a detailed analysis.)

Scott, Marion, *Beethoven*, Dent, London; Pellegrini & Cudahy, New York, 1934.

Elliot, J. H. *Berlioz*, Dent, London; Dutton, New York, 1938.

Barzun, Jacques, *Berlioz and the Romantic Century* (2 vols.), Little, Brown, New York, 1950; Gollancz, London, 1951.

12. *The Oratorio and Cantata Market: Britain, Germany, America*

Niemann, Walter, *Brahms*, Knopf, New York, 1946.

Latham, Peter, *Brahms*, Dent, London; Dutton, New York, 1948.

Gounod, Charles, *Autobiographical Reminiscences, etc.*, Heinemann, London, 1896.

Searle, Humphrey, *The Music of Liszt*, Williams & Norgate, London, 1954.

Radcliffe, Philip, *Mendelssohn*, Dent, London; Dutton, New York, 1954.

Semler, Isabel Parker, *Horatio Parker*, Putnam, New York, 1922.

Fuller-Maitland, J. S., *The Music of Parry and Stanford*, Heffer, Cambridge, 1934.

Chissell, Joan, *Schumann*, Dent, London; Dutton, New York, 1948.

Mayer, Dorothy Moulton, *The Forgotten Master: The Life and Times of Louis Spohr*, Weidenfeld & Nicolson, London, 1959.

Hughes, Gervase, *The Music of Arthur Sullivan*, Macmillan, London; St Martin's Press, New York, 1960.

13. *The Mass – from Rossini to Dvořák*

Doernberg, Erwin, *The Life and Symphonies of Anton Bruckner*, Barrie, London, 1960.

Newlin, Dika, *Bruckner, Mahler, Schoenberg*, O.U.P., London; King's Crown Press, New York, 1947.

Redlich, Hans F., *Bruckner and Mahler*, Dent, London; Farrar, Straus, New York, 1955.

Fischl, Viktor, ed., *Antonin Dvořák: his Achievement* (with a chapter, 'The Church Music', by Mosco Carner), Drummond, London, 1942.

Robertson, Alec, *Dvořák*, Dent, London; Dutton, New York, 1945.

Toye, Francis, *Rossini: a Study in Tragi-comedy*, 2nd edn, Barker, London, 1955.

Hussey, Dyneley, *Verdi*, Dent, London; Dutton, New York, 1940.

Toye, Francis, *Giuseppe Verdi: his Life and Works*, Heinemann, London, 1931; Vintage Press, New York, 1959.

14. *Chorus and Symphony: Liszt, Mahler, and After*

Hill, Ralph, ed., *The Symphony*, Penguin Books, London and New York, 1949.

Reik, Theodor, *The Haunting Melody*, Farrar, Straus, New York, 1953.

Nettel, Reginald, *Ordeal by Music: the Strange Experience of Havergal Brian*, O.U.P., London and New York, 1945.

Redlich, Hans, *Bruckner and Mahler*, Dent, London; Farrar, Straus, New York, 1955.

Dent, Edward J., *Ferruccio Busoni*, O.U.P., London and New York, 1933.

Vallas, L., *César Franck*, Harrap, London, 1951; O.U.P., New York, 1952.

15. *Britain from Stanford to Vaughan Williams*

Warlock, Peter (Philip Heseltine), *Frederick Delius*, revised edn, Lane, London; O.U.P., New York, 1952.

McVeagh, Diana M., *Edward Elgar: his Life and Music*, Dent, London, 1955.

Young, Percy, *Elgar O.M.*, Collins, London; Macmillan, New York, 1955.

Holst, Imogen, *The Music of Gustav Holst*, O.U.P., London and New York, 1951.

St John, Christopher, *Ethel Smyth*, Longmans, London and New York, 1959.

Greene, H. P., *Charles Villiers Stanford*, Arnold, London; Longmans, New York, 1935.

Day, James, *Vaughan Williams*, Dent, London; Farrar, Straus, New York, 1961.

Howes, Frank, *The Music of Ralph Vaughan Williams*, O.U.P., London and New York, 1954.

16. *Slavonic Nationalism from Dvořák to the Soviets*

Calvocoressi, M. D., and Abraham, Gerald, *Masters of Russian Music*, Duckworth, London; Knopf, New York, 1936.

Abraham, Gerald, ed., *Tchaikovsky: a Symposium*, Drummond, London. 1945.

Leonard, Richard A., *A History of Russian Music*, Jarrolds, London, 1956; Macmillan, New York, 1957.

Olkhovsky, A., *Music under the Soviets*, Routledge, London; Praeger, New York, 1955.

Polyakova, Lyudmila, *Soviet Music*, Foreign Languages Publishing House, Moscow, 1961.

Werth, Alexander, *Musical Uproar in Moscow*, Turnstile Press, London; Smithers, Toronto, 1949.

Newmarch, Rosa, *The Music of Czechoslovakia*, O.U.P., London and New York, 1942.

Robertson, Alec, *Dvořák*, Dent, London; Dutton, New York, 1945.

Stedron, B., *Leoš Janáček*, Artia, Prague, 1955.

Safranek, Milos, *Bohuslav Martinů*, Knopf, New York, 1944; Dobson, London, 1946.

Nestyev, Israel V., *Prokofiev*, Stanford University Press, California; O.U.P., London, 1961.

Shlifstein S., ed., *Sergei Prokofiev, Autobiography, Articles, Reminiscences*, Foreign Languages Publishing House, Moscow, 1959.

Seroff, Victor I., *Rachmaninoff*, Simon & Schuster, New York, 1950; Cassell, London, 1951.

Rabinovich, Dmitry, *Dmitry Shostakovich*, Lawrence & Wishart, London, 1959.

17. Four Revolutionaries

Stevens, Halsey, *The Life and Music of Bela Bartók*, O.U.P., London and New York, 1953.

Hindemith, Paul, *A Composer's World*, O.U.P., London; Harvard University Press, Cambridge, Mass., 1952.

Leibowitz, René, *Schoenberg and his School*, Philosophical Library, New York, 1949.

Newlin, Dika, *Bruckner, Mahler, Schoenberg*, O.U.P., London; King's Crown Press, New York, 1947.

Rufer, Josef, *The Works of Arnold Schoenberg*, Faber, London, 1962.

Craft, Robert, and Stravinsky, Igor, *Conversations with Igor Stravinsky*, Faber, London; Doubleday, New York, 1959.

Craft, Robert, and Stravinsky, Igor, *Memories and Commentaries*, Faber, London; Doubleday, New York, 1960.

Craft, Robert, and Stravinsky, Igor, *Expositions and Developments*, Faber, London; Doubleday, New York, 1962.

Vlad, Roman, *Stravinsky*, O.U.P., London and New York, 1960.

18. France from the Age of Fauré and Debussy

Cooper, Martin, *French Music*, O.U.P., London and New York, 1951.

*Raugel, F., *Le Chant Choral*, Presses Universitaires de France, Paris, 1958.

Lockspeiser, Edward, *Debussy*, 3rd edn, Dent, London; Pellegrini &
    Cudahy, New York, 1951.
Suckling, Norman, *Gabriel Fauré*, revised edn, Dent, London, 1951;
    Pellegrini & Cudahy, New York, 1952.
Hell, Henri, *Francis Poulenc*, Calder, London, 1959; Grove, New York,
    1960.
Demuth, Norman, *Albert Roussel*, United Music Publishers, London,
    1947.
Myers, Rollo H., *Ravel: Life and Works*, Duckworth, London, 1960;
    Yosseloff, New York, 1961.
Deane, Basil, *Albert Roussel*, Barrie & Rockliff, London, 1961.
Copland, Aaron, *Our New Music*, Whittlesey House, New York and
    London, 1941.

19. *Modern British Composers*

Frank, Alan, *Modern British Composers*, Dobson, London, 1953; Saunders,
    Toronto, 1954.
Mitchell, Donald, and Keller, Hans, eds., *Benjamin Britten*, Rockliff,
    London, 1952; Philosophical Library, New York, 1953.
Howes, Frank, *The Music of William Walton* (2 vols.), 2nd edn, O.U.P.,
    London and New York, 1947.

20. *A Mixed Modern Group*

Eimert, H., and Stockhausen, K., *Young Composers* (*Die Reihe*, vol. 4),
    Universal, London; Presser, Pennsylvania, 1960.
Hartog, Howard, ed., *European Music in the Twentieth Century*, Routledge,
    London; Praeger, New York, 1957. (New edn, Penguin Books, 1961.)
Myers, Rollo H., ed., *Twentieth Century Music*, Calder, London;
    McClelland, Toronto, 1960.
Vlad, Roman, *Luigi Dallapiccola*, Zerboni, Milan, 1957.
Weissmann, John S., *Goffredo Petrassi*, Zerboni, Milan, 1957. (English
    text.)
Eimert, H., and Stockhausen, K. *Anton Webern* (*Die Reihe*, vol. 2), Uni-
    versal, London; Presser, Pennsylvania, 1958.

21. *Twentieth-Century Americans*

Chase, Gilbert, *America's Music from the Pilgrims to the Present*, McGraw-
    Hill, New York, 1955.
Copland, Aaron, *Our New Music*, Whittlesey House, New York and
    London, 1941.
Cowell, Henry, ed., *American Composers on American Music: a Symposium*,
    Stanford University Press, California, 1933.
Ewen, David, *American Composers Today*, Wilson, New York, 1949.

Howard, John Tasker, *Our American Music: Three Hundred Years of It*, 3rd edn, revised, Crowell, New York, 1946.

Lang, Paul H., ed., *One Hundred Years of Music in America*, Schirmer, New York, 1961.

Smith, Julia, *Aaron Copland: his Work and Contribution to American Music*, Dutton, New York, 1955.

Cowell, Henry and Sidney, *Charles Ives*, O.U.P., New York, 1955.

Schreiber, Flora R., and Persichetti, Vincent, *William Schuman*, Schirmer, New York, 1954.

RECOMMENDED MUSICAL EDITIONS

MUSICAL editions listed here for Chapters 1–21 are vocal scores (i.e. with accompaniment, if any, composed or transcribed for piano or organ) unless the indication 'miniature score' (i.e. including full instrumental parts) is given. Scholarly collected editions are not mentioned unless they are the sole source available.

1. Choir and People in the Later Middle Ages

THE main sources for works of this period are given below. The letters in brackets following them are the abbreviations used in the second list, which gives the exact location for works mentioned by name in the text, or providing examples of a type discussed generally in the text. Finally, any modern editions available are given.

Davison, A. T., and Apel, W., *Historical Anthology of Music*, vol. 1, O.U.P., London; Harvard University Press, Cambridge, Mass., 1949. (HAM)

Husmann, H., *Die mittelalterliche Mehrstimmigkeit*, Volk, Cologne, 1955.

Rokseth, Y., *Polyphonies du XIII siècle* (4 vols.), Oiseau Lyre, Paris, 1935–9.

Schrade, L., *Polyphonic Music of the Fourteenth Century*. (In progress.) Oiseau Lyre, Paris, 1956–.

Marrocco, W. T., ed., *Fourteenth-Century Italian Cacce*, 2nd edn, Medieval Academy, Cambridge, Mass., 1961 (M.C).

Ramsbotham, A., Collins, H. B., and Hughes, Dom Anselm, *The Old Hall Manuscript* (3 vols.), Plainsong and Medieval Music Society, 1933–8. (OH)

Dunstable, John, *Complete Works*, edited by M. Bukofzer, *Musica Britannica*, vol. 8, Stainer & Bell, 1953. (JD)

Dufay, Guillaume, *Complete Works*, edited by G. de Van and H. Besseler. (In progress.) American Institute of Musicology, 1947–.

The Eton Choirbook, edited by Frank Ll. Harrison (3 vols.), *Musica Britannica*, vols. 10–12, Stainer & Bell, 1956–61. (EC)

Harrison, Frank Ll., *Music in Medieval Britain*, Routledge, London, 1958; Dover, New York, 1959. (MMB)

Reese, Gustave, *Music in the Middle Ages*, Norton, New York, 1940; Dent, London, 1941. (MMA)

Bukofzer, Manfred, *Studies in Medieval and Renaissance Music*, Norton, New York, 1950; Dent, London, 1951. (BS)

Feininger, L., Documenta Polyphoniae Liturgicae ... Societas Universalis S. Ceciliae, Rome, 1947 – (DPL).

REFERENCES FROM THE TEXT

1. HAM 27a	11. Schrade I p. 76	19. OH I p. 157
2. HAM 27b	12. Schrade III Nos.	20. DPL I No. 2
3. For editions see	21–3	21. JD p. 47
MMA p. 302	13. e.g. Schrade III	22. JD p. 35
4. Husmann, p. 24	14. See other Masses	23. JD p. 41
5. See MMB p. 143	in Schrade I	24. JD p. 88
6. HAM 57a	15. HAM 52; MC p. 93	25. JD p. 133
7. Rokseth III 340	16. OH I p. 34	26. HAM 65
8. BS pp. 30–3	17. OH III p. 1	27. EC I p. 43
9. HAM 57b	18. OH I p. 156	28. EC III p. 112
10. Schrade I p. 106		

MODERN AND PERFORMING EDITIONS

The Play of Daniel. O.U.P.; Plainsong and Medieval Music Society.
Dufay: *3-part Hymns.* Möseler, in 'Das Chorwerk', 49.
Dufay: *Ave Regina Caelorum.* Bärenreiter.
Machaut: *Notre-Dame Mass.* Rouart, Lerolle; Breitkopf & Härtel.

2. *From Ockeghem to Palestrina*

THE main sources for works of this period are given below. The letters in brackets following them are the abbreviations used in the second list, which gives the exact location for works mentioned by name in the text or providing examples of a type discussed generally in the text. Finally, any modern editions available are given.

Davison, A. T., and Apel, W., *Historical Anthology of Music* (2 vols.), O.U.P., London; Harvard University Press, Cambridge, Mass., 1949. (HAM)

Expert, H., *Les Maîtres musiciens de la Renaissance française*, Leduc, Paris, 1960. (MRF)

Schering, Arnold, *Geschichte der Musik in Beispielen* (*History of Music in Examples*), Broude, New York, 1950. (GMB)

Parrish, Carl, and Ohl, John F., *Masterpieces of Music before 1750*, Norton, New York, 1958; Faber, London, 1959. (MM)

Parrish, Carl, *A Treasury of Early Music*, Norton, New York, 1958; Faber, London, 1959. (TEM)

REFERENCES FROM THE TEXT

1. MM 17; HAM 73	6. GMB 66	12. HAM 128
2. MM 18; HAM 76, 77a	7. HAM 114	13. TEM 23
3. MM 19	8. HAM 125	14. GMB 128
4. GMB 55	9. MM 24	15. HAM 149
5. HAM 92	10. HAM 141	16. HAM 113
	11. GMB 122	17. GMB 104

18. HAM 126; TEM 25–26; GMB 142
19. TEM 31
20. MM 20
21. HAM 147
22. HAM 107
23. GMB 144
24. HAM 138

25. MRF 11
26. HAM 95; TEM 20; GMB 69–72
27. GMB 98
28. HAM 130
29. HAM 129
30. HAM 131
31. HAM 155

32. MM 27
33. HAM 145a
34. GMB 125
35. HAM 143
36. HAM 144
37. GMB 126
38. MM 23
39. GMB 127

MODERN AND PERFORMING EDITIONS

Palestrina: *Veni Sponsa Christi*. S.P.C.K. and O.U.P.
  Missa Papae Marcelli (Pope Marcellus Mass). Chester; Schirmer. Miniature score, Eulenburg.
Victoria: *O Magnum Mysterium*. Breitkopf & Härtel; Schola Cantorum; Gray.
  O Vos Omnes. Novello.

3. *Tudor England and After*

A new series announced in 1962 is: *Early English Chamber Music*, F. Ll. Harrison (ed.), Stainer & Bell.

Tudor Church Music, 10 vols. (O.U.P.), and *The English Madrigal School*, edited by E. H. Fellowes, 36 vols. (Stainer & Bell), are the main sources for this period, and the second of these is a performing edition. Other editions are given below.

Tallis: *Evening Service in the Dorian Mode*. O.U.P.
Merbecke: *Book of Common Prayer Noted* (1550).
  (Facsimile edition contained in *Cranmer's First Litany, 1544, and Merbeck's Book of Common Prayer Noted, 1550*, by J. Eric Hunt.) S.P.C.K. London; Macmillan, New York, 1939.
Gibbons: *Hosanna to the Son of David*. O.U.P.
  Behold Thou Hast Made my Days. Novello.
Morley: *Out of the Deep*. O.U.P. Also new edition in *Collected motets*, ed. Andrews and Dart. Stainer & Bell.
Byrd: *Collected Works*, edited by E. H. Fellowes (20 vols.). Stainer & Bell.
Ravenscroft: *Pammelia and other Rounds and Catches*, transcribed by Peter Warlock. O.U.P.
Dering, Weelkes, and Gibbons: *The Cries of London*. Novello.

4. *Germany and Northern Europe, before Bach*

Walter: *Geistliches Gesangbüchlein Wittenberg (Wittenberg Sacred Song-book)*. Bärenreiter.
Rhau: *Newe Deudsche Geistliche Gesenge (New German Sacred Songs)*, in *Denkmäler Deutscher Tonkunst*, vol. 34. Breitkopf & Härtel.

Sweelinck: *Works* (10 vols.), edited by Max Seiffert. Alsbach.

Praetorius: *Syntagma musicum* (*Musical Treatise*) (3 vols. Facsimile edition). Bärenreiter.

　Musae Sionae (*Muses of Zion*), in *Musikalische Werke von Michael Praetorius*. Kallmeyer.

Schein: *Opella Nova* (*The New Work*), in *Collected Works*, vols. 5–7. Breitkopf & Härtel.

Schütz: *Psalms of David*. Bärenreiter.

　Cantiones Sacrae (*Sacred Songs*). Bärenreiter.

　Symphoniae Sacrae (*Sacred Symphonies*). Bärenreiter.

　Kleine Geistliche Konzerte (*Little Sacred Concertos*). Bärenreiter.

　Passion according to St Luke. Bärenreiter.

　Passion according to St Matthew. Bärenreiter.

　Passion according to St John. Bärenreiter.

Buxtehude: *Jesu meine Freude* (*Jesus My Joy*). Hinrichsen.

5. At the Courts of Italy and France

Monteverdi: *A un giro sol; Hor che'l ciel e la terra*, and other madrigals, in *Collected Works*, edited by G. Malipiero. Universal.

　Madrigals, edited by H. Redlich, Schott.

　Mass in F, edited by D. Arnold, Miniature score, Eulenburg.

　Mass in G minor, edited by H. Redlich. Miniature score, Eulenburg.

　Vespers of 1610, edited by Walter Goehr. Full score, Universal. This includes the first version of the *Magnificat*.

　Vespers, edited by D. Stevens, Novello.

　Magnificat (second version), edited by Karl Matthaei. Bärenreiter.

Gabrieli: *Beata es Virgo*, contained in Winterfeld: *Johannes Gabrieli und sein Zeitalter*, vol. 3. Schlesinger.

　Beata es Virgo and *Exaudi Deus*, both contained in: *Gabrieli: Collected Works*, I, edited by D. Arnold. American Institute of Musicology.

　In Ecclesiis. Broude; Schirmer.

Cavalieri: *La Rappresentazione di anima e di corpo* (*The Representation of Soul and Body*). Ricordi.

Vivaldi: *Gloria*. Ricordi.

　Juditha Triumphans. De Santis.

Carissimi: *Historia di Ezechia* (*The Story of Hezekiah*). Istituto Italiano per la Storia della Musica.

　Jephtha. Novello.

Lully: *Miserere* (*Lord have mercy*). Éditions de la Revue Musicale.

Delalande: *De Profundis* (*Out of the deep*). Rouart, Lerolle.

Charpentier: *In Nativitatem Domini Nostri Jesu Christu; Canticum*. Heugel.

Couperin: *Quatre Versets d'un Motet Composé de l'Ordre du Roy* (*Four Extracts from a Motet Composed on the Order of the King*). Oiseau Lyre.

　Motet de Sainte Suzanne (*Motet in Praise of St Susanna*). Full score, Oiseau Lyre.

6. Church and State in England

THE best source for the works of Purcell is the Purcell Society edition, published by Novello and still in progress. This is the only source for the Ode for Queen Mary's Birthday, *Now does the glorious day appear*. Performing editions of other works treated in this chapter are given below.

Blow: *God is our hope and strength*. O.U.P.
  God Spake Sometime in Visions. Stainer & Bell.
  Ode on St. Cecilia's Day, 1684, *Begin the Song*. Hinrichsen.
Purcell: *Hear my prayer, O Lord*. Novello.
  In the midst of life. Novello.
  My heart is inditing, Schott.
  O sing unto the Lord, Novello.
  Te Deum and Jubilate, Novello; Schirmer.
  Come, ye sons of art, away. Schott.
  Ode on St Cecilia's Day, 1683. *Welcome to all the pleasures*. Novello.
  Ode on St Cecilia's Day, 1692, *Hail, bright Cecilia*, Novello.

7. Bach and his Time

Graun: *Te Deum*. Novello.
  Der Tod Jesu (*The Death of Jesus*). Novello; Peters.
Telemann: *Die Tageszeiten*. (*Times of the Day*). Bärenreiter.
C. P. E. Bach: *Magnificat*. Schirmer.
  Die Israeliten in der Wüste (*The Israelites in the Wilderness*). Bote & Bock.
J. C. F. Bach: *Die Kindheit Jesu* (*The Childhood of Jesus*), contained in *Denkmäler Deutscher Tonkunst*, vol. 56. Breitkopf & Härtel.
J. S. Bach: *Christmas Oratorio*. Novello; Peters; Schirmer. Miniature score, Bärenreiter; Eulenburg.
  Motets. Novello. Miniature score, Lea.
  Church Cantata No. 4. Novello; Peters; Schirmer. Miniature score, Eulenburg.
  Church Cantata No. 61. Novello; Peters; Schirmer. Miniature score, Bärenreiter, Eulenburg.
  Church Cantata No. 140. Novello; Peters; Schirmer. Miniature score, Bärenreiter, Eulenburg.
  Magnificat. Novello; Peters; Schirmer. Miniature score, Eulenburg.
  St John Passion. Novello; Peters; Schirmer. Miniature score, Eulenburg.
  St Matthew Passion. Novello; Peters; Schirmer. Miniature score, Eulenburg.
  Mass in B minor. Novello; Peters; Schirmer. Miniature score, Bärenreiter, Eulenburg.
  Easter Oratorio. Breitkopf. Miniature score, Lea.

8. *England in the Age of Handel*

Handel: Chandos Anthem, *O praise the Lord with one consent*. Novello.
 Messiah, ed. Watkins Shaw. Novello. Miniature score, Eulenburg.
 Samson. Novello; Schirmer.

 Note: Nearly all Handel's oratorios, anthems, etc., were printed by Novello during the nineteenth century, but see the note on reliability on page 152. A new German complete scholarly edition, which should in time give rise to new and reliable popular editions, is currently in progress, but so far (1961) the only work embraced by this chapter appearing in this series is *Alexander's Feast*, published by Bärenreiter.

Greene: *Lord, let me know mine end*. O.U.P.
Croft: *O Lord, rebuke me not*. O.U.P.
 Hear my prayer, O Lord. O.U.P.

9. *The Viennese Classical Period*

Pergolesi: *Stabat Mater*. Novello, and others. Miniature score, Eulenburg.
Haydn: *The Creation*. Novello; Schirmer. Miniature score, Eulenburg.
 The Seasons. Novello; Schirmer. Miniature score, Eulenburg.
 Missa Sanctae Caeciliae (St Cecilia Mass). Haydn-Mozart Press.
 Six Last Masses (for Novello Editions see text p. 170 ff. Other editions
  as undernoted).
 Missa in Tempore Belli. Breitkopf, and others.
 Missa Sancti Bernardi. Breitkopf, and others.
 Nelson (Imperial) Mass. Peters; Schirmer, and others.
 Theresienmesse. Peters, and others. Miniature score, Philharmonia.
 Schöpfungsmesse (Creation Mass). Breitkopf, and others.
 Harmoniemesse (Wind-Band Mass). Peters, and others.
 Stabat Mater. Breitkopf.
 The Seven Words. Novello; Schirmer.
 Te Deum in C. Doblinger, Novello, O.U.P.
Mozart: Mass in C, K. 317. Novello; Schirmer. Miniature score, Phil-
  harmonia.
 Litaniae Lauretanae. K. 195. Breitkopf.
 Litaniae de Venerabili Altaris Sacramento, K. 243. Novello.
 Mass in C minor, K. 427. Edited by H. C. Robbins Landon. Vocal
  and miniature scores, Eulenburg.
 Requiem. Novello; Schirmer, and others. Miniature score, Eulenburg
  and others.
Schubert: Mass No. 2 in G. Novello; Schirmer; Broude.
 Mass No. 5 in A flat. Novello; Breitkopf. Miniature score, Eulenburg.
 Mass No. 6 in E flat. Novello; Rieter-Biedermann. Miniature score,
  Eulenburg.
Cherubini: Missa Solemnis in D minor. Novello.
 Mass in C. Novello.
 Requiem in C minor. Novello; Schirmer, and others.

10. *After Handel – in Britain and America*

Boyce: *O, Where shall Wisdom be Found?* Novello.
　By the Waters of Babylon. Novello.
　O Give Thanks. Novello.
Arne: *Comus.* Stainer & Bell (as volume 5 of *Musica Britannica*).
Battishill: *Call to Remembrance.* Novello.
　O Lord, Look Down From Heaven. Novello.
Samuel Wesley: *In Exitu Israel.* Novello.
Crotch: *Palestine.* Novello.
S. S. Wesley: *The Wilderness.* Novello.
　Blessed be the God and Father. Novello.
Bennett: *The Woman of Samaria.* Novello.
Webbe: *Glorious Apollo.* Novello; Schirmer.
Pearsall: *O Ye Roses.* Novello.
　Great God of Love. Novello.
Billings: *Europe.* In *Landmarks of Early American Music*, edited by R. F.
　Goldman and R. Smith. Schirmer, 1943.

11. *The French Revolution: Beethoven and Berlioz*

Gossec: *Hymne à l'être suprème* (*Hymn to the Supreme Being*). (In *Musique des
　Fêtes et Cérémonies de la Révolution Française.*) Paris, 1899.
Beethoven: Symphony No. 9. Choral section, Novello; O.U.P., and
　others. Miniature score, Boosey, and others.
　Mass in D. Novello; Schirmer. Miniature score, Eulenburg.
Berlioz: *Grande Messe des Morts* (Requiem). Breitkopf; Schirmer, and
　others.
　Te Deum. Novello; Schirmer.
　Romeo and Juliet. Breitkopf. Miniature score, Eulenburg.
　The Childhood of Christ. Novello; Schirmer.
　The Damnation of Faust. Novello, and others. Miniature score, Costallat.

12. *The Oratorio and Cantata Market: Britain,*
Germany, America

Mendelssohn: *Elijah.* Novello; Peters. Miniature score, Philharmonia.
Schumann: *Paradise and the Peri.* Novello; Breitkopf & Härtel.
Liszt: *The Legend of St Elizabeth.* Novello.
　Christus. Kahnt.
Gounod: *The Redemption.* Novello.
Brahms: *A German Requiem* (*Ein Deutsches Requiem*). Novello; Schirmer;
　Peters, and others. Miniature score, Eulenburg; Rieter-Bieder-
　mann.
　Alto Rhapsody. Novello; Peters, and others. Miniature score, Phil-
　harmonia.
Parker: *Hora Novissima.* Novello.

13. *The Mass – from Rossini to Dvořák*

Rossini: *Stabat Mater*. Novello; Schirmer, and others. Miniature score,
    Eulenburg.
    Mass. United Music Publishers; Ricordi.
Verdi: Requiem Mass. Ricordi; Schirmer. Miniature score, Ricordi,
    and others.
    Four Sacred Pieces. Ricordi.
Bruckner: Mass in D minor. Peters. Miniature score, Philharmonia.
    Mass in F minor. Peters. Miniature score, Eulenburg.
    Mass in E minor. Peters. Miniature score, Philharmonia.
    Te Deum. Universal, Schirmer. Miniature score, Eulenburg.
    Psalm 150. Universal. Miniature score, Philharmonia.
Dvořák: *Stabat Mater*. Novello, Schirmer. Miniature score, Artia.
    Requiem. Novello.
    Te Deum. Simrock. Miniature score, Eulenburg.
    Mass in D. Novello.

14. *Chorus and Symphony: Liszt, Mahler, and After*

Liszt: *Faust Symphony*. Miniature score, Eulenburg.
    Dante Symphony. Full score, Breitkopf.
Franck: *Psyche*. Le Bailly; Bruneau.
Skryabin: Symphony No. 1. Full score, Belaiev.
Mahler: Symphony No. 2. Miniature score, Universal.
    Symphony No. 3. Miniature score, Universal.
    Symphony No. 8. Vocal and miniature scores, Universal.
Busoni: Piano Concerto. Full score, Breitkopf.
Bush: Piano Concerto. Williams (for hire only).
Havergal Brian: Symphony No. 2. Full score, Cranz.

15. *Britain from Stanford to Vaughan Williams*

Stanford: *The Blue Bird*. Stainer & Bell.
    Songs of the Fleet. Stainer & Bell.
Elgar: *The Dream of Gerontius*. Vocal and miniature scores, Novello.
    The Apostles. Novello.
    The Kingdom. Novello.
Delius: *Sea Drift*. Universal; Harmonie. Miniature scores, Boosey;
    Philharmonia.
    Songs of Sunset. Universal.
    Song of the High Hills. Vocal and miniature scores, Universal.
    Requiem. Universal.
    A Mass of Life. Universal; Harmonie.
    Appalachia. Universal; Harmonie. Miniature score, Boosey, and
    others.

Holst: *The Planets*. Miniature score, Boosey.
  The Hymn of Jesus. Stainer & Bell.
  First Choral Symphony. Novello.
  Choral Fantasia. Curwen.
Vaughan Williams: *A Sea Symphony*. Breitkopf; Stainer & Bell.
  Mass in G minor. Curwen; Schirmer.
  Flos Campi. O.U.P.
  Five Tudor Portraits. O.U.P.
  Sancta Civitas O.U.P.
  Dona Nobis Pacem. O.U.P.
Bantock: *Omar Khayyám*. Breitkopf.
  Atalanta in Corydon. Breitkopf.
Smyth: Mass in D. Novello.
Coleridge-Taylor: *The Song of Hiawatha*. Novello.

16. *Slavonic Nationalism from Dvořák to the Soviets*

Most modern Russian works are published in Moscow by the State
Music Publishers; English and American editions, where available, are
noted below.

Dvořák: *The Spectre's Bride*. Novello.
Janáček: *Glagolitic Mass*. Universal.
  Kantor Halfar. Full score, Hudebni Matice.
  Maryčka Magdanova. Full score, Hudebni Matice.
  The Seventy Thousand. Full score, Hudebni Matice.
Martinů: *Czech Rhapsody*. Melantrich.
  Field Mass. Melantrich.
Mussorgsky: *The Defeat of Sennacherib*. Boosey.
  Joshua. Boosey.
Rimsky-Korsakov: *Svitezyanka*. Belaiev.
  The Song of the Prophet Oleg. Breitkopf.
Tchaikovsky: *Legend*. Jurgenson.
  Vesper Service. Jurgenson.
  Three Cherubic Hymns. Jurgenson.
  Six Church Songs. Jurgenson.
Rakhmaninov: *The Bells*. Gutheil.
Prokofiev: *Alexander Nevsky*. Boosey; Leeds. Miniature score, Boosey.

17. *Four Revolutionaries*

Schoenberg: *Gurrelieder (Songs of Gurra)*. Universal.
  Three Satires, Op. 28. Universal.
  Moses and Aaron. Vocal and miniature scores, Schott.
  Modern Psalm. Full score, Schott.
Stravinsky: *The Wedding (Les Noces)*. Vocal and miniature scores,
  Chester.
  Oedipus Rex. Vocal and miniature scores, Boosey.

Symphony of Psalms. Vocal and miniature scores, Boosey.
    Mass. Vocal and miniature scores, Boosey.
    Cantata. Vocal and miniature scores, Boosey.
    Canticum Sacrum (Sacred Canticle). Vocal and miniature scores, Boosey.
    Threni (Lamentations of Jeremiah). Vocal and miniature scores, Boosey.
    A Sermon, a Narrative and a Prayer. Vocal and miniature scores, Boosey.
Hindemith: *Five Choruses for Male Voices.* Schott.
    When Lilacs Last in the Dooryard Bloom'd. Schott.
    In Praise of Music. Associated Music Publishers.
Bartók: *Cantata Profana (The Giant Stags).* Universal; Boosey, New York.

18. *France from the Age of Fauré and Debussy*

Fauré: Requiem. Vocal score, Hamelle; Schirmer. Miniature score,
    Hamelle.
Bruneau: Requiem. Dupont.
Roussel: *Psalm 80.* Birchard.
Schmitt: *Psalm 47.* Schirmer.
Koechlin: *L'Abbaye (The Abbey).* Editions de la Schola Cantorum.
Debussy: *L'Enfant Prodigue (The Prodigal Son).* Durand.
    La Damoiselle Élue (The Blessed Damozel). Durand.
    The Martyrdom of St Sebastian.
Honegger: *Le Roi David (King David).* Vocal and miniature scores,
    Foetisch.
Milhaud: *Cantate pour louer le Seigneur (In Praise of the Lord).* Universal.
    Pan et Syrinx. Salabert.
    Cantate de la Guerre (War Cantata). Schirmer.
    La Naissance de Vénus (The Birth of Venus). Heugel.
Poulenc: *Stabat Mater.* Rouart Lerolle.
    La Figure Humaine (The Human Face). Rouart Lerolle.
Migot: *L'Annonciation (The Annunciation).* Leduc.
    La Nativité de Notre Seigneur, (The Nativity of our Lord). Leduc.
    Le Sermon sur la Montagne (The Sermon on the Mount). Leduc.
    La Passion (The Passion). Leduc.
    Saint Germain d'Auxerre. Leduc.
    Le Petit Évangéliaire (The Little Gospel). Schola Cantorum.
    Requiem. Ouvrières.

19. *Modern British Composers*

Walton: *Belshazzar's Feast.* O.U.P.
    In Honour of the City of London. O.U.P.
    Coronation Te Deum. O.U.P.
    Gloria. O.U.P.
Dyson: *Nebuchadnezzar.* Novello.
    In Honour of the City of London. O.U.P.
    The Canterbury Pilgrims. O.U.P.
Bliss: *Pastoral.* Vocal and miniature scores, Novello.
    Morning Heroes. Novello.

Goehr: *Sutter's Gold*. Schott.
  The Beatitudes. Novello.
Howells: *Hymnus Paradisi*. Novello.
  Missa Sabrinensis. Novello.
Harrison: Mass in C. Lengnick.
  Requiem. Lengnick.
Rubbra: *Five Motets*. Augener.
  Missa Cantuariensis. Lengnick.
Lambert: *The Rio Grande*. Vocal and miniature scores, O.U.P.
  Summer's Last Will and Testament. O.U.P.
Berkeley: *Jonah*. Chester.
  Stabat Mater. Vocal and miniature scores, Chester.
Tippett: *A Child of Our Time*. Schott.
Britten: *A Boy was Born*. O.U.P.
  Hymn to St Cecilia. Boosey.
  A Ceremony of Carols. Boosey.
  Festival Te Deum. Boosey.
  Spring Symphony. Vocal and miniature scores, Boosey.
  St Nicolas. Vocal and miniature scores, Boosey.
  A War Requiem. Boosey.
Fricker: *The Vision of Judgement*. Schott.
Milner: *The City of Desolation*. Universal.
  St Francis. Novello.
Joubert: *Pro Pace*. Novello.

20. *A Mixed Modern Group*

Bloch: *Sacred Service*. Birchard.
Kodály: *Psalmus Hungaricus*. Boosey; Universal. Miniature score, Philharmonia.
  Missa Brevis. Vocal and miniature scores, Boosey.
Burkhard: *Das Gesicht Jesajas (The Vision of Isaiah)*. Hug.
Vogel: *Thyl Claes*. Ricordi (excerpts only).
Webern: *Das Augenlicht (The Light of the Eyes)*. Vocal and miniature scores, Universal.
  Cantata No. 1. Vocal and miniature scores, Universal.
  Cantata No. 2. Vocal and miniature scores, Universal.
Orff: *Carmina Burana*. Schott.
  Catulli Carmina. Schott.
  Trionfi di Afrodite (Triumph of Aphrodite). Schott.
  School-work. Schott.
Petrassi: *Psalm 9*. Ricordi.
  Coro di Morti (Chorus of the Dead). Suvini Zerboni.
  Noche Oscura (The Dark Night of the Soul). Suvini Zerboni.
Dallapiccola: *Canti di Prigionia (Songs of Prison)*. Carisch.
  Canti della Liberazione (Songs of Liberation). Suvini Zerboni.
  Job. Suvini Zerboni.

21. *Twentieth-Century Americans*

Ives: *67th Psalm.* Arrow Music Press.
  Harvest Home Chorales. Mercury.
Hanson: *Lament for Beowulf.* Birchard.
Thompson: *The Peaceable Kingdom.* Schirmer.
Harris: *Folk Song Symphony.* Schirmer.
Copland: *In the Beginning.* Boosey.
  Canticle of Freedom. Boosey.
Thomson: *Missa Brevis.* Weaner-Levant.
Sessions: *Turn, O Libertad.* Marks.
Cowell: *Lilting Fancy.* Broadcast Music Inc.
  John Brown's Body. Broadcast Music Inc.
  American Muse. Music Press.
Schuman: *A Free Song* (Cantata No. 2). Schirmer.
  Choral Étude. Fischer.
Dello Joio: *The Mystic Trumpeter.* Full score, Schirmer.
  Song of Affirmation. Fischer.
Barber: *A Stopwatch and an Ordnance Map.* Full score, Schirmer.
  Prayers of Kierkegaard. Schirmer.
Foss: *A Parable of Death.* Fischer.
Hovhaness: *Magnificat.* Vocal and miniature scores, Peters.
  Thirtieth Ode of Solomon. Peters.

RECOMMENDED GRAMOPHONE RECORDS

THE discography lists the recordings now available (mid 1962) of works referred to in the text. A few recordings of works not specifically mentioned, but of particular interest and relevance, are also included. Where several versions of a work are available, a number of alternatives are usually given, the selection depending on the general standing in the field concerned of the performers on each recording and on the consensus of critical opinion on the various versions. Recordings where the performers have not made at least an attempt to follow the composer's intentions, as far as they are known or understood, are excluded. Details of couplings are not given, unless they include other works relevant to the same chapter; the interested reader can easily discover them for himself by consulting current catalogues. Where an item occupies only a small part of a record some indication is given of that fact.

> *   = stereophonic recording
> (us) = available in u.s.a.
> (uk)= available in Great Britain
> hms = History of Music in Sound
>   (series issued by h.m.v. [uk]
>   Vic. [us])

Arc.	= Archive series (d.g.g.)	Lyr.	= Lyrichord
Bruns.	= Brunswick	Merc.	= Mercury
Cap.	= Capitol	Mus.-Lib.	= Music Library
Col.	= Columbia	Per.	= Period
d.g.g.	= Deutsche Grammophon	Phil.	= Philips
	Gesellschaft	Sup.	= Supraphon
Elec.	= Electrola	Van.	= Vanguard
Font.	= Fontana	Vic.	= Victor
h.m.v.	= His Master's Voice	Westm.	= Westminster
Lond.	= London	Soc.	= Society

1. *Choir and People in the Later Middle Ages*

Gregorian Chant. Collections on d.g.g. Arc. (uk, us); Lond. (us), Decca (uk); Per. (us); Gregorian Institute (us); Oiseau-Lyre ol 50209, sol 60040* (uk); also some in hms II, Vic. lm 6015 (us), h.m.v. hlp 3–4 (uk).

The Play of Daniel. Decca 9402, 79402* (us), Bruns. axtl 1086 (uk), sxa 4001; excerpt in hms II.

Léonin, Pérotin: *Organa.* Expériences Anonymes 21 (us); on d.g.g. Arc. 3051 (us), apm 14068 (uk); see also below.

Sumer is icumen in, Rosa fragrans, Alleluia psallat, in hms II.

Sumer is icumen in, on Gregorian Institute el 17 (us).

Machaut: *Notre-Dame Mass*, with secular works, on D.G.G. Arc. 3032 (US), APM 14063 (UK), Bach Guild 622, 5045* (US); Benedictus in HMS III, Vic. LM 6016 (US), H.M.V. HLP 5–7S (UK); Et incarnatus, on Gregorian Institute EL 17 (US).

Byttering: *Nesciens Mater* } in HMS III.
Dunstable: *Veni Sancte Spiritus* } in HMS III.

Dunstable: *O Rosa Bella*, in HMS III; with 5 motets, on D.G.G. Arc.3052 (US), APM 14069 (UK).

Dufay: *Ave Regina Coelorum*, in HMS III.

Dufay: *Alma Redemptoris Mater*, with other sacred works, on D.G.G. Arc. 3003 (US), APM 14019 (UK).

Davy: Passion Music } in HMS III.
Fayrfax: *Magnificat* } in HMS III.

2. *From Ockeghem to Palestrina*

Josquin: *Sanctus* from Mass, *L'homme armé* (with a motet and works by Ockeghem, Obrecht, and de la Rue), in HMS III, Vic. LM 6016 (US), H.M.V. HLP 5–7S (UK).

Palestrina: APM 14182, SAPM 198182* (UK) (with 8 motets); Pope Marcellus Mass. Vox PL 10020 (US, UK); D.G.G. Arc. 3074 (US); Epic LC 3045 (US); Westm. 18364 (US).

Palestrina: *Sicut cervus* (and 4 other motets). Angel 35667 (US).

Victoria: Motet, *O Magnum Mysterium* (with other works). Angel 35668 (US), Col. 33CX 1641 (UK).

Le Jeune: *Revecy venir du printans* (with chansons by Sermisy, Jannequin, Costeley, etc.). Decca 9629 (US), Bruns. AXTL 1048 (US).

Chansons by Sermisy, Costeley, etc., in HMS IV, Vic. LM 6029 (US), H.M.V. HLP 8–10S (UK).

Jannequin: 7 Chansons, D.G.G. Arc. 3034 (US), APM 14042 (UK); 18 Chansons. Vox DL 710 (US, UK), STDL 500710* (US).

Marenzio: 6 Madrigals. D.G.G. Arc. 3073 (US), APM 14045 (UK).

Marenzio: 1 Madrigal, in HMS IV.

Lassus: *Missa Pro Defunctis* and Motet, *In hora ultima* (with three other motets). Lyr. 87 (US).

Lassus: *Tristis est Anima Mea*, with 7 other motets and Mass, D.G.G. Arc. 3077 (US), APM 14071 (UK); with 2 other motets and secular works (see below), Vox DL 380 (US, UK).

Lassus: Seven Penitential Psalms. D.G.G. Arc. 3134–5, 73134–5* (US), APM 14129–30, SAPM 198014–5* (UK).

Lassus: Selections of chansons, *lieder*, villanelle, madrigals. D.G.G. Arc. 3076 (US), APM 14055 (UK); Vox DL 380 (US, UK).

Lassus: *Bon jour, mon Cœur*, on Decca 9629 (US), Bruns. AXTL 1048 (UK).

3. *Tudor England and After*

Taverner: *Benedictus* from Mass, *Gloria tibi Trinitas*, in HMS III, Vic. LM 6016 (US), H.M.V. HLP 5–7S (UK).

Taverner: Mass, *The Western Wynde* and 3 motets. Argo RG 316, ZRG 5316* (UK).

Tallis: Mass, *Lamentations of Jeremiah*, with motets, Decca 9404, 79404* (US); Argo RG 91 (UK).

Gibbons: *Behold Thou Hast Made My Days* (and other English church music), in HMS IV, Vic. LM 6029 (US), H.M.V. HLP 8–10S (UK).

Gibbons: *Hosanna to the Son of David* (with other anthems). Argo RG 80 (UK).

Gibbons: Anthems, Madrigals, and other works. D.G.G. Arc. 3053 (US), APM 14056 (UK).

Gibbons: Anthems and other works. Argo RG 151, ZRG 5151* (UK).

Weelkes: *Hosanna to the Son of David*, on Angel 3516B (US), Col. 33CX 1193 (UK); on Argo RG 237, ZRG 5237* (UK).

Morley: *My Bonny Lass She Smileth*, on Delysé ECB 3144 (UK).

Morley: Madrigals. Bach 577, 5002* (US); Esoteric 520 (US).

Byrd: Mass for 5 voices, Mass for 4 voices. EMS 234 (US).

Byrd: Mass for 5 voices, Great Service. Argo RG 226, ZRG 5226* (UK).

Byrd: Mass for 4 voices, 8 Gradualia. Argo RG 42 (UK).

Byrd: Mass for 3 voices, 2 motets. Argo RG 114 (UK).

Byrd: Great Service. Van. 453 (US).

English Madrigals. Collections on Bach 553–4 (US); Angel 35461 (US), Col. 33SX 1078 (UK); Decca 9406, 79406* (US); four in HMS IV.

The Triumphs of Oriana. Mus.-Lib. 7000–2 (US)

Cries of London. Bach 563 (US).

4. *Germany and Northern Europe, before Bach*

Hassler: *Teutsche Gesang.* D.G.G. Arc. 3075 (US), APM 14010 (UK).

Sweelinck: 3 Psalms. Cantate T 71881 (UK).

Praetorius: *8 geistliche Tricinien.* D.G.G. Arc. 3072 (US), APM 14003 (UK).

Schütz: Psalms (Nos. 84 and 121). Cantate T 71676K (US, UK).

Schütz: 14 Motets. D.G.G. Arc. 3122, 73122* (US), APM 14131, SAPM 198016* (UK).

Schütz: *St Matthew Passion.* D.G.G. Arc. APM 14174, SAPM 198174* (UK).

Schütz: Sacred Symphonies with Little Sacred Concertos, on Cantate 640212 (US); 2 each on D.G.G. Arc. EPA 37012 (UK). Cantate T 71679 F (UK) and T 72087 F (UK).

Schütz: Little Sacred Concertos, see above; also 4 on Cantate T 71680 F (UK), 3 on T 71675 F (UK), 1 (with Magnificat) on T 72029 K (US, UK).

Schütz: *Christmas Oratorio.* Vox DL 780 (US, UK), STDL 500780* (US).

Schütz: *The Seven Last Words.* Lyr. 91 (US); excerpt, and a cantata, in HMS V, Vic. LM 6030 (US), H.M.V. HLP 11–13S (UK).

Schütz: *The Resurrection.* D.G.G. Arc. 3137, 73137* (US), APM 14118, SAPM 198022* (UK).

Buxtehude: Cantatas. Cantate T 72098 K (US, UK); D.G.G. Arc. 3096 and 3103 (US), APM 14082 and 14088 (UK); Overtone 6 (US); Lyr. 96 (US); Urania 8018, 58018* (US).

5. *At the Courts of Italy and France*

Gesualdo: Madrigals, D.G.G. Arc. 3073 (US), APM 14045 (UK); Col. ML 5234 and ML 5341, MS 6048* (US).

Monteverdi: *A un Giro Sol* (with 10 other madrigals). Decca 9627 (US), Bruns. AXTL 1051 (UK).

Monteverdi: *Hor che'l Ciel* (with *Lament of Ariadne* and other madrigals). Angel 20 (US), H.M.V. COLH 20 (UK)

Monteverdi: *Lament of Ariadne* (*Lamento d'Arianna*), with madrigals. D.G.G. Arc. 3136, 73136* (US), APM 14132, SAPM 198021* (UK); on D.G.G. Arc. 3005 (US), APM 14020 (UK).

Monteverdi: *Vespers.* Vox VUX 2004 (US); Oiseau-Lyre OL 50021–2 (UK).

Monteverdi: *Magnificat.* Per. 558 (US).

Lotti: *Crucifixus*, on Epic LC 3359 (US); Mus.-Lib. 7065 and 7085 (US).

G. Gabrieli: *Exaudi Deus* (and other motets). Bach 581, 5004* (US).

G. Gabrieli: *Beata es Virgo* (and other motets). Bach 611, 5037* (US).

G. Gabrieli: *In Ecclesiis*, in HMS IV, Vic. LM 6029 (US), H.M.V. HLP 8–10S (UK).

Carissimi: *Jephtha.* D.G.G. Arc. 3005 (US), APM 14020 (UK).

Vivaldi: *Gloria.* Vox PL 10390 (US), GBY 11960, STPL 510930* (UK); Westm. XWN 18958, WST 14139* (US, UK).

Lully: *Miserere.* Oiseau-Lyre OL 50166 (US, UK); D.G.G. Arc. 3097 (US), APM 14100 (UK).

Delalande (Lalande): *De Profundis.* Vox PL 9040 (US, UK).

Delalande (Lalande): *Te Deum, Confitemini.* Oiseau-Lyre OL 50153 (UK).

6. *Church and State in England*

Tomkins: *Musica Deo Sacra.* Expériences Anonymes 27 (US).

Tomkins: Sacred Music. Argo RG 249, ZRG 5249* (UK).

Humfrey: *Hear, O Heavens*, in HMS V, Vic. LM 6030 (US), H.M.V. HLP 11–13S (UK).

Purcell: *O Sing Unto the Lord* (with another anthem and secular works). D.G.G. Arc. 3038 (US), APM 14059 (UK).

Purcell: Anthems and Sacred Songs. H.M.V. ALP 1766, ASD 335* (UK).

Purcell: *Come, ye Sons of Art.* Oiseau-Lyre OL 50166 (US, UK).

Purcell: *Hail, bright Cecilia.* Bach 559 (US), Nixa NCL 16021 (UK).

7. *Bach and his Time*

C. P. E. Bach: *Magnificat.* Bach 552 (US).

J. S. Bach: 6 Motets. D.G.G. Arc. 3040–1 (US), APM 14060 and 14133, SAPM 198019* and SAP 195002* (UK); Vox VUX 2010 (US), DL 512, STDL 500512* (UK).

J. S. Bach: Cantatas Nos. 4 and 140. Bach 598, 5026* (US).

J. S. Bach: Cantata No. 4, with No. 1, D.G.G. Arc. 3063 (US), APM 14079 (UK); with Nos. 54 and 59, Elec. 80573, S-80573* (US); with motet,

Jesus, priceless treasure, Vic. LM 2273, LSC 2273* (US).

J. S. Bach: Cantata No. 140 with No. 106, Westm. 18394 (US); with No. 11, H.M.V. ALP 1828 (UK).

J. S. Bach: *Magnificat.* Vox PL 8890 (US, UK); Angel 45027 (US), H.M.V. CLP 1128 (UK); Westm. 18465 (US); with Cantata No. 50, Bach 555, 5005* (US).

J. S. Bach: *St John Passion.* D.G.G. Arc. 3045–7 (US), APM 14136–8 (UK) (in German); Vic. LVT 3000 (US) (in English); Argo RG 270–2, ZRG 5270–2* (in English).

J. S. Bach: *St Matthew Passion.* D.G.G. Arc. 3125–8, 73125–8* (US), APM 14125–8, SAPM 198009–12* (UK); Angel 3599E/L, S3599E/L (US); Col. 33CX S1799–1803, SAX S2446–50* (UK); Vox VBX 200 (US, UK); Bach 594–7, 5022–5* (US); (all in German); Decca ACL 109–11 (UK) (in English).

J. S. Bach: *Mass in B minor.* D.G.G. Arc. 3177–9, 73177–9* (US), APM 14190–2, SAPM 198190–2* (UK); Vox VBX 7, STPL 511283* (US, UK); Bach 527–8 (US); Westm. 3305, WST 304* (US).

J. S. Bach: *Christmas Oratorio.* D.G.G. Arc. 3079–81 (US), APM 14101–3 (UK); Vox VBX 201 (US, UK); Elec. 80465–8S, S-80465–8S* (US); Oiseau-Lyre OL 50001–3 (UK).

J. S. Bach: *Easter Oratorio.* Vox PL 8620 (US, UK); Bach 507 (US).

8. *England in the Age of Handel*

Handel: *Acis and Galatea.* Oiseau-Lyre OL 50179–80, SOL 60011–2* (US, UK).

Handel: 'Honour and arms', from *Samson*, on H.M.V. DLP 1200 (UK).

Handel: 'Total eclipse', from *Samson*, on Cap. G 7170, SG 7170* (US), H.M.V. ALP 1575, ASD 291* (UK).

Handel: 'Return, O God of hosts', from *Samson*. Lond. 5083 (US), Decca LXT 5382, SXL 2234* (UK).

Handel: *Israel in Egypt.* Vox PL 11642, STPL 511642* (US, UK).

Handel: *Messiah.* Decca ACL 118–20 (UK); Westm. 3306, WST 306* (US); Nixa NLP 907 (UK); Kapp 8000, 8000S* (US).

Handel: *L'Allegro ed il Penseroso.* Oiseau-Lyre OL 50195–6, SOL 80025–6* (US, UK).

Greene: *Lord Let Me Know Mine End* } on Argo RG 247, ZRG 5247*
Croft: *God is Gone Up With a Merry Noise* } (UK).

9. *The Viennese Classical Period*

Haydn: *The Creation.* Elec. 80579–81, S–80579–81* (US), H.M.V. ALP 1834–6, ASD 409–11* (UK); Van. 471–2 (US) (all in German).

Haydn: *The Seasons.* Decca DX 123 (US), D.G.G. LPM 18486–8 (UK) (in German); Cap. CGR 7184, SCGR 7184* (US), H.M.V. ALP 1606–8, ASD 282–4* (UK) (in English).

Haydn: *Missa Brevis* in F; Mass, *St Joannis de Deo.* Lyr. 30 (US).

Haydn: Mass No. 2, *Great Organ*. Lyr. 84 (US).
Haydn: Mass No. 3, *St Cecilia*. D.G.G. LPM 18545–6, SLPM 138028–9* (US, UK).
Haydn: Mass No. 7, *In tempore belli*. Van. 1061, 2075* (US).
Haydn: Mass No. 9, *Nelson* ('Imperial'). Van. 470 (US); Record Soc. RS 10 (UK).
Haydn: *Stabat Mater*. Lyr. 89 (US).
Haydn: *Salve Regina* in G minor. Elec. 80055 (US).
Mozart: *Nascoso* (K. 557) and other canons. D.G.G. Arc. EPA 37091 (UK).
Mozart: Mass in F (K. 192). Lyr. 18 (US).
Mozart: Masses in D (K. 194) and in C (K. 220). Vox PL 7060 (US).
Mozart: Masses in D (K. 194) and in C (K. 257). Epic LC 3062 (US), Phil. A 00375L (UK).
Mozart: Mass in C (K. 317), *Coronation*. Vox PL 10260 (US, UK); D.G.G. LPE 17222, SLPE 133222* (US, UK); Elec. 80055 (US).
Mozart: Mass in C minor (K. 427). Vox PL 10270 (US, UK), STPL 510272* (US); D.G.G. LPM 18624, SLPM 138124* (US, UK).
Mozart: Requiem in D minor (K. 626). Vox PL 270 (US, UK); Westm. 18766, WST 205* (US, UK); Col. ML 5160 (US), Font. CFL 1000 (UK); Col. ML 5012 (US), Phil. A 01251L (UK).
Mozart: *Litaniae Lauretanae* (K. 195). Oiseau-Lyre OL 50085 (UK).
Mozart: *Litaniae de venerabilis altaris sacramento* (K. 243). Oiseau-Lyre OL 50086 (UK).
Mozart: *Ave verum corpus* (K. 618), on Westm. WST 205* (US, UK); Vic. LM 1117 (US); D.G.G. EPL 30447 (UK).
Schubert: Mass No. 2 in G. Lyr. 93 (US); Vic. LM 1784 (US).
Schubert: Mass No. 5 in A flat. Vox PL 9760 (US, UK).
Schubert: Mass No. 6 in E flat. Cap. P 8579, SP 8579* (US).
Schubert: Psalm 23 and Serenade (D. 921), on Decca DX 144 (US), D.G.G. DGM 18101–2 (UK).
Cherubini: Canons. Cherubini Soc. CSLP 1 (UK).
Cherubini: Requiem in C minor. Vic. LM 2000 (US); Cap. P 8570, SP 8570* (US); Phil. A 00428L (UK).

10. *After Handel – in Britain and America*

Arne: *Comus*. Oiseau-Lyre OL 50070–1 (UK).
Boyce: *O Where shall Wisdom be Found*, on Argo RG 247, ZRG 5247* (UK).
English Catches, etc. Elektra 162, 7162* (US).
Music of the American Moravians. Col. ML 5427, MS 6102* (US); Col. ML 5688, MS 6288* (US).

11. *The French Revolution: Beethoven and Berlioz*

Beethoven: Symphony No. 9 in D minor. Angel GRB 4003 (US), H.M.V. ALP 1286–7 (UK); Vox GBY 10000 (US, UK); Richmond 19083 (US),

Decca LXT 5645 (UK); Angel 3577B, S 3577B* (US), Col. 33CX
1574–5, SAX 2276–7* (UK); Westm. 2214 (US); Vic. LM 6009 (US),
R.C.A. RB 16106–7 (UK); Col. M2L 264, M2S 608* (US), Phil. ABL
3351–2, SABL 169–70* (UK).

Beethoven: Mass in C, Op. 86. Cap. G 7168, SG 7168* (US), H.M.V. ALP
1672, ASD 280* (UK).

Beethoven: Mass in D, Op. 123. Vox PL 11430 (US, UK); Vic. LM 6013
(US), R.C.A. RB 16133–4 (UK); Angel 3595B, S 3595B* (US), Col.
33CX 1634–5 (UK).

Berlioz: *Symphonie Funèbre et Triomphale.* Westm. 18865, 14066* (US); Lyr.
40 (US); Saga XID 5114 (UK).

Berlioz: *Grande Messe des Morts.* Vic. LD 6077, LDS 6077* (US), R.C.A.
RB 16224–5, SB 2096–7* (UK); Westm. 2227, WST 201* (US).

Berlioz: *Te Deum.* Col. ML 4897 (US).

Berlioz: *Romeo and Juliet.* Vic. LM 6011 (US).

Berlioz: Oiseau-Lyre OL 50201–2, SOL 60032–3* (US, UK).

Berlioz: *The Damnation of Faust.* Vic. LM 6114 (US); D.G.G. LPM 18599–
600, SLPM 138009–100* (US, UK).

12. *The Oratorio and Cantata Market: Britain,*
Germany, America

Mendelssohn: *St Paul.* Vox VUX 2006 (US).

Mendelssohn: *Elijah.* Lond. A 4315 (US), Decca LXT 5000–2 (UK); Angel
3558C (US), Col. 33CX 1431–3 (UK).

Brahms: Requiem. Col. 33CX 1781S–2, SAX 2430S–1* (UK); Decca
DX 136 (US), D.G.G. DGM 18258–9 (UK); Vic. LM 6004 (US).

Brahms: *Alto Rhapsody.* Lond. 5098 (US), Decca LXT 2850 or CEP 569
(UK); Vic. LM 1146 (US).

Brahms: *Song of Destiny.* Angel 35400, S 35400* (US), Col. 33CX 1429
(UK).

13. *The Mass – from Rossini to Dvořák*

Rossini: *Stabat Mater.* Decca DX 132 (US), D.G.G. DGM 18340 (UK);
Elec. 80607, S 80607* (US).

Rossini: *Petite Messe Solennelle.* Per. 588 (US).

Verdi: Requiem. Vic. LM 6018 (US), R.C.A. RB 16131–2 (UK); Cap.
GBR 7227, SGBR 7227* (US), H.M.V. ALP 1775–6, ASD 353–4* (UK).

Verdi: Four Sacred Pieces. Decca 9661 (US).

Bruckner: Mass in D minor. SPA 72 (US).

Bruckner: Mass in E minor, *Te Deum.* Elec. 80010 (US), H.M.V. ALP 1567
(UK).

Bruckner: *Te Deum,* see above; also on Col. ML 4980 (US); Phil. GBL
5629 (UK).

Dvořák: *Stabat Mater*. Artia 182–3 (US), Sup. LPV 228–9 (UK).
Dvořák: Requiem. D.G.G. LPM 18547–8, SLPM 138026–7* (US, UK).

14. *Chorus and Symphony: Liszt, Mahler, and After*

Liszt: *Faust Symphony*. Vox PL 10902 (US, UK); Cap. GBR 7197, SGBR 7197* (US), H.M.V. ALP 1737–8, ASD 317–8* (UK).
Liszt: *Dante Symphony*. Westm. 18971, 14152* (US).
Mahler: Symphony No. 2. Col. M2L 256, M2S 601* (US), Phil. ABL 3245–6, SABL 189–90* (UK); Vox VBX 115 (US, UK).
Mahler: Symphony No. 8. Epic SC 6004 (US), Phil. ABL 3024–5 (UK).

15. *Britain from Stanford to Vaughan Williams*

Stanford: *The Blue Bird*, on H.M.V. DLP 1128 (UK).
Elgar: *The Dream of Gerontius*. Angel 3543B (US), Col. 33CX 1247–8 (UK).
Delius: *Mass of Life*. Col. SL 907 (US), Font. CFL 1005–6 (UK).
Delius: *Appalachia*. Col. ML 4915 (US), Font. CFL 1009 (UK).
Delius: *Sea Drift*. Phil. ABL 3088 (UK).
Delius: *Midsummer's Song, On Craig Dhu, To be sung of a Summer Night on the Water*, etc. Argo RG 46 (UK).
Holst: *The Planets*. Whitehall WH 20033, S 20033* (UK); Cap. G 7196, SG 7196* (US), H.M.V. ALP 1600, ASD 269* (UK); Nixa NLP 903 (UK).
Vaughan Williams: *Sea Symphony*. Lond. CMA 7205 (US), Decca LXT 2907–8 (UK).
Vaughan Williams: *Mass in G minor*. Lond. 5634, OS 25271* (US), Argo RG 179, ZRG 5179* (UK).
Coleridge-Taylor: *Hiawatha's Wedding Feast*. H.M.V. ALP 1899, ASD 467* (UK).

16. *Slavonic Nationalism from Dvořák to the Soviets*

Janáček: *Glagolitic Mass*. Sup. LPV 251 (US, UK).
Janáček: *Miscellaneous Choral Works*. Sup. LPV 475 (US, UK); SUA 10064 (US, UK).
Foerster: *9 Choruses for male voices*, Op. 37. Sup. SUF 20010 (UK).
Tchaikovsky: *Liturgy of St John Chrysostom*. Westm. 18727 (US, UK).
Rachmaninov: *The Bells*. Col. ML 5043 (US).
Soviet Songs. Monitor 520, 540–1 (US); Col. 33C 1049–50 (US).
Prokofiev: *Alexander Nevsky*. Vic. LM 2395, LSC 2395* (US), (in English); Colosseum 228; Col. ML 5076, MS 6306* (in Russian).

17. *Four Revolutionaries*

Schoenberg: *Four Pieces*, Op. 27, and *Canon*, Op. 28 No. 1, with instrumental works, Col. ML 5244 (US).
Schoenberg: *The New Classicism*, Op. 28, with instrumental works, Col. ML 5099 (US).

Schoenberg: *A Survivor from Warsaw*, Op. 46, and *Kol Nidre*. Col. ML 4664 (US).

Schoenberg: *Moses and Aaron*. Col. K3L 241 (US), Phil. ABL 3398–9 (UK).

Stravinsky: *The Wedding* (*Les Noces*), Mass, *Pater Noster, Ave Maria*. Epic LC 3231 (US).

Stravinsky: *The Wedding* (*Les Noces*), with *Symphony of Psalms*, Lond. CM 9288, CS 6219* (US), Decca LXT 5639, SXL 2277* (UK).

Stravinsky: *The Wedding* (*Les Noces*). Van. 452 (US) (in Russian).

Stravinsky: *Symphony of Psalms*. Col. ML 4129 (US), Phil. ABL 3055 (UK); see also above.

Stravinsky: *Oedipus Rex*. Col. ML 4644 (US), Phil. ABL 3054 (UK); Lond. A 4106 (US), Decca LXT 5098 (UK).

Stravinsky: *Cantata*. Col. ML 4899 (US).

Stravinsky: *Canticum Sacrum* (Sacred Canticle). Col ML 5215, MS 6022* (US).

Stravinsky: *Threni* (*Lamentations of Jeremiah*). Col ML 5383, MS 6065* (US), Phil. ABL 3329 (UK).

Bartók: *Cantata Profana* (*The Giant Stags*), with 12 unaccompanied choruses, Bartok 312 (US); with Concerto for Orch., Vox PL 10480 (US, UK).

18. *France from the Age of Fauré and Debussy*

Fauré: Requiem. Lond. 5221 (US), Decca LXT 5158, SXL 2211* (UK); Epic LC 3044 (US); Cap. P 8241 (US).

Ravel: *Daphnis and Chloe* (complete ballet). Lond. CM 9028, CS 6147* (US), Decca LXT 5536, SXL 2164* (UK); Vic. LM 2568, LSC 2568* (US), R.C.A. RB 16266, SB 2137 (UK); Decca ACL 53 (UK).

Ravel: *The Child and the Spells* (*L'Enfant et les Sortilèges*). Lond. A 4102 (US), Decca LXT 5019, SXL 2212* (UK); D.G.G. LPM 18675, SLPM 138675* (US, UK).

Debussy: *The Blessed Damozel*. Vic. LM 1907 (US).

Debussy: *Nocturnes*. Lond. CM 9230, CS 6023* (US), Decca LXT 5426, SXL 2062* (UK).

Debussy: *The Martyrdom of St Sebastian*. Vic. LM 2030 (US); Col. M2L 266, M2S 609* (US); Decca LXT 5024 (UK).

Honegger: *Joan of Arc at the Stake*. Col. SL 178 (US).

Honegger: *Christmas Cantata*. Epic LC 3153 (US).

Milhaud: *The Choephori*. Decca 9956 (US), D.G.G. DGM 18385 (UK).

Poulenc: *Litanies of the Black Virgin of Rocamadour*. Pathé DTX 247 (US); Gregorian Institute S 205* (US).

19. *Modern British Composers*

Walton: *Belshazzar's Feast*. Angel 35681, S35681* (US), Col. 33CX 1679, SAX 2319* (UK).

Howells: *A Spotless Rose*, on Angel 3516B (US), Col. 33CX 1193 or SED 5553 (UK).

Rubbra: *Missa Cantuarensis.* Sanctus Benedictus, and Agnus Dei, in HMS X, Vic. LM 6092 (US), H.M.V. HLP 26–7 (UK).

Tippett: *A Child of Our Time.* Pye CGL 30114–5 (UK).

Britten: *A Boy was Born*; *Rejoice in the Lamb.* Decca LXT 5416 (UK).

Britten: *Ceremony of Carols.* Lond. 5634, OS 25271* (US), Argo RG 179, ZRG 5179* (UK).

Britten: *St Nicolas Cantata.* Decca LXT 5060 (UK).

Britten: *Hymn to St. Cecilia*, with other choral works, Oiseau-Lyre OL 50206, SOL 60037* (US, UK).

20. *A Mixed Modern Group*

Bloch: *Sacred Service.* Lond. 5006 (US), Decca LXT 2516 (UK).

Kodály: *Psalmus Hungaricus, Te Deum.* Artia 152 (US, UK) (in Hungarian).

Kodály: *Psalmus Hungaricus.* Decca 9773 (US), D.G.G. DGM 19073 (UK) (in German); Everest 6022, 3022* (US) (in English).

Kodály: *Missa Brevis* Gregorian Institute S 205* (US); H.M.V. ALP 1687 (UK).

Webern: *The Light of Eyes*, Cantatas Nos. 1 and 2 and other choral works, in Webern's complete works, Col. K4L 232 (US), Phil. L 09414–7 (UK).

Orff: *School-work.* Col. 33CX 1549–50 (UK).

Orff: *Carmina Burana.* Col. ML 5498, MS 6163* (US), Phil. ABL 3385, SABL 217* (UK).

Orff: *Catulli Carmina.* Decca 9824 (US), D.G.G. DGM 18304 (UK).

21. *Twentieth-Century Americans*

Ives: *Sixty-Seventh Psalm.* Mus.-Lib. 7071 (US); New Records NRLP 305 (US).

Hanson: *Lament for Beowulf.* Merc. 50192, 90192* (US).

Hanson: Songs from *Drum Taps.* Merc. 50073 (US).

Randall Thompson: *Alleluia.* Gregorian Institute EL 19 (US); Mus.-Lib. 7085 (US); Cambridge 403 (US).

Randall Thompson: *The Peaceable Kingdom.* Mus.-Lib. 7065 (US).

Copland: *In the Beginning.* Mus.-Lib. 7007 (US).

Virgil Thomson: *Psalms Nos. 123 and 126.* Overtone 2 (US).

Virgil Thomson: Mass for 2-part chorus and percussion. Cambridge 412 (US).

William Schuman: *Te Deum.* Aspen 1511 (US).

William Schuman: *Preludes for Voices.* Concordia 6 (US).

Barber: *Three Reincarnations.* Cook 11312, 11312* (US).

Foss: *A Parable of Death.* Educo 4002 (US); Col. ML 4859 (US).

Horhaness: *Magnificat.* Louisville 614 (US).

Harrison: *Four Strict Songs.* Louisville 58–2 (US).

Stevens: *Like as the Culver*
Claflin: *Lament for April 15* and other } CRI 102 (US).
American Madrigals

INDEX

*The numbers in **bold** type are the most important references.*

Some Penguins and Pelicans
on music
are described on the
following pages

THE SYMPHONY

Edited by Ralph Hill

A204

This volume devoted to the symphonies of the great composers is addressed to serious students of music, students who *think* about music as well as *listen* to it, and do not merely approach music sensuously, as one might a hot bath or a pipe of tobacco. We grant that the sensuous appeal of music is a vital and important part of appreciation, but it is only a part and not the whole. Our first reaction to music is an emotional one, after which, if we are intelligent listeners, we want to know something about its construction, how the composer obtains this or that effect, and the process of his thought. The purpose of this book is, therefore, to guide the intelligent and serious listener towards a deeper understanding of the masterpieces of symphony which he is likely to hear frequently in the concert hall, on the radio, or on the gramophone. In the first chapter the Editor outlines the early development of the symphony, after which there is a series of chapters, each written by a leading critic, containing commentaries on some or all of the symphonies of Haydn, Mozart, Beethoven, Schubert, Berlioz, Mendelssohn, Schumann, Liszt, Franck, Bruckner, Brahms, Borodin, Tchaikovsky, Dvořák, Mahler, Elgar, Sibelius, Vaughan Williams, Rachmaninov, and Bax.

THE CONCERTO

Edited by Ralph Hill

A249

The late Ralph Hill's symposium on *The Symphony*, first issued in 1949, has been since the day of its publication one of the most popular and successful of Pelican books. This companion volume, *The Concerto*, which follows the same plan, was completed before his death in the autumn of 1950, and, though he did not live to see it through the press, is in conception and arrangement as much his work as its companion volume.

It deals with all the well-known piano, violin, and cello concertos of the present-day repertoire, and its analyses are illustrated by a wealth of musical examples. The composers whose work is considered begin with Bach and end with William Walton; special chapters are devoted to English compositions, to the general lines of development of the concerto, and to variation forms.